The Arming of Europe
and the Making of the First World War

The Arming of Europe
and the
Making of the First World War

David G. Herrmann

PRINCETON UNIVERSITY PRESS

PRINCETON, NEW JERSEY

Library of Congress Cataloging-in-Publication Data

Herrmann, David G. (David Gaius), 1962–
The arming of Europe and the making of
the First World War / David G. Herrmann.
p.   cm.
Includes bibliographical references and index.
1. World War, 1914–1918—Causes.
2. Arms race—Europe.   3. Military readiness—Europe.
I. Title.
D511.H453 1995 940.3′11—dc20 95-11049 CIP

ISBN 0-691-03374-9 (alk. paper)

To my parents

CONTENTS

List of Maps	ix
Preface	xi
List of Abbreviations	xiii

INTRODUCTION 3

CHAPTER 1
The European Armies in 1904   7

CHAPTER 2
The European Armies and the First Moroccan Crisis, 1905–1906   37

CHAPTER 3
Military Effectiveness and Modern Technology, 1906–1908   59

CHAPTER 4
The Bosnia-Herzegovina Annexation Crisis and the Recovery of
Russian Power, 1908–1911   113

CHAPTER 5
The Second Moroccan Crisis and the Beginning of
German Panic, 1911–1912   147

CHAPTER 6
The Balkan Wars and the Spiral of Armaments, 1912–1913   173

CHAPTER 7
The European Armies and the Outbreak of the First World War   199

CONCLUSION   225

APPENDIX A
Peacetime Strength of the European Armies, 1904–1913   233

APPENDIX B
Army Expenditures of the European Powers, 1904–1914   236

Notes   239

Bibliography   289

Index   301

LIST OF MAPS

1. Europe in 1904   2

2. Projected Troop Concentration Areas on the Western
   Front, 1905   48

3. The Balkan Peninsula after the Annexation of Bosnia
   and Herzegovina   114

4. Withdrawal of the Projected Russian Deployment in
   the West, 1910   133

PREFACE

THIS IS a study of land armaments before the First World War, intended to complement the extensive scholarly work that has been done on the naval race. Battleship building, in its relationship to diplomacy, finance, and politics before 1914, has produced an impressive literature which explains many of the tensions that led to war. The importance of these conclusions raises the question of what the situation was on land. The continental powers expected their fates to depend on their armies when a great war broke out, not on their navies. The war proved that they had been right, although for the wrong reasons.

A major body of historical work exists on the European armies, but it mostly concentrates on individual countries. Essential as these contributions are, it is necessary to advance to a level of international comparison, covering the forces of all the great powers together—Germany, France, Russia, Austria-Hungary, Italy, and Great Britain—if the part played by armies in the events leading up to the war is to be understood. The work that has previously been done on the comparative level mostly deals with war planning, rather than with the armies for which the plans were made. The relationship between the means available and the way they were to be used is naturally an important one. It is crucial to know what the decision makers thought this relationship was: how strong they believed the armies were in relationship to one another, and how capable of undertaking a successful campaign at a given moment. Perceptions of power play a large part in this work.

Along the way, there is occasion for many observations about how armies functioned and changed in the decade before the First World War. What were these forces like? Authors on each country have identified problems in modernization during a time of technological transformation in warfare, and indicated reasons why particular states had trouble surmounting them. These historians have not been in a position to distinguish between difficulties endemic to the period and problems that were more pronounced in some armies than in others. Here, too, assessments by contemporaries provide an essential source of material.

Research for this project was assisted by grants from Yale University, the Council for European Studies, the German Academic Exchange Service (DAAD), the Joint Committee on Western Europe of the Social Science Research Council, and the American Council of Learned Societies, with funds provided by the Ford Foundation and the William and Flora Hewlett Foundation. The manuscript was prepared with the generous support of a John M. Olin Fellowship in National Security at Harvard University's Center for International Affairs, as well as a Tulane Committee on Research Summer Fellowship.

This research would not have been possible without the generous cooperation of the following archives, to the government authorities and staff of which I am deeply indebted for granting access to material and facilitating my work: the Service Historique de l'Etat-Major de l'Armée de Terre at Vincennes, the Archive du Ministère des Affaires Etrangères, and the Archives Nationales in Paris; the Politisches Archiv des Auswärtigen Amtes in Bonn, the Bundesarchiv in Koblenz, the Bundesarchiv-Militärarchiv in Freiburg, the Kriegsarchiv section of the Württembergisches Hauptstaatsarchiv in Stuttgart, and the Bayerisches Hauptstaatsarchiv-Kriegsarchiv in Munich; the Kriegsarchiv and Haus-, Hof- und Staatsarchiv in Vienna; the Archivio dell'Ufficio Storico dello Stato Maggiore dell'Esercito, Archivio Centrale dello Stato, and Archivio Storico del Ministero degli Affari Esteri in Rome; and the Public Record Office at Kew outside London. I am also grateful for the generous cooperation of the direction and personnel of the Bibliothèque Nationale, the Württembergische Staatsbibliothek, the Österreichische Nationalbibliothek, the Biblioteca per la Storia Contemporanea, the German Historical Institute in Rome, the British Library, the Institute of Historical Research at the University of London, the Library of Congress, and, most particularly, the Militärgeschichtliches Forschungsamt in Freiburg. In the quotation of documents and printed works from these collections, all translations are my own unless otherwise indicated, and all emphases reproduce those present in the originals.

My personal thanks are due first of all to my dissertation supervisor, Professor Paul Kennedy, whose learning, good-humored encouragement, and active promotion of the project have been indispensable throughout. I am grateful to Professor John Gooch of the University of Leeds, not least of all for suggesting the topic to me. I received advice and generous assistance from Michael Howard, Henry Turner, and many others, most importantly Martin Alexander, Volker Berghahn, Lisa Brandes, Wilhelm Deist, Jürgen Förster, Luigi Goglia, Brian Hammerstein, Daniel Hughes, Robert Jervis, Jack Levy, Sean Lynn-Jones, Bruce Menning, Manfred Messerschmidt, Williamson Murray, Tim Naftali, Douglas Porch, Giorgio Rochat, Gideon Rose, Heidi Sandige, Michael Schäfer, Eric David Schramm, Gerhard Schreiber, Dennis Showalter, Jack Snyder, David Stevenson, Hew Strachan, Brian Sullivan, Martyna Szalanska-Fox, Bruno Thoß, Stephen Van Evera, Hannelore and Hubert Wartenberg, Bernd Wegner, and Sam Williamson. Much credit for anything the present work may achieve is due to them, and any errors it contains are my own.

LIST OF ABBREVIATIONS

ARCHIVES

ACS	Archivio Centrale dello Stato, Rome
AN	Archives Nationales, Paris
ASMAE	Archivio Storico del Ministero degli Affari Esteri, Rome
AUSSME	Archivio dell'Ufficio Storico dello Stato Maggiore dell'Esercito, Rome
BA	Bundesarchiv, Koblenz
BA-MA	Bundesarchiv-Militärarchiv, Freiburg im Breisgau
BHStA-KA	Bayerisches Hauptstaatsarchiv-Kriegsarchiv, Munich
HHStA	Haus-, Hof- und Staatsarchiv, Vienna
HStAS-KA	Württembergisches Hauptstaatsarchiv Stuttgart-Kriegsarchiv
KA	Kriegsarchiv, Vienna
MAE	Ministère des Affaires Etrangères, Paris
PAAA	Politisches Archiv des Auswärtiges Amtes, Bonn
PRO	Public Record Office, Kew
SHAT	Service Historique de l'Armée de Terre, Vincennes

PUBLISHED DOCUMENT COLLECTIONS

BD	*British Documents on the Origins of the War, 1898-1914*
DDF	*Documents diplomatiques français (1871-1914)*
GP	*Die Grosse Politik der europäischen Kabinette 1871-1914*
Ö-UA	*Österreich Ungarns Außenpolitik von der Bosnischen Krise 1908 bis zum Kriegsausbruch 1914*

The Arming of Europe
and the Making of the First World War

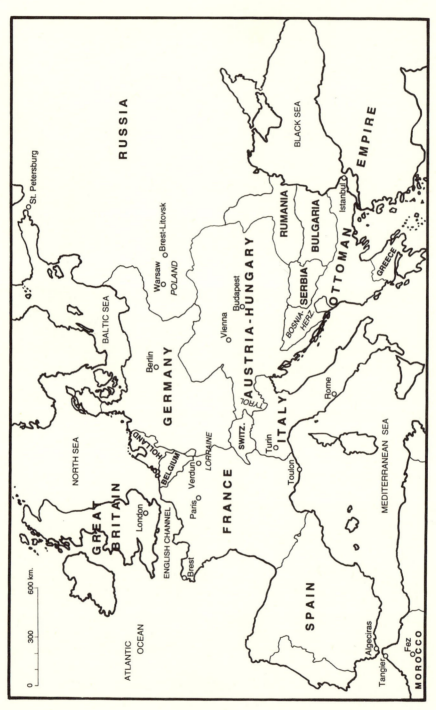

Map 1. Europe in 1904.

INTRODUCTION

When the European armies marched against one another in 1914, they did so after ten years of international crises had repeatedly brought threats of war. The present work is a survey of one major influence on international affairs in that decade: armies and land armaments. In an age of diplomatic confrontations when governments repeatedly contemplated war, the military strength of the European powers was a subject of increasingly vital interest to the public as well as to policy makers in Germany, Austria-Hungary, France, Russia, Great Britain, and Italy. This gave rise to a sudden surge of army expansions in the last two years before the war: an arms race. How this came about, what effect military strength had on crisis politics, and how these developments contributed to the outbreak of the world war in 1914 are the major questions addressed in the following pages.

The naval race between Germany and Great Britain was very much in the public eye during the same period, but in some respects it was less important than the development of armies. Fleets were far less vital to the security of the continental powers than land forces were. The colossal battleships and armored cruisers that the great powers had built with such fanfare in the decades around the turn of the century did not do the decisive fighting in the First World War. Nor did people expect them to. Most knew that the armies of millions, which stood ready to mobilize on the contiguous land frontiers of the European states, would be the principal combatants. Of course this assumption was as often as not based on the totally mistaken notion that the war would be over in a matter of months, before naval power had a chance to make itself felt. Nevertheless, it turned out to be fundamentally correct. Throughout the period, all the European states with the exception of Great Britain spent at least twice as much on their armies as they did on their fleets, and the military was in all cases by far the largest item in the state budget.

The decade that preceded 1914 brought repeated threats of a land war in Europe. With the Anglo-French Entente of 1904, the two alliance blocs began to coalesce, and ten years later they went to war against each other. A series of diplomatic confrontations in this period involved war scares, the threat of war used as a tool of diplomacy, and in some cases even the partial mobilization of forces. This was true of the first and second Moroccan crises, the Bosnia and Herzegovina annexation crisis, and the moves for intervention in the Balkan Wars of 1912 and 1913. At the same time, several wars were actually fought, involving the

European powers or closely touching their security. The Anglo-Boer War of 1899–1902 left the British army still in disarray by 1904, the year the Russo-Japanese War broke out in Manchuria. The Italian-Turkish War of 1911–12 was immediately followed by the Balkan Wars opposite the southern borders of Austria-Hungary. Other powers continually engaged in colonial fighting, such as the German suppression of the Herero rising in Southwest Africa and France's ongoing campaigns in its North African territories.

In view of these threats and actual conflicts, the question arises of how the balance of military power affected international affairs. Above all, the issue of perceptions is crucial. Did statesmen actually take account of military strength and the likely outcome of wars when they made decisions in crises? If so, when did this occur, what did they perceive the balance to be, and how did it affect their actions? Did assessments of the strategic situation influence the decision for war in 1914? How strong people thought armies were can often be easier to assess in retrospect than the actual strength available.

It may well be asked why it is necessary to add yet another item to the long list of causes of the First World War, interesting though the armies may be as subjects of study in themselves. The main reason is that perceptions of a changing balance of military power may have determined the timing of the outbreak of war: why it happened in 1914 and not substantially earlier or later. This does not diminish the importance of competing explanations for the origins of the war. The conflict probably would not have occurred—or would at least have been very different—if it had not been for a European ideological culture of international struggle, imperialism, militarism, and social Darwinism.[1] Diplomatic rivalries and the increasing isolation of Germany and Austria-Hungary as a result of their pugnacious foreign policies were obviously crucial too. These were all the more volatile when combined with domestic political strategies that exploited chauvinism in an attempt to subdue class antagonisms.[2] Several scholars have suggested that the very system of European international affairs had outgrown its nineteenth-century shape by the time war broke out.[3] The naval race contributed to almost irreconcilable antagonism between Germany and Britain.[4] On land, the codification of interlocking mobilization and war plans with a strong emphasis on the offensive were a destabilizing element in crisis decision making.[5]

Most of these influences were more fundamental and compelling as independent causes than the balance of military power was, but they all remained largely static from at least the turn of the century until the outbreak of war. It is hard to identify a particular crisis in any of these areas that made war more likely in 1914 than at another moment in the period. Aggressive ideology had a long history in the culture of the Victorian age and the Belle Epoque. Diplomatic crises had been endemic to the European system, particularly in the Balkans, long before the assassination of the Archduke Franz Ferdinand at Sarajevo. Berlin's international policy had been on an assertive course for decades before then. It is difficult to demonstrate that domestic political tension even in Germany or Austria-Hungary had reached a particular, decisive level in 1914 that caused statesmen to choose war as a solution. The naval race was past its peak after 1912, and army general staffs had been planning offensives against each other for more than a quarter of a century.

Where perceptions of military strength were concerned, however, Europe underwent a radical change between 1904 and 1914. For most of the early part of the decade, the armies of the great powers remained in a state of slow peacetime development, much as they had done since the wars of the mid-nineteenth century. Their size and budgets stood under constraints of one kind or another everywhere, with international competition playing only a small role in their modernization. The spate of technological innovations that armies had to incorporate at the beginning of the twentieth century, such as quick-firing artillery, machine guns, motor vehicles, aircraft, and telephone and wireless equipment, tended to restrict expansion in other areas during a period of only moderately increasing funds. Between 1912 and 1914, however, the principal European armies undertook a series of increases in both manpower and equipment, in a reciprocal dynamic of competitive armament measures directed explicitly against each other. This took place amid frequent alarms of imminent war and fear on all sides of military eclipse.

How this transformation took place, and how it affected international politics, is therefore a matter of substantial interest. The principal reasons for the change lay in perceptions of a changing balance of military power in Europe. These perceptions were dominated by the collapse of the Russian army as a result of the war with Japan, and by the subsequent recovery of Russian military capability. The extent of the Russian army's prostration in this period and its effects on crisis diplomacy were understood by contemporaries to a much greater extent than most historians have recognized. The comments of military officers and statesmen at the time show that these perceptions caused the First World War to break out in large part as a "preventive" war, undertaken primarily by Austria-Hungary and Germany but also to an extent by the Entente powers. Decision makers in Vienna and Berlin became resigned to risking an immediate war with a rival coalition they believed would only grow stronger in the future. In Paris, St. Petersburg, and London the fear prevailed that the Entente between them might fail in another crisis if they avoided the risk of fighting in 1914. The conflict originated at least as much from changes in the international strategic situation as from domestic political forces.

Many of the traditional arguments about the destabilizing effect of arms races on international relations apply to the case of the First World War.[6] Military competition helped to precipitate war because it made states that increased their armies appear aggressive. This was particularly true when the mobilization of state resources for armaments required a corresponding mobilization of political opinion and martial sentiment to support it. The process tended to create perceptions that "windows of opportunity" for successfully fighting a war were closing, due to the belief that a rival could draw upon immense resources in the future while one's own side was approaching the limits of its capacity.

Nevertheless, military competition itself depended upon international politics. The arms race did not inexorably bring about a war between otherwise benign states. Nor, on the other hand, was the outcome of an arms race entirely subject to international affairs.[7] The relationship between armaments competition and international politics was one of interdependence throughout. Without the military balance changing as it did, there might well have been no war, but without particular antagonisms between states, it would not have mattered how the military balance changed. The two reciprocal influences are impossible to separate.

Quite apart from its theoretical implications, the development of the European armies in the decade before 1914 was significant for what it showed about military institutions and attitudes to armed force at the time. Statesmen and officers continually assessed military power by the standards of their day and of their particular national, institutional, or personal biases. The armies themselves tackled rapidly mounting problems of modernization in tactics, organization, and equipment as they prepared for war on a twentieth-century battlefield that they increasingly realized would be very different from anything they had faced in the past. This was the period when the armed forces of Europe adopted quick-firing artillery, machine guns, motor vehicles, new communication gear, and aircraft. They had to procure these devices and integrate them into systems of organization and tactics. Their failure to meet these challenges adequately became notorious in the course of the world war and in subsequent historical writing and military thought. It is therefore all the more important to understand the limits and the sources of this failure.

Chapter 1

THE EUROPEAN ARMIES IN 1904

IN THE FIRST HOURS after midnight on 9 February 1904, the Russo-Japanese War began, with Vice-Admiral Togo Heihachiro's surprise attack on the Russian naval base at Port Arthur in northeastern China. The war was not only the first great military campaign of the twentieth century, employing many of the new technologies that were to transform warfare in that age. It was also the origin of a total collapse of Russian military power in Asia and Europe. Within a year, the struggle over control of Korea and Manchuria drew virtually all of the Russian navy and a large part of the army into a series of disastrous battles on the waters off the Chinese coast and in the Liaotung Peninsula. The Russian forces retreated from one line to another, and revolution broke out in St. Petersburg in January of 1905. The debacle was total. From a strategic point of view, one of the mightiest of the European armies was simply removed from the scales of international power. For several years Russia was incapable of taking part in a war. The history of the balance of military power in Europe in the decade between 1904 and the outbreak of the First World War was in large measure the story of Russia's prostration, its subsequent recovery, and the effects of this development upon the strategic situation. This was all the more important as it was a decade of international crises in which the European powers more than once threatened each other with war.

When the Russo-Japanese War broke out, the armies of the great powers were far from being involved in preparation for an imminent continental conflict. The Russians sent their troops eastward from a European theater where the land forces of Germany, France, Austria-Hungary, Italy, and Great Britain were engaged in steady peacetime development, more conscious of the constraints they faced than of any imperative for rapid expansion. Statesmen and diplomats seldom referred to military force in their international business. On the domestic front there were few elements working in favor of army increases, while many militated against them. The armies were in the process of adopting various technological inventions recently placed at their disposal by the ingenuity of the industrial age, but this process as often as not constituted a drag on the speed of army expansion. New equipment had to be evaluated, developed, and refined by special technical branches of the general staffs, then ordered by contract from government arsenals or private firms. Once produced, it went into service with units specially constituted and trained to use it. The whole process cost money, time, manpower, and precious training hours. It especially taxed the finite supply of officers and their subordinates, the experienced noncommissioned officers such as sergeants and corporals, who did much of the practical work of training the ordinary soldiers.

Military budgets did increase from year to year in most countries as a matter of course, and armies grew fractionally larger, but by 1904 this had become a standard feature of peacetime military forces. They were accustomed to keeping pace with technological innovation and expanding populations and economies. The armies engaged in a continual process of innovation and reorganization, but not in a true armaments race with rapid expansions in response to increases by rivals. This form of peacetime development for institutionalized standing armies was by 1904 a familiar state of affairs for the great powers. It was not the way things had always been, but it had become normal with the effects of the industrial and national revolutions of the nineteenth century.

Modern industrial states, as they had emerged between the Napoleonic Wars and the early 1900s, had placed extraordinary new resources at the disposal of armed forces, as well as imposing more burdens upon them.[1] New metallurgical techniques, the replacement of artisanal manufacture by mass production, and the invention of chemical explosives far more powerful than gunpowder had brought about a revolution in the deadliness of weapons. Muzzle-loaded smoothbore muskets and cannon, of a kind little changed since the end of the seventeenth century, had given way to rifled, breech-loading small arms and artillery of unprecedented range, accuracy, and rapidity of fire. Exploding shells had replaced cannonballs. Repeating rifles holding magazines full of brass cartridges had superseded single-shot infantry weapons. Fortresses had attained new levels of impregnability as bricks and masonry had been surpassed by underground concrete shelters with armored steel gun cupolas.[2] Steam power had brought railways, which could transport vast numbers of soldiers from every part of a country to a battle front in a matter of weeks, and then constantly deliver supplies and reinforcements during a campaign.[3] The governments of increasingly centralized, industrialized, and efficient bureaucratic states had gained the tax revenues and the organization to conscript, train, and equip mass armies. Vast peacetime forces were supplemented by reserves available for recall in wartime. Armies instituted permanent, professional general staffs to plan for mobilization and war instead of simply appointing commanders ad hoc for each campaign. At sea, navies had made the transition from wooden, sail-powered men-of-war, with broadsides of cannon firing solid shot, to armor-plated steel warships, steam powered and armed with guns that fired explosive shells to ranges clear over the horizon. Since the middle of the nineteenth century, fleets had competed in continual arms races to develop these vessels. Land warfare, however, was not dominated by large, complex weapons systems in the way that sea power depended upon the warship. Armies engaged less in arms races than in the steady improvement of existing forces and equipment. The nineteenth century had seen virtually no competitive army expansions among the European powers on land, except in the face of immediate war.

In their outward appearance and composition, the European armies of 1904 still looked very much like those of the nineteenth century. In spite of the continual state of development into which the late 1800s had forced them, they remained strongly traditional institutions. Most were more concerned with keeping the pace of events under control than with engaging in adventurous rivalries. Speculation abounded about how they would perform the next time they fought a major war, as well as about what numbers they would actually be able to field with their conscript-and-reserve systems, and what effect modern technology would have upon tactics. But for all the changes in their recruitment and weaponry, the armies still consisted fundamentally of large masses of men, horses, and guns.

They contained the conventional specialized branches, or "arms," of land combat. The infantry, as ever, accounted for the majority of the troops. In all armies the men carried magazine-fed, bolt-action repeating rifles of the basic types that remained in service from the late nineteenth century through the Second World War. All of these could be fired to a range of more than a thousand meters, or easily as far away as the soldier could see any kind of target. Cavalry still formed a substantial proportion of the fighting forces, the men being armed with rifles in addition to the traditional sabers and in some cases even lances. The artillery was still all horse-drawn. The most numerous type was the field artillery, which was expected to play the primary role on the battlefield. It operated with relatively light cannon that could be towed by their six-horse teams across country as well as on roads, followed by horse-drawn ammunition wagons, or caissons. The guns, breech-loaded and rifled, operated in batteries of four, six, or eight. They fired shells seventy-five to ninety millimeters in diameter to a range of approximately seven kilometers. This was in any case about as far away as the gunners could conceivably see where their rounds fell. The ammunition was sometimes regular high explosive, but more often consisted of shrapnel shells, set by a time fuze to explode in the air above enemy troops, scattering a burst of steel balls and fragments. Some armies also used light field howitzers: short-barreled guns with a larger caliber but shorter range, designed to lob heavier explosive shells in a curved trajectory over obstacles and into defiladed enemy positions.

More ponderous and much less numerous was the heavy field artillery. It employed cannon and howitzers of 100 to 155 millimeters' caliber, which would go into action at selected points to demolish fortifications or important targets in the path of large units. These longer-ranged guns often had to be dismantled into sections for transport and were generally not considered suitable for operation away from good roads. Their ammunition, in particular, was heavy, bulky, and hard to bring forward in large quantities. More cumbersome still were the various categories of siege and fortress artillery, a heterogeneous array of long-range guns and mortars firing very large shells. Transported by rail, set up on platforms for action, and aimed by laborious mathematical calculation, these weapons mostly remained in storage during peacetime. Soldiers regarded them as holding none of the glamour of the more dashing field artillery batteries. Since these gigantic guns were also extremely costly to design and manufacture, armies tended to keep them in service for as long as possible, perennially leaving the siege and fortress artillery with large proportions of obsolescent material.

In all armies the engineer arm performed its long-established duties of constructing field fortifications, clearing obstacles, building roads and bridges, and providing the expertise for other special technical tasks. The small but rapidly growing branch of the communication troops worked on rail and telegraph lines and operated signal and observation devices such as flags, balloons, and heliographs. It also experimented with new inventions, including telephones, bicycles, and motor vehicles, that might help in gathering and transmitting information. All armies arrived in the theater of operations by rail and received their support in the field from columns of horse-drawn wagons belonging to the supply corps. The troops wore traditional bold-colored uniforms: blue coats and red trousers for the French; blue tunics in Germany, Austria-Hungary, and Italy; and dark green uniforms in Russia. The only exception was Britain, where the experience of colonial wars had led to the adoption of khaki instead of the historic scarlet tunics, even for home service, in 1902.[4] In the continental armies, accoutrements were of leather, while headgear consisted of a picturesque array of caps, shakos, ornamented helmets, and, for the resplendent cavalry, even busbies and square-topped *czapkas* in the Polish style.

Despite these traditional features, however, the European armies had also undergone important changes since the mid-nineteenth century. Some of these transformations were quite evident, while others could only be guessed at, since their effects would only materialize when the armies actually went to war. Clearly the forces in every country were permanently institutionalized on a larger scale and with more articulated bureaucracies of command and administration than their predecessors. General staffs, dedicated to war planning in peacetime and to the conduct of operations in war, existed alongside the war ministries that handled legislative and administrative matters. More men than ever before were trained by a military apparatus that cost unprecedented amounts to maintain and to furnish with continually changing equipment, whether or not a country was at war or contemplated fighting one soon. But just what effect all of these transformations would have on actual fighting remained a matter of speculation and extrapolation at a time when the armies of the great powers had not fought one another for more than a quarter of a century. The Franco-Prussian War of 1870–71 and the Russo-Turkish War in 1877–78 had been the last major campaigns. Most of the armies had fairly recent experience of waging colonial wars or suppressing uprisings in their own territories, but this did not give an accurate indication of what a big European conflict would look like. Beneath the surface of armies' traditional exteriors lurked considerable mysteries for anyone who tried to predict how these forces would perform the task for which they were designed.

Where their numerical strength was concerned, the continental European armies by 1904 had become hard to evaluate because their peacetime composition was very different from the organization with which they would go to war. This was a result of the institutionalization of conscription applied to virtually the whole of the male population. Since the third quarter of the nineteenth century, all the great powers except Britain had adopted the system of organization that had allowed Prussia to mobilize vast and effective forces for the wars of German unification. The peacetime army functioned as a huge training camp for a wartime "nation in arms." It was chiefly an organization that instructed recruits for a short period—normally two or three years—before returning them to civilian life as reservists. There they might serve a few periods of refresher training, but above all they would be recalled to their units for duty in time of war. The "active army" at any time therefore contained only two to three years' worth of age "classes," in addition to a permanent training and leadership cadre consisting of the officers, the noncommissioned officers, and some other enlisted men who also chose to make the army their career.[5]

For war, the army would "mobilize" by calling up its reservists and adding them to the standing portion of the forces. It took at least two weeks to get the main body ready to begin operations, and much longer than that in many armies. Everything depended on how well the general staff had laid its plans in peacetime for organizing and transporting the troops called up, as well as on the availability of numerous and efficient rail lines, and the distances that had to be covered to assemble the army. The recalled reservists would travel from their homes to their depots, to be clothed, armed, equipped, and sent to join their units. These would reorganize to absorb the influx, combine into brigades, divisions, corps, and armies, and move up to their deployment positions to start the campaign. The units the men joined would not always be the same ones with which they had trained. Some reservists went to fill up the combat formations: infantry and engineer companies, cavalry squadrons, and artillery batteries. The most typical unit, the infantry company, had approximately 250 men in wartime and was supposed to have about one hundred in peacetime in most armies, although in practice it was often far below this strength. The difference was made up with reservists on mobilization. Other reservists formed actual "reserve" units, with only a small cadre of active peacetime troops. Still others filled up even larger proportions of the units farther from the center of combat, such as siege artillery, fortress garrisons, supply services, railway and communication troops, and administrative staffs. Many of these types of units consisted of the merest skeletons in peacetime, with their equipment mothballed or nonexistent, and plans for their constitution existing almost exclusively on paper. Armies therefore expected to take the field with many times more men than they had in peacetime.

Within this framework, it was not always clear what proportion of the mobilizable forces should really be counted as effective soldiers. As a rule, the younger classes of reservists joined the combat units while older categories took over duties progressively farther from the front line, less demanding and offering more time for retraining and reorganization before they would be seriously tested. This shaped the military life of a European male, who was theoretically subject to universal service in most countries, though in practice often exempted. He progressed from a brief period of full-time duty with the active army, through a number of years with the "reserve" proper, and thence through a series of home-guard and militia categories of steadily decreasing readiness as he grew older. These second- and third-line forces varied in composition and nomenclature from one country to another, but generally included a moderate-aged classification such as the Landwehr, Milice Mobile, or Milizia Mobile, followed by an array of catch-all classifications for the superannuated and the scarcely trained or untrained: Landsturm, Ersatzreserve, Milice Territoriale, Opolchenie, and Milizia Territoriale. Naturally the first-line units received the lion's share of the regular officers and NCOs. They also had the most reliably prepared mobilization schedules and stocks of uniforms, accoutrements, weapons, vehicles, animals, artillery, and ammunition. The rear echelons

would have to make do with scantier or outdated equipment and progressively larger proportions of retired officers, NCOs of the reserve,
and reserve officers.

It was therefore hard to judge exactly what sort of force a given peacetime army would produce when it mobilized for war. The standing units
would expand, others would come into existence, and the support services for all of them would spring into being from almost nothing. A
division or a corps of tens of thousands of men could not function without a vast array of higher command organs, supply columns, heavy artillery, communication troops, and other services that depended entirely
on how well the reserves had been trained and equipped. In the early
stages of mobilization the railway lines would be packed to capacity with
the trains for the first-line formations according to elaborately orchestrated timetables. As a result, nobody could be sure just how soon all the
auxiliary forces would be ready and how effective they would be. Consequently, estimates of how many men would really be available relied
upon a great deal of guesswork, as well as differing criteria. Statistical
tabulations might count only first-line troops, or range all the way up
to the full total of men of military age in the country who had theoretically received any sort of training. Assessments might also be phrased in
terms of units mobilized rather than numbers of men: battalions, squadrons, divisions, corps, or other formations. Such figures could be mis-
leading since these units often had widely varying strengths even within
the same army. International comparisons foundered on questions of
whether, for example, a German reserve corps of two divisions should
count as the equivalent of two French reserve divisions, which had different training, equipment, composition, and mobilization priority, and
were not organized into corps-sized formations.

It was also hard to know what proportion of an army would be able
to fight on a given battlefront, and how quickly. The German and Austro-Hungarian armies expected to divide their forces between various
fronts in Europe, with the proportions for each varying according to the
strategic situation. The Russian army had to deploy forces not only on
the several main sectors of its western border against Germany, Austria-
Hungary, and possibly Rumania, but also opposite the Caucasus, Finland, Japan, and its central Asian frontier territories. The French, Italian,
and British armies had varying totals of men stationed in their colonies,
and it was impossible to say what the situation would be on the outbreak
of a European war. The forces available to any country also depended
on timing. A certain number of units would be ready at the end of
two weeks from mobilization, and different additional ones would become available later, according to how quickly the army mobilized and

where the campaign was to be fought in relation to the main call-up areas. Given all of these imponderables about the strength of mobilized armies, it is perhaps not surprising that estimates varied widely, often depending on who was doing the estimating, and usually also on what point they were trying to prove.

Apart from the size of the new European armies, it was clear that in peacetime they also cost a great deal more than their predecessors. The expenditures constantly rose and were by and large expected to do so as a matter of course by the turn of the century.[6] It was no easier to compare the size of their budgets across national lines as a means of measuring relative power than it was to measure numerical strength. Some of the problems were the same as with calculating numbers of troops. The proliferation of different criteria for recording data defied precise tabulation.[7] Costs might or might not include such items as pensions, gendarmerie, colonial forces, military railroad construction, or coastal defense. The funds for these might appear in the army budget or lie hidden under headings for the ministry of the interior, colonies, public works, or other chapters. Each state had a different degree of latitude for tinkering with its military expenditures beyond the initial yearly vote in parliament that was printed in official publications. Under some systems of government, like the tsarist autocracy or the Dual Monarchy of Austria-Hungary, sovereigns could under certain circumstances spend money without prior legislative approval. Furthermore, in almost all states parliamentary procedures generally allowed changes to the initial appropriations. A typical case was France, where the Chamber of Deputies voted "supplementary credits" to the initial annual budget throughout the year, and even retroactively in succeeding years. Such votes might change the original budget by less than 1 percent in a year, or they might amount to an increase of over 20 percent.[8] It was equally hard to get a sense of proportion by comparing the impact of military spending in different countries.[9] The buying power of currency differed widely from one state to another, as did the degree of state intervention in the national economy, while consistent tabulations of gross domestic product were not available.[10] It was also not clear what proportion of the military budget of the Russian empire, for instance, really bought assets that would be used in a European war, rather than in some other theater. In all countries, war costs further muddied the waters. Military budgets might claim at one time or another to include them or to separate them out into a special extra-budgetary account. The dividing line was in any case largely an artificial one, leaving officials free to cook the books in order to disguise costs as well as to spread them out over many years to lessen their fiscal impact. This applied to major conflicts like the

South African war (which the British were still paying for in 1904), the Russo-Japanese War, and the Italian-Turkish War, just as it did to lingering colonial campaigns or to partial mobilizations during European crises in peacetime.

Despite the difficulties of assembling consistent data, however, general staffs did continually observe and assess foreign armies and try to compare their relative strengths, especially when crises threatened. This was the role of the intelligence sections of general staffs, performed by regular analysts and a network of military attachés accredited to embassies abroad, normally officers ranking between captain and lieutenant-colonel. Chiefs of general staffs normally reviewed reports from these attachés as well as estimates compiled by the intelligence section offices responsible for separate foreign countries or theaters of operations. They also received occasional observations from other branches of the general staff on specific matters such as fortress construction or artillery development. By these means, the European armies remained remarkably well informed about one another. Since highly sophisticated and secret weapons systems did not yet play a significant role, there was little a general staff knew about its own forces that its rivals did not at least conjecture. The resulting estimates were normally syntheses of information about numbers of men, time needed for mobilization and deployment on the battlefronts in question, guesses or intelligence concerning war plans, and more subjective judgments about inherent fighting power. In an age before machines had definitively taken over the battlefield, and when prevailing ideals emphasized heroic, voluntarist, and virile activity in any form of struggle, professional military men paid a great deal of attention not only to an army's numbers and equipment but also to its morale, discipline, appearance, and tactics.

Observers gathered their information on foreign military forces from a wide array of sources. These included newspapers, official publications of armies and governments, personal contacts, and a moderate amount of espionage. They also relied on observations made by military attachés during inspections, barrack visits, and training exercises. Most of all they concentrated upon the climactic event of the army year, the "grand maneuvers." The European armies held many field exercises of various types and sizes in all seasons, but the great display was the annual full-scale war game held at the end of the summer. Tens of thousands of troops formed two sides to fight a simulated battle lasting several days over many hundred square kilometers. The generals and staffs commanding each force underwent the rare experience of handling very large bodies of troops in the field. The high command could experiment with new equipment, regulations, and tactics. The troops and junior officers got a taste of sustained operations in unfamiliar terrain. Roads and villages teemed with columns of troops, horses, and vehicles. Officer-referees bustled back and forth, the men fired off blank ammunition, and the countryside blossomed with marker flags for simulated entrenchments and fire directions. The cost was colossal, the atmosphere festive, and the spectacle an attraction for heads of state, foreign dignitaries, the press, and the local population, all of whom turned out in force to watch the action. Only France and Germany managed to organize full-scale maneuvers regularly every year, but they were frequent enough in all countries to provide a major venue for military attachés and commentators to see what foreign armies could do.

Much more difficult for outsiders to learn about were the secret exercises carried out by each army high command to evaluate both the skill of its officers and the effectiveness of operational plans. These trials could take the form of "staff rides" or of map exercises. The former somewhat resembled grand maneuvers without troops. The officers representing the commanders and staff officers of a force would spend several days in the field, beginning with an assigned situation and task with allotted forces. They drew up orders for imaginary troop movements and traveled over the terrain where these were to take place. The details the participants wrote out for practice could range from overall operational directives down to supply schedules and marching orders for small units, to be reviewed later at a critique. The ride might involve two opposing sides or only one, and could simulate anything from a local operation up to the main part of a war plan for an entire theater. Less physically taxing, and more economical in time as well as cost, were map exercises or war games, which did much the same thing as staff rides but without the participants going out into the field. Instead the officers involved in a map exercise, usually in two opposing teams mediated by referees, moved forces on paper according to elaborate rules for simulating the constraints imposed by actual field conditions. Again, these exercises might cover operations all the way up to the size of general war plans, and could involve the drafting of detailed orders for each movement. Both staff rides and map exercises tested officers and planning at every level, including that of the central war plans that general staffs maintained for the mobilization, deployment, and initial operations of the country's forces for different war contingencies. With the new system of citizen-reserve armies, war plans had to be concerted in peacetime before an actual conflict threatened. The elaborate call-up schedules and railroad timetables that were necessary to mobilize the whole apparatus depended upon where and when the assembled units would have to be when operations started. A complete set had to be on file for each separate war plan in an army's repertory.

CHANGING TECHNOLOGY IN THE EUROPEAN ARMIES

Assessing the effectiveness of armies or war plans in the early twentieth century was all the more complicated because of the rapid changes in technology that had taken place since the last European wars. These innovations kept the capabilities of armies in constant flux. In this respect as in others, some of the changes in the armies of the great powers were quite apparent, while others could only be guessed at, even by their own side. That new equipment was available was obvious. How it would change even further in the future, and what effect it would have on combat, tactics, and the international balance of military power, were matters of lively debate.

The most conspicuous of the new technologies was quick-firing artillery. In the late nineteenth century the rate of fire of artillery had attained the upper limit set by the recoil of a field gun. No matter how quickly the crew could thrust in a shell and close the breech, when they fired the gun they had to stand clear to avoid it as it leaped backward with the force of the blast. No matter how accurately the new telescopic sights and calibrated aiming dials could point the gun at a target farther away than the eye could see, the gunners had to push the whole piece back into position and aim it again after each round. Partial recoil suppressors, such as springs in the mounting or a shovel blade at the back of the trail that dug into the earth to hold it in place, could alleviate the effects only fractionally. The basic problem of recoil remained. It was not until 1896 that two French officers, Captains Deport and Sainte-Claire Deville, finally solved it. In that year they presented a design, which the French army adopted, for a field gun carriage that remained stationary in firing. Only the barrel itself slid backward, along a track in the mounting. The shock was taken up by an intricate brake, a piston cylinder mounted parallel to the barrel, which used the action of the recoil to compress fluid. The compression and reexpansion of the brake first absorbed the recoil of the barrel and then pushed it forward again into exactly the position from which it had started. The new gun, firing a shell seventy-five millimeters in diameter, was a total success, and the French army began reequipping its entire field artillery with it in 1897.[11]

The French invention constituted a revolution in the deadliness of artillery. Suddenly the possible rate of fire quadrupled. The old guns were theoretically capable of firing up to five rounds a minute, though precise reaiming each time took longer. By contrast, the French 75mm gun could fire twenty rounds per minute once the shells began hitting the target. The gun remained stationary, with its crew ready to reload the instant a shell left the barrel. The aimer and gunlayer still occupied their seats on the mounting, and the sights stayed aligned. Once they found the right setting, they could fire off shells practically as fast as the crew could load them, deluging a target with explosive. The loaders could remain close to the piece, partially protected by metal shields bolted to the gun carriage and to the ammunition caisson that stood beside it in action. This meant that they could work faster and often continue serving the gun under fire when with earlier cannon they would have had to take cover.

As well as being faster, fire became much more accurate. With the barrel maintaining its alignment, the gunners could correct their aim to make each shell fall closer to its target than the preceding one. With the old guns, each round was bound to be almost as inaccurate as the first one fired. Above all, the 75mm gun could reliably hit targets its crew could not see. Artillery had used "indirect fire" before, but this had always been a laborious and erratic process. Guns emplaced out of sight of their target, behind the crest of a hill or some other obstacle, could be aimed by computation with the aid of a map and compass, as long as an observer who was in a position to see the target could signal its location back to the gunners. The projectiles, fired on a slightly curved trajectory, would fly over the intervening obstruction and drop into the target area beyond. With each round fired, the forward observer could indicate to the battery how far off target the shell had fallen and in what direction. But this information was of limited use to the old recoiling artillery, which had to aim afresh each time. For the new quick-firing gun, however, it meant that the gunners could aim each round with a correction from the sighting line of its predecessor to be more accurate, and once the shells began falling on target they could dispense with the elaborate aiming and signaling process. The French 75 had sophisticated new sighting, ranging, and fuze-setting apparatus, specially designed to help make this procedure rapid and precise. Suddenly it became practical to emplace an artillery battery in a secure position, out of sight of the enemy, and yet still to direct its fire accurately onto exposed targets. Artillerymen could now exploit the seven-kilometer range of a field gun in terrain that did not afford a clear field of vision for anything like that distance. Smokeless ammunition meant that almost nothing remained to betray the position of the battery. Guns no longer had to come under fire to come into action.

The significance of the French *soixante-quinze* was not lost upon other European armies. They could not imitate the invention at once, however, since the French kept its design rigorously secret. In 1904 the contest was still in progress to develop and deploy field artillery equipped with hydro-pneumatic recoil brakes of the French type. The German army had the misfortune to have adopted a new 77mm field gun without recoil absorption in 1896, manufacturing and distributing it at great expense just as the French 75 appeared. The war ministry realized its mistake and had to set about commissioning a conversion that incorporated a recoil mechanism. The result, a composite of designs by the Krupp and Ehrhardt steelworks, did not go into production until 1905.[12] The Russians had also recently adopted a gun with a partial recoil buffer, the Model 00, which relied on the compression of a stack of rubber rings inside the trail to cushion the impact. When this system proved clearly inadequate after a number had gone into service, the army canceled it. The Model 02 field gun, a 76.2mm piece with a hydro-pneumatic brake, went into production at the Putilov works in 1904, though it would take several years to reequip the whole army.[13] The Austro-Hungarian design for a quick-firing gun was still undergoing tests in 1904, and even when it was ready the following year there was no money to begin manufacturing it.[14] The Italians suspended production of their new Krupp 75A field gun in 1904, since it possessed only a spring recoil-absorption mechanism, whereas a true quick-firing type was clearly going to be necessary.[15] The British were producing a reliable eighteen-pounder field gun with a hydro-pneumatic recoil brake by 1904, but since the Indian army had first priority in delivery, the forces at home did not begin to receive it until 1905.[16] The French were in a position to gloat over the considerable head start they had gained over other European armies in the introduction of quick-firing artillery.[17]

Another new weapon that was just beginning to enter service, albeit at less expense and with less fanfare, was the machine gun. Several armies had used various multibarreled and manually fired types, such as the Gatling and Gardner guns and the French *mitrailleuse,* in the second half of the nineteenth century, but these had generally proven too unwieldy and temperamental to constitute anything more than a specialized auxiliary weapon. Hiram Maxim had patented the first effective, fully automatic machine gun in the United States in 1884, but it had not immediately gained acceptance for use in Europe. Most armies successfully tested it in colonial warfare, where its volume of fire could compensate for the small numbers of troops deployed. For use with the metropolitan forces, however, commanders judged it to be too cumbersome and costly. Most importantly, it consumed far too much ammunition, firing at a rate of six hundred bullets a minute, or ten per second. Before the early 1900s machine guns still did not fire the same cartridge as the rifles of the infantry, since designing fully automatic weapons that worked at all required that the rounds be made to suit the tolerances of the mechanism and barrel. This meant that machine gun ammunition had to be manufactured and brought forward separately. The guns and their mountings were heavy and had to be towed like artillery pieces on two-wheeled carriages, or at best packed on mule-back for movement across country.

Introducing machine guns into the infantry or cavalry consequently meant adding special miniature batteries, attended by officers and dozens of men, as well as a small train of animals to haul the guns and thousands upon thousands of rounds of ammunition. These formations required special training, equipment, stables, fodder, and space in the supply columns. They could not move as quickly across country as either infantry or cavalry. The flexibility, mobility, and simplicity that most officers regarded as the particular assets of these arms seemed as if they might be seriously compromised. There appeared to be no way of incorporating the still cumbersome and vulnerable machine guns into the tactical movements of troops who were supposed to advance rapidly in lines across the battlefield, and yet if the guns remained behind the attack they seemed likely to be left too far away from the enemy to offer effective covering fire.[18] War ministries did not wish to expend the men and money that the large-scale adoption of machine guns would require, especially at a time when the weapon's complex mechanism still broke down just often enough to remind skeptics of the dangerous unreliability of its crank-operated predecessors. The earliest employment of machine guns in continental Europe was for the defense of fortresses, where mobility and ammunition supply would not present problems, and where rapid fire could help defenders to hold off more numerous attackers.

Nevertheless, by 1904 most European armies had begun experimenting with a few special machine gun units. They often attached these to the cavalry to augment its firepower with something less cumbersome than artillery. The Germans set up five units with six Maxim guns each in 1901.[19] In the following year the French attached a section of two French-built Hotchkiss machine guns to each of four battalions of mountain infantry, probably with a view to their utility in rough terrain where small units would operate without much artillery support.[20] Also by 1902, the Russian army had three machine gun detachments in operation.[21] The Austro-Hungarians began testing in 1903, and set up three experimental units the next year.[22] Italy remained at the stage of experiments in 1904.[23] Alone among the European armies, the British had institutionalized the use of machine guns as part of standard formations by 1904, with a section of two Maxim guns constituting an organic part of each infantry battalion and operating together with the unit in the field.[24] The small size of Britain's professional army compared to the national-service forces on the continent made this transformation cheaper to carry out, as well as an obvious means of compensating for small numerical strength. The experience of colonial warfare, which had been the principal task of the British army and remained a likely employment for any of its regular units, may also have dictated its exceptional progress in the adoption of machine guns. Foreign military attachés noted it, but as yet few expected serious consequences for the great continental armies.

A few other technologies that would change the face of warfare in the twentieth century were only in their most experimental stages in Europe by 1904. The automobile, which the invention of the internal-combustion engine had recently transformed from a curiosity into a practical means of conveyance, was not yet in widespread service anywhere, though several armies had acquired a few for trials. By renting additional vehicles, the Germans, for example, were able to field twenty-two cars and thirty-five motorcycles for the use of the directors and the headquarters of the two sides at the imperial maneuvers of 1904.[25] Guglielmo Marconi's experiments in Italy had made it possible for many armies to begin using fixed wireless radio stations and make preliminary tests of mobile ones in the field.[26] Telephones, which promised to be more robust for campaign service and simpler for nonspecialist troops to use, were just becoming practical for military purposes. The communication links were being forged that would control units on the battlefield, direct artillery fire onto unseen targets, and pass information back to headquarters. Armies had regularly used tethered balloons to send observers aloft to survey the battlefield since the mid-nineteenth century, and by 1904 aviation pioneers were beginning to break the bonds of earth with powered flights that opened up wholly new possibilities. As yet, however, the fliers of dirigible airships had not gained enough success to attract the serious interest of the military. The Wright brothers were still experimenting with the remarkable invention they had tested at Kitty Hawk, North Carolina, in December of 1903.

TACTICAL AND OPERATIONAL THOUGHT: THE FUTURE OF WAR

The question remained what these new forces could actually do. To assess the strength of an army, observers had to take into account the way it would perform on a battlefield profoundly transformed by modern organization and technology. What would the war of the future look like? Colonial campaigns captured the public imagination, but they were not the real missions of the *Millionenheere*, the people's armies of millions that would mobilize for any struggle between the great powers on their own frontiers. A great European war might involve just two states or coalitions of states in a great continental test of arms. It was for such a conflict that all the European armies organized and trained, even though colonial distractions might temporarily subtract improvised formations from the metropolitan strength. The British alone maintained a regimental system that favored the regular rotation of units to overseas stations around the empire.

All European forces expected to fight mobile, mostly offensive actions. They took as their models the most successful campaigns of the Napoleonic Wars and the wars of German unification. Tacticians realized that firepower was deadlier than ever, but they often expected that this would, if anything, make attacks more effective and place a premium on rapid, decisive movements. The history of recent wars seemed to suggest that the side that seized the offensive would win.[27] Frederick the Great and Napoleon had gained their most spectacular victories by means of aggressive maneuvers that had repeatedly overwhelmed their opponents. Commentators tended to dismiss the protracted campaigns of the American Civil War as a struggle of hastily levied civilian armies, quite unlike the more thoroughly trained and professionally officered European forces.[28] The Union and Confederate armies operated over vast and often thinly settled areas at the extremity of long supply lines, under conditions that bore little resemblance to the narrow frontiers in Europe. The American experience also suffered a virtually total eclipse in the shadow of several major European wars that took place just before and after it. These tended to reinforce the idea that it was an anomaly. The Franco-Austrian, Austro-Prussian, and Franco-Prussian wars offered examples of decisive, fast-paced offensives overcoming sluggish, apparently irresolute efforts by the losing side. Even the Russian advance through the Balkans against the slow-moving Turks in 1877–78 presented evidence that an attacker could prevail in mountainous terrain against a series of powerful fortresses. The Anglo-Boer War of 1899–1902 suggested a contrary lesson, as the British army in South Africa repeatedly faltered in advances against rapid fire from the Boers' modern German-made rifles. However, even while observers debated the implications of this, the Russo-Japanese War seemed to prove once again that attacks would succeed. The Japanese suffered terrible casualties in 1904 and 1905, but ultimately their assaults went in to decide the day. Against the almost incomprehensible passivity of the Russian command, the Japanese won repeated victories with an aggressive strategy and a willingness to sacrifice men at decisive points. The victors throughout the second half of the nineteenth century had accomplished all of this in spite of a continual increase in the lethality of weapons. The results tended to silence critics of the offensive, and to confirm the axiom that only the attack could bring victory.

Military theory provided a continuous accompaniment to this development. Not only did it enthrone the virtues of the offensive; it tended increasingly to transfer the debate from the realm of material, technical considerations to that of morale, will, and interaction between people. The wars of the French Revolution had shown what an influence popular enthusiasm and political ideas could have, not only upon recruitment and the mobilization of society for war, but also upon fighting effectiveness. Napoleon himself had said that in war the moral is to the material as three is to one, a maxim that his disciples never tired of quoting. Carl von Clausewitz, writing in the aftermath of the Napoleonic Wars, acknowledged the power of the defensive in an age of firearms, but argued that nevertheless a commander would only win by seizing the initiative and boldly aiming at the destruction of the enemy's army, as Napoleon had done.[29] Most importantly, Clausewitz illuminated the terrible human side of combat: the roles played by fear, confusion, and the emotional and physical experiences of the combatants from the lowest level up to the commander on the battlefield. The visionary French officer, Charles Jean-Jacques Joseph Ardant du Picq, took up this theme in the 1860s, writing that a battle was more a contest of wills than anything else, and that it was much less important to inflict material losses than to persuade the enemy that he was beaten.[30] To achieve this, du Picq believed in sacrificing everything to the awe-inspiring momentum of an attack. Colmar von der Goltz, the influential German author of many works on strategy after the wars of unification, perpetuated these ideas.[31] For him, to defend was to let the enemy decide where, when, and how the battle would be fought. It was also to sacrifice the inestimable advantage in morale that an advancing army enjoyed over a retreating one. All of these ideas conformed well with those of popular nationalist writers in the Mazzinian and later Treitschkean traditions, who placed voluntarism and the power of feelings, especially experienced as a community, above mundane material constraints. The sociological, political, and psychological theory of thinkers like Nietzsche, Sorel, Weber, Durkheim, and Freud contributed to this preoccupation with will and emotion in a world that seemed to many by the turn of the century to have fallen prey to a dehumanizing materialism.[32] The whole also intermingled readily with Social Darwinist calls for vigorous action in an inexorable struggle for survival. Attitudes had moved a long way from the Enlightenment, when military thinkers had sought a universal and rational system of warfare, while tinkering with optimal solutions to problems of gunnery, engineering, drill, maneuver, and logistics.[33] General staffs still concerned themselves intensely with technical details, but where combat itself was concerned, the ethos of aggressiveness tended to prevail.

The result by the early twentieth century was that all European armies favored a fairly standard scheme of offensive maneuver.[34] Cavalry patrols would ride ahead of the main advance to screen its movements against attack and to watch the enemy. Once a force made contact, the infantry would go forward, in columns at first for easier movement along roads and defiles. It would disperse into looser formations as it came under fire closer to the enemy. Artillery was supposed to cover this advance, firing from commanding positions to keep down the heads of opposing troops and suppress the fire of the enemy's batteries. When the infantry reached a point a couple of hundred meters from the enemy (the distance varied from one set of regulations to another), the men were supposed to form a firing line of their own and blaze away until they had established what was vaguely termed "fire superiority" over the enemy. This achieved, the infantry was to fix bayonets, advance to a short distance from the opposing positions, and charge. Regulations celebrated the bayonet as the most fearsome of weapons and the symbol of aggressive will.[35] Cavalry, also approaching by marches as far out of sight as possible, could charge at the decisive moment against weak points in the enemy position, and was supposed to take over the task of pursuing or cutting off a retreating enemy. Debate raged among theorists as to whether the cavalry would be most effective staying in the saddle for "shock action" with lance and saber, or dismounting to fight like infantry with their rifles after riding swiftly to key positions.[36] Whatever the case, the orchestration of infantry, artillery, and cavalry in their mutually supporting roles, the "cooperation of arms," was the key to all of these movements.

Theoreticians generally agreed that the cooperation of arms would be more necessary than ever to overcome the increasing firepower of modern weapons. Everybody acknowledged that fire now dominated the battlefield. The consensus, given the power of modern rifles and the experience of the Anglo-Boer and Russo-Japanese Wars, was that there would be a nearly lethal zone, essentially uncrossable, between the opposing front lines, eight hundred to a thousand meters broad and swept by bullets. The difficulty was how to traverse, circumvent, or eliminate this fire-swept area. The Polish-Russian banker Ivan Bloch published a microscopically detailed treatise in 1899 entitled *War in the Future,* which concluded that it would be impossible.[37] Bloch's six volumes consisted of an exhaustive study of the lethality of modern weapons, the demands their effects would place upon manpower and industry, and the impact of total war upon modern societies. The work minutely examined everything from the impact of high-velocity bullets upon human tissue and bone to statistics on national production of grain. Professional officers dismissed Bloch's claims as the exaggerations of an amateur.

Many argued that the new armaments could make attacks easier. Certainly casualties would be heavy in the face of magazine-loaded rifles, quick-firing artillery, and, eventually, machine guns. However, these weapons might also make it impossible to hold defensive positions. If artillery could break up an advance, it could also slaughter troops who stood still and tried to defend ground. "The steady growth in the power of artillery always facilitates the attack," wrote the French gunnery expert Hippolyte Langlois in 1904.[38] The guns, in his phrase, would "open the door for the infantry."[39] Even Napoleon had relied on massed cannon fire to batter a hole in the enemy's line before launching an infantry column into the breach. As von der Goltz recalled, during the Franco-Prussian War the German commanders had quickly learned to let artillery pound a defensive position into silence before attempting to send the infantry forward.[40] Langlois and other specialists like the German General Heinrich von Rohne pointed out that the new artillery of the turn of the century could use its vastly increased range and accuracy to bring defending infantry under fire while itself remaining almost invulnerable, far out of rifle shot. More importantly, it would be able to give covering fire while friendly infantry advanced toward the enemy. In the past, the short range, inaccuracy, and unreliable fuzes of artillery had made this risky or impossible. The new guns, however, would be able to continue firing, over the heads of their own infantry, as the latter went forward. The defenders would be faced with the choice of either lying protected but helpless under cover as the attackers closed in, or else standing up to use their rifles and take punishing casualties from the rapid fire and the much more powerful shrapnel loadings of modern shells. The infantry had a dual role in closing with the enemy and in forcing him to expose himself to the artillery's fire. Even when the attacking infantry approached very close to the defenses, its artillery could fire at longer range to reach behind the enemy lines and hit reinforcements as they came up. Rapid small arms fire, for its part, could mow down troops in the open, but it also gave the attackers much more deadly firepower to carry forward with them. Within the eight-hundred-meter killing range, the advancing infantry could begin using their own rifles to beat down the fire of the defenders, often in the alternate rushes of "fire and movement" that were to become a familiar feature of twentieth-century tactics.

In this way, the theoreticians maintained, technology continually altered the grammar of an immutable language of war. The effects of weapons had always been present. These effects merely grew progressively more extreme, and in some ways canceled each other out. This was one reason why Bloch and other doomsayers met with so much criticism. Proper training, the cooperation of arms, and unflinching readiness to accept necessary casualties seemed to be capable of turning the new weapons into yet another asset to the perennial offensive. By and large, these schemes of tactics ignored the effects of such things as the enemy's artillery, the complexity of fighting engagements in which both sides were attempting to rush forward in an onslaught of this kind, and of course the best method of fighting a defensive action, a prospect that would surely arise from time to time in spite of the most aggressive will in the world. What did receive much attention instead was the manner of exploiting mobility, above all, to achieve surprise or reach around the enemy's flank. If possible, multiple attacks were supposed to converge on the adversary's front and flank at once, in order to minimize the need to approach positions directly where the enemy was prepared to respond with fire. The lethality of weapons, then, could be made to conform to a system of thought that stressed the energetic offensive and greater mobility than ever before.

It was in this light that critics interpreted the lessons of the latest wars fought with some of the new armaments. European observers minutely dissected the engagements of the Anglo-Boer and Russo-Japanese Wars, and found in them evidence to support their hypotheses. Where the combatants had followed proper procedures, they argued, the attack had succeeded. Where they had made mistakes, the result had been disasters of the kind Bloch had predicted. In South Africa, traditional British tactics had met with almost total paralysis in the face of murderous long-range rifle fire.[41] The Boers remained almost invisible in their defensive positions because they were far away, entrenched, and firing smokeless cartridges. The twentieth-century phenomenon of the "emptiness of the battlefield" made its appearance. The opposing forces could scarcely see one another, and yet to move in the open was practically suicidal. Only later in the war did the British prevail by bringing overwhelmingly superior resources to bear and staging methodical advances over enormous expanses of territory. French authors in particular argued that the British attacks in the early engagements had failed because they were conducted in complete disregard of accepted European doctrine. The British had customarily shelled enemy positions with artillery, ceased fire, and then sent the infantry forward. This had allowed the Boers to lie almost invulnerable in their trenches during the bombardment, and then rise to take aim at the attacking formations. When the Boers retreated, the British had not used cavalry aggressively to cut them off and annihilate them in the moment of greatest vulnerability. Especially after the first battles, little cavalry had been left in the saddle toward the end of engagements, due to the increasing tendency for the troopers to dismount and move forward to fight on foot, leaving their horses out of reach at the decisive moment. The British had clearly not achieved proper cooperation of arms in their assaults at Talana Hill, Colenso, Magersfontein, or Spion Kop. This left authors in Europe free to speculate on the successes that might have followed if they had, especially using large amounts of quick-firing artillery instead of their limited number of guns mostly designed in 1883. Langlois, Georges Gilbert, and Henri Bonnal, all French officers writing analyses of the Boer War in 1903 and 1904, heaped criticism on the British for what they regarded as these almost incredible tactical blunders, which would have guaranteed low marks in any European military exercise.[42] In fact, argued Bonnal, there was nothing new about the supposed "lessons" of fire on the battlefield or the impossibility of direct frontal assaults against firmly held positions. All of this, he maintained, had been clear at least since the Franco-Prussian War, and indeed frontal cavalry charges against unbroken infantry or artillery had been an acknowledged recipe for disaster even in the Napoleonic Wars. Nobody in Europe was proposing these methods of assault in their crudest form any more.

The Russo-Japanese War seemed to offer far more edifying examples to European observers. The French general staff intelligence office, the Deuxième Bureau, concluded, "a point which cannot be refuted by example, since it emerges clearly from all operations, is the dazzling confirmation of the superiority of the offensive as a form of combat, of the value of maneuver, and, conversely, of the impotence of the defensive and above all of the passive defensive."[43] This appeared to be the case even without the aid of truly quick-firing field guns on either side. The Japanese had none of these and the Russians had only a small proportion of rather ineffective early-model ones. The field artillery suffered frequent breakdowns, fired many defective shells, and was poorly handled on both sides. It hung back at extreme range because it was not equipped with shields and could not fire accurately by indirect laying from defiladed positions.[44] The Deuxième Bureau concluded in its report on field guns that the results simply showed that artillery could be much more effective than this if properly used.[45] The Prussian general staff agreed that, "according to all observations, neither the Russian nor the Japanese artillery achieved remotely what we expect from our own." The Germans judged that "it may be assumed for certain that the laborious progress and the long duration of attacks observed in almost all battles was in large part due to the inadequate artillery preparation."[46]

Even in the face of modern small arms fire and without up-to-date artillery support, the Japanese infantry had ultimately succeeded in getting forward. It had done so mostly by approaching to short ranges along defiladed routes, or by entrenchment and nighttime movement. Sometimes it had advanced by accepting very heavy losses. A Russian officer writing for the authoritative French *Revue militaire des armées étrangères* in 1906 went so far as to derive the lesson that the charge with the bayonet remained the essence of combat, and that "it is force of morale which will bring victory."[47] By his account, authors like Bonnal and Langlois had been exactly right: the ranges of engagement had increased tremendously, but the final decision was still the same as ever. The Japanese infantry had displayed precisely the qualities European officers sought from their own troops, pressing attacks home in spite of terrible casualties and behaving with unshakable discipline and a fervent spirit of patriotic self-sacrifice enjoined by a warrior code.[48] In fact, the long duration of the battles in Manchuria and the devastating effect of modern weapons prefigured the shape of engagements in the First World War, as many of the nineteenth-century campaigns had done. At the time, however, it was easy for predisposed observers to interpret the manner of Japan's victory as a confirmation of the effectiveness of the offensive tactics. In the early twentieth century these were being preached perhaps most conspicuously by Lieutenant-Colonel Ferdinand Foch. He delivered his famous lectures *On the Principles of War* at the French staff college, the Ecole Supérieure de la Guerre, in 1903.[49] Foch took up all of the points raised by earlier advocates of the offensive and of the psychological advantage, illustrating his views with a metaphor: "A purely defensive battle is a duel in which one of the fencers does nothing but *parry*. It would not occur to anybody that he could get the better of his opponent with this game. On the contrary, and despite the greatest of skill, he exposes himself to being struck sooner or later, to succumbing to the blows of the other, even if the latter is weaker."[50] It was enough to smash any part of the enemy's army, Foch argued, and the entire organism would cease to function. To do so "is to arrest the functioning of the hierarchy, to transform the units into formless masses of men, to make the execution of orders impossible, to annihilate the will of the command, to stop all action."[51] All of this had become crucial, Foch argued, with the change wrought by the Napoleonic Wars and recognized since Clausewitz. The wars of the future would be wars of entire peoples, aimed not at the capture of fortresses or territory but at the total destruction of the enemy: "absolute war," as Clausewitz himself had defined it.

The concern with the scale of future wars added to the urgency of fighting great, decisive battles early in a campaign, although military men seldom defined the connection explicitly. An aggressively fought war was a short war. A static war was a long one that in the future would drag in appalling masses of men and resources, reducing states to economic ruin, starvation, and perhaps revolution. The Napoleonic Wars had burned upon the European consciousness the scourging effects of wars that toppled thrones and unleashed the power of populations. The

Franco-Prussian War lingered for a ghastly winter in the throes of another *levée en masse* after the early swift campaigns and the overthrow of
Louis Napoleon. The French provisional government threw the nation's
last resources into a desperate effort to wear down the invaders and finally found itself faced with the nightmare of popular insurrection in the
Paris Commune. Von der Goltz warned that a struggle of nations might
only begin with the destruction of the enemy's army and continue until
the victor had crushed every power of resistance out of the defeated
state.[52] Ivan Bloch was more explicit, showing by his encyclopedic calculations that most European economies would quickly be devastated by
the strains and consumption of a full-scale war with modern weapons,
paving the way for revolution on the home front even by a victorious
population.[53] To accept this aspect of Bloch's work, it was not necessary
to believe what he wrote about the tactical impossibility of a decisive
battle at the outset. Certainly it was more comprehensible to military
men than the notion put forward by idealistic antimilitarist authors such
as Guglielmo Ferrero and Norman Angell at the turn of the century:
that the interdependence and economic sophistication of modern industrial states meant that war between them had become contrary to reason, and therefore impossible.[54] For strategists in imperial Germany,
faced with the prospect of a war on two fronts and against the long purse
and naval power of Britain, the problem of a prolonged war appeared
real enough, and indeed particularly severe. The only solution seemed to
be to destroy at least one opponent, France or Russia, quickly and decisively in order to free the forces to beat the other. Only a rapid offensive
such as that designed by Count Alfred von Schlieffen, the chief of the
Prussian general staff from 1892 onward, stood a chance of bringing
this about: a "battle of annihilation" at least on one front, waged from
the outset.[55] On every level, from the infantry skirmish to the national
war plan, the future of war in the twentieth century seemed to be the
offensive.

CONSTRAINTS ON THE GROWTH OF ARMIES IN 1904

Despite these efforts to apply the products of technological progress
and military experience to the modernization of warfare, the European
armies were far from being engaged in a headlong armaments race
against one another in 1904. As a result of a combination of domestic
and international pressures, each could at most sustain a process of slow
development. While officers might look across the frontiers at neighboring armies and shape their own practices as far as possible to counter
those of likely opponents, the dominant concerns were the constraints
they faced.

The French army, for example, lived under a cloud of governmental suspicion and political animosity. The Dreyfus affair of the 1890s had discredited the military establishment by exposing its bigotry, exclusivism, and corruption. The conviction of a Jewish officer, Captain Alfred Dreyfus, by a court-martial on fabricated charges of spying had bitterly divided society as well as the officer corps. Religious and political antagonisms had hardened as the falsehood had come to light while the high command had desperately tried to defend its initial position. The scandal had swept into power a Radical government under Prime Minister Emile Combes, dedicated to secularization and aggressive reform, particularly of the army. Under the zealous eye of the new war minister, General Louis André, the government scrutinized officers for anti-Republican tendencies and deprived them of perquisites in an effort to democratize the service. The government was in no mood to boost military spending.

Indeed, to the horror of the generals, the Radicals introduced a bill to the Chamber of Deputies to reduce the term of military service from three years to two. This passed in March 1905. By extending conscription even to those groups that had previously been exempted, the measure was supposed to implement true principles of equality, to maintain a peacetime strength close to that under the three-year law, to pass more men every year through the army and into the reserves for wartime, and to provide an incentive for more educated young men to volunteer to become officers since they would now face conscription into the ranks if they did not do so.[56] In accordance with the established axioms of the European Left, shortening and expanding the basis of service was designed also to erode the praetorianism of a caste-ridden long-service military. Instead, France was to have a "citizen army" of civilian reservists for national defense in wartime. The generals in the Conseil Supérieur de la Guerre, the group of army commanders and planners that met with the war minister and sometimes the president and prime minister to discuss military policy, saw only a blow against the strength and cohesion of the army. Short service meant more disruptive turnover of men in the units, lower physical standards for soldiers as the army reached deeper into the available pool, more raw recruits to be trained by fewer experienced men, and, in the long run, a lower peacetime strength.[57] The latter would have to be dealt with by a series of "cadre laws" (lois des cadres) that reduced the official strength of units and shuffled officers and men between them to cover the most urgent needs.[58] France might possess the magnificent 75mm field gun, but the army was in no position to think of expansion and was receiving no encouragement from the council of ministers.

France's principal ally, Russia, which had the largest army in the world, was in even worse condition, especially after war broke out with Japan in 1904. Since the larger and better-equipped part of the Russian forces normally stood in the garrisons on the western frontier opposite Austria-Hungary and Germany, it was from there that much of the modern weaponry and many of the reinforcements and specialist units had to come for the campaign in Manchuria. The high command at first tried to meet its needs with the Siberian corps and reserve forces east of the Urals, but it quickly found that supplementary men and equipment from the west would be indispensable.[59] By the end of the war, Russia sent more than half a million soldiers to East Asia. This involved stripping away numerous units stationed in the European theater. What was worse, the mobilizations took place in a haphazard manner that left the remaining forces quite unready for war. Instead of filling up the departing formations with the reservists and equipment designated for them in wartime, the military authorities simply skimmed off the best personnel and hardware from the units that were not being put on the trans-Siberian railway for the journey east. The mobilized force therefore contained much of the army's best material, but it was jumbled together from different sources rather than possessing the homogeneity of units that had trained together. The part of the army that still faced westward yielded up all of the new Model 00 and Model 02 field guns it had received, vast quantities of the mobilization stores in its magazines, and assorted other assets from siege guns to engineer battalions.[60] Much of this process had already taken place by the end of 1904.[61] Nor did the morale or the international credibility of the army as a whole improve with its dismal performance on the battlefields in Manchuria. Not once did the Russians mount a successful offensive operation, falling back instead from one defensive position to another in the face of Japanese forces of comparable size and armament.[62] When defeat at the front turned into revolution at home at the beginning of 1905, the disaster for the army was complete. The society and government that supported it fell into turmoil, while the principal tasks of the military became the maintenance of order in its own ranks and the suppression of civilian unrest throughout Russia.[63]

France's other ally was a more recent one, and likewise in no condition to undertake serious military competition on land in Europe. Great Britain signed the *entente cordiale* with France in April of 1904 precisely in the hope of reducing the pressures of strategic competition. By resolving its colonial disputes with France and putting to rest any lingering possibility of naval rivalry across the Channel, Arthur James Balfour's Conservative government set itself free to invest its resources elsewhere. This chiefly meant concentrating on Britain's perceived conflicts of interest with Russia in Afghanistan and Persia, and an increasingly costly naval race with Germany in the North Sea.[64] The competition in battleship building consumed the majority of new British defense spending and took priority over the army since the navy still appeared to be the principal guarantor of the country's security. The army had to spend much of the money it did get on liquidating the consequences of the Boer War. Although Britain had finally won the conflict in South Africa, it had only done so at the cost of a three-year military effort involving the bulk of the regular army as well as the improvised mobilization of large additional volunteer formations that had never been designed to leave the home country.[65] For a small, professional, long-service army like Britain's, the dislocation caused by fighting a war on such a scale had been severe. The expenses and casualties had been depressingly high, and failures on the battlefield had prompted a total overhaul of the army's organization, equipment, tactics, and organs of command and administration.[66] This was still in progress in 1904. What was more, the army still existed and planned essentially for wars outside of Europe, functioning chiefly as a source of replacements and potential reinforcements for the Indian army. The war plans formed by the new general staff and the civil-military Committee of Imperial Defence were exclusively for non-European contingencies, such as the defense of Egypt or the northwest frontier of India.[67] The *entente cordiale* with France was a striking departure from Britain's avoidance of continental entanglements in peacetime. Nevertheless, it did not include a military convention and it certainly did not mean that the British army was preparing to fight an enemy in Europe.

Imperial Germany, France's main rival on land and Britain's at sea, was likewise disinclined to contemplate any great military expansion in 1904. The most rapidly growing part of the state budget was, as in Britain, for the navy. Admiral Alfred von Tirpitz, the ambitious state secretary for the Reich Naval Office, had secured backing from a parliamentary majority of agrarian conservatives, industrial interests, and the Catholic Center Party for his plan to build a fleet large enough to threaten the Royal Navy's supremacy at sea. With this he proposed to conquer for Germany the position of colonial and commercial power that he imagined would flow from naval strength. Reich Chancellor Bernhard von Bülow was for the time being content to follow this policy, which enjoyed the vigorous support of the patron upon whom he depended, Kaiser Wilhelm II. Bülow owed his position to his political adroitness as a courtier who catered to the emperor's taste for flattery and procured parliamentary coalitions that would reliably uphold the interests of the throne and the social and political elite. The naval program assured a unified grouping in the Reichstag to support the government while excluding the left-liberal and Social Democratic parties. However, the soaring costs of battleship building wrought havoc with Treasury Secretary Hermann von Stengel's efforts to carry out a systematic finance reform and balance the state budget. One thing on which the parties supporting the naval program could agree was that there should be no taxes on private property, so Bülow had to fund the bills precariously with a mixed bag of tariff and commodity tax increases.[68] There was certainly no money left over for ambitious army programs, especially after the outbreak of the Herero rising in the German colony of Southwest Africa in October of 1904, the bloody suppression of which made further demands on military budgets.[69] The Social Democrats' large gains in the 1903 Reichstag elections further enjoined caution in proposals for spending on the army.

Germany's principal ally in Europe, the Dual Monarchy of Austria-Hungary, faced domestic disputes that practically paralyzed its military development. Under the three-tiered system of state administration, policy formed by the government in Vienna had to be approved by votes in the separate parliaments of both halves of the monarchy. This made the single common army of Austria-Hungary into a principal arena for the struggle of the Hungarians to assert their independence from the Austrian-dominated center. Indeed, as the main joint institution of the monarchy, the army functioned as a barometer for the pressures of separatist impulses in general. Since the turn of the century, the Kossuthist Independence Party had begun blocking votes of Hungarian funds and recruits to the army as a means of gaining increased recognition for Budapest's claims to separate representation. Where the army was concerned, the autonomists called for the designation of special Hungarian regiments with their own officers, speaking Magyar and carrying the Hungarian tricolor flag. These were to be distinct from the army's existing formations, which were of mixed nationality, spoke a variety of the monarchy's ten languages, used German as a *lingua franca* for command and administration, and carried the black-and-gold double eagle flag of the House of Habsburg. The emperor Franz Joseph had found himself obliged to use emergency decrees to call the Hungarian annual contingent of recruits to the colors in the face of obstruction in the Budapest parliament in 1899, 1900, and 1901.[70] The 1903 class did not report for training until May of 1904, seven months late.[71] Military spending practically stood still from one year to the next, with proposals for increases dying in endless legislative battles. But Franz Joseph and his military entourage considered the unified, German-speaking army to be an institution so vital to the cohesion of the heterogeneous monarchy that they resisted almost all concessions. The emperor was an austere old soldier who had spent the majority of his seventy-four-year life in the army and was deeply preoccupied with the integrity of the institution at the heart of his realm. The general staff went so far as to draw up plans in April of 1905 for a possible military occupation of Hungary in case the emperor decided to resolve the deadlock by an open coup.[72]

Nor were Vienna's concerns limited to the joint forces. Besides the common army, Hungary and the Austrian-dominated section of the monarchy each had their own separate volunteer military forces, the Honvédség and the Landwehr, respectively. These would operate alongside the common army in wartime, but the men served only two years instead of three and were recruited on a national basis. Beginning in 1904, the Hungarian moderate leader and minister-president, Count István Tisza, renewed earlier efforts to turn the Honvédség into a self-sufficient Hungarian army. He did this by reviving the demand that it be allowed to form artillery units of its own to support the existing infantry and cavalry, in return for the passage of military legislation in the Budapest parliament.[73] Austria-Hungary might be free from worries about an armed conflict with Russia, its historic rival in the Balkans, but the army was in no state to embark on adventures or dramatic increases in size.

Vienna had even more reason for concern because new adversaries had lately arisen on the international scene. The assassination of King Alexander Obrenović in Serbia in 1903 had brought to the throne the Karadgeorgević dynasty, hostile to Austria-Hungary and soon the target of a bitter campaign of trade sanctions on the part of the Dual Monarchy. Serbia remained weak for the time being, but its enmity and its ambition to unify the South Slav lands of the Balkans and of the frontier regions in Austria-Hungary made it appear to Vienna as a dangerous enemy for the future. To the southwest, Italy had veered away from its position in the Triple Alliance with Austria-Hungary and Germany in the first years of the twentieth century, having patched up its Mediterranean quarrels with France in a series of diplomatic agreements. By 1904, Italy seemed most likely to end up an enemy of the Dual Monarchy, which still contained Italian-speaking areas that had not been incorporated into Italy upon its unification in 1861. The Austro-Hungarian army began shifting troops southward and strengthening its unit establishments and fortifications opposite Italy.[74]

The Italian army, for its part, was not in a position to engage in an armaments race with its northeastern neighbor. All of its fortifications, troop deployments, and mobilization plans were directed against

France, the probable adversary until the turn of the century. The bulk of the land forces did not face Austria-Hungary and could not get there quickly along Italy's sparse roads and rail lines. The northeastern border was virtually without modern defense works.[75] When the general staff played out a map exercise in 1904 representing an Austro-Hungarian invasion, the Italians suffered total defeat. Their forces could not deploy in time at their main defensive position before the enemy overran it, even though this was a hundred kilometers inside Italian territory on the Piave river.[76] Nor was there any prospect of the government spending money for the army to make the changes that could meet this contingency. The military in Italy still languished in the disgrace of its appalling defeat at the battle of Adua in Ethiopia in 1896—until that time by far the worst loss ever inflicted on a European colonial army by indigenous forces. The rout had signified not only the end of Italian colonial expansion in East Africa but also a drastic fall in military spending, prestige, and morale. In 1904 the liberal statesman Giovanni Giolitti took office as prime minister in the first of a series of his governments that were to dominate Italian politics until the First World War. Giolitti was above all a pragmatist, a former finance minister with little interest in foreign policy and with a sense of priorities that placed domestic reforms ahead of military demands. He was certainly not the man to respond to calls for increased funds for an army that did not as yet seem to face a serious external threat.[77] Italy, like the other European powers, was not preoccupied with military expansion in 1904.

The beginning of the prewar decade found the European armies in a steady state of development, but far from engaged in an actual armaments race with each other. They were the largest and most expensive peacetime forces yet seen, containing complex institutionalized bureaucracies for planning wars, incorporating technological innovations, and assessing each other's strength. Experts engaged in continual discussion of what the tactics of a future war might look like under the influence of a constantly changing arsenal of ever more lethal weaponry. The armies presented in some ways a peculiar spectacle of essentially traditional institutions caught up in perpetual innovation and development. They were not, however, in the process of rapid or competitive expansion. The Russian army had its hands full with the campaign in Manchuria, which was quickly turning into a disaster. The British were still recuperating from the Boer War, while both they and the Germans found that most new funds had to go to pay for the ever-escalating costs of the naval race. In France the Radical government of the Dreyfusards made certain that the military remained on a short leash. Giolitti in Italy

Chapter 2

THE EUROPEAN ARMIES AND
THE FIRST MOROCCAN CRISIS, 1905–1906

IN THE SUMMER OF 1905 the German government threatened France with war. It did not actually intend to fight, and the real danger of a conflict flickered only for a moment. But the menace, made at the height of a dramatic diplomatic confrontation over French efforts to secure colonial control of the Sultanate of Morocco, raised the question of whether the armies of the biggest European powers were ready. The war scare that accompanied the first Moroccan crisis caused statesmen and members of the public to look to the armies and weigh their relative strength as they had not done since the Balkan crisis of 1887. The Moroccan confrontation, which hung in balance for eleven months, marked the beginning of a series of diplomatic trials of strength that continued until the outbreak of the First World War, each escalating from its predecessor and helping to drive the European powers into two opposing and increasingly armed camps.

The balance of military power in 1905 was the main thing that made it possible for Germany to pose a credible threat of war against France. The military situation was not a significant element in the considerations of the Reich foreign office on the Wilhelmstraße during the decision to challenge French aspirations in Morocco in the first place, but it came to hand as a weapon of opportunity when the situation grew tense. Because Germany found itself in a position to face its adversaries with the prospect of a war in which it would enjoy a distinct advantage, it played the military card in negotiations. The menace was a bluff, since the makers of policy in Berlin had no intention of going to war over tenuous colonial claims in North Africa. However, it worked in the first phase of the crisis because of the strength of the German army. In the later phases the threat lost its force as Germany's opponents seemed prepared to call the bluff and as Kaiser Wilhelm in particular made public his desire to avoid a war over the remaining issues. Germany went down to diplomatic defeat in the crisis, but not before the military question had been raised. The process exposed the helplessness of the Russian army, the unreadiness of the British to fight in a continental war, and the vulnerability of the French while their allies were unable to help them.

The diplomatic crisis arose early in 1905, when the French foreign minister, Théophile Delcassé, declared France's intention to take over from the Sultan of Morocco various rights to regulate customs and trade and to organize border police forces in the country.[1] Delcassé asserted that these measures were necessary to insure freedom of commerce and to guarantee public security on the borders of the French colony of Algeria and more generally in northwest Africa, a region where the French claimed to exercise special interests because of its geographic location and previous French exploitation of the area. Delcassé was an ardent nationalist, committed to antagonism against Germany, and a proponent of an active colonial policy for France.[2] The German foreign office spotted in his declaration an opportunity to thwart Delcassé's design and use the issue to isolate France diplomatically. Delcassé had made an elementary mistake that exposed him to this pressure: he had announced his intentions without first consulting Germany. This made him vulnerable because Germany was a signatory to the 1880 Treaty of Madrid, by which the European powers claiming interests in Morocco had arrogated to themselves the right to decide jointly on any intervention in the affairs of the sultanate. Reich Chancellor von Bülow, who at the time functioned in practice as his own foreign secretary, guided by the influential councillor Friedrich von Holstein at the Wilhelmstraße, peremptorily warned the French against making any attack on Morocco to impose their "reforms."[3] He persuaded Kaiser Wilhelm to visit Tangier in the course of a Mediterranean cruise on 31 March 1905 and make a speech in the city declaring his support for the "complete independence" of the Sultan from foreign interference. The German emperor, normally a protagonist of vigorous measures in foreign policy designed to assert his country's claims to world power status, entered upon this particular venture with some misgivings. He was concerned with maintaining smooth relations with France and Britain while he and Admiral Tirpitz built the battle fleet.

Nevertheless, the imperial performance at Tangier, a dramatic entrance in full uniform, unmistakably signaled to the world Germany's intention to make an issue of the Moroccan question. Bülow demanded that the French convene a European conference to decide on the measures to be taken in Morocco, on the premise of upholding the "open door" there. Bülow and Holstein hoped to prevent France from securing through unilateral intervention even more power than it already possessed in North Africa. When Delcassé refused to accept a conference, the crisis reached its height. Under the threat of a Franco-German war breaking out over the deadlock, the cabinet in Paris decided to renounce intervention on its own and forced the foreign minister to resign on 6 June 1905. This represented a symbolic victory for Berlin. But by the time the international conference convened at Algeciras in southern Spain in January 1906, it was clear that Bülow had been quite wrong to expect the powers to oppose French intervention and grant Germany equal participation in taking over the running of Morocco's affairs. It turned out to be Germany that was isolated, with only Austria-Hungary and Morocco supporting Berlin's demands. After moments of fear that Germany would throw over the table and resort to a test of strength— perhaps even a military one—with France alone, the conference concluded by giving the French more or less what they had claimed for themselves at the outset. Bülow was left with a stinging diplomatic rebuff.

In challenging France over Morocco in the first place, the planners of German foreign policy never meant to provoke a war.[4] Nor did they take the balance of military power into account. Bülow did not refer to the possible outcome of a conflict or to the strategic situation when he wrote to the kaiser on 26 March 1905, urging him to land at Tangier and make the German démarche.[5] He did not even mention the obviously favorable circumstance of the Russian army's being completely out of action as a result of the war with Japan. The German scheme had been maturing since June 1904, before the Russian military collapse had become apparent. At that time Holstein had first suggested something of the kind, based entirely on the prevailing diplomatic configuration of Europe.[6] The plan he and Bülow concerted thereafter, and set in motion on the occasion of Delcassé's provocative step in Morocco in 1905, aimed to discredit the French foreign minister and his ambitious designs. The government also hoped to score a prominent national success that would bolster its prestige at home. The planners of the Moroccan démarche attempted to play upon British fears of French imperial expansion, and by this means to break up the *entente cordiale* of the previous year, which worried Holstein considerably. They expected by the same means to call attention to Russia's lack of interest in engaging in bruising conflicts on behalf of France over colonial matters in which St. Petersburg had no stake at all.[7] These expectations that the powers would generally be hostile to Delcassé's move were the reason why Bülow hoped that making an international issue of Morocco would work out to Germany's advantage. France had to be forced to accept the participation of other powers in its intervention, and Bülow realized he might have to make threats to achieve this. Actual war, however, would not be necessary. In advising the kaiser on what to say at Tangier, he wrote:

> The question of whether Your Majesty will risk a war with France on account of Morocco cannot be considered. But on the other hand also, it is

more than questionable whether the present French civilian government, for which a victorious general would be almost more dangerous than the external enemy, will dare to make war on Morocco as long as there is even the slightest possibility that Germany will intervene sooner or later. For this reason we must leave our intentions unclear.[8]

But two months later Bülow did explicitly threaten the French with war if they acted in Morocco without waiting for a conference. "If French troops cross the Moroccan frontier," the German foreign ministry informed Delcassé by a circuitous route via Italy on 4 June, "German troops would at once pass the French frontier."[9] The slightly bizarre threat was chiefly a means of speeding the French along in their protracted internal debate over whether or not to accept a conference.[10] In fact it was almost certainly pure bluff, since it was never repeated and since Bülow was convinced that the French would not go to war. He had been receiving word from his ambassador in Paris, Prince Hugo von Radolin, that Prime Minister Maurice Rouvier was determined to avoid a conflict and spoke of the possibility as "quite out of the question."[11] Even Delcassé, the Reich chancellor judged, would ultimately shrink from war.[12] Bülow shrewdly timed his démarche to coincide with a French cabinet meeting at which he knew that the issue of a conference was to be decided between Rouvier's conciliatory policy and Delcassé's hard line, which Bülow judged to be without support in France.[13]

THE OPPOSING FORCES IN THE CRISIS

Whether or not the German challenge was anything more than a bluff, the balance of military power in Europe hung heavily enough against France to make the threat seem plausible: sufficiently plausible, at any rate, to make the French give way in the face of the German challenge. The French government seriously wondered if it faced a war over the dubious issue of Morocco. It also knew that this was a war that France would almost certainly lose. France's allies, Russia and Britain, were hesitant in offering military support, and were in any case in no position to provide it if a conflict did break out. This left the French army, riven by internal disputes and by disagreement over what its adversary's war plans were, facing a German army that would be able to field significantly greater forces. The situation forced statesmen in Paris to hesitate.

In the first place, it looked as if France would have to fight alone against Germany. The French army counted heavily on the intervention of Russia on its side in the event of an attack by Germany. Ever since the ratification of the Franco-Russian alliance in 1893 the French general staff had eagerly looked forward to making the Germans fight on two fronts at once when the time came for the war of the *revanche*, the equalizing contest that they hoped would efface France's humiliating defeat in the Franco-Prussian War. The military convention attached to the treaty explicitly committed the signatories to mutual support in any war where one of them was attacked by Germany (or, in Russia's case, Austria-Hungary supported by Germany). But this was impossible in June 1905. The Russians were already involved in a war of their own, and General Kuropatkin's army was in the process of being beaten in Manchuria. Port Arthur had fallen in January, the imperial fleet had been sunk to the bottom of the Tsushima Strait in May, and the Russian cities were in revolution.

The French as well as the Germans were fully aware of these Russian weaknesses. The French military attaché in St. Petersburg, Brigadier-General Moulin, had been reporting on the feeble performance of the Russian army since early in the Manchurian campaign.[14] On 27 June 1905 he wrote to Paris that he found himself forced to endorse the words of the chief of the Russian general staff, General V. V. Sakharov: "If we were to get into a war with Germany, our storehouses in Poland would be empty and we would not even have shells to put in our guns. There would be nothing for us to do but kneel down and beg for mercy."[15] As early as April 1904 the chief of the Prussian general staff, Count Alfred von Schlieffen, had replied to Bülow's inquiries about the strength of the Russian army in the west by reporting on the disarray caused by the mobilization for the East Asia campaign.[16] On 4 June 1905, as Bülow transmitted his threat of war to France, he again asked for Schlieffen's opinion of Russia's military strength.[17] The chief of staff wrote back that those troops still available were so hopelessly ill-trained and underequipped that "they are incapable of standing up to another army, and are completely useless for an offensive. The East Asian war has shown that the Russian army was even less good than had generally been supposed, and as a result of the war it has become worse rather than better. It has lost all spirit, confidence, and discipline."[18] Bülow also realized that he could easily make France look like the aggressor in Morocco, giving Russia an excuse to declare that the mutual defense provision of the Franco-Russian treaty would not apply to such a war, which would in any case be far removed from Russia's actual European interests in the Balkans and the Turkish straits.[19] At the same time the French ambassador in St. Petersburg, Maurice Bompard, reported that Russia's weakness as a result of the war with Japan was merely confirming the predisposition of the Russian foreign minister, Count V. N. Lamsdorff, to stay out of any Franco-German dispute over Morocco.[20]

Nor did France have a serious hope of aid from its other principal ally, Great Britain, in a land war with Germany. Prime Minister Rouvier harbored suspicions about London's attitude, and even went so far as to tell Radolin in May that he on no account expected the British to take up arms in behalf of France.[21] And in fact the French had very little reason to think that they would. The British Foreign Office had assured Delcassé at the start of the crisis that it supported the French position, and then proceeded to back Paris in discussions with Germany.[22] But there was no assurance that this would translate into effective help if a war broke out. Apart from the mild affirmation of support in Morocco that had accompanied the *entente cordiale,* all the French had in their hands by the time Bülow threatened them with war in June was a declaration from Lord Lansdowne, the British foreign secretary, expressing his wish

> that the French and British Governments should continue to treat one another with the most absolute confidence, that we should keep one another fully informed of everything which came to our knowledge, and . . . that there should be full and confidential discussion between the two Governments, not so much in consequence of some act of unprovoked aggression on the part of another Power as in anticipation of any complications to be apprehended during the somewhat anxious period through which we are at present passing.[23]

In days when a European land war was expected to be decided in a matter of weeks, this was hardly a confidence-inspiring offer.

Even if the intentions of the Balfour government had been unambiguous, it was clear that Britain had nothing much with which to fight alongside the French in a war on land. The Royal Navy was the most powerful force afloat, but Rouvier did not believe this could save France, as Radolin learned from a confidential source, "for he knew that the English ships have no wheels." Bülow agreed that this would leave the French high and dry.[24] As for the diminutive British army, in June 1905 it was still engaged in reorganization and reequipment in the aftermath of the Boer War. An experiment with reducing the term of service from five years to three was resulting in an unprecedentedly rapid turnover of recruits for training. The new quick-firing field guns were being sent to India first as they came off the production lines, leaving most of the home forces with obsolete field artillery, while there were no up-to-date heavy guns either. The cavalry was being reorganized and half of it was quite unready to take the field. High-level units, such as the corps that formed the building blocks of continental armies, were not organized or assigned commanders and staffs in peacetime.[25] The French intelligence service, the Deuxième Bureau, recognized that Britain was groping its way, "not without a certain amount of trial-and-error," out of the traumatic crisis of the South African War and into "a complete reorganization of its army."[26] The Prussian general staff considered that, "with regard to the value of the field army, it may be said without doubt that in terms of unified training, quality of replacements, and trained leadership, it will not be the equal of German regular troops."[27] Furthermore, any army the British did send to France, whatever its quality, would be almost insignificantly small. The expeditionary force that the general staff eventually proposed consisted of approximately 115,000 men, compared with French and German field armies each with closer to 600,000 troops from peacetime as well as vast numbers of reservists.

Most importantly of all, no plans or preparations existed for transporting any force Britain did decide to send to the continent in time to take part in a war there. In setting out the goals of the reform of the British army in 1904, Balfour had written that the forces should be prepared to maintain garrisons in the colonies, to send reinforcements to India in case of a Russian attack from central Asia, and to defend the British Isles themselves from invasion.[28] There was no mention of a role for the army in continental Europe. Evidently under the influence of the *entente cordiale* and the earliest Moroccan tensions, the British general staff first played out a war game assuming the dispatch of an expeditionary corps to help the French by landing at Antwerp only in March to April of 1905. This was, however, a personal initiative of the new director of military operations, Major-General Sir James M. Grierson. There were no talks with the French military authorities, who did not find out about it until December, long after the German threat in June.[29] The results in any case showed that the British would arrive too late to have any effect upon a French defeat unless their transport could be carried out very quickly. The members of the British Committee of Imperial Defence did not even discuss measures for sea transport to the continent until January 1906, while full preparations together with the Admiralty and the French did not get under way until 1911.[30]

The Prussian general staff guessed rightly that a British expeditionary force would head for Antwerp, but was unsure whether any plans existed for the actual transshipment. Even if they did, the Germans estimated that it would still be an absolute minimum of seventeen days before the British could all be ashore and ready to march to the battle area, whereas the French and German armies expected to go into action only two weeks from mobilization. The British would be reluctant to hitch their destinies to participation on the left flank of a French line of battle, the Germans thought. They would be too weak to have any effect by landing in southern Denmark or on the north German coast in the hope of drawing off German forces. They might be capable of forming a significant diversion later by attacking south from Antwerp.[31] As late as November 1905, the French military attaché in London, Lieutenant-

Colonel Huguet, estimated that a British expeditionary force could not be ready for action in Europe until four or five weeks after the outbreak of war, too late to participate in the decisive battles. "It is doubtful," he reported, "that its cooperation could be of truly effective use, or could be capable of seriously influencing the course of events."[32] The other European powers had no reason to contemplate intervention in a possible war over Morocco. As long as Russia did not attack Germany, Austria-Hungary's alliance obligation to move against Russia did not take effect. At no time in the crisis did the Italian government contemplate joining Germany in a Triple Alliance war against France, with which Rome was eager to cultivate its newly improved relations. France and Germany faced each other alone. Bülow summed up his view of the situation in a telegram to Holstein in May 1905, predicting that the British would confine themselves to their current diplomatic declarations in France's behalf, while Russia would stay out of any conflict: "England's harassment makes no impression on us. In the event of war the match would be played out between Germany and France. Russia would not become embroiled with us for the sake of Morocco even if it were able to do so. We are in a position to await any further developments with confidence."[33]

This left France in what looked like a very risky position. In the first place, its army was smaller than Germany's. The numbers in peacetime were in theory not very different: in 1905 the French metropolitan forces consisted of approximately 595,000 officers and men, while the Germans had 609,552.[34] Both sides expected to deploy their main forces for the opening battles in about the same amount of time, two weeks from the first day of mobilization. However, the German army tended to stay closer to its nominal peacetime strength than the French, since it conscripted only a limited proportion of the men available each year, unlike the situation in France with its smaller population. The Germans could therefore periodically draw in replacements for recruits who dropped from the muster rolls for various reasons in the course of their service. This yielded active forces of twenty-one corps for France and twenty-three for Germany—twenty-six counting the three "*Kriegs-korps*" that would be formed from surplus smaller peacetime formations on the outbreak of war.[35] Each side was prepared to mobilize a corresponding proportion of reservists in wartime in order to fill out these regular units and to compose their rear-line services.

The Germans, however, would have a superiority of far more than five corps in the initial battles because of the way the two sides planned to use their reserves. The Germans planned to put reservists into further "reserve" corps that would march and fight in the first line, whereas the French did not. The general staff in Paris had abandoned the idea of forming reserve corps and of incorporating reserve divisions into the main fighting forces when they designed their 1898 mobilization and deployment scheme, "Plan XIV."[36] The decision rested on fears that such formations would be a liability, lacking adequate training, officers, and equipment. They had performed badly in the Franco-Prussian War, and Plan XV of 1903 grouped them well to the rear of the main deployment as reinforcements.[37] The Germans, however, took the risk the French shunned. General von Schlieffen planned to use every available man for the initial advance, including reserve divisions and corps. Germany could, at least nominally, equip its reserve units with a minimum of artillery, support, and command elements.[38] German reserve divisions had only half the field artillery complement of their regular counterparts, but, like French reserve formations, they were at least scheduled to reach full mobilization and deployment at the same time as the active army. Schlieffen calculated that by the time they actually made contact with the enemy after their long approach march they would have gained sufficient cohesion to be effective in combat.

The result was a dramatic numerical advantage for Germany. Twenty-one French corps would face the equivalent of thirty-six German. The French Plan XV provided for twenty-one corps on the eastern frontier, with a few further units to watch the Italian front on the Alps. The German deployment plan that went into effect on 1 April 1905 was for an advance by twenty-six corps and twenty reserve divisions (the equivalent of a further ten corps, though only about half of them were actually organized into corps-sized formations).[39] The Prussian general staff counted on this superiority, expecting to mobilize a field army of 1,950,000 soldiers.[40] The French military authorities disagreed about what they would be confronting. The chief of the general staff, General Jean Pendezec, counted organized reserve forces on both sides, and sent a note to Delcassé saying that the French army would deploy the equivalent of twenty-four corps of all types (presumably including the weight of the ten reserve divisions in the rear as a further three corps), against a German total of thirty-eight. This amounted to 840,000 men against 1,330,000.[41] Pendezec's estimate slightly exaggerated the number of corps for the Germans but fell somewhat short in the total of their soldiers. Nevertheless, it accurately expressed the general proportions of the two sides. Pendezec's immediate superior, however, did not believe that the Germans would make such bold use of their reserves. General Henri de Brugère, as president of the Conseil Supérieur de la Guerre, would be the commander in chief in wartime, and therefore had ultimate authority over war plans. Brugère dismissed the notion that the Germans could equip and maneuver reserve corps quickly enough to fight in the initial battles. He, like many French military experts, ruled out the use of reserves by Germany for the same reasons as he did for his own forces. It was in vain that Pendezec warned that "we are poorly informed about the numerical potential of the German armies. . . . The *Ersatz-* and reserve corps may hold some formidable surprises for us."[42]

But even those who, like Brugère, did not believe that the Germans would use many reservists in the front line, had their reasons for fearing that France would be weaker in the opening battles. They guessed that the German army's regular strength would allow it to make a preemptive attack, before the French were ready. As many French officers pointed out, German units, especially those based on the border, had higher complements of men and noncommissioned officers in peacetime than their counterparts in France, and in some cases could reach combat strength more quickly because they drew their reservists from the areas where they were stationed, unlike French units with their anti-regional recruitment system. This led skeptics to worry that these frontier corps would immediately advance into the French deployment areas in a so-called "*attaque brusquée,*" possibly without even waiting for their reserves to join the ranks. This would allow them to brush aside the *corps de couverture* that were supposed to protect the French mobilization, and march westward to disrupt the assembly of the entire army before it was ready to fight. In 1904 one of the designated army commanders for wartime, General François de Négrier, concluded an inspection report by writing that a vital part of the eastern fortresses and covering forces were completely unready to parry such an incursion.[43] Négrier caused a sensation on the eve of the Moroccan crisis by publishing his results in the *Revue des deux mondes* and arguing the point in a session of the Conseil Supérieur de la Guerre convened expressly for the purpose.[44] The president of the Republic and the prime minister both attended the meeting and expressed their alarm at the state of affairs. President Loubet concluded that "it is clear from the discussion that, although much has already been done, much more nevertheless remains to be accomplished if we are to be completely free from fear." Rouvier agreed to seek extra credits for defense preparations, since he said the gravity of the situation had not been brought home to him before. Of course, Négrier was completely wrong. An early blow against the French *couverture* was exactly the reverse of Schlieffen's plan to attack only after mobilizing an overwhelming mass of reservists. Nevertheless, it meant that French leaders feared the strength of the German army whether or not they believed the general staff's estimate about reserves in the front line.

France found some consolation in the technical domain, although even this was an uncertain advantage. The Germans had nothing to match the new French 75mm field gun. The French field artillery with its quick-firers would have the upper hand over the Germans' obsolete pieces without recoil-absorbing systems. By June 1905 the German army had only equipped a few regiments with the quick-firing version of the 77mm gun.[45] The Prussian war ministry was aware of the disparity and during the crisis ordered production of the new type to be sped up.[46] The French were confident in the superiority of their material, about which the army took every opportunity to boast.[47] There did remain the problem that the Germans had 50 percent more field guns for each of their army corps than the French: 144 per corps to France's 92.[48] The French had been forced to lower the number of guns when introducing the quick-firing system because the new artillery used up shells at such an unprecedented rate. Instead of being followed by a single towed ammunition caisson and sharing another that belonged to the battery, each of the quick-firing guns and its limber had to be assigned three caissons. This meant that bringing a single gun into action now required four vehicles and horse teams instead of two and a half. The French had therefore reduced their field batteries from six guns to four in order to avoid unmanageably long columns of march and maneuver. Nevertheless, most soldiers agreed that even the smaller number of modern guns was still preferable to a larger array of non-quick-firers. On the other hand, in the realm of heavy field artillery the French army was greatly inferior. The Germans had a much larger number of heavy guns and howitzers. Unlike their French counterparts, the German heavy field batteries were easily mobile and trained from peacetime to take an active role on the battlefield.[49]

War Plans in the Crisis

Where it was a matter of what the two sides actually planned to do in a war involving these forces, the German war plan offered considerably better prospects. The French general staff's Plan XV provided for the deployment of the whole army on the heavily fortified Franco-German frontier between Verdun and Belfort (see Map 2).[50] The scheme was suitable for defense or for attack. An offensive would be possible if the Russians joined the war against Germany, as the operations bureau had expected when drawing up the plan between 1901 and 1903. In this case, the French would strike into the Saar to threaten the flank and rear of the expected German advance from Metz toward Toul and Nancy.[51] There were two problems with this in June 1905. In the first place, the Russians were not going to come in, so the French would bear the brunt of a German attack. The general staff realized this, and in the revision of the plan it drew up in 1905–6 in view of the crisis, it recognized that it would have to abandon the offensive in favor of a strategic withdrawal.

Map 2. Projected Troop Concentration Areas on the Western Front, 1905

Sources: France, Ministère de la Guerre, *Les Armées françaises dans la Grande Guerre*, vol. 1, *La guerre de mouvement* (Paris, 1922), i: Carte No. 2; Friedrich von Boetticher, "Der Lehrmeister des neuzeitlichen Krieges," in *Von Scharnhorst zu Schlieffen 1806–1906. Hundert Jahre preußisch-deutscher Generalstab*, ed. Friedrich von Cochenhausen (Berlin, 1933), 267.

"The Germans will be able to face us with superior, or at least equal, forces *at every point*," the new addendum concluded. "If we do not wish to abandon territory, we will be drawn little by little into throwing in everything down to our last battalion to sustain a battle sought and planned by the enemy."[52] At most, there might be a chance for a counterattack later against the German lines of communication.

The other difficulty was that Plan XV was wrong about where the enemy would attack. In predicting a German offensive against the main French fortress belt, the scheme completely ignored the possibility that the Germans might infringe the neutrality of Luxembourg and Belgium in order to send part of their forces through these countries and simply go around the northern end of the French line. The only French troops deployed north of Verdun in the Plan XV dispositions were four cavalry divisions, posted between the Meuse and Luxembourg. The general staff in Paris did in fact worry about this prospect, since already in 1904 intelligence reports had been making it clear that the Germans might indeed be preparing to turn the French flank via Belgium. They were building a suspiciously large number of railway lines and unloading facilities near the Belgian frontier, especially around Aachen.[53] The operations office proposed that Plan XV be modified to deploy some forces further north to meet the contingency. General Pendezec was greatly alarmed at the prospect of a German swing through Belgium and kept the foreign ministry informed of his fears throughout 1904 and 1905: "Do I need to tell you that we could not resist such an attack?" he asked one official in April 1904. "We would be immediately overwhelmed."[54] Delcassé was briefed on the matter. The designated commander of the northernmost French army near Verdun pointed out in the February 1905 meeting of the Conseil Supérieur de la Guerre that he would find himself "in a very unfavorable situation" if an attack around the left flank did materialize.[55]

But General Brugère did not believe in a wide German sweep through Belgium. Brugère consistently dismissed the idea in meetings of the Conseil Supérieur, to Pendezec's despair. In June 1905 the generalissimo did not think the Germans could get enough of their units to the front early enough in the war to make a large-scale swing around the French flank at the same time as a frontal holding offensive.[56] This opinion was a product of his conviction that the enemy would not use reserve divisions in the first line. At the end of 1904 the chief of staff had reported that Brugère "refuses to believe that the Germans would take the risk of violating Belgian neutrality so flagrantly; he admits at most that they might spill over a little into Luxembourg."[57] Brugère expected to meet this threat using the group of four reserve divisions that would gather at Reims behind the French left flank: "If the Germans advanced by way of Luxembourg, this reserve would immediately be directed upon the Argonne to extend and consolidate our left wing." In truth the French, with their more limited forces, faced a serious dilemma over thinning out the armies that faced Germany directly in order to cover their flank. They did not make even the most minor northward adjustment to Plan XV until 1906, when Brugère had been replaced as designated commander in chief.

While the generals in Paris argued over where the enemy would attack and what use he would make of his reserves, the Germans were ready to do almost exactly what Pendezec was afraid of. According to the 1905–6 mobilization plan that was in effect in June 1905, approximately one-third of the German army would deploy opposite the French frontier from Luxembourg southward to between Saarburg and Strassburg. The other two-thirds would occupy a wide sector opposite Luxembourg and Belgium with their right wing resting on Aachen.[58] The plan was for a frontal attack against the northern part of the French frontier, accompanied by a vast enveloping movement through Luxembourg and southern Belgium, wheeling around Verdun to turn the northern flank of the whole French defensive position.[59] Schlieffen's objective may still have been the French armies to the south, as in earlier versions, or he might have tried to march all the way westward to Paris, as in the ultimate scheme he drew up at the end of 1905. Since 1897 he had been planning to decide a future war against France by an envelopment at least via Luxembourg, and his designs for this move had grown more daring with each successive draft.[60] Schlieffen became steadily more pessimistic about the prospects of battering a path through the French fortress belt and army concentrations along the common frontier, at Belfort, Epinal, Toul, and Verdun, and he grew increasingly fascinated by the possibilities of an outflanking move. During the June 1905 crisis he still had not reached the final stage of stripping virtually all forces from Lorraine, though the projected deployment clearly showed his intention to put most of his weight behind the outflanking thrust north of Verdun. From the number of corps deployed there, as well as from remarks he made on the general staff ride of 1904, it seems likely that Schlieffen already planned to cross to the north bank of the Meuse in Belgium with at least some forces, probably electing to bypass and mask the powerful fortresses of Liège and Namur that guarded the main crossings. The latter was his intention when he wrote the December 1905 plan, and the army did not yet possess enough very heavy siege artillery to destroy the defenses quickly.[61]

It was the military collapse of Russia that made this plan possible. Schlieffen attained the extraordinary numerical superiority necessary for his outflanking maneuver in 1905 partly by allotting no forces at all to the eastern front. This was a direct result of the Russian army's incapacitation in the war with Japan and the subsequent revolution. The 1905–6 plan was the first to go so far as to send virtually the entire German army westward, although since 1894 Schlieffen had been assigning ever greater proportions of it to an offensive against France as he contemplated the difficulty of either fighting on two fronts simultaneously or securing a decisive victory early on in the vast spaces of western Russia.[62] The Russian defeat in Manchuria finally gave him the chance to take his ideas to their logical conclusion. The problem of a two-front war was effectively, if temporarily, resolved by Russia's complete elimination. Schlieffen seized the opportunity with the alacrity of a staff officer who had dedicated a long and assiduous career to the practically obsessive refinement of operational calculations. The result was a very dangerous military situation for France during the Moroccan crisis.

If a war had broken out in 1905, the Germans would probably have won it. They would have deployed a substantially larger army than the French and, unperturbed by any need to leave forces facing Russia, thrown a crushing offensive against the French northern flank where there was nothing prepared to meet it. The Belgian army was even less ready to resist than it was by 1914. The advance through Belgium might have been somewhat slowed, on the other hand, by a decision to leave Liège and Namur undefeated astride the communications of the northernmost corps, instead of destroying the forts with heavy artillery as the Germans did in 1914. There would have been no British expeditionary force to help shore up the French left wing. The French armies, deployed opposite the German frontier in Lorraine, would either have pulled back in the face of the secondary enemy offensive there, or else launched their own attack headlong into the German one in the same sector. In combat the French would have been able to inflict punishing losses on the Germans with their technically far superior, though much less numerous, field artillery. Modern rifles would also have lent their rapid, long-range fire to the power of the defensive as in 1914, though machine guns were not yet present in sufficient numbers to add their devastating effect. By 1905 the German army possessed six very powerful 305mm siege mortars, kept secret from the French, which would have been useful against the casemates of Toul and Verdun, much as they and more guns like them later reduced the Liège and Namur forts to rubble in 1914.[63] The Germans did not depend upon sending as many corps forward along the limited roads and rail lines of Belgium as they did in 1914, and if the scope of the Germans' planned maneuver had not reached all the way to Paris this might have alleviated the logistical problems of the massive German right wing. Both sides would have lacked any form of aerial reconnaissance to reveal the enemy's (or their own forces') movements, throwing them back upon the perennially inadequate resource of cavalry patrols. The chief result of this would probably have been to enhance the surprise effect of the German turning maneuver. Movement on both sides would have been at a nineteenth-century pace, as yet virtually unassisted by motor transport or by telephone and wireless communication. While this would have slowed the German advance north of Verdun, it would likewise have delayed any French redeployment in reaction to it. Had the war not resulted in a quick German victory, the British would probably have intervened, sending a very small land force to Belgium and blockading the German coast with their overwhelmingly superior navy. But only in the case of a very prolonged war would this have had any effect, as the results of naval operations showed when war did eventually break out.

There was not going to be a war in 1905, and most people knew it. But the balance of military power helped to make the German threat in June just plausible enough to convince the French that the risk might be real. Bülow had checked with the military authorities to satisfy himself of the situation before he moved on the diplomatic front. Not only had he canvassed Schlieffen's opinion of Russia's military capabilities; he summoned the war minister, General Karl von Einem, in the spring of 1905 to ask about Germany's own preparedness. "Is the army ready for war?" was the chancellor's critical question. Von Einem answered decisively in the affirmative and assured Bülow that he could count on the army: "You may always depend upon it, Herr Graf, and base your policy upon it entirely."[64] Bülow did not mean to provoke a war, but the military situation was of a nature to persuade him that he could credibly threaten France, and even rely upon success if a conflict came about by mistake in the dangerous game he intended to play.

The man who consistently saw through Bülow's bluff, and therefore ignored the military balance, was Delcassé. He originated and championed the policy of the hard line against Germany from the beginning of the crisis. France's claim to intervene in Moroccan affairs without having to ask permission from Berlin was for him a matter of national prestige and a test of strength between France and Germany.[65] At the cabinet meeting on 6 June that decided the question of the German war threat, he insisted vigorously on holding out against it. One of the ministers in attendance reported Delcassé's speech: "Certainly Germany is menacing, but he believes that this is an empty threat, a bluff; that Germany does not want a war and that it will not start one, this being the thrust of all the information he has gathered as well as of the opinions of all our Ambassadors abroad."[66] In fact the diplomatic reports had been ambiguous. Georges Bihourd had written from Berlin at the end of April that the kaiser had little stomach for war but that his military advisers surely would urge it, and that ambassadors from other countries by no means discounted the possibility of a conflagration.[67] In London, Paul Cambon was more inclined to discount Bülow's menaces as an attempt to unseat Delcassé rather than provoke a war, while Camille Barrère transmitted the German threat of war from Rome on 4 June with the advice that it be treated "with perfect *sang froid* and without pointless alarm."[68]

But many others in France were not so sure. Delcassé's policy received an icy reception in the Chamber of Deputies, where neither the Left nor the Right liked the idea of risking a war, whatever the result, over the issue of whether French claims to Morocco should be submitted to an international conference. Jean Jaurès, the indefatigable orator of the Socialists, denounced Delcassé's refusal to compromise.[69] Above all the prime minister, Rouvier, feared that Bülow might really let it come to a war, which would result in a disaster for France and would not enjoy the support of opinion at home or of allies in London. Rouvier tried to persuade Delcassé of the need to accommodate German demands lest a war break out over a matter that was, after all, of no great importance to either side.[70] After the foreign minister refused to take Bülow's threat of war seriously, Rouvier told a group of ministers on 5 June 1905: "We shall have it out with Delcassé in the cabinet. What he is trying to do is insane. He runs the risk of unleashing war upon our country, and in the state we are in, it would be a crime to expose ourselves to it."[71] The next day the decisive meeting of the council of ministers convened, after earnest discussions between Delcassé, Rouvier, and President Loubet.[72] In front of the cabinet Delcassé argued his case about Germany's bluff, and then Rouvier took the floor. Germany, the prime minister declared, was aiming to break the ring of hostile powers that was beginning to close around it, and had chosen the Moroccan affair deliberately as the opportunity. The German government, he argued, "knows of our talks with England, it knows that the moment would be well chosen to attack us at present, and from all the communications we have received, of which the authority and seriousness cannot be doubted, it is clear that its threats are not empty, but rather very much in earnest." Consequently the military situation was decisive. Rouvier put the question to the cabinet:

> Now, are we in a position to fight a war? Evidently not. Our forts in the east are in need of refurbishment, our armaments likewise. Since General Négrier's inspection, we know that our *couverture* units in the east do not have their full complements. Morale is bad in the army, anarchist propaganda has begun its ravages among the soldiers; among the civilian population, too, the state of opinion betrayed by the strikes that have lately

broken out in so many parts of the country gives us grounds to fear difficulties in mobilization and, in the event of a setback at the start of the
campaign, disorders in Paris and other cities. It is easy to see that England,
on its island free from the fear of invasion, wants to drag us forward for its
own purposes. Our combined fleets would get the better of the German
navy, and the German trading ports would certainly be destroyed, but
meanwhile French territory would be invaded and the struggle against Germany on land would be very unequally weighted against us, if not disastrous. The country would not understand why it was being forced to
engage in such an adventure on the grounds of our disagreements in
Morocco.

The prime minister's view carried the day, and Delcassé resigned on the
spot.

The immediate threat of war was over. The Germans celebrated the
fall of their archenemy, while his successors began negotiating for a conference over Morocco. Bülow was vindicated for having pressed hard
upon the divergence of views between Delcassé and Rouvier, exploiting
a crack in the French position of which Radolin in Paris had kept him
well informed all along.[73] Kaiser Wilhelm conferred the title of prince
upon him for his triumph. The issue of war had been a bluff, but the
chancellor had been able to count on the military superiority of Germany on land to make his menacing tone plausible. Not even Rouvier
would have been likely to believe in the risk of a conflict if it had not
been for the ominous balance of forces on the frontier. Nobody wanted
to unleash the armies, whatever the outcome of a war was likely to be.
But in the tense atmosphere of the crisis the relative strength of the Germans made it hard to rule out any action by the harsh-tongued statesmen in Berlin.

Throughout the remainder of the first Moroccan crisis there was not
such a scene in the French cabinet again. The Germans did not renew
their threat of war after the fall of Delcassé, while the French did not
consider backing down a second time. The reasons for this had little to
do with the military situation. The relative power of armies in Europe
did not change significantly between the fall of Delcassé and the end of
the crisis, and yet Germany suffered a complete diplomatic defeat at the
Algeciras conference. In the June 1905 confrontation, the military situation had lent plausibility to a German bluff. Thereafter, it did not matter
whether a German threat was militarily credible or not, for two reasons.
In the first place, the French were resolved to fight rather than give in
again, whatever the cost. Secondly, the Germans had no more desire
than before actually to start a war, and therefore refrained from bluffing
again. Indeed, Kaiser Wilhelm explicitly renounced war over Morocco,

lending corresponding backbone to French intransigence. Under these conditions it did not matter who had the stronger army. What counted was who was prepared to fight at all over the issue at hand. Furthermore, the issue had changed. The confrontation that led to Delcassé's resignation had been over whether or not an international conference would convene to discuss the future of Morocco. Once France accepted the conference, the issues were whether Germany would receive compensating territorial or administrative rights in Morocco that Berlin demanded, and whether Britain and France were prepared to stand together to prevent Germany from dictating affairs in Europe. This not only called forth the deeper enthusiasm of the French political classes; it stirred the British Foreign Office into stern declarations of solidarity in the hope of deterring any further German threat to France.[74]

The military situation on land scarcely changed during the remainder of the crisis. On the frontier in Lorraine, the French did what they could. A series of extraordinary military expenditure bills passed in the Chamber of Deputies, while the readiness of the defenses and *couverture* units improved by early 1906.[75] But the basic ratio of forces remained the same. The revision of Plan XV that went into effect in March of 1906 merely redeployed a single army corps to the north of Verdun, spread along the line of the Meuse.[76] It was this same version of the plan that warned of the need to start the war with a general withdrawal.[77] Throughout the crisis, the Russian army remained as incapable as ever of offering any help.[78] The British never reached the stage of being able to offer prompt assistance on land. Only in December 1905 did a series of conversations begin, at first secretly and unofficially, between General Grierson and the French military attaché in London, Major Huguet.[79] From this time onward, the British general staff, Admiralty, and Committee of Imperial Defence began improvising preparations for the actual formation and transport of an expeditionary force to the continent in case a war broke out.[80]

The crisis had the effect of stimulating Franco-British military cooperation for the future. It was not until the new Liberal government of Henry Campbell-Bannerman took office in January 1906 that long-term preparations began. The purpose of these was to redesign the British army so as to give it a permanent organization capable of sending a cohesive force to assist France rather than an ad hoc array of independent formations. The scheme was the brainchild of the new foreign secretary, Sir Edward Grey, and the secretary of state for war, Richard Burdon Haldane, two energetic members of the "liberal imperialist" faction within the new cabinet. Grey and Haldane did not regard their party's progressive domestic policy as incompatible with an international strategy aimed at counterbalancing the power of Germany on the continent.

Their plans involved a complete program of military reorganization, which did not reach Parliament until March 1906.[81] The zealous Grierson had meanwhile been promising the French approximately 115,000 men arriving within a period varying from sixteen days to a month from mobilization.[82] Haldane could tell that, without proper organization and transport arrangements, it would take two months to get even 80,000 men across the Channel. In November 1905 the Committee of Imperial Defence decided to start directing the newly produced quick-firing field guns to the home forces instead of to the Indian army, although the artillery would not be wholly reequipped until April 1906, by which time the crisis was over.[83]

On the German side, the Prussian war ministry and the kaiser fretted somewhat over the continuing rearmament of their own field artillery with quick-firing guns and over the modification of the infantry's rifles to fire a new, sharp-tipped, high-velocity bullet.[84] At sea, the German naval staff remained as before without any plan for fighting the overwhelmingly superior combined French and British fleets.[85] From the point of view of Paris, however, this was not going to save the French army any more than it would have done in the June 1905 confrontation. Bülow and Holstein remained ready to gamble on the British being uncertain and the French unwilling to fight, so into the early months of 1906 the Wilhelmstraße pressed its demands and managed to keep a tone of crisis in the air.[86]

The man whose opinion mattered most in the end was the mercurial Kaiser Wilhelm II, and after the fall of Delcassé he vetoed any more threats of war. Never having been enthusiastic about Bülow's Moroccan policy in the first place, he greeted Delcassé's resignation with relief. He regarded the defenestration of the obstreperous minister at the Quai d'Orsay as a triumph for German diplomacy, and wanted to leave it at that. At the first opportunity he got, on the very day of Delcassé's defeat, the kaiser took aside General Henri de Lacroix, the French military representative at the state wedding of Crown Prince Wilhelm of Prussia, and announced to him that the real source of conflict was now removed. Germany, he declared, would on no account fight France over Morocco.[87]

On New Year's Day of 1906, the kaiser pronounced his final ban on any further thoughts of war in the crisis. By that time he had become convinced that France and Britain were ready, and even eager, to declare war if Germany challenged them.[88] The emperor was evidently deeply shaken by the mass strikes and the Social Democratic Party's political action in Germany that had followed the Russian revolution of 1905 and the tsar's granting of a constitution in October. At the turn of the year these were producing some of the most violent political strife the Reich had seen since Bismarck's chancellorship.[89] The Social Democratic Party congress at Jena in September had adopted a resolution proposing to use the mass political strike as a weapon against a Franco-German war.[90] To the kaiser, everything spoke against challenging France: a diplomatic situation likely to bring war, an unfavorable constellation of powers, changes in the army's equipment, a fragile navy, and the danger of revolution at home.[91] The agitated emperor delivered his traditional New Year's address to the assembled commanding generals with the conclusive declaration that there would be no war over Morocco.[92] Bülow went on to make strident demands at Algeciras and ultimately to suffer a bitter diplomatic defeat. At the conference Germany was outvoted because Russia stood beside France and Britain. The tsar had no army at all to set against Germany, but in 1906 the conference table was not functioning as a surrogate for a battlefield.

At the time of the first Moroccan crisis the balance of military power did not dictate the course of international affairs in Europe, although it exercised a certain influence. Although the notion is tempting in retrospect, there is no evidence that Bülow and Holstein precipitated the Moroccan crisis to take advantage of a window of German military superiority. Instead, they based their considerations upon the diplomatic constellation of Europe. They neither envisioned nor desired a war over the issue. The one important moment when the balance of military power came into play was in the June 1905 phase of the crisis, when the relative supremacy of Germany, the complete prostration of Russia, and the weakness of France tempted the German leaders to resort to the threat of war, and lent the plausibility the bluff needed in order to succeed. On the other hand, the balance of forces was almost irrelevant to the period of the Algeciras conference, when Kaiser Wilhelm was determined that Morocco was not worth the risk of a war of any kind, no matter what the outcome.

But even if the military balance did not control events for the most part, the confrontation of 1905 did bring it out into the light, with ominous consequences for the future. The threat of war that Germany launched as a result of its military advantage had more effect on the later course of international affairs than it did on the outcome of the first Moroccan crisis. Quite apart from the outburst of bellicose language that filled sections of the press in France, Germany, and Britain for the better part of a year, the strength of armies was weighed, both in decision-making circles and in public. Instead of looking chiefly inward, as they had been accustomed to doing when contending with political and financial constraints, the largest European armies were momentarily forced to compare their strength with that of potential adversaries in

Chapter 3

MILITARY EFFECTIVENESS AND
MODERN TECHNOLOGY, 1906–1908

THE YEARS following the first Moroccan crisis did not bring any great expansion of armies in Europe, despite the strategic concerns the confrontation had raised. Once the dispute over Morocco was settled at Algeciras, discussions of conflict dropped from the agendas of ministers while no other issue even remotely threatened to provoke a war. Domestic constraints continued to keep the armies on short financial leashes in all countries. In Britain and Germany in particular, the naval race spiraled into evermore astronomical costs with the inauguration of a whole new class of vessel, the Dreadnought-type battleship. What money did reach the armies in all countries had to go in large part to the modernization of existing forces rather than the creation of new ones. This applied not only to the Russian army, devastated by the losses and deficiencies of the Manchurian campaign, but to land forces everywhere, as they contended with the adoption of the new equipment and tactics that the Russians' dearly bought experience had shown to be necessary on the modern battlefield. If anything, the introduction of new technology made it harder for armies to challenge each other with expansions. Only in the southeastern corner of Europe, on the border between Italy and the Dual Monarchy of Austria-Hungary, did an explicit military competition gather momentum between 1906 and 1908. It assumed the form of redeployments, planning, and rhetoric, rather than expansion in manpower and equipment, since the participants possessed the weakest armies of all the great powers and almost completely inelastic financial resources. Its origins were not related to the Moroccan crisis, in which neither Italy nor Austria-Hungary took an active part. Rather, it was the result of a changing diplomatic alignment and of the rise of a new type of political and strategic calculation in the crisis-ridden Habsburg Monarchy that was later to lay the foundation for Austro-Hungarian action in July 1914.

CONSTRAINTS ON MILITARY EXPANSION
AFTER THE MOROCCAN CRISIS

Of the countries that had been involved in the crisis over Morocco, France had experienced the greatest alarm, but it did not devote substantially increased resources to its army. The spate of extraordinary spending bills that had poured from the Chamber of Deputies during the emergency ceased afterward. Old wounds continued to fester in the army and society as a civilian court tried Alfred Dreyfus for the last time, partially exonerated him, and reinstated him in the army in July 1906. Georges Clemenceau, who became prime minister at the end of the year after another Radical election victory, was a popular politician of patriotic and Jacobin stamp who hoped to do much for the national defense. He found his efforts counterbalanced, however, by the growth of the antimilitarist movement, both under the leadership of the Socialist Gustave Hervé and within broader sectors of the French Left to which Clemenceau owed his support. His policies also bogged down in the controversy stirred up by his authoritarian style of leadership and his use of the army against striking workers. All Radicals in any case agreed that universal two-year military service was an achievement that should not be reversed. More men served, but for less time, which resulted in the army growing very gradually while the number of experienced men in the units fell drastically in proportion to the less-trained and the untrained. The Conseil Supérieur de la Guerre began devising *lois des cadres* in September 1907 to reallocate its thinning contingent of officers, NCOs, and experienced soldiers to the units that would need them most. This task was especially difficult because the army simultaneously had to increase the number of field artillery batteries by more than 50 percent so as not to be left hopelessly inferior when the Germans completed the rearmament of their far more numerous artillery with quick-firing guns by 1908.[1]

Realizing the impossibility of substantially enlarging its own forces in the prevailing political climate, the French general staff turned its attention after the Moroccan crisis to insuring that its allies would be able to offer effective support in the future. Although the French generals had sought military aid from Britain during the confrontation, it was still upon Russia that they pinned their hopes for the future. During the Moroccan crisis the French general staff began to revive discussion of military cooperation with St. Petersburg. The chiefs of the two general staffs had met in 1900 and 1901 to discuss the practical aspects of the aid their countries had pledged in case either was attacked by Germany. Relations had remained dormant since then, but in January 1906 the French military attaché in St. Petersburg, Brigadier-General Moulin, began persuading the chief of the Russian general staff, General F. F. Palitsyn, to reopen discussions with his French counterpart.[2] In April the first meeting between Palitsyn and General Jean Brun took place in Paris. From then onward, the staff talks were an annual institution every summer, the venue alternating between the capitals of the two allies. According to the 1892 military convention to the Franco-Russian alliance, Russia was supposed to mobilize 800,000 men against Germany in the event of a German attack on either signatory. The French hoped to reaffirm this condition and secure some kind of pledge to an early offensive from Russia.

Palitsyn avoided committing himself to deploying the forces stipulated, let alone to taking the offensive, in his talks with the French general staff between 1906 and 1908. All he said was that the Russians would do their best, and that they would at least be capable of mobilizing in the west if necessary, although they would do so much more slowly than their opponents.[3] In a moment of rare candor in 1907, Palitsyn told Moulin that he refused even to prepare for taking the offensive against Germany.[4] He argued that "the Russian army at present has neither the cohesion nor the tactical instruction necessary to a good offensive instrument." Equipment of all types was lacking, and the army would have to be ready to fight Austria-Hungary at the same time as Germany, while detaching forces to keep order in the Caucasus and to cover other fronts such as Rumania and Finland. Palitsyn pointed out that the French themselves hardly seemed to be in a position to mount an offensive on their side either, and that both allies might do best to plan a defensive strategy. But for the French this was not the point. Their aim was to deter Germany by making sure that in a war it would be forced to divide its forces from the first day, a result that could only be achieved by threatening the Germans with actual attacks from two sides simultaneously. The French knew that their allies were in no condition to participate in a scheme of this kind at once.[5] The hope in Paris, however, was that they could be prepared for such a role in the future. "For the moment and for a certain amount of time to come, the Russian general staff cannot afford us *de facto* the support that it is engaged to give us," Moulin wrote to his chief when negotiating for the first staff talks during the Moroccan crisis; "nevertheless it is important to do nothing that could erode the *de jure* force of this engagement."[6]

Military experts everywhere in Europe agreed that Russia was incapable of fighting an offensive war throughout the period from 1906 to 1908. Moulin reported that Russian military opinion considered that "Russia will for a certain time be almost valueless as a military ally against Germany."[7] Palitsyn estimated in March 1906 that it would be three and a half years before the Russian army recovered fully, provided that enough money flowed to keep the factories in production.[8] Moulin, too, judged that it would take at least three years, or until 1909, for the Russians to get their artillery, fortresses, supplies, and mobilization preparations back into working order.[9] Helmuth von Moltke, Schlieffen's successor as chief of the Prussian general staff, periodically wrote summaries for Bülow showing the unreadiness of the Russian army.[10] The German military attaché in St. Petersburg, Major von Posadowsky-Wehner, doubted even in 1908 that the Russian high command could pronounce the army "*schlagfertig*" for a European war, while the general staff in Berlin continued to comment on the persistent lack of progress in Russian rearmament and training.[11] The annual reports of the chief of the Austro-Hungarian general staff discounted the Russian army as being out of action "for the coming years."[12]

These were not unfounded opinions. It is doubtful whether the Russian army would have been capable of mobilizing coherently, as Palitsyn had promised the French, let alone fighting a war successfully.[13] To begin with, it took nearly a year to get the troops back from Manchuria.[14] The logistics of retransport along the tenuous trans-Siberian railway represented a colossal task, especially after the supply of rolling stock and locomotives had worn out in two winters of intensive operation.[15] To make matters worse, the army needed to get cadres of long-service troops back westward first in time to train the new 1905 recruit class. This left behind masses of reservists who joined forces with the revolution and seized control of part of the railway, interrupting traffic for nearly six weeks before fresh troops recaptured the line.[16] Outbreaks of indiscipline racked the army even after many units had returned, most notoriously in the sensational mutiny of a battalion of the Preobrazhensky Guards, an ancient and favorite regiment of the tsar, in St. Petersburg in June 1906.[17] By 1908 the disorders had petered out, but morale nevertheless remained low.[18] Even when the army ultimately showed itself ready to support the forces of reaction, this role marked it out for a ruinous task. Its cohesion suffered terribly from the constant detachment of contingents to suppress revolution and perform police duties against the rest of the population in the years following 1905. This was the principal employment of the forces, and it gutted the units on the frontier, scattering troops throughout the interior of the empire. It consumed time, administrative energy, and resources, while eroding the army's popularity and morale still further. Worst of all, it left the army practically unable to train its troops.[19] Even those units that remained at their garrisons were too weak for proper instruction. The reserves received no training at all through 1908, and not until that year did even a few districts hold larger field exercises up to corps level with the regular troops. There were no grand maneuvers at all to pit corps or armies against each other.

Another obstacle to reconstruction of the army was lack of money. The revolution had saddled the autocracy with a parliament it did not want, the Duma. In 1906 and 1907 this was dominated by parties of the Center and Left. The result was a tumultuous struggle between the

Duma and the tsar's reactionary ministers, led by Piotr Alexandrovich Stolypin, over domestic priorities and the means of handling demands for reform. The army interested the Right only as an instrument of repression and the Left only as a bastion of the old regime to be weakened. In practice, as the tsar rapidly dissolved the first two Dumas for their unruly behavior, the military budget remained in the hands of the finance minister, Vladimir Nikolaevich Kokovtsev. His main concerns were liquidating the costs of the war with Japan and coping with the financial chaos the revolution had caused. The war minister, General A. F. Rediger, kept a low profile in the fray and remained perennially short of money for reforms.[20] Even the appropriation of such funds as could be produced was complicated by the competing jurisdictions of the service ministers, of the influential Grand Dukes who held many important military inspectorates, and of the Council of State Defense, founded in 1905 by the tsar's uncle, the Grand Duke Nicholas Nikolaevich. The council was designed to set priorities for spending but instead became entangled at once in quarrels with the military chiefs, who resisted its intrusion upon their purviews.[21]

Due to a combination of scarce funds and inefficient management, the material reconstruction of the army dragged on slowly. The emptied mobilization storehouses had to be refilled to make up for the appalling losses of material in Manchuria.[22] The rearmament of the field artillery with quick-firing guns, originally scheduled to be completed in 1908, was still not finished in 1909.[23] As for wholly new armament, there was practically no progress in procuring modern heavy field artillery of the kind the Germans had. The army accumulated 120mm light field howitzers of various types in the course of tests, but did not equip all of its units with a standard model.[24] The inability of Russian industry to design suitable weapons had to be reconciled with the finance ministry's insistence that contracts be awarded to domestic manufacturers to the fullest extent feasible in order to win independence from "colonization" by western finance and industry.[25] This policy distorted the judging of test competitions for new artillery types and resulted in exhaustive comparisons of French, German, and Russian models. These contests generally ended with French and German steelworks selling designs and prototypes to strike-plagued Russian firms, which in turn passed on the astronomical costs to the government and proceeded, slowly and inexpertly with the unfamiliar construction.[26] The army had stripped the fortresses in the west of many of their guns in the Russo-Japanese War, and the Russian siege artillery remained universally recognized as obsolete while only vague plans existed to order new guns for it.[27] The French general staff had to reserve all its hopes for a more or less distant future.

The generals in Paris had no alternative but to hope, however, for they did not witness any great outburst of army expenditure from their other allies across the English Channel either. The Liberals had taken office in 1905 hoping to reduce military costs, but had nevertheless found themselves drawn into a colossal upswell in the naval race with Germany. The Moroccan crisis had called forth a naval war scare of its own, just as Admiral Sir John Fisher, the First Sea Lord, announced that a wholly new type of battleship would be necessary in future wars at sea. HMS *Dreadnought*, launched in 1906, was the first of these, designed around an armament consisting almost exclusively of very heavy guns.[28] The Dreadnought class was tremendously expensive, but promised to make all earlier battleships obsolete. As a result, the British and German navies soon found themselves involved in a costly race to build them as quickly as possible.[29] Worried at the soaring expenditures and the ferocious rivalry this race produced, the Campbell-Bannerman government hoped at least to hold a lid on costs for the army, in keeping with the Liberals' election slogan of "Peace, Retrenchment, and Reform" after the Boer War.[30] British army budgets continued to decline until 1909 as the residual costs of the South African war dwindled away.[31]

Within the limits of the budget, Haldane as secretary for war devoted himself to preparing the army for one role in particular, the one that had emerged from discussions over the first Moroccan crisis: the dispatching of an expeditionary force to the European continent.[32] The naval race and Germany's aggressive policy were making it increasingly likely that the British army might have to do this in the future. Rather than perpetuating the global improvisations with which Britain had met the needs of its small wars and the fears of invasion in the nineteenth century, Haldane redesigned the country's military system to make it capable of sending a cohesive field army across the Channel. He created a peacetime structure of divisional organization, which the British army had lacked until then, but which it needed if it were to field large combined-arms formations quickly like the continental powers. He eliminated the archaic proliferation of auxiliary forces designed for home defense and converted them into a useful reserve. This reserve would provide support services to the regular army, as well as forming more divisions that could complete their training and follow the first-line forces overseas after a war broke out. Haldane's reforms began to make it feasible to furnish France with the kind of aid against Germany that the general staff had discussed in 1905 and 1906 but at the time would not have been able to provide. This thoroughgoing reconstruction of the British army took years, however, and was in any case a matter of reorganization rather than of any great increase in size or expenditure from which the French would have been able to derive comfort.[33]

"Monsieur Haldane's project is as satisfactory and as wisely conceived as could have been hoped, given the economic conditions that were imposed upon him," the Deuxième Bureau reported toward the end of 1906, noting with regret, however, that the scheme "is in reality nothing but a program of army reduction."[34]

The Germans were not engaged in any major army expansion either in the years after the Moroccan crisis. Like the British, they devoted most new resources to the snowballing naval race, a practice that put them in far worse financial straits than their rivals. Building Dreadnought-type battleships placed even more strain on the Reichstag coalitions that Bülow tried to maintain to pay for them.[35] Under the circumstances, more money for the army was out of the question. Schlieffen, singlemindedly devoted to attaining overwhelming force at the decisive point, had always demanded a bigger army to realize his ambitious war plan against France. After Schlieffen's retirement in 1906, Helmuth von Moltke played a more subtle game. He maintained the strategic plan of his revered predecessor but devoted himself to politically more practical methods of acquiring the forces for it. He argued in favor of the "internal strengthening" of the army in order to fit it for a major offensive. By this he meant training, equipping, and organizing the second- and third-category troops to take over many duties from the active forces in wartime, increasing the technical units within the larger regular formations, and procuring more modern weapons and equipment.[36] Moltke had to exercise creativity in implementing costly procurement programs, such as the development of very heavy siege artillery. It had come to his attention in 1906, through reports from his artillery and fortress intelligence departments, that existing French and Belgian fortifications with concrete vaults and steel gun cupolas could only be breached by hits from the German 305mm mortar, of which the army possessed six. Works then under construction in France, using concrete reinforced with metal rods, would be even tougher.[37] For an offensive in the west, Moltke evidently hoped to be in a position to demolish the fortresses that Schlieffen had planned to bypass, particularly on the Meuse in Belgium, since he insistently pressed for the construction of even more powerful artillery. Denied the necessary funds for such colossal weapons, the general staff secretly persuaded Krupp in 1907 to undertake the research and development for an elephantine 420mm mortar at the firm's own expense, in the assurance that the army would sooner or later be in the market for such a piece.[38]

The war ministry, because of its particular responsibilities, had its own reasons for restraining the general staff's demands for funds.[39] The minister, General von Einem, certainly did his share of chafing at the navy's astronomical demands and the government's limitations on army expenditure.[40] On the other hand, he did not believe in rushing precipitously into the acquisition of armaments before they had been thoroughly tested.[41] New equipment cost money, and so did the new units that would operate it. It was von Einem's job to get the money from the Reichstag. He was concerned with the continued improvement of the army's equipment and presided over the completion of the conversion to quick-firing artillery by the end of 1908.[42] However, there were limitations to how fast new inventions should go into service, as he put it in a memorandum to Bülow in 1906: "Machine guns, telephones, signal equipment, and telegraph installations can all be procured quickly as long as money is available. More important, and immeasurably more difficult to provide, are the formations that are necessary to make this technical equipment effective. . . . These can only be set up by an increase in the peacetime strength. The question, then, is when we should or must create them."[43] The general staff and the technical services, von Einem observed, wanted the new units right away and could afford to ignore costs and political considerations. "But for me," he argued, "the matter cannot be settled with such a simple solution to the question. I have to consider it from the financial and political point of view, and additionally bear in mind that the military administration can only improve its image the less it changes the opinions it lays before the legislature. It must therefore approach the latter only with properly matured projects." The war minister had to defend military appropriations in the Reichstag, and knew well how any request for extra funds after a budget had been passed was greeted with charges of improvidence.

The army depended upon the authority of its public image for the privileged position it enjoyed. It was not merely a question of the difficulty of securing the funds; it was a matter of preserving the army's unchallenged status as the most prestigious organ of the state, immune to parliamentary interference and as insulated as possible from the political debates that surrounded and penetrated all other European armies. The war ministry above all, responsible for peacetime administration rather than for war plans, historically regarded itself as the guardian of the army as an institution. It viewed the military as the ultimate bulwark protecting the power of the throne and the landholding aristocracy in a constitutional monarchy that threatened with every election to turn into more of a democracy. Von Einem particularly resisted changes that might weaken the institution that gave the army a special degree of autonomy: the five-year budget, or *Quinquennat*. The Reichstag voted on the scale of military funding only once every five years, according to a modification of a provision that Bismarck had designed to insulate the army from the spending authority of the legislature. The most immediate danger von Einem saw in proposals for supplementary funding measures at other intervals was the possibility that they might set a precedent for parliamentary review of the army's budget within the period of the Quinquennat, and perhaps call into question the whole system that shielded the army from minute control by the Reichstag. An army increase in 1906 would make this a serious possibility, he wrote: "In this case we would be breaking with the Quinquennat and running the risk of losing it, perhaps never to regain it, which would have regrettable consequences for the calm and steady development of the army. . . . That the Quinquennat ties our hands in certain respects is obvious. Should we give it up because of this? I do not think it would be expedient, since the savage and persistent agitation against the existence of the army, which arises with every military expansion, would only become all the more dangerous if it were a yearly occurrence."[44] The war minister therefore proposed to save any extraordinary increase in the peacetime strength for the next Quinquennat, due to begin in 1910. In the meantime the war ministry could continue to meet the need for technical units by the expedient of skimming small numbers of men from all over the existing regular forces. Bound by the twin constraints of Tirpitz's fleet and the preservation of the army's special status in German politics—both components of the way in which conservative elites hoped to hold the line against political change—the kaiser's army remained confined to a stately rate of development. It certainly did not set the pace for a rush to arms in the wake of the Moroccan crisis.

The Influence of New Technology on Military Development

Adding to the pressures on European armies was the need to modernize their equipment to reflect the changing demands of warfare as it had been waged on the battlefields of the Anglo-Boer and Russo-Japanese Wars. These two recent conflicts gave military technicians much to think about, employing at last many of the new weapons that European armies had been developing for a quarter of a century. As usual, observers tended to derive the lessons they wanted, and in putting changes into practice they seldom had as much money as they needed. The result was a gradual modernization of equipment and an inclination toward battlefield tactics that emphasized the power of gunfire particularly as an offensive asset. The soldiers kept an eye on these developments in rival countries, and often found their existing judgments of foreign armies reinforced by what they saw. The results provided a constant spur to development at home as well as a yardstick for estimating how different armies would perform in combat. Broadly speaking, the French often appeared to be the most energetic pioneers of new technology, fertile in invention and inclined to be the first to field a new type of equipment that would not only add military capability but redound to the glory of the nation. The Germans, with their cautious and traditionalistic war ministry, tended to demand longer periods of testing before adopting new equipment, but when they did so it was invariably with methodical thoroughness. The Russians actually made many important adaptations during the Manchurian war itself, but in other respects they tended to lag behind, reliant as they were upon contracting from the west at great expense for most sophisticated technology. The British likewise came away from their South African experience with many changes firmly ingrained, but were much slower to adopt entirely new equipment because they usually attempted to develop it on their own in much smaller-scale programs. Austria-Hungary and Italy struggled along behind, limited by virtually static military budgets and by dependence chiefly upon France and Germany for cues.

Although European military experts differed on the exact implications of the Anglo-Boer and Russo-Japanese Wars, they could at least agree that technology would be important in a future war, and that firepower would be crucial. Since all armies had already adopted magazine-loaded rifles by 1904 and were working as fast as they could to incorporate quick-firing artillery, the principal innovation to emerge from the Russo-Japanese War was the machine gun. Neither the Boers nor the British had used significant numbers of these in South Africa, but in Manchuria a few years later their effects were devastating. The combatants possessed scarcely any at the outset, but by the end both sides put into the field every one they could get their hands on, and observers all agreed on their fearsome power. The Deuxième Bureau set it out in a classic report at the end of the war:

> *The Manchurian war has shown the incontestable value of machine guns. Opinions are unanimous concerning the great material and morale effects which they produced. . . . It was above all in the defensive that these weapons displayed their terrible effectiveness,* particularly at the point when, with the two adversaries being a few hundred meters from each other, the men become nervous and aim too high although their fire could be more effective if it were properly adjusted. In these circumstances machine guns, soulless devices without nerves, literally mow down the attackers.[45]

Nor, to their surprise, did the French observers in the Russo-Japanese War find that machine guns consumed a prohibitive quantity of ammunition, a discovery that silenced one of the principal objections to widespread use of the new weapon. The Russians emerged from the war with over eight hundred machine guns. Officers who had been at the front on both sides called for their introduction all the way down to battalion or even company level.[46] It was at once clear to all other powers that they had to procure machine guns. "After this war," wrote General Moulin from St. Petersburg in 1906, "—and especially with soldiers more nervous and less phlegmatic than the Russians—like it or not, one must encumber oneself with this new device if one is likely to face an adversary who possesses it."[47]

The French and German armies worked to get machine guns into service with a constant eye to what was happening on the opposite side of the frontier. The Germans gave detachments to all of their cavalry divisions, prompting the Conseil Supérieur de la Guerre to extend its own equipment to all of the mountain infantry in June 1905, since, despite continuing worries about adopting a reliable type, "we cannot wait any longer without exposing ourselves to being left behind."[48] For Moltke in October 1906, the French action was "grounds enough not to let the further development of machine guns in our own forces come to a halt," quite apart from their obvious necessity after the experience of the Russo-Japanese War.[49] The impending introduction of machine gun companies in the Prussian Guard infantry in turn caused General Brun to advise the Conseil Supérieur de la Guerre in September 1907 that all infantry units should receive machine guns. "Under these conditions," he wrote, "it seems difficult not to provide our Infantry with comparable weapons, lest it be left in a position of material as well as morale inferiority with respect to its eventual adversaries, even given equality of numbers."[50]

And so it went. Between 1905 and 1908, all of the European armies moved from the stage of experimenting with machine guns to their adoption throughout the infantry, at least in principle. The general proportion was a two-gun section for each regiment or each independent light battalion, with the eventual aim of giving a section to every battalion of the infantry as soon as possible. Machine guns were expected to operate most advantageously in sections of two in order to take advantage of their mutually supporting fields of fire, and to insure against the loss of a single gun in the case of a breakdown in its mechanism or ammunition supply. After the Russo-Japanese War, military experts never disputed the desirability of machine guns, but the armies proceeded at different speeds in the actual implementation of rearmament according to their resources. The British already had two guns per battalion and therefore did not perceive a need to change. The Russians managed to give a section to each regiment in 1908, and the French and Germans were not far behind. The Austro-Hungarian army as usual made slower progress due to lack of funds for any new equipment or formations at all, but eventually settled on a serviceable design by the Austrian firm of Schwarzlose.[51] Lack of money slowed down the Italians, too, and in

1908 they were still stuck with a batch of 220 Vickers machine guns from Britain and mired in the question of whether to buy more from the same source or to hold out for the perfection of a superior, cheaper type being designed by the Italian firm of Perino.[52] In this period armies also resolved the questions of which arm should use the machine guns and of what their specifications should be.[53] By 1908, after experiments with wheeled mountings, cavalry detachments, and hand-carried automatic rifles, the consensus had settled around perfected, medium-weight designs. These were mounted on tripods or sledges, and could be carried on animal-back or wagons on the march, and by teams of soldiers in action. They were assigned primarily to the infantry and fired the same bullet as the service rifle. All of this cost much debate and testing time, and most armies still had to squeeze the troops and officers for machine gun detachments out of existing units, since parliaments voted for scarcely any new formations.

But while military experts concurred that machine guns would be necessary, it was harder to agree on just what they would be necessary *for*. It was clear that they would be essential for defense against an enemy armed with machine guns. They were also obviously ideal for holding defiles against superior numbers of assaulting troops. But this was not what most officers were interested in doing. The Russians and Japanese, by what observers in the West regarded as tactical errors, had used machine guns mostly to protect positions. European soldiers were concerned instead with how the new weapons could help to lever attacks forward. The maneuver fields witnessed all manner of expedients, ranging from machine guns operating in batteries at long range like artillery in support of assaults, to the guns being carried forward with the advancing infantry and fired from successive positions reached by the skirmish line.[54] Nobody was quite satisfied with these obviously inadequate efforts, and the machine gun remained chiefly an asset to be acquired in the expectation that awful consequences might follow if it were not.

On the fire-swept battlefields of the Veldt and East Asia, it also became abundantly clear that the traditional brightly colored uniforms would have to go. Under the merciless fire of Boer rifles, the British had resorted to painting over or dulling the buttons, buckles, accoutrements, and insignia even on their khaki colonial-service uniforms, in order to suppress anything that might reflect the sunlight and betray a position. Officers had begun to dress as much as possible like their men, tucking away binoculars, sometimes carrying rifles, and abandoning the swords and distinct uniform elements that set them apart from the ranks. These now simply made them irresistible targets for sharpshooters. The same things occurred in Manchuria. After seeing in the early battles how crucial concealment had become and how desperately vulnerable to fire at all ranges the troops were in their boldly colored uniforms, both sides scrambled to get into something less conspicuous. The Japanese switched from blue with bright unit facings to whatever supplies of khaki they could procure quickly. The Russians replaced their varied panoply of green, black, and summer white with anything they could get their hands on: gray, olive, tan, or brown. In winter new materials came to cover up anything that stood out too much against the snow. The French Deuxième Bureau learned about all of this from its observers in the theater of war, who predicted that European armies would have to follow the example of the combatants. "From the experience of the Russo-Japanese War," concluded its principal report on the subject of uniforms, "*it seems that there is an urgent need to proscribe from our order of dress all shiny objects* (scabbards, helmets, breastplates, aiguillettes, etc.) . . . ; *to give the officers the same uniform as the troops and to adopt a single neutral color, at least for the headgear and coat,* if not also for the trousers."[55] Military attachés consistently commented favorably on the low visibility and the practicality of the British army's khaki field uniform, similar for all arms of service, at maneuvers.[56]

But even in the face of evidence from the battlefields, the principle met with fierce resistance from many officers. They considered the uniform to which they had dedicated their careers to be far more than just a practical working dress. It was an important symbol of tradition, as well as a prestigious and becoming attire that constituted one of the compensations for the hardships and unremunerative character of the military profession. They regarded it as a vital means for inspiring soldiers with pride and with a constant reminder of the distinct nation and corps to which they belonged. This applied equally in the public glamour of a parade or in the heat of battle, where greater sacrifices than ever would be called for. To change the uniform was one thing, and it had been done often enough before; but to make it dull-colored, similar to work clothing or to the uniforms of other countries, and generally unattractive, was to sacrifice many of its functions and all of its *cachet*. General Henri Bonnal, writing about the South African war in 1903, had ridiculed a proponent of a khaki uniform for the French army even on the grounds that it would subvert the glorification of the manly physique and bearing that the advocates of national preparedness continually propounded: "The uniform of his dreams no doubt consists of a smock that would conceal the thinness or deformities of the torso, and a broad-brimmed hat to hide the eyes. In this way, ill-built people would have nothing to envy handsome men, for both would be equal in their ugliness."[57] The Prussian war minister knew he was headed for an ordeal when he approached Kaiser Wilhelm with the general staff's proposal for a gray-green field uniform in the light of the experiences of the Russo-Japanese War: "As I had expected, the Emperor was outraged; it was scandalous, he said, to lay such a suggestion before him. He reminded me that the army had won all its great victories in the blue uniform, and that this would now represent a form of attack upon our entire glorious tradition. . . . His Majesty did not agree with my arguments, and in particular discounted the East Asian experience on the grounds that completely different conditions had prevailed there."[58]

Nevertheless, the European armies gradually began to swallow their disgust at adopting neutral-colored uniforms, prompted by the realization that the loss in terms of morale would be more than compensated by the tactical advantages and the reduction of casualties. General von Einem persuaded the kaiser to accept the idea, and settled on a "field gray" uniform of a gray-green color that later went on to become the symbol of the German soldier as blue had been for the Prussians since the days of the Great Elector. As a compromise, the commissariat at first merely procured the new uniform for stocks, to be issued on mobilization, while the peacetime army continued to go about its business in the old style.[59] The Austro-Hungarian army chose the pale, blue-tinged "pike gray" (*Hechtgrau*) that the Tyrolean Jägers, or light infantry, had traditionally worn in the Alps. "Practical but anti-aesthetic" was the Italian military attaché's comment on the resulting field uniform.[60] The army officially adopted it in 1907 but it did not appear in most units for several years due to lack of money for implementing the change.[61] The cavalry in any case remained exempt to assuage the traditionalists, riding on in its dazzling array of hussar, lancer, and dragoon uniforms. The Italians fired bullets at dummies dressed in various colors and discovered that a figure clad in their regulation blue coat received seven times as many hits at standard ranges as one in grayish green. A service order of this color underwent tests in units of the Alpini, the elite mountain troops, starting in 1906. It soon began appearing even at maneuvers and officially became the uniform for the whole army in 1908.[62] Polished leather shakos and hats, cockaded, pompommed, and plumed, gave way to plainer fabric caps in gray-green. The Russian army toyed with various efforts to institutionalize the expedients of the Manchurian campaign, it but had still not properly outfitted the troops with a standard field uniform by 1909.[63] In all countries the task of reclothing armies of hundreds of thousands was a laborious one, as quartermasters took the opportunity to redesign every item of uniform and accoutrements. It invariably took many years to procure and pay for new fabric, leather, and manufacture in sufficient quantities not only for the active army but also for the wartime reserves, while waiting for economy's sake until the troops used up existing stocks of the old material. Not until about 1913 did the European armies regularly turn out in recognizably twentieth-century field kit. The only ones to resist all change were the French, unwilling to relinquish the blue coats and the red trousers and képis they had worn since the days of Louis-Philippe: the uniform of the victories of the Second Empire, of the debacle of 1870, and—it was fervently hoped—of the *revanche*. The adherence to this symbol of pride in the army may have seemed all the more vital to the generals in the wake of the Dreyfus affair, as the Radicals in parliament assailed other aspects of military tradition.

The increased range of gunfire and the growing size of armies and battlefields made a number of other kinds of equipment necessary, much of it having come into use in the Russo-Japanese War. Some of these innovations were relatively minor. Optical equipment like binoculars, aiming telescopes, and range-finders, for instance, proved vital for observation and for directing gunfire under new conditions of distance and concealment. Field kitchens, towed on wagon wheels, were invaluable for bringing the economies of scale to the preparation of food for men on the march or in the combat area who were otherwise reduced to foraging, hunger, and time-consuming fatigues.[64] Support and technical units in general, and especially engineers and railroad troops, were crucial to keeping forces in operation in the Russo-Japanese War, and all European armies realized that they would need to raise more of these at the first opportunity.

Particularly significant, however, was the development of communications to link units on the far-flung and fire-swept battlefield. Messengers on horseback could no longer cover the requisite distances in time, and they, as well as flag or heliograph signalers, easily fell victim to the omnipresent fire of the enemy whenever they exposed themselves to view. The solution lay in the telephone. Armies had used the telegraph since the mid-nineteenth century, but for instantaneous communication on the battlefield, the new technology of the telephone was the only practical means. Marconi's experimental wireless sets remained too bulky for use by any but the highest headquarters. The Japanese began the Manchurian war with a considerable array of telephone equipment and the Russians hastened to acquire as much as they could once operations started. The French observers with the armies noted that the disjointed nature of Russian operations on the vast battlefronts was often due to the breakdown of communications. Generals rode up to the fighting line and their staffs dispersed to carry dispatches. Japanese headquarters, by contrast, remained stationary, well to the rear, following and controlling operations through a dense network of telephone and telegraph wires unrolled by the troops.[65] The European armies at once set about expanding their telegraph services for high-level communications, but above all devoted themselves to developing and introducing practical field telephones. Durable, simple, and portable sets and switchboards had to be designed and supplied with wire that was well enough insulated so that signals did not become inaudible over longer stretches and multiple branchings. At the same time, the cable still had to remain light and strong enough to be carried forward in sufficient quantity with the fighting units. Between 1906 and 1908, most of the European armies introduced field telephones on at least some level in their combat units, to link headquarters or artillery batteries.

Other technologies that had not made themselves felt in the Russo-Japanese War began to appear in the European armies in these years as well. Motor transport, in particular, came to be regarded as a likely solution to the problem of mobility as armies confronted the prospect of bringing forward supplies for forces of hundreds of thousands moving in columns more than a day's march in length. Since there were no good roads in Manchuria, neither side had used cars there. But with the development of a practical internal-combustion engine, the European armies set about exploiting the rapid and powerful means of transportation that it provided, at first for liaison and later for carrying supplies forward beyond the rail lines. The main problem was standardization, since it was vital that military vehicles have interchangeable parts for field maintenance, as well as similar performance for relay or convoy purposes. However, it seemed unwise to settle on any particular type too soon at a time when every year brought revolutionary improvements to the new machines. The answer in these early years was generally for armies not actually to purchase vehicles, for which there was in any case no money. Instead, war ministries hired them for exercises, registered them for requisition upon mobilization, and paid subsidies to private vehicle owners who kept automobiles or trucks that conformed to specifications laid down by the military. Automobile clubs received government support, and in most countries corps of civilian motor volunteers formed, sometimes consisting of reserve officers, pledging to place their vehicles and their services as drivers at the disposal of the army for exercises or in wartime. The practice drew upon the glamorous and intrepid aspirations of early automobile owners while providing an economical source of interim motor transport until the military could settle on reliable vehicle types to procure in quantity. Motor rallies, some of which were sponsored by armies in order to test vehicles for military specifications, attracted broad public enthusiasm.

Progress came about at comparable rates in all the west European armies, though the Italian and above all the French auto industries displayed the most impressive products.[66] By 1906 all the major west European countries had volunteer organizations or subvention systems for mobilizing the national automotive power, and Russian officers formed one in 1907.[67] The French gave a remarkable demonstration of their progress by using forty-two motor lorries of various types, mostly hired, to supply one side in the grand maneuvers of 1907, while most other powers were still conducting small-scale experiments with load-carrying trucks.[68] By 1908, all armies could be expected to field approximately fifty motor vehicles at the annual maneuvers, except in Austria-Hungary and Russia, where the scarcity of good roads and of motor-owning civilians kept the numbers down to a fraction of this. A few armored cars were even tested, for instance in Austria-Hungary in 1906 and in Germany the next year, although without significant results.[69]

By far the most spectacular new invention to be adopted by armies between 1906 and 1908, however, was the dirigible airship. The astonishing appearance of flying machines at the dawn of a new century of technology captured the attention of the public as did no mere refinement of field equipment. When armies began to furnish themselves with dirigibles, this public enthusiasm transferred itself to the military sphere as well, where progress in aviation came to be a popular yardstick of national prowess. What the awe-inspiring battleship had done for the navy, the majestic cruiser of the air now did, in a more faddish and exotic way, for the army. With the conversion of the dirigible into a potential weapon of war, the conquest of the air became a military struggle that could be waged in peacetime. The armed forces could neglect this contest only at the peril of losing public confidence and perhaps sacrificing a crucial armament of the future. Balloons powered by steam or electric motors had achieved some limited successes in the last two decades of the nineteenth century, amid numerous disasters. Nobody could build really practical dirigibles until the development of the internal-combustion engine. Only this furnished a motor that was sufficiently light, compact, and powerful to propel a shaped balloon through the air fast enough for its crew to steer it by means of the currents passing over its hull and control surfaces. In 1900 the ex–cavalry officer Count Ferdinand von Zeppelin launched the first of his highly successful series of giant airships. Other pioneers followed closely, most notably the French balloonist Alberto Santos-Dumont and the wealthy sugar refiners Paul and Pierre Lebaudy. Within a few years the possible military utility of dirigible flying machines became apparent, and by 1906 the French, German, Italian, and British armies were each sponsoring the costly experiments of at least one inventor.[70]

The most significant step came when the French army actually acquired a Lebaudy airship in 1906. The galvanizing effect, particularly upon Germany, was immediate as news spread in the press. "Thanks to its dirigible airship, France is far ahead of us in the adoption of balloons," Moltke wrote: "it can only be a question of time until this important means of liaison, observation, and reconnaissance also joins the ranks of offensive weaponry."[71] The French widened their lead by purchasing a second Lebaudy ship in December and commissioning the construction of others.[72] The significance of the machines as instruments of national power enthralled the public on both sides of the Rhine when this dirigible, significantly named *La Patrie*, appeared at the 14 July parade in 1907. Eight days later it cruised over Paris with Georges Clemenceau aboard, accompanied by the war minister, General Picquart. The newspapers enthusiastically reported the event as well as an interview with the ex–war minister Maurice Berteaux, extolling the military potential of the dirigible.[73] There was nothing for the Germans to do but to reveal at once one of the dirigibles that had been under construction with the sponsorship of the war ministry. It was a question of national pride by now, wrote Jules Cambon from Berlin to the Quai d'Orsay:

> The appearance of the dirigible balloon "Patrie" at the 14 July review, its maneuvers aloft, the ascent of the President of the Council and of the War Minister, and the press articles devoted to this balloon, a new testimony to our genius in engineering, have attracted the lively attention of the Germans. The government has hastened to display the balloon that the military authorities were preparing in the strictest secrecy, and the newspapers have all declared that it worked better than the Patrie. . . . the solicitude with which the government felt impelled to reassure public opinion and its promptness in doing so are to my mind very significant. . . . the German public believes in our strength. The government devotes itself constantly to suppressing anything that could erode popular confidence in the invincibility of the empire and deprive the country of any part of its capacity for energy.[74]

The problem that the Germans faced in matching the French successes was not an easy one. The war ministry was reluctant to rush into the purchase of types before they had proven their viability, and two major alternative designs existed in Germany. The less successful of these were the machines being built by Captain Hans Groß under the auspices of the army's airship battalion, and by Major August von Parseval with its support. These were respectively "semi-rigid" and "nonrigid" constructions, like the French types of the day. They consisted of a large, elliptical gas envelope, from which the nacelles, engines, and control surfaces hung. The semi-rigid dirigible maintained its shape by means of a keel, or girder frame along the bottom of the envelope. The nonrigid blimps had an elongated profile simply due to the shape of the bag and the pressure of the gas inside. These designs seemed particularly suitable for military use because a ground crew could deflate them for transport or for safe stowage in stormy weather. Parseval and Gross, however, were still engaged only in test ascents by the summer of 1908.[75] Far more viable were the gigantic rigid airships that Zeppelin's private venture was routinely flying. The problem was that these were not what the army had initially invested in since they seemed in many ways less suited to military requirements. Over a hundred meters long, the Zeppelins were twice as big as the nonrigid or semi-rigid types in all countries, and extremely expensive. They consisted of a vast, cigar-shaped, canvas-covered aluminum skeleton containing internal sacs inflated with hydrogen for lift. The whole construction, with its engines and gondolas, was so heavy that it required the thrust of engines to pass air over its hull and elevating planes in order to gain altitude. Such a machine was therefore in serious danger if its temperamental motors failed, especially over enemy territory. Nor did deflating it reduce its bulk, which made it impossible to transport except under its own power. This also meant that it could only be safely berthed at fields equipped with enormous and expensive hangars to protect it from the winds that continually threatened to snatch up dirigibles and whisk them off to unintended destinations or dash them to the earth. None of these characteristics seemed to qualify the rigid airship as a handy and versatile companion to advancing armies.[76] In June 1908 General von Einem told the French military attaché in Berlin, Colonel Laguiche, that he wanted to wait for more convincing results from Zeppelin's flights before investing in the machines.[77]

However, the caution of the military authorities succumbed to a wave of nearly hysterical enthusiasm in the German public for matters aeronautical and for Zeppelin's feats in particular. In the summer of 1908 the inventive count made a series of impressive flights in his native Württemberg, arousing euphoria in the population, the royal parliament, and the press. He topped off the display by carrying the king and queen of Württemberg aloft during one ascent.[78] Laguiche reported that "all Germany has been seized by a wild enthusiasm for Count Zeppelin. . . . All trace of common sense and self-control seems to have vanished from this people for the moment."[79] The climax arrived in August, when a gust of wind tore a Zeppelin from its moorings at Echterdingen outside Stuttgart and swept it through the air until it crashed and burst into flames.[80] From Mannheim, the French consul wrote, "This news, falling in the midst of joy, in the midst of enthusiasm, is giving rise here to general consternation—I have seen people in tears; there is talk in all the newspapers of raising a national subscription to permit Count Zeppelin, who has been completely ruined, to build a new balloon and resume his experiments as soon as possible."[81] A subscription was indeed forthcoming, and a tremendous success—so much so, indeed, that the kaiser himself telegraphed to Zeppelin to impress upon him in grandiloquent terms a sense of the patriotic responsibilities his task had assumed:

> Inspired by great national spirit, the German people and its Princes have unanimously gathered through voluntary contributions the sums that will offer you the means of making a new airship available. The people has hereby made your enterprise its own. The future airship will therefore be not merely yours but a national one, that of the German nation. It therefore goes without saying that no accident or design flaw may be allowed to interfere with this national enterprise, whose outcome the German people and the entire world will follow.[82]

The army's own airship battalion found itself "permanently besieged" by the press, as the Inspector of Communication Troops reported to the war ministry in August. Efforts to maintain security around the air station or to appeal to the journalists' sense of patriotism about publishing the results of theoretically secret experiments were useless in the face of the hunger of the main Berlin papers for news of aeronautical feats. "No exercise can take place," wrote the Inspector, "without one or more of these reporters at once appearing by automobile on the public road that runs past the barracks, from which they cannot be sent away."[83] By the end of 1908, the German army finally accepted a Parseval dirigible for active service, and in February 1909 it bought one of Zeppelin's ships, designated "Z1."[84]

Not to be outdone, the British army experimented with its own non-rigid dirigible, ambitiously christened *Nulli Secundus*. A series of short trial flights in September 1907 all ended in engine failures. In October a storm wrecked the airship, and a successor came out of the workshops at Farnborough the following year.[85] The Italians had two successful dirigibles flying by that time, one of them constructed at the army's own installation on Lake Bracciano near Rome.[86] Also in 1908, the Russians began constructing an experimental dirigible of their own while commissioning a Lebaudy ship to be built in France.[87] Austria-Hungary still had no significant aviation program to report in January 1908.[88] The French army lost the *Patrie* in 1907 to a storm that blew it out into the Atlantic, but the war ministry bought three other dirigibles by the end of 1908.[89]

The early proponents of aerial warfare expected dirigibles to be useful chiefly for reconnaissance over enemy lines. They could fly from the bases to which they were soon assigned at frontier fortresses, such as Metz and Verdun, and plans took shape for eventually attaching them to field armies as well. The Germans conducted tests with dropping dummy bombs from the air in 1908, but found it impossible to hit targets even from 100 to 150 meters up, well below the altitude at which dirigibles would have to fly in order to stay out of range of fire from the ground.[90] Aeroplanes, for their part, had still not become practical for military purposes by 1908. Nevertheless, the new technology of aviation had begun to drive warfare into the third dimension. Curiously enough, it was in the conquest of the air that international competition in land armaments first captured—and was even driven forward by—a significant measure of public excitement.

Perceptions of Military Effectiveness: Training, Modernity, and "National Character"

The quality of the European armies naturally did not depend only on numerical strength and modern technology. Observers at the time were acutely aware that training, tactics, cohesion, and morale would be crucial to effectiveness in combat. This was all the more true in an age of intense nationalism and racialism, pervaded by vulgarized social Darwinist ideas about the importance of "national spirit" in an imagined struggle between nations or races. Military officers were particularly susceptible to this ethos. In the late nineteenth century many of them had begun to associate it with their unique role as servants and defenders of their society. Officers received little pay and considered themselves followers of a unique calling that demanded a particular dedication to national ideals. The armies of the early twentieth century were the most tangible embodiment of the nation, recruited from the entire population, officered largely by its elite, and celebrated as the instrument of national protection, power, and public display.

When assessing an army's effectiveness, observers were therefore particularly given to judgments based on perceived qualities of military spirit and bearing in the ranks and the officer corps, both in barracks and on the maneuver field. Evaluations of an army depended almost more than ever on considerations that transcended the material. Such judgments were not irrelevant. Managing any force in the field, especially on the scale of the armies that the European powers would mobilize, did depend on cohesion, dedication, and high levels of education, training, and initiative down to a low level in the chain of command. Observers watched for signs of good morale among the troops, as well as hardiness, leadership, spit-and-polish, precision of drill, marksmanship, discipline, and loyal political attitudes. In these matters, military men of all the European nations developed remarkably consistent impressions of the strong and weak points of each army.

In doing so, they also betrayed prejudices about the "national character" of the populations involved. To some extent existing biases about what to expect from people of different nationalities affected observers' assessments of what they saw. Shortcomings and strengths could be fitted into preexisting notions of what Frenchmen, Germans, or Italians were like, for example. The approach could take on a pseudoscientific dimension in some contexts, and staff officers often reached for this tone when writing reports for their new bureaucratic masters in attempts to quantify the performance of armies. Racialist attitudes were widely accepted on the level of popular prejudices, a development from earlier nineteenth-century ideas about the unique spirit of different nations. In the case of armies, the distinct history, traditions, and culture of military institutions in each of the European states made such generalizations even more tempting. Perhaps the most surprising characteristic of these subjective observations was their consistency over time and from one commentator to another, irrespective of nationality. Officers making remarks about perceived national traits were inclined to agree with foreign observers even about the inclinations of their own countrymen. They often acknowledged what they regarded as the weaknesses of their national tendencies as well as the strengths. No army considered itself to possess a monopoly on the military virtues, and national stereotypes extended from questions of political loyalty to approaches to tactical problems.

In the years after the turn of the century the French army remained one of the chief models for military standards, still the heir to Napoleonic traditions and the product of an astonishing revival after defeat in 1871. Both at home and abroad it was regarded as a force distinguished by inspiration rather than thoroughness, against a background of political turmoil. In some respects, everybody agreed that it performed magnificently. Above all the field artillery, of which the French themselves were so proud, consistently earned the admiration of foreign observers. This remained, in the words of the Austrian military attaché in Paris in 1904, "an elite arm of the very first rank."[91] The 75mm field gun, in service for longer than the hastily adopted quick-firing types of other European armies, was already functioning with perfect smoothness by 1904 in its compact four-gun batteries. The French field artillery almost always fired by indirect laying, with the guns emplaced "in defilade" behind the crests of hills or woods, out of the line of enemy fire. Only the battery commanders or forward observers stationed themselves in positions where they could see the targets, and the gun crews aimed by a detailed, meticulously rehearsed series of geometric calculations and range settings, the basis for all subsequent twentieth-century field gunnery.

In some other respects, though, the French army struck observers less favorably. Above all, it functioned according to a rule of brilliance over method, which carried with it serious drawbacks. French military men prided themselves on the fiery, enthusiastic temper they believed to be a particular asset of their nation, a racial characteristic, and one they sought to exploit in everything from operational doctrine down to the training of the individual soldier. They exalted above all the virtues of "*souplesse*," a quick-minded, adaptable approach they contrasted with what they regarded as the rigid habits of the Germans. In the conduct of battle, for example, Colonel Foch and his disciples advocated a flexible formation in the attack, which appeared constantly at maneuvers. A unit would move forward on a broad front as a screen, spread out so as to engage the opposing force at many points in the front and flank at once. The commander held back a reserve, to launch in a decisive attack when the enemy had shown his hand. The French relied on disorienting the enemy as to their own intentions and then hitting where they found him weak. "To the brutal and schematic tactics of the Germans," wrote General Lacroix after watching an imposing German cavalry exercise in 1906, "we must oppose the resources of the more alert and flexible [*souple*] French spirit."[92] German observers, like the military attaché in Paris, Captain von Mutius, were inclined to skepticism, acknowledging that French tactics would expose German commanders to "dangerous deceptions," but nevertheless observing that in practice the senior officers—and in fact the whole system—were often overcautious. The method of the French commanders "is dedicated in the first place to guarding their own forces," wrote von Mutius after the 1907 maneuvers, "and only thereafter do they begin to wonder if they might be able to do something to the enemy. . . . troops are split up for security on all sides, and never is the whole force engaged for a single goal, even for the final decision itself."[93]

The tradition of *souplesse* defined the whole tenor of military life. The 1904 infantry training manual became a rallying point for the advocates of exploiting the initiative and imagination of the individual soldier and of leaders down to a low level.[94] The approach was self-consciously rooted in the French Revolutionary tradition, updated to respond to the needs of dispersal and movement on the modern battlefield. Many of the elaborate drills of the parade ground disappeared from training. Instead, recruits learned the bare essentials of moving and fighting. For combat, the authors of the 1904 regulations stressed the use of terrain cover above all as a means of approaching the enemy, a reflection of the effect of small arms fire in the Boer War. Troops would no longer advance in orderly skirmish lines and files so as to remain under control of their leaders and well arrayed for volley fire and the bayonet charge. Instead, the new combination of individual, dispersed maneuver and aggressive motivation generally won praise from observers.[95] The Deuxième Bureau concluded that the Russo-Japanese War fully vindicated the tactical forms of the 1904 regulations, while it also "throws into relief to the greatest possible extent the qualities of initiative inherent in our race."[96] The French military attaché in Berlin came home to watch the French grand maneuvers of 1908 and commented with pride on the French infantry: "On the march it is less splendid, less brilliant than German troops, that is undeniable; but as soon as it leaves column to deploy, to take up support positions, to thread its way through fields, to move forward in the open, then everything comes alive. The stragglers and the men bringing up the rear of the platoon in disorder catch fire again, and it is a pleasure to see how each man works with genius to exploit the resources of the moment and of the terrain."[97] Von Mutius, the German attaché in Paris, had acknowledged much the same thing the preceding year: "The strength of the French infantry lies in the individual soldier's unusual skill in the use of terrain. This is born into the blood of the people and evidently derives from speed of comprehension and action linked with great physical agility. Its most characteristic feature is that great order never prevails, but that nevertheless each man reaches the most suitable position in the shortest time."[98]

However, not everybody regarded this natural élan as a substitute for thorough training and efficiency. Von Mutius wrote to Berlin in 1906 on a favorite theme of his: "The 'souplesse' of the race, which the French proudly and justifiably exalt, has a reverse side: superficiality. This appears in every realm of activity." The rank and file enjoyed a casual lack of discipline that was almost incredible to foreign observers. "It makes a very peculiar impression," von Mutius remarked, "when one occasionally sees a squad in the afternoon at Vincennes playing football instead of training."[99] In the midst of a simulated battle at the 1908 maneuvers he witnessed a spectacle still stranger to the Prussian military eye: "I even came upon a skirmish line in which a newspaper vendor was successfully offering his wares. The newspaper-reading riflemen presented a bizarre picture. The officers looked on in acquiescence."[100] Newspapers themselves had a suspect connotation for many officers as an instrument for the diffusion of political ideas in the barracks, where soldiers were encouraged to think about such things as little as possible. The appearance of such reading matter as a distraction from duty even in the firing line was stupefying to von Mutius. The Italian attaché at the French 1908 maneuvers came away with the same impression of indiscipline in the field: "It was not rare to see troops in the firing line reclining in careless postures, just as it was not unusual to hear the officers repeat the same warning order, given in any case in a tone more of advice than of command."[101] "Drill in particular," the German attaché noted, "gives more the impression of a compromise with the good will of the troops than that of a serious school of obedience."

All of this told in combat performance, where the French infantry received low marks for training. Columns on the march dropped stragglers along the route. "One encountered many who had fallen behind, probably mostly reservists," observed von Mutius at the 1907 maneuvers; "These filled the ambulances and other vehicles, without appearing really exhausted." Soldiers often unloaded their packs onto the regimental wagons.[102] Fire discipline was bad at close ranges, and marksmanship poor. Men under fire trotted forward from one cover to the next instead of sprinting at the double and throwing themselves flat like German infantry. The realism of maneuvers suffered badly from a daily pause in the action, usually lasting from the middle of the day until early evening, to allow the troops to regroup and recover from their exertions. For the night, the men marched back to billets in villages rather than bivouacking in the field like the Germans.[103]

In seeking the causes for the French army's untidy standards of discipline, both French and foreign observers blamed the political situation. The annual reports of the Austro-Hungarian chief of staff never failed to disparage the progress of the army as it struggled with religious and political questions and the imposition of two-year service. The latter was also part of the basis for the simplified drill of the 1904 regulations: there were fewer months and cadres to make smart soldiers of the recruits. This was certainly not unwelcome to the mildly antimilitarist Radicals of the Chamber who passed the law, and it was to their "regime" that von Mutius attributed many of the troubles of the French military. "Radical-democratic propaganda," he asserted, had "dangerously loosened discipline in the army." The government treated the conscript forces with kid gloves to preserve its popularity, out of what von Mutius regarded as a weak-spined democratic fearfulness.[104] Indeed, he took the argument even further during the mutinies over the suppression of strikes in 1907, pointing to what he considered to be signs of decadence: "For this the guilt falls upon the entire French people, and at its head the government and parliament, which for years has undermined authority and pandered to popular passions. In these last eight days it has been proven once again that the modern people's army is a mirror of the people itself, and that it is impossible, in spite of honest exertions by the officer corps, to keep an army up to standard as long as the moral strength of the people itself is not upheld."[105] Articles by French officers indicting the two-year service law shared this contempt for a parliament that seemed to them determined to destroy the martial spirit of the nation.[106] The British general staff's handbook on the French army, published in 1905, remarked upon an array of divisive tendencies:

> the almost superhuman efforts of French officers to set the national defenses in order have been to a great extent nullified by the introduction of questions of politics and religion into military matters, and by the dissemination of socialist propaganda amongst the rank and file of the army. . . . It may well be asked what is the value as a fighting machine of an army, however well armed and equipped, in which such sentiments are prevalent. Frenchmen are renowned for intense patriotism, but more than this is required in order to wage war successfully, and unless early steps are taken to eradicate from the French army the existing spirit of indiscipline, France, in spite of her stupendous military preparations, may one day have to learn a more bitter and humiliating lesson than that of the war of 1870–71.[107]

The real concern was the loss of training time and unit cohesion, rather than any fear that the army would actually refuse to fight. "The infantry are, without doubt, quite first-class and absolutely reliable," the British handbook went on to say, "and they will probably move forward to the attack with all their old dash and impetuosity." Everyone agreed that the fervent spirit of the French revolutionary armies and the *furia francese* of the Second Empire would still inspire the soldiers of the Third Republic. When pressed about antimilitarism in the French army after the 1908 maneuvers, General Palitsyn told the German military attaché in St. Petersburg "that enough internal strength still lived on in the French troops to absorb these elements even today if they were to creep into the rank and file."[108] Von Mutius, despite his acid comments on the level of French training and discipline, always emphasized that the French soldiers would fight when it came to a reckoning with the "hereditary enemy." "The great bravery with which every French army has fought for centuries still exists today," he wrote: "Despite Socialism and antimilitarism, every French soldier will fight outstandingly and with passion in the future, too, from the moment when he actually stands on the battlefield opposite the enemy. It is in his blood."[109]

Germans and French in particular often viewed what they considered to be the martial qualities of their peoples as mutually complementary. Von Mutius reflected in 1906 that the loose discipline of the French army was in some ways appropriate: "Perhaps the Frenchman can only be treated in this manner, and certainly in his case temperament, especially in the face of the enemy, replaces much that can only be cultivated by routine and discipline in people with more slowly flowing blood."[110]

Colonel Laguiche, in Berlin, almost exactly mirrored the views of his counterpart in Paris when he wrote in 1908: "We are incapable by nature, by civic and moral education, of assuming the machinelike character of the German; we are beaten in advance by the numbers; so we must make up for it with other qualities. The value of a single French soldier must make him capable of holding his own against many Germans."[111]

The German army presented an image that was almost exactly the converse of the French. Virtually all military men admired its martial appearance, solidity, and thoroughness, but many observers both at home and abroad concluded that these systematic virtues came at the cost of flexibility and imagination. The troops looked magnificent on parade and on the march, smartly turned-out and meticulously drilled. French, Italian, and Russian commentators routinely praised the extraordinary order and endurance of German units in the field.[112] Colonel Laguiche's description of German infantry on the march at the 1904 maneuvers was typical: "Until the very last day the pace was brisk and steady, without the appearance of fatigue. . . . Order is perfect, without the stretching-out of columns, the men bringing up the rear as well aligned as those at the head. . . . Columns cross paths without difficulty; *three* columns can pass each other, march abreast, or move in opposite directions along the same road in admirable order, with impressive ease. . . . The men have a fine bearing, do not look untidy, speak little, and nothing is heard."[113] What a contrast, Laguiche lamented, with the French infantry: "With us, after a march of any length the heads of the columns remain in good order while the tails of these same units follow with difficulty. . . . If it is true that battles are won with the soldiers' legs, the situation leaves us no small grounds for reflection." In the firing line or on the drill ground, German troops executed movements with far greater precision, alacrity, and order than the French. In Britain, the Inspector General of the Forces held up the Germans as an example: "The most noticeable feature of the magnificent German Infantry is the absolute uniformity of drill throughout."[114] The cavalry was no different. Its discipline and training allowed it to maneuver on the battlefield in compact formations, riding in solid ranks over rough ground in fast and complex evolutions that other European cavalry could not execute without scattering into ragged swarms. General Lacroix watched them at the kaiser's annual cavalry maneuvers at Döberitz in 1905: "The cavalry troops that maneuvered at the Döberitz camp give the impression of extremely *homogeneous* squadrons and regiments, well-trained, with a very pronounced offensive spirit, constituting above all *an arm for shock action*, formidable in the mass of its effectives, in its offensive armament (the lance), in its perfect cohesion and in the extreme rapidity of its charges.

The lower cadres are solidly constituted; the leaders are young and vigorous."[115]

The French attributed this military smartness to the German army's luxury of being able to select its recruits rather than having to take virtually every available man. Conscription boards could afford to reject men who showed any sign of physical unfitness, as well as workers suspected of holding political views hostile to the state, the army, or the ruling class. This produced a more vigorous, loyal force with a predominantly rural and politically unquestioning culture. French observers also noticed the much higher proportion of NCOs to trainees, which helped to insure detailed individual instruction and tight discipline.[116] Above all, however, commentators pointed to a difference in national traditions that they did not hesitate to define in words like those of Laguiche in 1908: "The German conception of turning the man into an automaton is a powerful tool for the maintenance of good order; it is all the stronger for being more than simply a culture invented in the army; it is the object of the continual care of the entire administrative machinery of the country."[117] The empire's bureaucratic rigor, the "*Gründlichkeit*" ("thoroughness") on which German military men prided their system, contributed to a military atmosphere radically different from that in France. So did the degree of political consensus achieved within the forces. When commenting on the disorderly appearance or political fractiousness of the French army, German officers were also warning against the consequences of a breakdown of "order" in their own society.

But, like French *souplesse* and patriotism, German smartness in the popular imagination also had its accompanying drawbacks: rigidity and traditionalism. These appeared in the tactics of the German army at maneuvers. Instead of arraying units in depth for the advance, with feint attacks across a broad front, commanders had a predictable way of massing all their forces for a single heavy blow against the enemy's flank. Artillery assembled in the chosen sector to pound a breach, and when the assault went in, the commander held back no significant reserve.[118] To the Germans, this was the only way of ensuring success and being certain of throwing in every possible resource at the decisive point. To foreign officers it looked like a crude formula, exposing the forces to crippling counterattacks. Laguiche expressed the French hope of finding here the scope for the superiority of *souplesse*:

> I believe that we, for our part, will be able to assure ourselves of good advantages if we manage to profit from this rigidity, which corresponds so well to the German idea of force. The straight punch, to which I have referred, is good when it finds its mark; but it remains to be seen whether it will hit home against a flexible [*souple*] enemy, or whether, when thrown

off balance by the energy deployed, striking into emptiness and unaccustomed to responding to the unexpected, the Prussian army will be capable of putting to use that power which it possesses and which it would be puerile not to admire.[119]

At the level of combat drills, this rigidity manifested itself in the persistence of old-fashioned massed tactics. Most often, military attachés at maneuvers saw the infantry approach the battlefield in dense columns even where these could not stay out of sight. They were slow to deploy into skirmish lines, generally waiting to do so until they were about a thousand meters from the enemy. Even then, the lines were too dense, with the men only some four paces apart, keeping strict alignment and disregarding the folds of terrain and other cover. Military experts deplored the overschematized results of such drill-ground tactics. "Certainly," wrote the Italian military attaché in 1904, "to see them in one field action after another advancing in dense lines or in columns under enemy fire, and for long distances, one is not induced to express too favorable a judgment on the manner in which they intend to lead their troops on the terrain of an attack."[120] The Russian military attaché found German tactics in 1907 "sometimes archaic and bearing little relation to the situation," while the Grand Duke Nicholas, visiting the maneuvers that same year, told the French "that he had been far from expecting such a disappointment in the state of tactical preparation of the German army."[121] The *Revue militaire des armées étrangères* routinely sneered at German attack formations as being designed primarily for their dramatic effect upon the spectators, and witheringly described the scene at the climax of the imperial maneuvers in 1904: "The onward march of these dense masses over many kilometers, the one side pushing the other literally with their swords in their backs, to the music of the bands, only feebly evokes the idea of a *Kriegsgemäss* pursuit."[122]

The Germans themselves realized that something had to be done, but could not decide what changes to make. This was a struggle that had been going on since their sobering experiences in the face of breechloading rifle fire on the battlefields of the Franco-Prussian War. It continued with varying results even after the South African and Manchurian campaigns. In 1902 and 1903 the Germans tried a new system of "Boer tactics" at the imperial maneuvers, using dispersed movement and terrain cover, but these then disappeared.[123] Kaiser Wilhelm himself actually called for more dispersed infantry formations in 1905 after seeing what had happened to massed attacks in the Russo-Japanese War.[124] At the 1907 maneuvers the emperor caused a sensation in his final critique by telling the assembled officers "among comrades" that the massed advance of one division under enemy fire was, frankly, "the biggest

Schweinerei" he had ever witnessed.[125] The general staff hesitated to order too much dispersal because its officers drew from the Russo-Japanese War the lesson that "the attainment of fire superiority" was the only means of succeeding in the attack, and this required getting large numbers of men concentrated well forward.[126] Observers noted periodic improvements, as at the 1906 and 1908 maneuvers.[127] However, they considered it far more typical when the German army lapsed, as in 1904 and 1907, into old-fashioned linear formations.[128] New drill manuals, like one that the Prussian general staff issued in 1906, did not convince the French, among others, that fundamental change was at hand in such a tradition-bound army.[129] Even the Germans themselves considered that the problem had something to do with "national characteristics." The Bavarian military representative in Berlin often heard from German generals that dispersed tactics were poorly developed, but "that at any rate we can still make considerable progress in this, even if the natural talent of the Germans on average does not exactly favor the training necessary for it."[130]

The field artillery was no better. Only slowly and erratically did it begin to adopt the techniques of indirect fire from defiladed positions as practiced by the French. Foreign attachés watched as each year at the imperial maneuvers the guns were deployed differently: sometimes exposed on the crests of hills, to fire directly at their targets or even move forward with the infantry; sometimes well defiladed in valleys or on reverse slopes; and sometimes only partly concealed, with the muzzle flashes and dust clouds from the firing shocks revealing their positions to the enemy. The Germans drew contradictory conclusions from the Russo-Japanese War about the relative advantages of keeping the guns out of the enemy's sight on the one hand, and being able to shoot accurately on the other.[131] In truth, since neither side in Manchuria had possessed fully modern pieces or employed artillery to its full effect, the results were hard to interpret clearly. The Germans seem to have used the excuse to persist in old habits. These were reinforced by the later introduction of quick-firing guns in Germany than in France.[132] The German field artillery's resistance to scientific methods of gunlaying and its eagerness to maintain a dashing role in the forefront of battle elicited glee from Laguiche, who expected French gunners to outfight their opponents easily: "If the German artillery as I know it were called upon to operate against us, it would be quite helpless. It would not even know upon what or upon which area to direct its fire."[133]

The most widely criticized arm of service, however, was the German cavalry. Perhaps its very splendor made foreign observers eager to find fault, but certainly it did little to belie accusations that it remained stuck in a long-past era. At least the general staff banished the ritual charge of the massed cavalry of both sides at the grand finale of the imperial maneuvers, led by the kaiser in person, starting in 1904.[134] The elite of the mounted troops, however, continued to hold its own annual exercises at Döberitz under the proud eye of the emperor. In the imperial maneuvers it might be relegated to the same peripheral role as other European cavalry, with the commanders not really knowing what to do with it and the attachés unable to judge very clearly how effectively it carried out its tasks of reconnaissance and security patrolling. But the German cavalry maintained a high enough profile elsewhere to attract the attention of observers to its enduring fascination with the mounted charge. It was not that the cavalry of other armies did not also often prefer this role; it was rather that the Germans performed it with so much conviction and publicity. General Lacroix's report from Döberitz in 1906 summarized what foreign observers loved to disparage about the kaiser's mounted troops, so splendid in their appearance and drill:

> the *manner* in which these squadrons and regiments were used, particularly at the level of larger units (Brigade and Division), did not seem to produce the *results* one might have expected from elements individually so well trained: the error lies in the *rigidity* of their evolutions, most of which are *linear*, and also in a perhaps excessively schematic conception of cavalry combat, which amounts to a *frontal* attack by a very strong first line, which the support of several successive lines tends to render irresistible. . . . The large units (in particular the 4-Brigade Guard Division) march and maneuver in *compact* formations, lacking lightness and flexibility; from a distance, they appear in the form of blocks, extremely vulnerable to artillery fire and exposed to being easily outmaneuvered on their flanks. The maintenance of *order* and *cohesion*, at all gaits and in any terrain, seems to be the constant preoccupation of the leaders.[135]

All of this left little room for the form of action that many theorists in Europe considered to be the most likely role for cavalry on the modern battlefield: dismounted combat with carbines. The cavalry would use its horses to reach positions quickly, and then function as infantry once it got there. At the annual maneuvers the German cavalry wavered between shock action and foot combat, according to the will of the kaiser and the influence of his successive cavalry inspectors.[136] Foreign observers, however, most often came away with the impression of its preference for massed charges. After watching some spectacular examples at the Döberitz exercises in 1906, the Japanese military attaché remarked to Laguiche: "I saw a lot of things in Manchuria; I never saw that."[137]

In many respects, though, the German army displayed remarkably modern characteristics. It was the first to develop the practice of continuous action in annual maneuvers, in 1906, when Moltke did away with suspensions of hostilities at night or for periods of the day and minimized interventions by referees that made operations conform to prepared scripts.[138] These new practices could lead to disorder, hardships for the troops, scattering, and loss of control in less disciplined armies. Other countries lingered on with various degrees of organizational breaks in operations, and sometimes preassigned battle plans to ensure that certain tactical situations would arise so that they could be practiced. The Germans also used entrenchments very extensively at maneuvers, far more than other armies. Sometimes pre-dug by the engineers and sometimes shoveled out by the infantry during operations, large trench systems in the defense attracted the attention of military attachés at maneuvers as early as 1904.[139] The Russo-Japanese War, where both sides dug furiously to protect themselves from enemy fire whenever they stayed in position for any length of time, convinced the Prussian general staff that field fortifications would be crucial for defending conquered objectives against counterattack.[140] From 1906 onward, foreign observers noted that German defensive positions frequently consisted of several successive trench lines linked by communication saps, often with barbed-wire entanglements strung in front of them, as in Manchuria. They were deep enough for standing riflemen, and provided with well-protected dugouts for field telephones that assured communications throughout the network.[141] These arrangements elicited little fanfare at the time, but they prepared the German army well for taking up the defensive at the end of 1914. They were easier to carry out in Germany partly because of the political status of the army, which made it more acceptable than in other countries for troops to dig deep trenches through people's agricultural land, and partly because there were more engineer units than in most other armies. Another modern feature Laguiche noticed was the increasingly thorough training of reservists after Moltke became chief of staff—a mission that most armies grossly neglected.[142] The Germans also won praise from foreign observers for their generally excellent complement of technical equipment, from binoculars and range-finders to motorcycles and communication gear. Laguiche was prompted to admit by 1908 that "the use of recent technical inventions is far more developed in Germany than in France."[143]

The most significant technological advantage of the German army after the turn of the century was its development of large quantities of mobile heavy artillery.[144] In 1900 the war ministry adopted a wheeled 150mm howitzer for general service and began converting its carriage to a recoil-absorbing version in 1903.[145] Most armies relied almost entirely on lighter field guns for artillery support, but the Germans believed that the heavier caliber, greater range, and plunging fire of the 150mm piece would be essential for demolishing tougher targets and silencing enemy artillery batteries. This "1902" howitzer, unlike most other heavy artillery of the time, could be towed on its wheeled mounting like an ordinary field gun without being disassembled, and the Germans decided that the difficulty of bringing up its much heavier ammunition would be compensated by its power. Von Einem ordered in 1904 that, since each corps would mobilize a heavy field howitzer battalion in wartime, the forces must constantly practice with the guns and bring them along to all maneuvers. "In this way," he directed, "all unit commanders and troops can be shown that the heavy field artillery is capable of being used like any other weapon in open battle, and must be brought in for the decision."[146] While this was going on, the French were still debating whether or not to introduce a mobile 155mm quick-firing heavy howitzer of their own for use with the field army. In the Conseil Supérieur de la Guerre almost everyone agreed on the desirability of such a gun, but several preferred to use it simply for the siege artillery, to be placed at the disposal of army commanders in wartime. "It would be difficult to drag them along constantly with the field vehicles," objected General Hagron, "and thus needlessly to lengthen the 15 km of vehicles that already overload our corps."[147] "Such weapons are obviously not made for field campaigning," agreed General Langlois, asserting that the 75mm gun was "perfectly sufficient" for destroying the usual obstacles of the battlefield. Even a 155mm howitzer, he reported, had proven in tests to be scarcely more effective than smaller calibers against troops in trenches, the main form of field fortification. The French remained preoccupied above all with the mobility of their field forces, emphasizing as they did flexibility and ease of movement and perhaps recalling the chaos into which their logistical efforts had repeatedly collapsed during the Franco-Prussian War.[148] The complexities of ammunition supply for more and heavier calibers spoke against their adoption in the first line. The French eventually settled on constructing 155mm howitzers—but only six of them per corps—for assignment as a group to army commands. The howitzers did not appear at maneuvers, and the commanders generally ignored them even after they had been produced (between 1904 and 1908).[149] The Germans, meanwhile, gave their heavy howitzers a prominent role in maneuvers, with sixteen of them assigned to each corps in peacetime. Secrecy surrounded them at first, although gradually attachés began to report on their proliferation and on the evident ease with which their horse teams towed them in all terrain in spite of their weight.[150]

The Russo-Japanese War gave rise to conflicting interpretations of the utility of heavy artillery. It was practically absent in the first stage of the campaign, and only improvised in insufficient quantities later, mostly in the form of naval guns brought ashore from ships. This left room for observers to believe what they wanted. French officers in Manchuria, noting little effective use of heavy guns and the difficulty of moving the clumsy pieces that eventually arrived, reported that such weapons were a useless impediment.[151] The Germans, for their part, blamed the poor performance of the heavy artillery on its misuse, and considered that the combatants could have achieved far more with it, especially if it had been present in adequate quantities.[152] The Japanese devoted much effort from early on in the campaign to hauling off captured Russian 150mm naval cannon, and relied heavily upon huge 280mm Krupp howitzers shipped from Japan to batter the elaborate defenses of Port Arthur with devastating fire that allowed the infantry to capture one position after another. The Prussian general staff reported that entrenchments and dugouts made large calibers all the more necessary: "For months both armies lie opposite each other in such strongly fortified positions that attacks upon them require heavy artillery and the means of siege warfare."[153] It was a portent of the crucial role heavy guns were to assume in the fighting on the western front after 1914. Apart from the French and Germans, most European armies did not yet have the resources to procure mobile heavy artillery, and had more urgent needs in the conventional line. They continued to rely on obsolete siege guns, sometimes converted to wheeled mountings, while the design of quick-firing heavy field howitzers remained confined to experiments or lists of desiderata.[154] The Russians watched the German development with apprehension and, unable to acquire mobile heavy guns yet themselves, advised their French allies in 1906 that they, at least, should get their own into service in the greatest numbers possible.[155]

The Russian army was judged by almost all observers to perform very badly. Its disastrous showing in the war with Japan merely reinforced existing assessments of it as a vast, clumsy organization of little offensive value. The officer corps and higher commands incurred particularly harsh criticism, both during the war and afterward. Russia's repeated defeats at the hands of the Japanese, despite the relatively equal forces engaged on both sides, were a result of long-standing defects, especially among the officers, according to Lieutenant-Colonel Lauenstein of the Prussian general staff, who had spent many years in St. Petersburg and followed the operations in Manchuria. "They were devoid of morality, of any sense of duty or responsibility," he wrote. "Their willpower was not steeled: they simply had no conception of being hard with themselves. The tendency to seek comfort made itself apparent everywhere."[156] Baggage and servants weighed down the columns, drunkenness and malingering were rife, and an obsession with rewards and decorations seemed to Lauenstein to be all that drove officers to distinguish themselves under fire—or at least to compose exaggerated reports.

Kuropatkin was a "feeble character," and even the men showed little stomach for fighting and a continual concern with making themselves comfortable. "An outspoken indolence," wrote Lauenstein, "a shrinking from hardship and effort, slackness, a repulsion for anything burdensome or unpleasant for one's own person, a lack of consistency in thought and action, all mark the Russian national character."

After the war, General Moulin in St. Petersburg emphasized that reform would come slowly due to "the immense force of inertia, the enormous friction of the entire machine."[157] In his opinion, like Lauenstein's, the problem was one of leadership: "the weakest point in the Russian army is the mediocrity of its command."[158] The Austro-Hungarian intelligence service blamed the Russian army's poor training on the "lack of interest and passivity of the *officers* . . . , who either do not report for duty at all or else display the most deficient comprehension of the instruction of the troops."[159] The British general staff pronounced a devastating verdict in its 1907 handbook on the Russian army, condemning the officers above all as society's rejects:

> The Russians are not a military nation. In all classes of the population there is a disinclination to serve in the army, and a still greater disinclination to adopt it as a profession. . . . a very large proportion of Russian officers serve mechanically and apathetically and even dislike their profession. . . . To crown all, the disastrous war with Japan deprived the corps of officers of its last shreds of prestige and laid bare its defects, not only to the world at large but to itself. The disturbed state of the country is reflected in the army, causing political dissensions among the officers, insubordination among the rank and file, and disgust in all ranks at the police work which they have to do.[160]

Where the enlisted men were concerned, observers generally agreed that the reservists proved ill-trained and unreliable and the NCOs inadequate, whereas the regular soldiers displayed what was regarded as a traditional Russian hardiness, fatalism, and toughness in defense.[161] But these traditional strengths held little value in the eyes of military experts who sought the decision of a future war in vigorous offensives by inspired and resourceful soldiers. Colonel Lauenstein commented that the stolidity of Russian troops often translated into "obstinate complacency" on the battlefield, especially in the absence of officers with initiative.[162]

Russian tactics and regulations after the Manchurian campaign became considerably more adapted to the demands of the fire-swept battlefield. All observers at maneuvers noticed how the artillery fired exclusively from defiladed positions while the infantry advanced in dispersed formation and took full advantage of terrain cover.[163] The British were

more impressed than other commentators since the changes reflected
what they themselves had been doing since the Boer War, as their attaché in St. Petersburg remarked in 1908: "There is no doubt that great
advances are being made in the training as a result of the experience of
war, and this is especially noticeable in the work of the infantry. The
changes bear a striking resemblance to those made in our training after
the South African War. The artillery possesses the best instructed officers and the use of covered positions is almost invariably adhered to."[164]
Observers from other armies were less convinced of the value of the
changes. Moulin reported in 1906, "*the offensive spirit is dead in the
Russian army after the misfortunes of the war.*"[165] Even Palitsyn confessed as much to Moulin earlier that year, and at maneuvers the French
attaché found the whole conduct of operations too slow and cautious,
partly due to what he regarded as the failure of initiative at all levels
among the Russian officers: "they take very strong account of the effects
of modern weapons and concentrate above all on minimizing casualties.
This is by no means the same point of view as a system which, taking the
power of modern weapons most strongly into account, would have concentrated above all upon obtaining the maximum results of this power
used against the enemy."[166] It became the orthodoxy of the Ecole
Supérieure de la Guerre that Russian soldiers "have a passive character
and it would be well if they added to it more offensive spirit than has
generally been the case in the history of Russia."[167]

According to Moulin, the Russian army's inability to follow a system
of tactics combining dispersal and aggressiveness like the French ultimately depended upon what he viewed as inherent characteristics of the
men themselves. He asked rhetorically: "What is the national temperament of the Russian infantryman? Extreme solidity in the defensive, lack
of dash and élan in the attack; he is strong, but not very agile, he is
obedient, but without individual initiative." Even new tactics and training, in his opinion, would yield no more than "a hybrid product, limp
attacks, unintelligent and ineffective riflemen; in short, a poor instrument for the offensive."[168] The Prussian general staff commented, "It
is obvious that modern infantry combat is unnatural and uncomfortable
to the Russian," and speculated that any improvement was unlikely:
"Against this speaks their scarce ability to train riflemen capable of acting independently, as well as the difficulty of keeping up the supply of
noncommissioned officers, which will be compounded by the shortening of the service term."[169] Besides the issues of tactics, initiative, and
the offensive, foreign observers noted mistakes and disorderly conduct
of operations everywhere at Russian maneuvers, such as cavalry charges
into the teeth of lethal fire and the persistence of fire by volleys in the

infantry. The Austro-Hungarian intelligence bureau attributed much of this to "the carelessness of the Russian national character."[170] General Moulin offered a gloomy prognosis in November 1906 in case no radical change in military organization took place: "Otherwise, the Russian army will continue to obey what has until now been the law of its history. Born the last, it remains even today the last among the armies of Europe in respect of organization, technology, training, and tactics. It will undoubtedly make certain steps forward; but other armies will profit even better than it will from the lessons of the Manchurian war. At any rate, without a very serious internal revolution it will never be able to face its enemies with the exalted patriotism of the Japanese and of the armies of the French Revolution."[171] The French attaché was saying more than he knew, but he summed up what most observers expected of the million men who stood under arms in the east.

The other European army with recent experience of war, the British, also brought back many expensive tactical lessons from the battlefield, and in applying them in training it likewise often fell afoul of French and German critics who accused it of having lost the offensive spirit. The British, however, had won their war in the end, and verdicts on the resulting habits were less harsh. What visitors at maneuvers noticed most often was the outstanding use of terrain cover and concealment. "The English Infantry has made great progress in the art of moving under cover, and in the science of using terrain," wrote the French military attaché in 1904; "Its combat formation, however, remains the same as ever, a succession of very thin lines without any rigidity of alignment."[172] A Prussian general staff report in 1907 gave an impression of what a British advance looked like from the defender's point of view as it moved forward with maximum care to avoid enemy fire:

> At great distances, fourteen hundred to two thousand meters, field glasses can discern individual riflemen, widely spaced out and carefully using every patch of terrain cover. They offer all the less of a target because the gray-green color of their uniform blends well with the terrain. As soon as effective fire makes further progress difficult, the men go to ground. At irregular intervals of fifty to three hundred meters follow further sparse lines, so that for a time the battlefield appears as if sprinkled with riflemen. The foremost line opens fire when it has been sufficiently reinforced by its successors. After this point, any movement in the open takes place either at the crawl, or in rushes that are so short and rapid that it is scarcely possible to bring fire to bear on them. . . . If further advance appears to risk excessive casualties, the infantry digs in while lying prone and awaits nightfall to continue the attack.[173]

The men were universally acknowledged to be well trained in marksmanship and rapid reloading. The artillery, once it got its quick-firing guns, fired exclusively from defilade, receiving criticism only occasionally for its reluctance to change position and dash forward to keep up with the advance, as French and German batteries were expected to do.[174]

As with the Russians, continental observers found fault with the British army for having been, as they saw it, cowed into excessive caution by its experience of war. Defilade and dispersed advance were all very well, but missing was the sense of aggressive enthusiasm that most European officers sought in a fighting force. "The tactical training of the army for the defensive is good and thoroughly modern," noted a Prussian general staff report in 1904, "but the training for the offensive by contrast unquestionably suffers from the impulse, out of the fear of incurring casualties, to deploy far too broadly, a circumstance that will undoubtedly bring disadvantages in its train when large formations move in country without good visibility."[175] The feature most often noticed was the use of cavalry almost invariably in the dismounted role, or at most for mounted reconnaissance, even after the special mounted infantry units formed for the Boer War disappeared from the Home Army shortly after the end of the campaign in South Africa. On the one hand, some observers admired this as modern. Colonel Huguet was able to report to Paris in 1907: "In the cavalry, excellent use of terrain, whether on the march or on security patrols; great aptitude for foot combat."[176] But the cost was a slackening in standards of horse care, of riding skills, and above all of ability to engage in shock action. The latter was obsolete, but military experts still considered it a crucial capability and an indicator of the appropriate cavalry spirit. "The English Cavalry is turning progressively into mounted Infantry," wrote the French attaché in London with disgust in 1904.[177] The verdict of the Prussian general staff in 1907 was typical: "All movements at exercises display a lack of compactness and order. In wheeling or deployment, especially at the gallop, everything flies apart. . . . In mounted combat the cavalry is decisively unequal to its German counterpart. As a result of the strong emphasis on dismounted combat, the sense for action in the saddle has receded."[178] British officers continually debated whether it might not be wise to prepare the cavalry more traditionally for action with the *arme blanche,* and much effort went into the design of a new sword.[179]

But for many observers, the issue as usual went beyond tactics to the question of supposedly inherent characteristics of the army. As General Michel of the Conseil Supérieur de la Guerre put it after watching field exercises in 1907, "Telephone cables and other lines multiply on the ground in the course of each maneuver, but the moral spark that places the commander in communication with his firing line, that draws toward him every spirit and every will, that makes everyone obey him at the smallest sign, does not exist. . . . the habits of mind of the English army will have to change if it wishes to measure itself against European armies."[180] The recruitment of the British army, being voluntary, of course put it in a category of its own. Colonel Huguet phrased the consequences of this in a common fashion when he reported in 1905 that "the English soldier, although he has the qualities of *sang froid*, of cold and steadfast bravery which distinguish the race, does not stand up to fatigue unless he is well fed and clothed. . . . Although he is a national mercenary, he remains nonetheless a mercenary who has neither the energy nor the moral valor of a truly national soldier."[181] British officers were often faulted for treating their profession as a "sport" more than as a patriotic calling. Indeed, continental observers themselves had difficulty taking the army as a whole very seriously because of its diminutive size and its remoteness from the soil over which the great battles would be fought. Foreign military experts often found British senior commanders relatively unacquainted with the handling of large, articulated forces in the field simply because they very seldom had a chance to practice. When they did, march columns were disorderly and showed a distressing lack of experience in moving en masse.[182] Even though the British army developed a highly effective, mobile, quick-firing heavy field howitzer of 120mm caliber (the 4.7-inch 60-pounder), and gave each division four of them by 1907, there were simply not enough divisions for this to add up to a very impressive weight of firepower—all together fewer barrels than the 150mm howitzers of two German corps, in fact.[183] Surveys of the European armies with their strengths and equipment, compiled by general staffs from Paris and Berlin to Vienna and Rome, very often simply left the British out altogether, regardless of how professional the forces might look in many respects.

Among the big continental armies, the Austro-Hungarian military continually amazed observers simply by continuing to function at all. Indeed, it appeared to perform impressively well, remaining united in its loyalty and improving its tactics gradually in spite of the obstacles that the political antagonisms of the Dual Monarchy presented to recruitment, expansion of the forces, or the acquisition of new equipment. Its commanders agonized incessantly over its future in a politically paralyzed system. General Friedrich von Beck, the chief of staff, laid a typical protest before Franz Joseph in his 1905 annual report, frustrated at the Hungarian parliament's continual refusal to vote for increased funds or for the prompt call-up of the annual recruit class for training. The situation, he warned, "must awaken all the greater worry when one compares our backwardness with the progress of foreign armies":[184]

> For these reasons we can point not only to no progress in our military readiness this year, but rather on the contrary to a substantial increase in the stagnation of which we have complained for years and which a living organism like an army, constantly in need of development, cannot bear any longer without collapsing into ruin. . . . All training, but especially that of new noncommissioned officers, has suffered badly from this, particularly in the mounted and technical services, and has perceptibly damaged the quality of the troops throughout their period of service. . . . The *insufficiency of available funds* leads to complete stasis in all areas of military activity. Even important, burning questions can only be "studied," or at most brought forward to the stage of "projects," while every new scheme, even in the case of very small extra resources, must be postponed to a later future "for lack of budgetary means."

Beck's pessimism helped to bring about his dismissal in 1906, but his successor, Franz Conrad von Hötzendorf, quickly took up the same tune and chafed at the "persistent stagnation" imposed by budgetary limitations and the divisiveness of Hungarian separatism.[185] Foreign commentators continually wondered how long this could go on. Captain Girodou, the French military attaché in Vienna, reported in 1905 that existing functions could at least continue at present levels for the time being, but that if the crisis were to stretch on for yet another year it would make even the daily routine of military life impossible.[186] Girodou still expressed the same sense of impending disaster two years later even though nothing had changed in the meantime: "It is upon the common army that all the weight of the vicissitudes of the dualist organization falls at present; it is its very existence, or at least its unity, which is at stake."[187] Girodou's Italian colleague in Vienna, Captain Alessandro Sigrai Asinari di San Marzano, judged in 1908 that the army was robust for the time being, but that the ethnic problem was "fatally destined in a more or less distant future to weaken its compact limbs."[188]

And yet, the worst never actually seemed to happen. Indeed, in the very same report San Marzano summed up a common view when he wrote that the delay in issuing modern artillery equipment was the only vital problem: "In all other respects, the army is organized on very solid bases. A compact officer corps, of disciplined intellect, keen, active: an army perfectly administered, well armed, and solidly disciplined, which is beyond doubt a powerful instrument for war." This applied as much to the Landwehr and the Honvédség as to the common army, and as much to the loyal spirit of the officers as to the material from which the rank and file were recruited. In 1906 Girodou remarked that, despite the acrimony of Vienna's disputes with Budapest over questions of language and administration in the army, "so far the officer corps seems to remain completely indifferent to the flow of particularist chauvinism."[189] This persistence of a unifying professionalism and *Kaisertreue* in an officer elite drawn from all the nationalities of the monarchy ranked as an achievement all the more astounding when compared to the divisiveness of the French officer corps over political issues in the post-Dreyfus republic. Until the last days of the Dual Monarchy, a military career continued to signify membership in a unique corps whose essence derived from constituting the only truly supranational institution of the imperial and royal state.[190]

As for the enlisted men, they did not resist military service to any considerable extent, or mutiny periodically like French, Italian, or Russian troops. They actually presented an impressive military appearance, looking consistently well turned-out, hardy, and disciplined. After watching a day of exercises in 1904, Girodou commented upon "the smart appearance of the landwehr regiments (not to mention the regiments of the common army, on the part of which only the contrary would be surprising) . . . . from the point of view of correctness of bearing and regularity of evolutions they seemed in no way inferior to units of the common army."[191] The French attaché considered that the 1907 imperial maneuvers "showed once again the excellent discipline that reigns from top to bottom in the Austro-Hungarian army, the good will of everyone, the endurance and spirit of the soldier; in this respect I believe that this army can bear comparison with the best."[192] Girodou sought one explanation for this in the fact that the Dual Monarchy "possesses in abundance excellent elements of manpower, robust, healthy, steadfast and disciplined; from this point of view it is in an altogether enviable situation." San Marzano tempered his admiration by cautioning that the army's obedient character came at the cost of "lack of initiative and of élan among the troops, who, by temperament and as a consequence of formal discipline, must always be commanded and guided in their every action."[193] With the Austro-Hungarian army it was less a question of national character in a land of such ethnic diversity than a matter of economic, social, and educational development in a state that still recruited a high proportion of peasants accustomed to subservience.

In their tactics on the maneuver field, Austro-Hungarian units took time to learn. Although disciplined and orderly, they displayed little evidence of having learned the lessons of dispersal from the Russo-Japanese War, adhering instead to dense formations.[194] Starting in 1907, this began to change. In that year, Conrad instituted the practice of omitting daily rest periods from the action at imperial maneuvers, and Girodou drew up a favorable report on the assault tactics employed. The previous year, he noted, he had commented on "the progress accomplished by the infantry since the 1905 maneuvers from the point of view of *souplesse*, adaptation to the terrain, and ability in seeking defilade. This year, too, I found this progress more marked: no masses to be seen; skirmishers, supports, and reserves advancing in sparse lines by small groups in short, rapid rushes and throwing themselves flat at once. I believe that in this respect the Austro-Hungarian infantry has nothing to envy any other."[195] The cavalry, for its part, looked magnificent and began to perform reconnaissance and foot combat effectively after the Russo-Japanese War, although it attracted criticism for its unreadiness for shock action. Girodou reported in 1907: "The Austro-Hungarian cavalry is an elegant arm, well in hand, splendid to look at; its horses are in excellent condition, its maneuvers correct; but it lacks dash, it does not gallop. Its junior officers do not have all the outward daring one could desire; its captains and colonels lack initiative or are too often held back by the fear of tiring out their horses."[196]

The most remarkable transformation came about in the artillery, where hopelessly outdated tactics remained in use until the new quick-firing field guns arrived in 1908. Until then, there seemed to be little incentive to reorganize and retrain the batteries before the modern material was available, so the gunners seldom practiced indirect fire from defiladed positions. San Marzano offered a typical report after the 1907 maneuvers: "I often observed a massing of guns that could have been fatal in real combat. I saw, for example, an entire brigade of artillery in battery in the open with the pieces at intervals of not more than two meters from one another.—Similarly on another occasion I observed two lines of artillery in battery on a forward slope facing the enemy, one on the crest and the other half way down."[197] Not until the following year did these suicidal practices begin to disappear with the introduction of the new field gun and regular use of indirect fire techniques.[198] It was in such areas, where the Austro-Hungarian army depended upon new technology—and therefore upon funding increases—that it was known for its weakness. Reporting on the cautious testing of machine guns in 1905, Girodou passed the common verdict: "in this as in all things, the Austro-Hungarian military administration is proceeding with parsimony and slowness."[199] On the other hand, he observed, it did get there in the end: "The Austro-Hungarian army always arrives after those of the principal military powers, but in return it profits from their experiences and saves itself unnecessary costs and efforts."[200] As long as it defied the disputes that tore at the society behind it, it seemed, the heterogeneous army of the Dual Monarchy could present a remarkably efficient spectacle of military power, which all observers considered worthy of respect.

The same could not be said of the force that seemed increasingly likely to become its opponent. The Italian army, whether on the maneuver field or in barracks, seemed to be able to do nothing right. Underfunded for its inflated size, and burdened with a legacy of relatively low national pride in its military traditions, the army of the Kingdom of Italy looked significantly less effective than its potential adversaries in the years following the Russo-Japanese War and the first Moroccan crisis. The troops struck foreign observers in some respects as hardy, but otherwise their appearance on exercises was a disaster. "The order of march defies description," wrote the German military attaché in Rome, Baron von Hammerstein-Equord, in 1905; "every man does as he likes, and I saw stragglers in masses, troops who broke ranks without permission in order to buy things for themselves."[201] The infantry performed abysmally in action, as the chief of the Italian general staff himself, General Tancredi Saletta, noted in his blistering critique of the grand maneuvers that year:

> In its tactical employment the infantry did not show itself to possess the degree of instruction that the exigencies of modern combat require. Often units were seen proceeding in column on roads effectively swept by artillery and rifle fire; and, even leaving the road, remaining in formations that were far too dense. . . . Account was not always taken of the necessity of exploiting terrain cover for moving protected from enemy observation and fire, which should by now be a matter of habit in all circumstances. Units were seen opening fire without control or judgment, at a prodigal rate, which the officers were only able to stop with difficulty. Little care was taken to keep in touch with the overall progress of the actions in which the units were directly involved, even when doing so was vital and easy. Nor was there any lack of instances of troops which, advancing without the prescribed security measures, found themselves in the midst of enemy troops without realizing it.[202]

The situation did not improve significantly in succeeding years.[203] The French attaché, Lieutenant-Colonel Messier de St. James, reported after the 1907 maneuvers that the soldiers sometimes allowed their rifles to get so dirty that the mechanism did not work properly.[204] Messier watched one attack in which the infantry completely missed an opportunity to approach the enemy unseen, moving instead laboriously up a succession of slopes "in compact masses" in the face of enemy fire, to mount a frontal assault on a strongly held position. At one point, on a ridge crest, they "remained bunched together under fire for nearly an hour and a half in a formation that did not in any way resemble a combat deployment." The Italian field artillery practically never fired from defiladed positions during maneuvers. Cavalry was hard to use effectively in Italy, since the terrain was in many places mountainous and the native breeds of horses small in stature. Even taking these handicaps into account, however, the army's mounted troops looked bad to all observers. According to Saletta in 1907, the cavalry still "did not show itself very expert" in the use of foot combat. Nor was it effective for shock action, as Messier judged in 1904, when it exhibited "ponderous charges without élan, much confusion during evolutions, and disorder after the charges."[205]

All observers agreed that the Italian cavalry failed to provide proper combat reconnaissance and security, consistently allowing units to collide without warning and causing chaos on the maneuver field. After the 1907 grand maneuvers, Messier reported that two brigades of the same force had lost touch with one another in the course of the action, and that later the two opposing sides had become hopelessly mixed together: "we discovered once again that the blue and the red units became entangled to an incredible extent. The reds carried out their advance without reconnoitering ahead while the blues retired from one position to the next, halting at points where they could not survey the ground for more than 100m to their front."[206] In the end the maneuvers had to be suspended several days ahead of schedule. The official reason was the onset of rain, but the French attaché thought it more probable that "the Directors of the maneuvers judged the situation to be too tangled up for order to be reinstated and for the maneuvers to be continued with any appearance of realism." The infantry throughout "seemed paralyzed in the field" to Messier; "the instruction of the troops appeared to me to be of the most neglected sort, and one might even doubt, when watching them maneuver, whether they had received any training whatsoever in open country."

Such doubts were not entirely unfounded. The Italian army had begun holding large "German"-style grand maneuvers, setting two sides against one another, only in 1903. Thereafter it could only afford to do so in approximately alternate years, so the troops and their commanders had little experience of large-scale operations. General Saletta blamed the army's terrible performance at maneuvers on the utterly inadequate level of training that resulted from the lack of money and therefore of personnel available.[207] He based his assessment on a study the general staff drew up in 1905, comparing the level of training in the Italian army with that of the Austro-Hungarian and French forces.[208] Italian units were weaker in manpower because, unlike its northern counterparts, the entire army was in reality far below its official strength. It had some 207,000 men under arms instead of the 265,000 that would have been necessary to maintain all units at their paper establishments. This was a long-term consequence of the decision to expand the army from ten corps to twelve in 1896 to approximate the corps-to-population ratio of other countries chiefly for reasons of prestige. The parliament did not vote sufficient funds to man the proliferation of units that this increase had created. Companies contained an average of only 52 men in peacetime, compared to approximately 70 in Austria-Hungary and 107 in France. All were supposed to field a total of about 250 in wartime, which gave the Italians by far the most unrealistic numbers for peacetime exercises. The frequent release of men for budgetary savings before the end of their full term of service left the army for up to eight months of the year without enough men to carry out training at all, its cadres barely sufficient to cover basic administrative and fatigue duties. The constant detachment of contingents for "public security" service against strikers or riots further contributed to the inadequacy of the available strength. Troops were not likely to receive more than two weeks of training per year as part of a large unit such as a brigade or division, and would only spend a few days actually on maneuvers in open country with a unit of any size whatever. Despite its great dependence upon reservists to fill up the companies on mobilization, the Italian army could only afford to call up some 50,000 of them for refresher training in any given year, compared to 423,000 in Austria-Hungary and 590,000 in France. On a regular basis, the Italian army received little more training than did the Russian army in the years of turmoil that followed the war with Japan and the 1905 revolution, and the general staff blamed this for a formidable array of evils.

But what struck foreign observers far more often was the low morale of the army, the lack of that elusive *esprit militaire* in which the age placed such critical faith. In Italy, discontentment in the army took on a uniquely institutionalized form in the early 1900s. The junior officers protested vociferously against the hardships of military life, the slowness of promotion, the erosion of perquisites, and other conditions of service. Between 1903 and the outbreak of the world war they published their grievances in a journal, *Pensiero Militare,* which called for a total overhaul of military organization in Italy to lend new prestige and influence to an officer corps that hoped to take on a less isolated role in a rejuvenated state. The army court-martialed and cashiered the founder of the *Pensiero Militare,* Captain Fabio Ranzi, after a trumped-up incident in 1904.[209] None of this, of course, escaped the attention of foreign attachés and general staffs, who wrote extensively of this *cause célèbre* and its roots. Messier de St. James judged such behavior among the officers to be "one more proof of their absolute lack of military spirit and sense of self-abnegation."[210] In Vienna the intelligence service interpreted the Ranzi case as a manifestation of "the visibly dissolving spirit of discipline and obedience."[211] In 1907 Messier noted even at maneuvers "the scant self-respect displayed by the officers, above all in the presence of foreign officers."[212] The French attaché reflected in 1906: "One is truly entitled to ask whether the military spirit as we know it in France is compatible with this race, leaving aside the Piedmontese whose military atavism is unquestionable. Italian officers have the character of functionaries."[213] They were often lenient in the application of discipline, and their principal tool for enforcing it, the corps of noncommissioned officers, engaged in a protest movement of its own in the same years.[214]

The rank and file were no easier to handle. The French attaché was horrified by the demonstrations that resulted when the army called up the 1904 recruit class at an inconvenient time of year.[215] Such displays, he wrote, were "certainly not the sort of thing that will maintain in the mass of the people that military spirit without which one cannot hope to have a powerful army." On the maneuver field, Hammerstein-Equord noted, "The Italian soldier does not exactly give the impression of possessing a particular relish for his job; and discipline, by our military standards, is unquestionably inferior."[216] The men served out their time apparently without enthusiasm or any sense of patriotic ideals, Messier de St. James reported in 1906, and "under these conditions it is hardly surprising if many of them lack the *feu sacré*; although it is only fair to acknowledge that they are in general conscientious and devoted."[217] Even more alarmingly to military men, lurid accounts of Socialist propaganda and mutinies made their appearance in Austro-Hungarian intelligence reports, which imputed these to an international conspiracy that allegedly involved the French army as well.[218]

Such disorders were particularly conspicuous when the authorities called up reservists and the older Milizia Mobile for retraining or maneuvers. It was upon these second-line forces that the Italian army would depend more than any of its rivals in wartime. In 1904 there were widespread demonstrations among reservists called to the colors in September, with red ties worn in some instances, the singing of the *Internationale,* and outbreaks of violence. In the judgment of the Austro-Hungarian army intelligence bureau, "the danger which threatens the discipline of the Italian army in the form of socialist agitation is not to be underestimated."[219] When a full-blown mutiny occurred in camp at Cuorgné near Turin among reservists recalled in 1906, the NCOs barely escaped harm while the officers failed to intervene, prompting Messier to report to Paris that, "whatever the motives for their conduct, the situation is nonetheless disquieting and in certain circles it is asked what would happen in the case of an actual mobilization."[220] Saletta excoriated his reserve officers at the 1905 maneuvers for being "unequal to their task because they were deficient in professional qualities and devoid of that ascendancy which is vital to the exercise of command."[221] The Milizia Mobile he pronounced insufficiently trained after it appeared at the maneuvers, and also in totally inadequate physical condition, due to "the lack of a virile national education and the present tendencies of society."

In 1908 a new French military attaché in Rome, Lieutenant-Colonel Jullian, tried to explain the "crisis of morale that the Italian army is presently undergoing."[222] He attributed it to the lack of a sense of purpose: "This numerous army seems to have no *raison d'être* at present except to permit Italy to play the role of a great power that it has assumed. . . . The Italian army today cannot but be aware that nobody is planning an attack upon its country; on the other hand military, political, and geographic reasons make any plans for an offensive campaign of its own futile." The war ministry might make whatever reforms it liked, according to Jullian, "but only events in foreign policy, which are for the moment impossible to predict, in giving a purpose to the work of the Army and a goal for its hopes, could restore to it that confidence in itself which it seems to have lost." Hammerstein-Equord shared this gloomy view of the Italian army's morale, but was not so sure that developments in foreign policy would leave it time for effective reforms. In one report at the end of 1908, he warned, "The Italian army today finds itself in a very precarious situation" due to the stirring-up of antagonism with its northeastern neighbor: "were Italian policy to force the *ultima ratio,* and were the army to have to fight the Austrians in the foreseeable future, one does not have to be a prophet to predict that . . . , not only due to its inadequate state of organization but above all due to its moral decadence, it would be headed for a third Custozza."[223] Few in Europe would have argued with him.

THE GROWTH OF MILITARY RIVALRY
BETWEEN ITALY AND AUSTRIA-HUNGARY, 1904–1908

The question raised by the French and German attachés, of the Italian army's effectiveness in a war against Austria-Hungary, had actually grown increasingly relevant to the general staffs in Rome and Vienna in the years since 1904. It was here, in fact, that the only significant competition between armies after the Moroccan crisis took shape. A rivalry developed between Austria-Hungary and Italy, accompanied by a whole new set of military consequences. Although no major expansion of armies resulted, Italy turned sharply away from the Triple Alliance, changing the strategic situation substantially. Partly in reaction, the Austro-Hungarian general staff began the highly destabilizing practice of proposing a "preventive war" as a means of solving domestic and international problems. This was the beginning of a policy that later drove the Dual Monarchy to touch off the world war.

As a political matter, the antagonism was no more than a realignment within the European alliance system. The process had its origins in Italy's shift to Liberal government and increasing friendship with France in the first years of the twentieth century. This was accompanied by a recrudescence of irredentist agitation and rhetoric against Austria, the traditional outlet for the nationalism of the Italian left. At the same time Austria-Hungary, free from its customary rivalry with Russia in the aftermath of the Manchurian war, was at liberty to look to its southern defenses. Tsar Nicholas II met King Victor Emanuel III at the Italian resort of Racconigi in 1907 in a sign of rapprochement, while Kaiser Wilhelm privately vented to Austrian statesmen his anger at Italy as well as Russia for failing to support Germany at Algeciras.[224] None of this was in itself a serious challenge to either Rome or Vienna, let alone cause for a war, but it represented a considerable departure from the spirit of the Triple Alliance.

Military leaders in both states readjusted their plans to the new rivalry, but they could do little to strengthen their forces materially. The Italian general staff had last made a thorough plan for deployment against Austria-Hungary in 1889, having directed its military preparations in the 1890s entirely against France. Only in 1904 did it distribute an up-to-date mobilization scheme for the northeastern frontier.[225] Since there were no modern fortresses opposite the Austro-Hungarian border, the army had to set about constructing some. In 1903 General Saletta staged the army's grand maneuvers on the Alps, and in the following year he laid out exercises for the mountain troops hypothesizing an Austro-Hungarian attack in the Tagliamento valley. None of this escaped attention in Vienna, where the general staff revived its war plans against Italy in 1903 after having concentrated against Russia since the 1880s.[226] The mobilization plan for the southwestern front was complete by the end of 1904.[227] A relatively static balance of forces meant that these schemes remained the same for years afterward. General Conrad made ambitious but unrealistic war plans for knocking Italy out in thirty-five days, no matter where else his forces might be engaged.[228] The Italians never had enough troops or rail lines to be able to plan an offensive, and all of their deployments envisioned a defense along the line of the Piave River, abandoning most of northeastern Italy to the enemy.[229] Intelligence reports showed that the Austro-Hungarians were simply too strong, and the Italian left flank would always be threatened with attack from the salient of the Tyrol.[230]

Apart from the redeployment of some existing units, neither side could do much to increase its strength on the Alpine frontier. No great expansion was possible in Italy because the government refused the money.[231] There were proposals for new military spending, which caused suspicion on the opposite side of the border, but these mostly died in parliamentary wrangles. Fortress construction programs had a menacing aspect but took many years to produce results in concrete. The railways to the northeastern deployment areas were hopelessly few, and new ones could only be laid slowly, keeping the possibilities for mobilization there within very strict limits. The army itself could not readily raise its effectiveness without securing more men or facing the prospect of a fundamental reorganization in order to improve the standards of training and readiness. Above all, the field artillery remained without modern quick-firing guns. This was a typical result of Italy's dependence upon foreign industry for designs and for the requisite quality of manufacture. A Krupp field gun adopted in 1906 proved to be a failure, and the international design competition for a better one in 1908 was held up by a late entry. The latter emanated from Colonel Deport, one of the inventors of the French army's 75mm gun, who not only submitted a design considerably more advanced than the Krupp and Schneider types under consideration in Italy, but also offered to sell the patent and allow it to be constructed almost entirely by Italian industry. This prospect appealed strongly to Giolitti and the Chamber of Deputies, who, like the Russian government, preferred to bolster the fledgling domestic steel industry rather than depend on expensive contracts abroad. By the end of 1908 Deport's prototype was still not ready and the Italian army remained equipped with two different kinds of non-quick-firing artillery and a small number of the defective Krupp 1906 quick-firing type.[232] In 1908 the Italian army decided to order 149mm heavy field howitzers from Krupp to use against the Austro-Hungarian fortifications in the Tyrol, but even the first of these were not delivered until 1911.[233] Torn between the hazards of depending on self-interested foreign suppliers or attempting to nourish its own far inferior industrial base by means of military contracts, Italy found its economic position hindering the armament of its soldiers. By 1907 enough questions about military preparedness had been raised in the Chamber of Deputies to force Giolitti to appoint a parliamentary committee of inquiry to make recommendations on the needs of the army. In the following year he himself began to preside over sessions of the Joint Supreme Council for State Defense, which in subsequent years allotted money to army reforms.[234]

The Austro-Hungarian army, for its part, still could not grow significantly because of the political deadlock between the nationalities within the monarchy. The Hungarian parliament's persistent refusal to pass increased military credits without receiving concessions to autonomy for its own forces meant that one military expansion bill after another failed in the Delegations or the joint council of ministers.[235] Although the army adopted a serviceable quick-firing 80mm field gun in 1905, there was no money to begin manufacturing it until the following year, and only in 1908 did it reach the troops.[236] The necessary reorganization of the field artillery into six-gun instead of eight-gun batteries could only take place by stripping more men from the infantry. Unable to procure more mountain artillery, the Austro-Hungarian army began training its field and siege batteries for Alpine operations in 1906.[237] In the same year the siege artillery began studying the possibility of constructing an extremely heavy 305mm mortar to smash the Italian frontier forts, and Conrad called periodically for funds to build such a weapon; but by 1908 he still had not secured them. The arrival of Hungarian recruit contingents continued to be delayed by several months each year, shortening training time and repeatedly forcing the emporor to call up classes of the Ersatzreserve to bring the infantry companies up to strength.[238]

This paralysis of the army gave rise to a dangerous impulse on the part of the general staff in Vienna to seek a solution by some dramatic move, a decisive blow that would sweep away internal dissensions and external threats at once. The handiest victim for these schemes was Italy. General Beck first hinted in 1904 that it might be desirable to provoke a war against Austria-Hungary's southwestern neighbor in order to put it out of action before it became a threat.[239] This would eliminate the danger of Italy joining any future coalition war against the Dual Monarchy, a possibility Beck foresaw in a future conflict with Russia and the Balkan states, perhaps as part of a general European conflagration. But the man who articulated the full implications of such a preemptive attack and called for it with increasing stridency was Beck's successor, General Franz Conrad von Hötzendorf. Conrad took office in 1906 with a bleak view of the army's "stagnation and retrogression," determined to grasp what he regarded as the root of the problem. He hoped to eliminate the divided identity of the army, and possibly of the monarchy itself. This might be accomplished by a coup against Hungary that would liquidate the dual system of government. Failing that, he favored a war to eliminate one or more of the foreign enemies who made the army's weakness a liability. At the same time, he hoped that a victory would rally patriotism within the Dual Monarchy. He agreed fully with Beck's analysis that Italy would take any opportunity to stab Austria-Hungary in the back the moment Vienna became involved in a war against other enemies.[240]

In April 1907 Conrad went so far as to send Franz Joseph two memoranda explicitly calling for either a preemptive war against Italy or a coup against Budapest. On 6 April he set out his plans with brutal candor.[241] Italy was as yet unready for war, he argued, with its forts unfinished and its artillery ill-equipped: "nevertheless the danger lies nearest precisely on this side, since in the event of internal complications within the monarchy, Italy would probably intervene to exploit them. Absolutely certain guarantees must therefore be established to ensure that such an action by Italy does not take place—or else to take a preemptive role and ourselves bring about a conflict with Italy, in order to seek a decision there first." A week later, Conrad gave a broader survey of the reasons for his proposal, and admitted frankly that he did not base them upon any fear that Italy would attack in the immediate future:

> For the time being the Monarchy as well as Italy are both utterly backward in their armaments. Italy is nevertheless proceeding with every means at its disposal to make good these deficiencies in railway construction, fortification, artillery rearmament, fleet building etc. . . . In the Monarchy, by contrast, the desperately necessary development of the army as well as of the fleet are immobilized. With respect to the latter, Italy is at present already materially far superior to the Monarchy, whereas it can be said that with respect to land forces the preponderance *still* lies on the side of the Monarchy. However, with every passing day this relationship deteriorates to the detriment of the Monarchy as long as it does not at once proceed with substantial means to the development of the army.
>
> Therefore the only choices remaining are, either:
> At once and decisively to set about this development and to remove the forces of resistance against it, if necessary with violence,
> or else:
> The sooner the better to strike out against Italy.[242]

Conrad included a list of emergency ammunition production measures to be completed "by the time of the start of operations" in July 1907.

He thought it would be even better to attack in two years, however, as he had explained with chilling cynicism the week before:

> As far as the solution of the question by means of a preventive action against Italy is concerned, it would probably not be advisable until next year, since only by then would organizational preparations be finished that would correspond to the needs of substantial operations. . . . But the chance could nevertheless still be taken in the current year, as long as the aforementioned operational preparations were taken in hand with the greatest speed. From a purely military point of view, considering the state of rearmament of the artillery, the best date would appear to be the spring of 1909. By that time our field artillery should be fully reequipped, while the rearmament of Italy's artillery could not yet have been completed.[243]

Of course, Conrad added, it would be possible to avoid all of this if Franz Joseph acted against Hungary and its obstructionism first. This would arrest the decline he perceived, and allow the army to expand to meet future foreign threats: "It would in all probability suffice to undertake the domestic political action with all decisiveness, in order to break the resisting forces that aim at tearing apart the army and the monarchy, before external complications arise. I have regarded it as my duty at the present juncture especially to emphasize the close interdependence of the military situation (both operational and organizational) and the state of domestic and foreign policy." The internal crisis of the Dual Monarchy was prompting the army to seek violent solutions, including aggressive external war.

The emperor vetoed the idea. The military calculations of a few generals were still far from being a decisive influence on the actions of statesmen. The Archduke Franz Ferdinand, like the emperor, opposed a foreign war, although he shared many of Conrad's views about the unity of the army and his opinion counted as Inspector General of the Combined Armed Forces.[244] The emperor also heard arguments from his new foreign minister, Alois Lexa Count Aehrenthal, who had come to the Ballhausplatz in 1906 with a policy of enhancing the prestige of the monarchy and especially dealing decisively with its border problems in the Balkans. Aehrenthal responded to Conrad's proposals with a firm memorandum to Franz Joseph, agreeing that a war with Italy was possible in the future, but rejecting the chief of staff's immediate suggestions.[245] "I wish to speak out absolutely against the thought of a preventive war," he wrote. "Such a course would not only go against Austrian traditions, but would also not be understood in our time, when wars must be waged with people's armies; the indispensable moral cooperation between army and population would not be present. I also ask myself what the objective of such a war would be. Larger acquisitions of territory in Italy would be a misfortune for the Monarchy, as history teaches us." And there the matter rested. There was no preemptive campaign against Italy, and Vienna decided to seek an aggressive solution to the nationality question later by actions in the Balkans instead. Conrad nevertheless continued to warn of a rising danger from Italy and to call for strangling it in its cradle.[246] Successive war ministers pleaded with the joint council of ministers for increased funds by pointing to the danger of Italy overtaking the Austro-Hungarian army. All such appeals failed due to the combination of Hungarian opposition and the realization that the Italian army remained weaker and was certainly not on the point of storming the Alpine passes.

Nor did Italian politicians seriously believe that the Austrians were about to invade. Here, too, diplomats regularly refused to be swayed by the alarmism of military men. The general staff continually pestered the foreign ministry with allegations of military preparations on the other side of the frontier, but undersecretaries routinely wrote back to say that there was no reason to expect that these forces would attack in the near future.[247] The Italian ambassador in Vienna reported characteristically in 1906: "There is no doubt that Austria-Hungary is proceeding and will continue to proceed with the greatest possible activity to complete its armaments opposite the Italian frontier and its southeastern border, but such armaments, in my judgment and also in that of my colleagues, have no purpose but a purely defensive one, and do not betray a deliberate intention on the part of the Imperial and Royal Government to undertake for the moment any military operation beyond its frontiers."[248] The foreign minister, Tommaso Tittoni, allowed the Triple Alliance to be renewed in July 1907. In the same month he met Aehrenthal at Desio to agree that they would both work to damp down the talk of military rivalry in their countries and try to calm the agitation of irredentists over the Italian provinces of the Dual Monarchy.[249] Giolitti, for his part, did not take the military threat seriously and certainly had no desire to spend more money on the army or see a war break out over the question of whether an Italian university would open at Trieste.[250]

Still, without any significant growth or diplomatic rupture, the Italian and Austro-Hungarian armies went from being allies to being enemies in all but name. German diplomats and military attachés reported with dismay on the sharpening rivalry from 1904 onward.[251] Military competition developed in a mutual dynamic even though neither side had much to throw into the effort. The influence of Austria-Hungary's internal politics upon Conrad's personal foreign policy contributed to the antagonism, but for the most part the domestic situations of both powers constrained rather than propelled competition in armaments. Funds were limited, governments were disinclined to burden their populations with military sacrifices, and industrial capability was taxed even by the limited production that could be paid for. Nevertheless, an attitude of mutual hostility solidified, exacerbated by the need of early twentieth-century armies to make war plans and preparations for mobilization against each other in peacetime. Such measures were impossible to keep completely secret and were in the hands of professional general staffs that operated largely according to perceived technical military imperatives. Most dangerously of all, these military experts in the Austro-Hungarian case began to let technical calculations about the relative strength of armies drive them to advocate starting wars in order to adjust the balance and to solve even nonmilitary problems within the Dual Monarchy.

In the years following the first Moroccan crisis, the European armies did not engage in a headlong armaments race on land. There were no particular motives for doing so, while domestic politics and naval competition restrained military expenditure. All armies had their hands full with the adoption of new technology and tactics, partly emerging from the recent wars in South Africa and East Asia, and partly pushed forward by the mere availability of useful inventions. Even in a climate of technological change, armies continued to rely also on subjective impressions for judging military effectiveness, based on martial bearing and perceptions of "national character" that they sought as a means of explaining the performance of troops in the field. Observers gauged armies by two kinds of standard in an age when technology was obviously transforming human activity while racialist and radical nationalist thinking also exerted particular power. By both measures, the French and German armies dominated the stage in the perceptions of military experts. Italy lagged far behind, Austria-Hungary remained unexpectedly solid, and the combat-influenced configurations of the tiny British and colossal Russian armies elicited mixed judgments. In the years from 1906 to 1908 the naval race attracted the principal attention of the governments in the west, but the most conspicuous features of the military scene on land did not involve the powers that had faced each other in the Moroccan crisis. Rather, the weakness of Russia and the growing antagonism between Austria-Hungary and Italy were the most noticeable changes in the landscape. Russia remained unable to take part in a European war with any hope of success, while the general staff in Vienna increasingly committed itself to the notion of a preventive war as the answer to an entire array of perceived challenges. These changes also played a central part in the Balkan crisis of 1908–9.

Chapter 4

THE BOSNIA-HERZEGOVINA
ANNEXATION CRISIS AND THE RECOVERY
OF RUSSIAN POWER, 1908–1911

ON 9 JUNE 1908, Aleksandr Ivanovich Guchkov, a leader of the Octobrist party, stood up to make an extraordinary speech in the Russian State Duma. Guchkov launched a devastating attack on the failure of all attempts at rebuilding the army since the war with Japan, heaping most of the blame upon the Imperial Grand Dukes who controlled the ineffectual Council for State Defense.[1] There was no overall plan for the renewal of Russia's military strength, Guchkov charged, and the principal obstacle to the formation of one was the deadening influence of the royal personages in every crucial position. It was an astonishingly bold accusation to make, but the warm reception it received from the center and left benches of the Duma showed that it was a challenge to be reckoned with. Guchkov's speech was a shocking indictment from a bourgeois party that was in principle loyal to the throne and strongly nationalist. The Octobrists had won a plurality of seats in the Third Duma thanks to a restriction of the franchise instituted by Stolypin in 1907 with the intention of bringing precisely such elements to power. Guchkov, an intensely patriotic businessman turned politician, who had volunteered to fight alongside the Boers against British imperialism in South Africa and who had worked with the Red Cross in the Manchurian campaign, brought a new concern for national defense to his party's drive for reform in 1908.[2] In doing so, he laid open Russia's military weakness for all to see.

Guchkov's Duma speech found a ready audience both outside Russia and within the country. Diplomats and military attachés reported on it as a confirmation of the divisiveness and military unpreparedness in St. Petersburg.[3] This sign of weakness was a vital condition for Austria-Hungary's annexation of the Balkan provinces of Bosnia and Herzegovina from the Ottoman Empire three months later. It clearly suggested that Russia would do nothing if Vienna made such a move, despite St. Petersburg's interest in supporting Serbia's efforts to prevent these Slavic lands from being absorbed into the Dual Monarchy. The powerlessness of the Russian military, denounced by Guchkov and dramatized by the annexation crisis that followed, spurred the Duma to enact a fresh

Map 3. The Balkan Peninsula after the Annexation of Bosnia and Herzegovina

round of military reforms and expenditures from 1909 onward. This effort ultimately brought a resurgence of Russian power that added decisive weight to the Entente and posed a growing threat to Germany and Austria-Hungary. In the process, the crisis of 1908–9 gave rise to the prospect of a localized "preventive" war in Europe in the form of an Austro-Hungarian campaign against Serbia. Even the possibility of a great-power war, involving Russia against Germany and Austria-Hungary, crossed the minds of some planners. Although none of these conflicts materialized, the passage of the crisis left Europe in a state of heightening military tension and the Russians and Serbs in a mood of bitter revanchism.

The dominant issue in European international affairs at the end of 1908 was the Austro-Hungarian annexation of Bosnia and Herzegovina.[4] The Dual Monarchy had occupied and administered these two provinces of the Ottoman Empire since 1878, when the Treaty of Berlin had assigned it the right to do so as part of the great powers' settlement of their spheres of influence in the Balkans at that time. Bosnia and Herzegovina had remained under the nominal sovereignty of the Sultan, however, despite Vienna's ambitions eventually to take full possession of them in order to keep their largely Slavic populations and their strategic territory out of the hands of the increasingly powerful Kingdom of Serbia. Serbia's desire to embody the provinces into a greater South Slav state, which would eventually also incorporate Montenegro and detach Slavic Eastern Orthodox regions from the south of the Dual Monarchy, only made the acquisition of Bosnia and Herzegovina seem all the more vital to statesmen in Vienna. To them, the integrity of the multi-ethnic monarchy was at stake.

The main thing that prevented Austria-Hungary from doing what it liked before 1908 was Russian support for Serbia's claims. St. Petersburg had many motives for acting as the patron of a greater-Serbian client state. Russia was the self-appointed protector of the Slavic and Orthodox peoples, the rival of the Dual Monarchy in southeastern Europe, and an eventual aspirant to power extending from the Balkans to the Turkish Straits so as to secure egress for its navy from the Black Sea. For Vienna, to challenge Belgrade was to defy St. Petersburg as well. Because of Russian hostility, Austria-Hungary had depended on German support for any move in the Balkans since 1878, in case a war with Russia should result. Traditionally, the German government had vetoed Vienna's ambitions in order to avoid complications with Russia. This changed in 1908. Berlin signaled its approval of an annexation in the knowledge that the Russian army was incapable of offering resistance, no matter how strenuously Serbia and Montenegro might appeal for aid.

The Balance of Military Power and the Outbreak of the Annexation Crisis

The Dual Monarchy declared its annexation of Bosnia and Herzegovina on 5 October 1908, with scarcely any warning to the other powers. There were numerous reasons for the timing of the move, and many of them had nothing to do with the military situation in Europe. The Austro-Hungarian government was experiencing increasing difficulty in keeping pro-Serbian agitation in the territories under control. In December 1907 the joint council of ministers discussed the idea of bringing Bosnia and Herzegovina fully under the sovereignty of the Dual Monarchy in order to allow the imposition of Vienna's authority.[5] The foreign minister, Count Aehrenthal, favored a more assertive policy to reestablish the prestige of the monarchy. General Conrad called for an aggressive "solution" to the ethnic problems of the state. Bülow hinted from Berlin that Germany would support such a move. In July 1908 the coup of the Young Turks in Istanbul brought a group of nationalist military officers to power around the Sultan, determined to impose reforms and assert stronger central control over his dilapidated empire. To forestall any Ottoman attempt to repossess the administration of provinces such as Bosnia and Herzegovina, Aehrenthal decided to annex the two territories at once.[6] On the pretext that the provinces were ripe for a constitution, and that Franz Joseph could not grant one if he did not have sovereignty over them, the annexation went ahead.

Apart from these political considerations, however, the timing of the Austro-Hungarian move in 1908 also depended upon the balance of military power. Above all, the military situation allowed Vienna to make its action unilateral rather than first having to muster a diplomatic consensus in Europe. The condition of the Russian army left St. Petersburg completely incapable of deterring an Austro-Hungarian action backed by Germany. Under the circumstances, Russia's western partners in the Entente were less disposed than ever to contemplate supporting it in a war over Balkan complications. The situation gave scope for General Conrad to air his ruthless notions about how to solve the Dual Monarchy's domestic and strategic problems by striking a blow against its weaker neighbors to the south. It also allowed Berlin and Vienna to terminate the crisis with the threat of unleashing an Austro-Hungarian war against Serbia.

Conrad, who was one of the principal instigators of the annexation, began from the premise that Russia would not intervene against an Austro-Hungarian move in the Balkans. He argued to this effect in a conference with Aehrenthal on 18 November 1907.[7] Whereas he portrayed Italy as the monarchy's "natural enemy" and urged the annexation of Bosnia and Herzegovina as part of the "preparations" for war on the Alps, he and the foreign minister agreed that they could take the step with Russia's compliance in return for promising to support an eventual Russian bid to secure free passage for its warships through the Turkish straits. The chief of the general staff persisted in bombarding Aehrenthal and the emperor with calls for moves against Italy, Serbia, or simply Bosnia and Herzegovina first, but he always assumed Russian neutrality. He was quite prepared to take on both Italy and Serbia, and Montenegro too, all at the same time if necessary, and he made war plans for each of these contingencies.[8] When the joint council of ministers asked for his professional opinion in the meeting where the annexation was discussed, he affirmed that, "according to his knowledge of the facts, Russia was presently not capable of fighting a war."[9] This belief had ample basis in Austro-Hungarian intelligence reports on the Russian army, which continued to present a picture of little or no renewal in 1907 and 1908.[10]

The other architects of the annexation also believed that Russia's military disarray would prevent it from offering any resistance. Aehrenthal wrote to his ambassador in St. Petersburg in June 1908 that, even if the Duma undertook major reconstruction programs, "the transformation and reform of the army and navy administrations as well as the replacement of the war material lost in the last war and the reconstruction of the fleet will proceed slowly due to the financial situation, so that throughout the entire period of transition Russia will be unable to contemplate any major external action."[11] Earlier that month, Aehrenthal had expressed the same view in a letter to Bülow, who himself confided to the Austrians his estimation of the "lamentable condition" of the Russian army.[12] The German Chancellor's encouragement to Vienna probably rested at least in part on the scathing reports his military attaché in St. Petersburg routinely sent in. Major von Posadowsky-Wehner blamed corrupt leadership and administration, as well as shortages of funds, for the inadequacy of modern drill regulations, machine guns, artillery, small arms ammunition, officer salaries, and above all mobilization supplies. By 1908, he noted, the latter were still depleted from the Manchurian campaign, and "as good as nothing" had been done to replace them. The German attaché concluded in March: "I do not think that the present War Minister and Chief of the General Staff would answer in the affirmative the question whether the army is ready for a European war. If, however, anyone could be found who would undertake such a responsibility lightly and without an adequate knowledge of the facts, it could only be welcome to Russia's enemies."[13]

THE POWERLESSNESS OF RUSSIA IN THE CRISIS

Once the Austro-Hungarians had decided on the annexation and carried it out, the balance of military power virtually determined the outcome of the ensuing Balkan crisis. The Russian army's impotence allowed Vienna, supported by Berlin, to dictate the terms of a unilateral action. The efforts of the Russian foreign minister, Aleksandr Petrovich Izvolsky, to bring diplomatic leverage to bear were thwarted for six months by his opponents' absolute refusal to back down from their position of military superiority. In the end there was nothing for the Russians to do but retreat. It was a bitter disappointment for Izvolsky, who did not at first recognize the impossibility of his situation. The first news of the annexation of Bosnia and Herzegovina came as a brutal shock. The Austro-Hungarian move was a blow to Serbia, and consequently to Russia too. Izvolsky had considered the possibility that it might happen, but ever since a somewhat ambiguous conference with Aehrenthal at Buchlau in September 1908 he had assumed it would take the form of a compensation to Vienna in return for Russian gains at the Turkish straits.[14] Izvolsky had expected to sell out the Serbs in Bosnia and Herzegovina, not give them away. Instead, the Dual Monarchy effected the annexation as a fait accompli, with no word about the straits. Infuriated, Izvolsky embarked on a series of increasingly desperate attempts to convene an international conference that would either reverse the annexation or else secure compensations to Russia at Istanbul and to Serbia in the Balkans. The French and British were amenable and the Italians were eager to claim compensations of their own, but Vienna and Berlin refused adamantly.

In this refusal, Aehrenthal enjoyed unswerving encouragement from Germany because the Russians were weak. Bülow realized that Austria-Hungary was Germany's only certain ally, and would have to receive wholehearted backing if it were to remain reliable.[15] He believed that a show of strength abroad would bolster his sagging political fortunes at home, and he feared a diplomatic failure. A conference could result in a disastrous repetition of Algeciras. Bülow's only hope of avoiding a diplomatic defeat for Austria-Hungary was to prevent a conference on the annexation and restrict the confrontation to a test of military power between the Austro-German bloc and Russia. In such a contest, Bülow knew that Russia would back down. In October he assured Count Laszlo von Szögyény, the Austro-Hungarian ambassador in Vienna, that there was nothing to fear from pursuing a hard line over the annexation. "Even in case difficulties and complications should arise," he wrote, "our ally may count on us. Besides, I find it hard to believe in the advent of serious complications. From Russia no hostile, let alone warlike, attitude is to be feared, since it is restricted to calm and peaceful development after the terrible shocks it has undergone."[16] Two months later the Reich chancellor scoffed to Szögyény at the Russian foreign minister's threats of intervention: "Despite the excited and bellicose language of M. Izvolsky, which we know so well, one may be certain that neither he nor any other serious Russian statesman is thinking of war. The internal situation of Russia and her need for money cannot permit it."[17]

Even the Russian military authorities betrayed their anxiety, and Bülow's confidence rested on intelligence reports from St. Petersburg that portrayed the army in the bleakest light. General A. F. Rediger, the Russian war minister, told Posadowsky-Wehner in December 1908, "It is out of the question for Russia to fight a war on account of the Serbs."[18] The German attaché reported after this conversation that Rediger would regard war as "the greatest misfortune that could befall the Russian army. He knows that it is not ready for war, and he fears for his whole beloved work, the internal reform of the army, the effect of which he does not expect to see for some 8 to 10 years." The other officers of the Russian army, the German attaché reported, "know that Russia cannot fight a war either now or next spring." He said they were perfectly right:

> This view corresponds entirely to the facts. It is enough to take account of the following. The army has no field howitzers, no heavy field artillery, and completely obsolete fortress- and siege artillery. The rearmament of the

field artillery is still not quite complete; those guns that have been manufactured have neither shields nor panoramic sights. The infantry does not
have modern small arms ammunition. The fortresses are obsolete. . . . The
army has severe shortages of young officers and as good as no serviceable
noncommissioned officers at all. The reserves have not trained for three
years. The reorganization of the supply service has only just begun. The
new field uniforms consist only of lengths of dyed fabric.[19]

There was not enough personal equipment, such as pots, canteens,
shovels, and haversacks, even for peacetime needs. "For the procurement of modern technical gear, as good as nothing has been done."
Even if a mobilization could be carried out, Posadowsky-Wehner remarked, "substantial forces" would have to stay behind for internal police duties against the threat of revolution, and indeed many were still
detached from the western frontier for this purpose in peacetime. These
observations accurately reflected the state of the Russian army, which at
the time planned to fight a defensive campaign if it were actually attacked, and was in no position to mount any kind of an offensive against
Germany or Austria-Hungary.

Nobody in the German leadership believed that Russia would fight.
When reports crossed Kaiser Wilhelm's desk saying that Izvolsky was
warning that pro-Slav public opinion might push him into action over
Bosnia and Herzegovina, the emperor was fond of writing "Bluff" in the
margins.[20] He avidly read his military attaché's reports from St. Petersburg, and also placed considerable faith in his personal relationship with
his cousin Tsar Nicholas and in the latter's earnest desire to avoid a
war.[21] It would probably have been difficult in any case for the Russian
government to secure broad public support for a war over the relatively obscure issue of the Balkans in 1908. Germany's acting state secretary for foreign affairs from November onward, Alfred von Kiderlen-
Wächter, also supported the view that there was no chance of Russia
going to war over the annexation.[22] Russia's international isolation contributed to this conviction in Berlin. The British public's unwillingness
to plunge into a war for the sake of Serbia was well known, especially
while the much-publicized imperial disputes with Russia in Persia remained unresolved.[23] Sir Arthur Nicolson, the British ambassador in St.
Petersburg, abruptly retreated from his encouragements to Izvolsky
after learning of the distressing state of the Russian army. The German
ambassador, Count Friedrich von Pourtalès, found out and relayed the
information to Berlin.[24] Bülow judged that there was nothing to fear
from the French either, who persistently attempted to persuade Berlin
to join them in an attempt to mediate between the adversaries in eastern
Europe. Paris was trying to link a new financial loan to Russian strategic
railway construction for the future, and tied this to the requirement that

Russia not go to war in 1909.[25] French military intelligence reports on
Russian readiness for war remained pessimistic throughout the period of
the crisis, and the Quai d'Orsay sought a diplomatic solution above all
else.[26] In January 1909 Bülow advised Wilhelm II:

> France's thought of mediation arises purely from the fear of a military
> conflict in the East. [The kaiser noted: "for that, *la belle France* does not
> wish to plunge into the fire, no enthusiasm for it there!"] . . . But the
> French absolutely do not need a general conflagration; they have no de-
> sire to fight with us just because the Russians may eventually wish to pre-
> vent Austria from disciplining Serbia by means of an attack on it; further-
> more they know precisely that their ally is in no way prepared for a war, and
> they naturally fear, last but not least, for the money they have lent to the
> Russians.[27]

Bülow saw that refusing to join any mediation effort could have only
one effect: to force France to make the Russians give in to Vienna's
policy.

From the start of the crisis, Bülow assured the Austrians of Germany's
absolute support, and continually urged upon Vienna a policy of intransigence. He called it "firmness" (*Festigkeit*). In his own determination to
face down the Entente's pressure for a conference, he made certain to
impress upon his allies the importance of maintaining a strong front, and
the safety of doing so in the face of Russia's weakness. By and large,
Aehrenthal remained convinced. He received all of Bülow's information
through Szögyény in Berlin, as well as supporting evidence from his own
ambassador in St. Petersburg, Count Leopold von Berchtold. Speaking
to Conrad, the Austro-Hungarian foreign minister dismissed Izvolsky's
threats of intervention as "merely a bluff."[28] To Bülow as well, Aehrenthal wrote that he doubted whether Russia was in a position to oppose
any action by the Dual Monarchy against Serbia:

> The question now arises of what attitude Russia will take toward our step
> in Belgrade. Berchtold's latest reports indicate that the Emperor Nicholas
> and his government will be prepared to do anything to prevent military
> complications. The prevailing view, particularly in military circles there, is
> still that Russia could not allow itself to get into a war in which it would
> have to reckon with the armies of Germany and Austria-Hungary. Public
> opinion likewise seems to be more or less without exception in favor of the
> preservation of peace, so that the warlike outbursts that can occasionally be
> noted may be regarded as a deception without any real basis.[29]

To back up his reassurances, Bülow allowed the chiefs of staff of the
German and Austro-Hungarian armies to consider joint war plans
against Russia during the crisis. This meant resuming communications

about the eventuality that had lapsed since 1896. For Bülow, it was part of the strategy of doing whatever was necessary to stiffen Vienna's resolve. Once the Austro-Hungarian foreign minister requested the staff correspondence, Bülow could hardly refuse without making his constant avowals of support for Vienna sound hollow. Aehrenthal requested it with reluctance, insisting that it remain secret and confined to written communications between Conrad and Moltke, without face-to-face meetings or lower-level contacts that might excite public alarm.[30] The correspondence took place entirely at the instigation of Conrad. He admired the Germans above all others as a military nation, and regarded consultations with them as a means of securing guarantors for his aggressive notion of the Dual Monarchy's future foreign policy. Moltke, for his part, put little faith in the deal, which concerned a war contingency that he considered improbable. Nevertheless, the joint planning and the resulting German military guarantee to Austria-Hungary outlasted the annexation crisis and played a significant part in sending the coalition to war against the Entente in 1914. It is therefore particularly ironic that the arrangement arose from a situation where both parties agreed that a war with Russia was virtually impossible.

The agreements did nothing to change the military calculus in the crisis. Conrad had pestered Aehrenthal with requests for staff talks with Moltke for months before the annexation, since June 1908.[31] The crisis finally caused the foreign minister to relent and propose the matter to Bülow in December 1908. This was a month after the move on Bosnia and Herzegovina, at the moment when Aehrenthal began to think that the Dual Monarchy might get involved in a war with Serbia.[32] The German chancellor agreed, although remarking that "any warlike action on Russia's part is wholly out of the question."[33] The political situation gave Conrad the chance he wanted, to make certain of German military support for the future. The correspondence between him and Moltke consisted of little more than this, and was not a plan for any war they feared might break out over the annexation crisis. The two chiefs of staff exchanged nine letters between January and March of 1909.[34] The main result was Moltke's promise that Germany would mobilize against Russia if Russia attacked Austria-Hungary over the issue of a war with Serbia. He wrote to Conrad that with any Russian move against the Dual Monarchy "the *casus foederis* for Germany would be given. . . . At the same moment when Russia mobilizes, so too will Germany mobilize, and with its entire army."[35] The two generals negotiated the number of divisions to be deployed by each against Russia, and Conrad managed to extract a promise of a joint offensive in the east. Moltke, however, made no secret of his conviction that France would not stand idly by in any war, and that therefore Germany's main offensive would go westward.

This was an improbable scenario in 1909, when France was not supporting Russia, and when Germany was engaged in conciliatory diplomacy with the French. The governments in Berlin and Vienna paid only cursory attention to the correspondence of the generals. Conrad and Moltke themselves kept their respective war ministries in the dark and did nothing to make the agreements practicable.[36] No contacts took place between subordinates to coordinate the details, no maps were exchanged to enumerate sectors, units, or objectives, and there is no evidence that either general staff made actual deployment plans corresponding to the chiefs' correspondence.

Moltke's real interest was in an eventual Schlieffen-plan offensive against France, and Conrad devoted his attention to mobilizations against Serbia, Montenegro, and Italy.[37] Russia, they both firmly believed, was not about to fight. In laying out his war planning guidelines in October 1908, Conrad discounted the need to include an eastern front contingency. "An intervention by Russia would probably bring about a general war," he observed; "it is hardly to be anticipated that this corresponds to Russia's intentions *at present*."[38] By February 1909 Conrad was articulating the belief that the mere knowledge of Germany's support for Austria-Hungary would continue to deter the Russians. The German military attaché reported to Berlin after a talk with him: "Germany alone, according to the Chief of the General Staff, can cast the deciding vote in the confrontation. If the strongest military power were to state plainly and clearly in St. Petersburg that it would answer an attack by Russia upon Austria with a deployment on its own eastern frontier, Russia would presumably guard against letting matters come to a showdown."[39] This was exactly the way the crisis turned out in the end.

THE PROSPECT OF PREVENTIVE WAR
AND THE END OF THE CRISIS

Although leaders in Berlin and Vienna traded confidently on Russia's military weakness in the crisis, they did not take matters to their logical conclusion and decide to attack Russia itself while it was nearly defenseless. The thought of preventive war certainly crossed the minds of many decision makers besides Conrad. This in itself was a significant change in mentality concerning the future of Europe, although the ultimate choice not to fight also showed that purely military considerations were not yet decisive. The Russian war minister, General Rediger, told the German military attaché in December 1908 that he suspected the whole annexation crisis of being designed as an excuse for a conflict, and that Germany "wanted by means of it to touch off a great European war, in order to decide all pending questions together."[40] When Kaiser Wilhelm read Major Posadowsky-Wehner's report on this and on the most glaring weaknesses of the Russian army, he wrote at the end of it: "So, from a military point of view this would be the best moment to settle accounts with the Russians."[41] But in spite of the realization that Russia might well grow stronger, there was no serious move in Berlin or Vienna to strike it while it was down. A war would have been very hard to justify to the public in an age when popular support was vital to any major conflict, and of course a direct attack would almost certainly have roused the Russians to a considerable effort in self-defense. Besides, Russia had capitulated, and there were other ways of exploiting the period of weakness. Bülow and Aehrenthal were fixated on the notion of using it as an opportunity for annexing Bosnia and Herzegovina and administering a blow to the South Slavs, which Franz Ferdinand also preferred. Conrad agreed with this, but added the prospect of crippling an isolated Italy. Neither he nor his superiors really wanted to take on a campaign against Russia and possibly risk a world war for the sake of having a better chance in the present than in a future conflict. This attitude was to change by 1914.

The war Germany and Austria-Hungary did contemplate, and which nearly broke out late in the crisis, was an Austro-Hungarian invasion of Serbia and perhaps Montenegro. Russia would have been powerless to stop it, and in Conrad's view it would have eliminated the South Slav threat to the integrity of the Dual Monarchy at a stroke. The army was in a position to smash Serbia and Montenegro easily, and Italy too if necessary. Austria-Hungary had more than 360,000 men under arms in 1908. Serbia was well below its nominal peacetime strength of only 20,000; Montenegro possessed a militia-style army with a very small peacetime cadre; and Italy had a little over 200,000 men.[42] Conrad calculated at the outset of the crisis that this would translate into a mobilized strength of over 700,000 for the Dual Monarchy against 120,000 for Serbia, 30,000 for Montenegro, and 417,000 for Italy.[43] Even though his estimates rose to over 240,000 for Serbia and 43,000 for Montenegro by the spring of 1909 due to the hasty preparations of those powers, Austria-Hungary still enjoyed a crushing numerical superiority over them and parity even when Italy was added to the calculation.[44]

In qualitative terms the Dual Monarchy was in a better position still. Foreign observers as well as the Austro-Hungarian army's own commanders agreed that it performed solidly in the field. The Delegations passed a new spending bill in the face of possible hostilities while the military administration made huge strides in completing equipment and training.[45] The new quick-firing 80mm field gun designed in 1905 had been issued in small numbers in 1908 for crew training, but in the winter of 1908–9 a tremendous effort resulted in its actual distribution to the whole of the army, along with telephones for fire control. At the 1908 autumn maneuvers the field artillery suddenly displayed modern tactics, firing entirely from defiladed positions and generally impressing foreign observers.[46] A series of special decrees led to the rapid distribution of machine guns, attaining the level of one section per regiment (per battalion in the *Jägers*) by early 1909, with more to come.[47] Ammunition production increased and the specially called-up reservists received realistic training with combat-ready formations throughout the winter war scare. Conrad pushed ardently for the transfer of more units to deployment areas near the southern frontiers, achieving what he thought was an adequate covering force for mobilization there by the time the start of operations appeared likely in March 1909.[48]

By contrast, the Serbian and Montenegrin armies were in terrible condition.[49] Serbia was in the process of distributing some French-made Schneider quick-firing artillery to its field batteries in the course of the crisis, but would be far from fully equipped with it by March 1909. Montenegro had no modern field guns. The Serbian army was barely able to equip its first-line units with magazine-loading rifles; the reserves would take the field with single-shot small arms. The Montenegrin militia had even lower stocks of modern rifles. It did at least possess sixteen machine guns by 1908, though; Serbia had none at all. Austro-Hungarian intelligence credited the Montenegrin troops with being hardy and reasonably well organized, although without advanced training. Many reservists had no training whatsoever. The Serbian army's morale and training received extremely low marks in Vienna, as it had done ever since the military-led coup that toppled the Obrenović dynasty and installed King Peter in 1903. In 1908 the Austro-Hungarian army intelligence bureau reported in a characteristic analysis: "The struggle between conspirators and counterconspirators, which has been in progress for years, continues unabated and has completely buried all discipline and authority in the army; progress in training is out of the question under these conditions."[50] Companies had as few as fifteen or twenty men on active duty in some periods. The consequences made themselves painfully obvious in 1905, during the only autumn maneuvers held in Serbia between 1902 and the annexation crisis. The Austro-Hungarian observer reported: "The infantry is not trained for modern combat; the cavalry is completely passive and incapable of offensive enterprises; the artillery made the best impression, as always; its tactical training, however, also leaves a very great deal to be desired."[51] The second-line formations presented "a picture of total disintegration." The Serbian and Montenegrin forces were still far from being the sizable and determined armies that the Austro-Hungarians later watched grow and emerge battle-seasoned from the Balkan Wars.

Conrad could have defeated them overwhelmingly in 1909 if the politicians in Vienna had let him. His initial offensive might have bogged down since he at first planned to keep ten of his fifteen army corps in reserve for a possible campaign against Italy. But since Italian intervention was out of the question, he would have found himself with ample forces in hand to throw in behind his first deployment. Even as it was, his plans gave him a solid margin of numerical superiority over the ill-equipped and poorly trained South Slav armies.[52] Belgrade lay exposed directly on the southern frontier of Hungary. Conrad expected his offensive to take three months and to extend as far as Niš, with the total destruction of the Serbian army.[53] With Germany resolved to prevent Russian intervention or a European conference, the South Slav states would have been at Vienna's mercy.

The statesmen in Berlin and Vienna toyed with the idea of unleashing Conrad's plan for an invasion of Serbia. Aehrenthal considered it, as a means of attaining the monarchy's diplomatic objectives in case negotiation failed. At times he played along with Conrad's bloodthirsty schemes for conquests to the south, and found the chief of staff an opportune ally against the caution of moderates such as the ever-reluctant ministers-president in Vienna and Budapest.[54] When it came to a test, however, he infuriated Conrad by ruling out a preemptive attack against Italy. "Today," he chided the general, "one does not fight preventive wars."[55] He broached the subject of a war against Serbia to Bülow in December 1908, writing that he would try all possible peaceful means first:

> We do not, however, propose to continue this policy of patience and conciliation ad infinitum. Should the attitude of Serbia give us cause for serious complaint in the next two months, then the time would come when we would have to make a decisive choice. You may be assured, honored friend, that I would give you prompt notice beforehand. In such an eventuality I intend, in order to work against a further expansion of the conflict, to issue a declaration at once to the other powers that we are only carrying out a perfectly justifiable act of self-defense, but otherwise have no intention of infringing the independence and territorial integrity of Serbia and Montenegro.[56]

At the height of the confrontation in March 1909, Archduke Franz Ferdinand told the First Secretary of the German embassy in Vienna that if Austria-Hungary's opponents remained intransigent, the opportunity would be a good one for fighting a war against the South Slavs, and conceivably Russia too if it intervened: "The international situation is favorable to us ["Yes," noted Kaiser Wilhelm], militarily we are better armed than ever, and therefore as long as the conflict is unavoidable we cannot let the decision be drawn out with half measures and inadequate promises; for it must come some time, and in a few years the situation may easily have changed to our disadvantage."[57] "Good," noted the kaiser at the bottom.

The Germans supported Austria-Hungary warmly. Bülow told Szögyény in Berlin that his views "fully agreed" with those expressed by Aehrenthal.[58] Moltke wrote to Conrad at the outset of their correspondence: "It is to be foreseen that the moment may come when the patience of the Monarchy in the face of Serbia's provocations will come to an end. Then nothing will remain but for the Monarchy to march into Serbia."[59] In that case, the chief of the Prussian general staff assured his colleague, Germany would offer its full support. Franz Joseph and Kaiser Wilhelm exchanged similar assurances.[60] The German emperor displayed an aggressive attitude equal to Conrad's, filling the margins with exclamations of "correct!" when he read his military attaché's report from Vienna on a general staff conference that determined: "From the military point of view, the only *certain* means remains the overthrow of the Serbian armed forces together with the destruction of their armament. Only then will there be peace for decades to come in this eternally turbulent neighboring state. *Such a favorable opportunity for disciplining the unruly Serbs will not come again soon.*"[61]

In the event, the imbalance of military forces against Russia allowed Vienna and Berlin to score a victory in the crisis without recourse to war. The Wilhelmstraße ended the crisis by means of a peremptory ultimatum to St. Petersburg and Belgrade. Germany and Austria-Hungary managed to coax the Ottoman Empire into acquiescing in the annexation, but the Russians and Serbs still held out. Although they made some concessions, Izvolsky continued to demand a conference while the Serbs insisted on leaving the annexation in the hands of the great powers rather than recognizing it outright themselves. When Aehrenthal appeared to waver, the Germans intervened vigorously to force a solution. Kiderlen-Wächter composed a stiff démarche on 21 March 1909, announcing that Germany would stand behind any Austro-Hungarian move to secure Bosnia and Herzegovina.[62] The Germans demanded "a precise answer—yes or no" as to whether Russia would recognize the annexation.[63] The German government warned: "We would have to regard any evasive, conditional, or unclear answer as a refusal. We would then draw back and let matters take their course; the responsibility for all further developments would then fall exclusively upon Herr Izvolsky." This was a threat to let Austria-Hungary invade Serbia with German protection. The Russians had no choice but to yield. In the face of such a blunt declaration, Izvolsky agreed to acknowledge the annexation and to join the powers in presenting Belgrade with the text of a declaration that Serbia must issue to the same effect. The Serbian note was published on 31 March, renouncing all claims and objections. The crisis was at an end.

In setting the ultimatum, the Germans had even St. Petersburg's assurance that there was nothing Russia could do. The military leaders had admitted their powerlessness in December 1908 and expressed the same opinion early the following March, as they contemplated a complete reorganization of the army's mobilization system and begged the civilian authorities not to get the country involved in a war in the meantime.[64] The government went ever further at the climax of the crisis. On the night of 8 March 1909, two weeks before the German ultimatum, the Duma met in a special session, presumably due to the army's intelligence reports which correctly warned that the moment for Austro-Hungarian military action was at hand.[65] The session resolved that Russia simply could not fight over the Bosnian issue. The meeting was supposed to be secret, but its proceedings quickly leaked out.[66] Guchkov revealed in the debate that Izvolsky had told the main parliamentary leaders that Russia could not oppose the annexation by force and must compromise. The Octobrist leader then went on to support this policy wholeheartedly on the grounds of the army's weakness: "I am convinced that the caution, reflection, and moderation that guide our policy are dictated above all else by the consciousness of our unreadiness for war; and, unpopular though this foreign policy may be, . . . I believe it is the right one."[67] Guchkov embarked on a new excoriation of the deficiencies of the army, as in the previous summer blaming them on the Grand Dukes. General Rediger made no effort to challenge Guchkov's denunciation. The Duma approved some new credits for military improvements and Izvolsky emerged with support for his policy from the normally vociferously pro-Slav parliament.

The Germans and Austrians were stunned. They had known of Russia's weakness, but could hardly believe their luck in hearing their adversaries confess it out loud. Captain von Hintze, the German military plenipotentiary in St. Petersburg, wrote to Berlin of the amazing "assertion by the leader of the strongest and presently the decisive party in the Duma, uncontested from any direction, not even by the government, that *the army is not ready for war*."[68] The German embassy had been reporting consistently on the emptiness of Russia's threats. "The surprise," Hintze observed however, "lies not in the fact, but in its open and uncontradicted admission." The consequences were obvious to him: "I would like to underline the significance of the Duma session of 8 March. *In it, Russia has abandoned the policy of bluffing with war* for

the present and expressed its hopes in the future. I do not fear any re-
lapse into threats of war; *the renunciation is final.*" "Outstanding!"
wrote Kaiser Wilhelm at the end of the report. A few days later the Germans learned that a crown council at Tsarskoe Selo had decided to follow the path indicated by Guchkov, and Izvolsky himself told the Austro-Hungarian ambassador in St. Petersburg that "if it were to come to
an Austro-Serbian conflict, Russia would under no circumstances step
out of neutrality."[69] The Germans could not have wished for a clearer
signal to go ahead with their ultimatum on 21 March. Kiderlen and
Bülow delivered it in the full knowledge that Russia would capitulate.

As it was, Germany and Austria-Hungary did not make all the use
they could have of this preponderance, contrary to the wishes of Conrad. The final word rested with Franz Joseph and his government, who
decided that the military advantage had served its purpose once it had
forced the Serbs to capitulate without a war.[70] They had been ready to
invade Serbia if it proved necessary to secure the annexation, but they
preferred to obtain victory without fighting. The war minister, General
Franz von Schönaich, had the same opinion, and Archduke Franz Ferdinand had never been enthusiastic about the prospect of a war.[71] The
joint council of ministers briefly swung in favor of an expedition against
Serbia when Belgrade dragged its feet about responding to the March
ultimatum, but on the whole the ministers of the two halves of the
monarchy were eager to avoid foreign conflicts when they had to deal
with political environments that were volatile enough at home.[72] They
chose to let the future determine whether a war really was inevitable or
whether a turn to a policy of internal consolidation might serve to de-
fuse tensions in Europe and further solidify the position of the monarchy. Their vision was not yet strictly that of a window of military opportunity as Conrad perceived it and as Kaiser Wilhelm occasionally
liked to think of it. Had it been otherwise, there would have been a war
in the Balkans in the spring of 1909, and Serbia would probably have
disappeared from the scene as an external threat to the integrity of the
Dual Monarchy.

The specter had been raised, however, and it remained after the crisis
had passed. Aehrenthal, Bülow, and the German and Austrian emperors
were content to rest on the laurels of the annexation and congratulate
one another on their triumph. But while they exulted over Izvolsky's
debacle, the chiefs of their general staffs became far less sanguine. They
increasingly viewed Europe in terms of two armed camps that, after Russia's humiliations, must sooner or later fight in a general war. Conrad
was furious at what he regarded as Aehrenthal's betrayal of earlier
thoughts of striking out at Italy, Serbia, and Montenegro.[73] He painted

a grim picture of the future to Franz Joseph in a call for more military funds immediately after the crisis:

> While the opportunity for a final settlement of these affairs went unused, a situation has been created that seems likely in the future to force the Monarchy into a war on several fronts,—or, if it is incapable of fighting one, into extensive submissiveness. . . . Italy is systematically continuing its military development and appears to be orienting everything toward the year 1912; Russia cannot and will not accept this diplomatic failure—but instead will bring its armed forces back to their full level if only for reasons of prestige;
>
> Serbia unquestionably emerges strengthened from the present situation, and:
>
> Montenegro as before has at its disposal its well-armed, capable, and quickly mobilizable militia.[74]

Some of this was merely the chief of staff's customary hyperbole designed to extract more funds from the finance ministry. His real opinion of the Italian and Montenegrin armies, at least in their current forms, was considerably lower. But he did begin to plan increasingly for a possible war against Russia, probably involving Italy and the Balkans as well.[75] Conrad took his correspondence with Moltke as the point of departure for this contingency, as he wrote to his colleague in Berlin in April 1909: "Even though at present the probability of an immediate conflict with Russia has receded, such a conflict appears all the less to be excluded in the future, since Russia will presumably devote every effort to reestablishing its position in the eyes of Europe, and especially of the Slavs, and also to reviving its Balkan policy. Given this prospect, the military agreements arising from the alliance between Germany and the Monarchy retain . . . their full present value and I shall take them as the basis for related war-planning activities."[76] Until the outbreak of the world war, Conrad wrote periodically to secure Moltke's confirmation of the plans for the eastern front.[77]

The Prussian chief of staff agreed that Germany and Austria-Hungary had missed a chance and would need to stand firmly together to face future threats. In a private reply to Conrad later in 1909, Moltke wrote: "An opportunity has passed by unused that can scarcely offer itself again under such favorable circumstances in the near future. I am firmly convinced that the war between Austria-Hungary and Serbia would have been successfully localized and that after waging it victoriously, the monarchy, solidified within and strengthened externally, would have won a preponderance in the Balkans that would not easily have been shaken thereafter."[78] Moltke went on to extend his ideas to the notion of Austro-German solidarity in the face of a strengthening ring of enemies. This was the first time he wrote so explicitly on a subject that later became familiar: "Even if Russia had intervened and started a European war, the preconditions would have been better for Germany and Austria now than they probably will be in a few years. Nevertheless, Excellency, let us face the future with confidence. As long as Austria and Germany stand shoulder to shoulder, each prepared to recognize the 'tua res agitur' in the affairs of the other, we will be strong enough to break any ring. On this Central European bloc a good many may break their teeth." The retired Count Schlieffen had expressed similar sentiments in his "War in the Present" article published in the *Deutsche Revue* at the beginning of that year: Germany was being encircled by enemies in an environment of steadily increasing armaments, but together with Austria-Hungary it could still hope to deter its adversaries if it kept its army strong.[79] Kaiser Wilhelm went so far as to read out a copy of Schlieffen's text in his New Year's address to the commanding generals in 1909, telling them that it corresponded with his own opinions.[80] Only Conrad was deeply pessimistic in the wake of the annexation crisis, but for many other military chiefs in Berlin and Vienna the empty threats made during the crisis had begun to translate themselves into a beleaguered mentality.

REACTIONS TO THE ANNEXATION CRISIS

The threats of war also had a tangible effect on those against whom they were directed. Russia and Serbia capitulated to *force majeure,* but their reaction to being bullied by more powerful armies was outrage and revanchism. Political as well as military imperatives drove them to seek a more active policy and more impressive means for backing it up the next time. France and Britain regarded the conduct of Berlin and Vienna as an ill omen for future relations with them, and Italy's enforced inactivity goaded its government into a renewed quest for effective military power to throw into the next weighing of forces over the Balkans. In the absence of any conciliation, Conrad's fears fulfilled themselves.

During the crisis itself the Russians served notice that they would fight back next time. In January 1909 Izvolsky remonstrated with Pourtalès at Aehrenthal's unilateral action as an infringement of a long-standing practice of settling Balkan disputes by negotiation. "Do not forget one thing," Izvolsky warned the German ambassador: "the Eastern Question cannot be resolved except by a conflict. . . . Perhaps this conflict will not break out for five or ten years, but it is inevitable, and the blame for having destroyed the only prospect of adjourning it for the unforeseeable future falls upon Baron Aehrenthal alone."[81] The German military plenipotentiary in St. Petersburg reported similar opinions from the Russian army, as in October 1908 just after the annexation: "At the moment the solution seems to be: Austria has inaugurated a policy of surprises; now we will see how far it gets that way; hopefully we have been the victims only this time. In some three to five years we will be ready for war. In this affair the last word will fall not to the conference but to the sword, presumably not for another two or three years."[82]

The Duma expressed similar hopes and later translated them into deeds. Exasperation was the principal note in debates during the crisis, and the South Slav cause was extremely popular. In endorsing Izvolsky's policy of capitulation in March 1909, Guchkov qualified his remarks with the demand for military revitalization to support a stronger policy in the future: "But, gentlemen, we cannot forever regard the issue of foreign policy entirely from the standpoint of weakness. You know, if our toleration knows no end then the appetite of our neighbors will grow. . . . We cannot be put in the same position as Turkey was in."[83] Kaiser Wilhelm did not improve the mood in Russia when he announced triumphantly that Germany had stood beside its ally like a knight "in shining armor." The response was a rapid increase in Duma appropriations for the army, starting with sharp rises in 1908 and 1909 and remaining at a high level thereafter. General Rediger's virtual admission of the Duma's accusations when he was interpellated during the debate led the tsar to dismiss him at the end of the annexation and replace him with a new war minister, Vladimir Aleksandrovich Sukhomlinov.[84]

General Sukhomlinov was an inveterate enemy of the Grand Dukes against whom the Octobrists inveighed, even though he fervently supported the autocracy itself. His appointment seemingly suited the Guchkov program of prying the army out of the grip of the imperial personages and their system of patronage. In the event, Sukhomlinov had an uphill struggle against the Grand Dukes, and simultaneously turned out to be hostile to any parliamentary control over the army, an institution he regarded as being outside politics and directly loyal to the sovereign. The resulting struggle over spheres of authority, the limits of imperial power, and the openness of the highest military ranks to career soldiers of nonaristocratic origins did much to impede Sukhomlinov's reforms.[85] Nevertheless, the new influx of funds and the tsar's decrees subordinating the general staff and all other military authorities to the war minister gave a powerful impetus to Sukhomlinov's reforms in the following years. The humiliation over Bosnia and Herzegovina provoked a genuine rise in Russian military power that at last began to bring the army close to readiness for a European war, watched by the other European states.

The most prominent feature of Sukhomlinov's program was a total reorganization of the army's mobilization and deployment scheme.

Plans to strengthen and rationalize Russia's strategic position had been in the air as early as 1903, but it took the shock of 1909 and the advent of Sukhomlinov to put them into effect officially at the end of 1910. Without substantially increasing the numbers of men in military service or the mileage of roads and railways, the design produced a larger effective force for wartime, more quickly mobilized when the time came. Above all, it made the reserves into a useful force rather than a liability. The old system relied chiefly on units of the active army, based near the western frontier and concentrated in Poland where they were expected to fight. Reservists either reached these units by means of the sparse railway network, which in wartime would be clogged with emergency transports of material, or else joined together in large, scarcely trained reserve and "fortress" garrison units in the interior, based on tiny cadre formations. Sukhomlinov redistributed the regular army to bases all over the empire, in corps areas as in other European countries. Each corps would draw its reserves from its own region, and then move up to the front ready to fight. This would avoid some of the congestion of the rail lines into Poland that had been expected to slow mobilization considerably, even though most corps would initially mobilize farther from the front. The war ministry dissolved the useless independent reserve and fortress units and converted them into a pool of manpower to be trained and embodied into a reserve division for each corps. Suddenly the creaky tsarist army began to take on more of the characteristics of a west European nation-in-arms system. This was especially true once the 1906 reduction of the term of active duty from six years to three or four (depending on the arm of service) had been fully phased in. This meant a larger contingent of recruits each year, a younger average age in the active army, and a bigger deposit of trained soldiers into the reserves every year. In the future, Russia's reserves would have to be counted.

The most controversial aspect of the new system was the geographical shift (see Map 4). The weight of the army under the new "Mobilization Schedule 19" stood more toward the center of the country. The corps based on the frontier thinned out and, most importantly, the actual forward line of deployment for a European war withdrew almost entirely from Poland. No longer were the foremost concentrations to be astride the Vistula and Narev rivers and the great fortress belt that included Warsaw. Instead, the main line was to run through Brest-Litovsk, over a hundred kilometers farther back in some places. On the one hand, the redeployment to the center of the empire would make the army's job easier in another war with Japan, with shorter lines of communication to the east.[86] On the other hand, it also reduced many dangers in the west. It eliminated the great bulge of the Russian line into Poland, which had invited an Austro-German pincer attack from East Prussia and Galicia to

------- Forward line of projected Russian deployment before 1910
••••••••••••• Forward line of projected Russian deployment after 1910

Map 4. Withdrawal of the Projected Russian Deployment in the West, 1910

envelop it while the Russians carried out their much slower mobilization. Instead, the new deployment formed a shorter, straighter front, separating the sectors that Austria-Hungary and Germany would have to attack by means of the Pripet marshes. It placed the Russian forces out of range of a crippling enemy offensive at the outset and gave them the prospect of mounting their own attack in greater strength later. It rid the Russians of reliance upon fixed fortress defenses to cover their mobilization at a time when the Polish strongholds were clearly obsolete, with their largely above-ground brick and masonry fortifications and outdated artillery. But the redeployment also drew back the threat of an early Russian offensive down the Vistula that might cut off East Prussia or menace Berlin. It clearly enhanced Russia's own defenses, but it also seemed to reduce even further the prospect of an attack on Germany in time to relieve the pressure on France in a European war.

Sukhomlinov ran into difficulties when it came to dismantling, or even simply abandoning, the fortresses in Poland that lay to the west of his new deployment and would therefore not be needed. Traditional attitudes, prestige, and enormous past investment all demanded that the works of Warsaw and the other main western forts not be simply razed or handed over to the enemy. One of Sukhomlinov's most prominent enemies was the Grand Duke Sergei Mikhailovich, the Inspector-General of Artillery, who used every means to control the vast funds that were necessary to modernize the fortresses and outfit them with new guns. The war minister was not enthusiastic even about building up and arming the forts that would buttress his new deployment line, such as Brest-Litovsk. They consumed disproportionate sums that Sukhomlinov would rather have spent on the field army.[87]

Sukhomlinov took a number of other measures to make mobilization faster and the resulting army more effective.[88] The new war minister created a central supply service from virtually nothing. This promised some sort of logistical support in wartime by making a single quartermaster service responsible for issuing uniforms and equipment rather than leaving procurement up to individual military districts as had been done with deplorable results in the past. By 1912 the budget no longer had to contain funds for replacing mobilization stores consumed in Manchuria. To test the system, Sukhomlinov ordered some regular and reserve units to carry out "trial mobilizations" from time to time beginning in 1908. They called up their reservists, equipped them, and conducted musters or exercises, to the alarm of the general staffs in Berlin and Vienna. Most importantly, training of all forces, including the reserves, commenced again on a large scale. This began with the imperial maneuvers of 1908 during the annexation crisis and broadened at all levels in the following years.

The Russians made substantial progress after 1908 in modernizing all their equipment, the most dangerous of which the Germans and Austro-Hungarians considered to be the artillery. In 1909 all remaining units finally received the Model 02 quick-firing 76.2mm field gun, although there were lingering difficulties with such matters as the provision of shields and panoramic sights.[89] The field artillery also finally began to acquire light howitzers with recoil-absorbing mountings from Krupp and Schneider-Creusot.[90] The Germans valued field howitzers especially for their ability to lob shells over obstacles into defiladed positions, and tended to disparage all armies that did not possess an up-to-date type. The Russians did not immediately solve the problem of heavy field artillery to accompany corps and divisions, but they made progress here too in Sukhomlinov's first years. Some Schneider 150mm howitzers that the army acquired proved too heavy and ended up in the far eastern theater, but the authorities kept up continual tests of new designs. By 1910 they chose a number of types and sent out orders for production: 150mm howitzers, 107mm heavy field guns, and an array of siege howitzers and mortars in larger calibers.

Except for the heaviest types, all of these were to be built in Russian factories according to foreign designs. The Duma and the finance ministry were adamant about developing the domestic armaments industry, even though it usually meant paying more and waiting longer while commissions chose designs and while factories accustomed themselves to the complex new processes. The Russians also shifted their sources of supply in this period from an emphasis on Germany to an almost exclusive patronage of France in the artillery market. This was partly because Schneider-Creusot was willing to go further than the German companies in merely selling designs and letting the customers construct the material themselves. Despite Russian protestations to the contrary, it probably also had much to do with St. Petersburg's increasing alignment against Germany and its financial dependence upon France.[91]

Foreign observers all thought these changes would make the Russian army much more effective, though they agreed that it would take time. For the short term, estimates of Russian power remained low. As late as 1910, Moltke believed that "as a result of its ongoing changes in organization and deployment, the Russian army is either incapable of mobilizing at all with any hope of success, or else could only do so with the greatest of frictions."[92] Kiderlen-Wächter, by then foreign secretary, took the same view, telling Aehrenthal later that year that there was no danger from the east "because, as everyone knows, the Russian army will still be incapable of undertaking major military actions abroad for years to come."[93] Bülow's successor as Reich chancellor, Theobald von Bethmann Hollweg, accepted these propositions. Acting as if Russia would remain weak for the foreseeable future was to prove disastrous for German foreign policy.

The prognosis for the longer term was that Russian power would grow formidably with the new era. Posadowsky-Wehner in St. Petersburg lamented the Third Duma's inclination to encourage rather than limit military spending. "Even more than the lost war," he noted, "the acknowledgment that Russia had to back down in the Bosnian crisis simply due to its inadequate readiness for war is responsible for this."[94] The Prussian general staff estimated at the end of 1910 that "the reorganization has brought the Russian army a more unified structure and a better provision of curved-trajectory artillery and technical troops; and hence altogether a significant increase in readiness."[95] By then the staff had forgotten its initial glee over the withdrawal of the Russian deployment line in Poland.[96] Instead, it had begun to realize that the redeployment did not in fact result in a reduction of the number of corps that would march against Germany, and that the new effectiveness of the reserves and better rail lines would actually mean more enemy forces in the east: "Therefore there can be no question of a lightening of the burden on Germany, but rather of a stronger threat."[97] Reading his military attachés' reports attentively, Kaiser Wilhelm began to grow uneasy at the mounting strength in the east by 1910.[98] Conrad was pessimistic about the future, especially as he watched Serbia and Montenegro switch to a trajectory of more rapid military development after the humiliation of 1909. The Austro-Hungarian intelligence bureau in 1910 called the changes in Russia "such a vast and radical enactment of army reforms as would scarcely have been possible anywhere else."[99] Conrad gloomily observed that Russian agreements with Japan and redeployments meant that "the days are over when the Austro-Hungarian military command could direct its attention exclusively to the strengthening of its position against Italy."[100] The French military authorities gradually overcame their initial alarm at the withdrawal of the forward line in Poland.[101] After explanations from Sukhomlinov, and his promise that an offensive would now take place with a million men rather than the 800,000 stipulated in the military convention, they became persuaded that "the new distribution of the Russian forces, if it has not increased the offensive value of our allies, has not reduced it either."[102] The British military attaché in St. Petersburg was impressed with Sukhomlinov's changes and in 1911 expected that, although the second-line troops and fortresses still needed much work, the Russian army "should, by the close of 1912, have a strong, efficient, and well-equipped force of first-line troops disposed on sound strategical principles."[103] Sir Arthur Nicolson predicted at the end of 1909 that, considering the speed of the military recovery and the "almost unlimited" resources of the country, Russia would soon regain the prestige lost in the annexation crisis: "Her land forces are in rapid course of reorganisation; for defence she is invulnerable, and for offence she will soon be most formidable. Sober and moderate men anticipate with confidence that in two, or at most three, years, if internal and external peace is preserved, Russia will be in a position to take the place in Europe to which she is rightly entitled. She will then be able to throw into the scales a great weight, and it will be a new Russia which will have appeared on the scene."[104]

Germany, Britain, France, and Austria-Hungary all confined themselves to modest military development in the years immediately after the annexation crisis. In Germany, Chancellor von Bethmann Hollweg was stuck with Tirpitz's 1908 naval law, which perpetuated fearsome expenses as the cost of building four Dreadnought-strength capital ships every year soared beyond all previsions. Bethmann's treasury minister, Adolf Wermuth, fought hard against military increases under the slogan "no expenditures without revenues."[105] The new Prussian war minister, General Josias von Heeringen, found it prudent to postpone renewal of the Quinquennat for two years in a row, waiting for a time when he might stand a better chance of winning the Reichstag's approval for increases. When he did finally put through a new five-year budget in 1911, it called for only a relatively limited rise in manpower.[106] This so-called "Technical Quinquennat" made good the previous transfers of soldiers from conventional units to specialist detachments, and provided funds for new levels of modern equipment such as heavy artillery, field uniforms, and communication gear. Britain likewise continued to invest chiefly in the Royal Navy in order to retain its lead over Germany. Haldane carried out his reorganization of the army with a nearly static budget. Preparations for the actual use of the new force on the continent lay nearly dormant until Major-General Sir Henry Hughes Wilson became director of military operations in 1910. Wilson began a one-man campaign to concert plans with a somewhat diffident French general staff for operations in France, which the Committee of Imperial Defence decided in 1909 were the only means of having any serious influence on the course of a European land war.[107] The French army worked on technological innovations and devoted resources above all to the *loi des cadres* that reorganized and increased the field artillery at the expense of the other arms. In Austria-Hungary the old parliamentary deadlock set in again after the annexation crisis had subsided, and the Delegations refused to allot more funds for the army. Aehrenthal proceeded with a policy of internal consolidation and external conciliation as planned after the absorption of Bosnia and Herzegovina, while General Conrad fulminated incessantly about the need to fight a war against somebody before it was too late.

Of the western powers, only Italy embarked on significant military reforms in the wake of the annexation crisis. Although the government had not contemplated war, the confrontation in the Balkans had thrown into relief Italy's total inability to influence events there, in large part due to its lack of military power.[108] The reports of the parliamentary Inquiry Commission on the Army from 1909 onward resulted in higher pay for officers and other improvements, aided by a steady rise in military appropriations in the Chamber.[109] General Paolo Spingardi, the new war minister, undertook a long-range program of modernization together with the chief of staff, Alberto Pollio.[110] However, the appalling tangle of field artillery procurement denied Spingardi and Pollio really far-reaching success. When a prototype of Colonel Deport's quick-firing gun did finally arrive for evaluation in 1910, it proved to be an extraordinarily advanced piece of ordnance. It incorporated a split-trail design, which allowed the barrel to elevate to higher angles than a conventional single-trail gun carriage did. This feature also permitted the barrel to traverse through a much wider arc to aim at new targets, without the crew having to lift up the trail and swivel the whole carriage into a new position. Most subsequent artillery designs of the twentieth century were to follow this pattern. At the time, the Italians could not resist acquiring it, especially since Deport agreed to let Italian factories undertake most of the manufacturing process. His competitors—chiefly Krupp and Schneider-Creusot, supported by the German and French embassies respectively—wanted a larger share of the contract for their own workshops.[111] The Italian army finally adopted the Deport 75mm gun in 1912, but production delays in both France and Italy meant that this modern weapon was not in the hands of the troops by 1914. The continuing struggle to bring the forces up to date, as well as the enduring shortage of rail lines in northern Italy, confined war planning to a defensive deployment on the line of the Piave.[112]

AVIATION: THE AEROPLANE SUPERSEDES THE DIRIGIBLE

In all countries, new pressures on military budgets and establishments continued to come from the progress of technology. Rifle and artillery ammunition, machine guns, heavy artillery, optical gear, motor transport, field uniforms, and communication equipment all improved steadily and had to be procured in increasing quantities, together with new units and specially trained personnel. The debates surrounding every military budget in Europe in the years after 1908 brought struggles over these matters. But no subject mobilized so much interest, let alone public emotion, as the development of aviation. Dirigible airships continued their spectacular ascents, but in 1909 heavier-than-air flight suddenly began to eclipse them. Aeroplanes, until then the apparatus for exotic experiments or a dangerous sport, became machines with serious potential for military reconnaissance. The French led the way as usual, and a general European scramble for aeroplanes followed.

Dirigibles remained popular, and all armies continued to develop them and increase their numbers. Both the German and the French grand maneuvers featured the participation of one in 1909, and two in the following year. In Germany the military Groß II airship flew on reconnaissance for one side in 1909, but had to make an emergency landing behind enemy lines on the first day, and was only able to take off on one subsequent day due to bad weather.[113] The same year, the

French Lebaudy ship *République* worked for both sides on alternating days, but was grounded by wind on one day and hampered by fog the rest of the time. It flew only three hundred to six hundred meters up, which would have made it vulnerable to ground fire under combat conditions.[114] On the flight back to base after the maneuvers, a propeller blade broke loose and destroyed the dirigible, killing the crew.[115] Nevertheless, both Germany and France continued to expand their airship fleets, followed by the other European powers, including Russia from 1908 onward and Austria-Hungary in 1909. The British and Italians developed some serviceable types of their own, while the Russians and Austrians depended chiefly on French and some German manufactures.[116] With the formidable rigid Zeppelins, in which only the Germans invested, the Reich remained the acknowledged leader in airship strength, and the government fostered the public's delirious enthusiasm for this national achievement.[117]

The switch to aeroplanes had not yet begun in 1908, when the French and German armies first granted subsidies to a few private pioneers, but it started with a sensation in 1909. On 25 July Louis Blériot, a civilian, flew a monoplane of his own design across the English Channel. The exploit transformed him into a hero throughout Europe overnight and contained an obvious portent for the military future of his machine. More significant still from the point of view of the armies was the privately organized *Grande Semaine de l'Aviation* held at Reims on 22–29 July 1909. The Communication Troops Inspectorate of the Prussian army reported with awe that thirty-six aircraft had taken part in the week-long competition, all of them French with the exception of eight American Wright and Curtiss biplanes.[118] The pilots were all French, except for Frank Curtiss and the Englishman, George Cockburn. The German military attaché in Paris, Major von Winterfeldt, spent a few days at Reims and confessed that the French had made "enormous progress" in aviation.[119] The sheer number of aircraft assembled in one place astonished him, "and for an entire array of machines it was not just a question of timid, short experiments like those for instance of Herr Armand Zipfel in Berlin; but instead really serious performances were achieved with respect to stability, speed, maneuverability, endurance, and altitude, . . . so that one may clearly maintain that aviation technology has overcome the stage of playing around or of fruitless experiments. Without a doubt the French will continue to work energetically in this area." The Inspectorate of Communication Troops in Berlin argued that "the much-doubted *development capacity of the flying machine* overall has shown itself plainly to the world at Reims, and makes even a military utility of aeroplanes in the foreseeable future appear entirely possible."[120] The French army at once bought seven planes (two Blériots, two Farmans, an Antoinette, and two Wright machines), ordered more for 1910, and began to pay for flying lessons for selected officers.[121]

Above all, 1909 was a triumph for French national pride. The Reims show had been, in the words of the Prussian technical section's report, "an unforeseen success, not only for its organizers, but above all for *France*, whose further advantage in this realm appeared more clearly than ever."[122] Winterfeldt described the wild enthusiasm of the French press: "In recent weeks French vanity has practically glutted itself with rapture. First Blériot's Channel flight and then the unparalleled success of the 'Grande semaine d'aviation' at Reims: that was almost a surfeit of joy."[123] With the exception of Curtiss and the Wright brothers, all of the most famous aviators were French: Blériot, Hubert Latham, Maurice and Henri Farman, Louis Paulhan, and Eugène Lefèbvre. Private individuals as well as organizations, military and civilian, rushed to sponsor aeroplanes. Blériot's Channel flight had captured for him the London *Times'* £1,000 prize for the feat. *Le Temps* raised a subscription to buy four planes for the army after the Reims show, and another private sponsor contributed a fifth. At the same time, the newspaper *Le Matin* offered 100,000 francs for a multistage flight from Paris with landings in Dijon, Belfort, Nancy, and Lille; presumably by no coincidence along the military front line of France's eastern frontier. Donors gave 290,000 francs for prizes for the 1910 Reims air show.[124]

"Germany has shamefully little to show in the face of the French achievements," admitted the Inspectorate of Communication Troops in Berlin.[125] Private entrepreneurs and organizations had offered prizes for aeronautical feats, but with few results.[126] The German army had sponsored experiments by a few pioneers but they barely managed to fly at all in 1909.[127] The private Deutsche Flugplatz-Gesellschaft, noting that Reims had shown the aeroplane to have "limitless significance as a military weapon of war," immediately organized its own *Flugwoche* at Johannistal outside Berlin two months later.[128] Designed to challenge German aviators to match French feats, this event only turned out to be an embarrassment.[129] Five French competitors entered, as well as an Englishman, a Belgian, and two Chileans, but only one German. The latter never managed to take off. All the aeroplanes were French and all the prizes went to Frenchmen. The kaiser, his suite, and therefore Berlin society shunned the proceedings, but the military experts were all there. Baron von Lyncker, inspector of the communication troops and hence in charge of the German military air section; Majors Groß and Parseval; and members of the technical department of the general staff, all took a lively interest. The French military attaché, Lieutenant-Colonel Pellé, reported: "The disappointment and humiliation experienced by German *amour-propre* were very severe. . . . We may be *certain* that Germany will make *serious efforts* to emerge from its inferiority in matters of aviation. . . . As happened with dirigibles, the Germans will patiently and in secret perfect our inventions and in a few years they will have at their disposal some very good military aeroplanes. At present, our head start is considerable. How shall we preserve it?"

Pellé was right about the Germans' ambitions, though it took them some time to transform these into accomplishments. The war ministry remained skeptical, as always, of investing heavily in inventions before they were ready to be deployed. General Franz von Wandel, head of the General War Department, the most important branch of the ministry, spent a day out at Johannistal and acknowledged that the foreign achievements should spur German pioneers to greater efforts, but he also noted serious shortcomings from the military point of view: "If one bears in mind that all the inventors who appeared here pronounced flying impossible as soon as the wind speed exceeded three meters per second, that the motors are still highly unreliable, and that accidents happen every day, it is advisable to hold expectations low for the near future and to encourage further development through experiments of all kinds."[130] This the war ministry did, through subsidies and private contributions, as well as the purchase of aeroplanes from the Wright brothers and even the French.[131] German aircraft and competitions were mostly failures, well into 1910.[132] The main problem was that the French were the first to design the compact, powerful engines that made heavier-than-air powered flight possible, and it took years for other inventors to catch up.[133] Many of Germany's first successful aeroplanes used French motors, such as the famous Gnôme designs. Kaiser Wilhelm preferred dirigibles, where Germany enjoyed a comfortable lead, but acknowledged grudgingly "that nevertheless, for the sake of public opinion, one must keep up with other nations."[134]

By the end of 1910 the Germans began to meet with success. The Johannistal air week in October showed signs of a revolution in German aviation. Foreign pilots were excluded, and only seven of the forty planes were French (although among the remainder, which were all German, most were based on French designs, and the German engines were inferior). The French military attaché was particularly impressed by the criteria the organizers set, all oriented toward military utility rather than general record-breaking, as with most competitions. The war ministry contributed most of the prizes, paying little attention to speed but setting a premium on altitude, endurance, and weight carried. Results were cumulative over the entire week, as a test of reliability. Two-seaters attracted the most military interest since they were more useful for observation at a time when a pilot still had to devote much of his attention to keeping his machine airborne and steady.[135]

Nevertheless, the French remained the unmatched masters of the aeroplane. After spectacular successes throughout Europe, they organized an independent air inspectorate in the army in 1910 under General Pierre Auguste Rocques. He performed a tour de force by mustering fourteen planes to take part in the 1910 grand maneuvers in Picardy. The operations, as the German attaché observed, "have often been referred to in the press not untruthfully as 'les grandes manoeuvres aéronautiques.' In point of fact, not only for the spectators but also among the troops the interest in the feats of the fliers was generally livelier than in the development of the combat operations."[136] The French war ministry played the public enthusiasm for all it was worth, sending planes aloft even on days when the weather was too poor for serious observation. Winterfeldt gave a wry explanation:

> Besides, it was in the interest of the army administration not only to gather practical experience, but also to present the eyes of the public and the troops as often as possible with the appealing—and for the French especially inspiring—spectacle of officers in flight. As a result, in my opinion, a large number of flights were made that were designed less to fulfill particular military missions than to serve simultaneously as advertisements. Among these exploits I count, for example, the much-publicized flight of the famous Latham on the day when the president of the republic visited the maneuver field.

Despite numerous breakdowns, enough aeroplanes took part so that sufficient machines were in service throughout operations. Significantly, they managed to fly more and produce much better reconnaissance results than the four dirigibles present.

German experience in 1910, as well as the results of both the German and the French 1911 maneuvers, supported this evidence that aeroplanes were rapidly becoming more effective than dirigibles. In April 1910 one of Zeppelin's dirigibles was destroyed when a wind tore it from its moorings and flung it against an escarpment.[137] At the *Kaisermanöver* that year a Parseval and a Groß ship took part, one on each side. The latter had to land behind enemy lines on the first day after an engine failure, and neither dirigible yielded much useful information to its ground forces in spite of clear weather. Indeed, the airships transmitted many erroneous reports, some of which led to mistakes on the battlefield, as many officers admitted in spite of triumphant accounts in the press.[138] At the annual maneuvers in 1911 the French used only one dirigible and the Germans two, of which both were grounded due to mechanical failures within the first two days, and one exploded upon landing at the end of operations.[139] In the same year's maneuvers the French fielded more than twenty aeroplanes, while the Germans made their debut with eight, and in both cases the fliers delivered highly useful intelligence to the ground commanders.[140] The French nourished their ecstatic enthusiasm for their heroes of the air, and even Kaiser Wilhelm began to speak out in encouragement of aeroplanes as his war ministry devoted increasing attention to them.

Dirigibles had been the first into the air, but for most military tasks aeroplanes proved better as soon as they became practical. Airships had several obvious advantages that made them seem attractive at first. They were available several years earlier and many could stay aloft for twelve hours or more, far longer than aeroplanes. They could cruise for great distances from secure bases and stay over the battlefield or deep behind enemy lines for many hours. Their low speed meant that their crews had time to examine what they were passing over on the ground below and, in theory, minimize the difficulties that immediately became apparent in identifying landmarks, obstacles, and friendly-versus-enemy forces from the unfamiliar vantage point of the air. Perhaps most importantly, dirigibles could carry a large payload, allowing for abundant fuel, possibly armament or photographic equipment, an articulated crew with trained observation officers and engine mechanics, and a wireless set to provide instantaneous communication with headquarters on the ground. German airships already had radios in the 1909 maneuvers, although the French did not.[141] This kind of reporting was obviously superior to that from aeroplanes, which were confined either to furnishing information only after landing or else to dropping written messages, attached to streamers for visibility, over friendly positions. Before the First World War, planes were barely powerful enough to carry one or two people, and could not attain anything like the altitude or endurance of dirigibles. Dependent on a single motor that the pilot could not repair in flight, aeroplanes were extremely vulnerable to engine failure, unlike airships that often had several motors, invariably carried mechanics on board to handle breakdowns, and could in any case remain airborne under little or no power. Planes passed over the terrain at high speed, making it difficult for the aviators to get a steady look at what they were supposed to be observing below.

But in the 1910 and 1911 maneuvers and other tests, the French and Germans discovered many crucial advantages of aeroplanes. In the first place, they were less vulnerable to the weather. Fragile though they were, they could already fly in stronger winds without the lighter-than-air machine's risk of being blown off course or stymied by headwinds. On the ground they did not require the vast, expensive, and only occasionally portable hangars that dirigibles needed as protection against being whisked away by storms. They depended on fewer other kinds of ground support too: no hydrogen inflation equipment and no vast ground crews to hold tether lines during take-off and landing. Indeed, early planes with their low airspeeds could land on almost any field or road in an emergency—an added insurance against bad weather or mechanical failures. They could be rapidly dismantled and loaded onto vehicles for transport to repair shops or new take-off points. All of this made them far more flexible for operations with ground troops, which was naturally the main role for which army leaders were interested in adopting aircraft. In the annual maneuvers, commanders found that this more than made up for their short endurance and inability to carry radios. They flew numerous, quick sorties, returned with up-to-date observations, and were ready to take off again in a relatively short time. If necessary, they could often improvise a landing near friendly troops or headquarters to deliver information promptly. Furthermore, they cost a fraction of the value of a dirigible (approximately £1,000 each, compared to £35,000 for even a semi-rigid airship),[142] and could therefore soon be produced in incomparably greater numbers. Crashes and mechanical failures were less of an obstacle to effectiveness when fresh aircraft and pilots were always available. The relatively accessible cost also meant that private individuals began to become aeroplane owners, creating potential reserves of machines and pilots that armies could call upon in wartime. Planes arrived over the combat area sooner, more often, in greater numbers, and at less cost than the slow dirigibles from distant ground stations.

Once over the battlefield, the small size and higher speed of aeroplanes made them almost impossible to shoot down, in contrast to the majestic airships.[143] Artillery, infantry, and machine gun officers reported after maneuvers that their units would have had many good shots at dirigibles under real combat conditions, but would have had little hope of hitting aeroplanes due to the problems of aiming and range-finding against such a fast-moving target. This relative invulnerability carried with it the invaluable advantage of allowing aircraft to fly low over enemy positions. As soon as dirigibles appeared at exercises, it became clear that their minimum realistic altitude was eight hundred to one thousand meters. The large, slow-moving ships presented tempting targets, and, being filled with hydrogen, were desperately vulnerable to explosions. From a kilometer up in the sky, it was difficult to discern details of troops and features on the ground. Aeroplanes, on the other hand, could fly low over enemy lines, allowing their crews to glimpse the ground closely with near impunity. Numerous air competitions in 1910 and 1911 involved simulated reconnaissance flights, which required fliers to navigate over prescribed courses and report on what they saw. As battlefield reconnaissance and artillery spotting defined themselves as the province of air observation, aeroplanes quickly showed themselves to be best suited to the task. The great airships in which all countries had invested were relegated to long-distance missions at high altitude, or to maritime patrols, where range and endurance were at a premium.

Italy, Russia, Austria-Hungary, and Britain followed well behind France and Germany in aviation, but imitated the same patterns of development. In 1909 all of their armies offered subsidies to private aeroplane pioneers and purchased dirigibles, mostly of French types.[144] The Austrians and the Italians bought isolated aeroplanes for some tentative experiments. A few dirigibles took part in the Italian and Russian fall maneuvers in 1910, although the British still enjoyed little success with them. In 1910 all of the armies acquired planes and began training pilots.[145] Wright, Farman, and Blériot types enjoyed particular favor, although all governments naturally tried to foster domestic manufactures. In 1911 all three armies embarked on substantial efforts to procure aeroplanes en masse and to train aircrew. Several aeroplanes took part in the Italian and Russian grand maneuvers that year.[146] Aviation of both types was to have been a feature of the Austro-Hungarian maneuvers too for the first time in 1911, but was canceled due to poor terrain conditions.[147]

All over Europe, air clubs and leagues, much like their automotive counterparts, helped to channel public enthusiasm for aerial sports and warfare. They served as both a spur and an auxiliary to armies in the quest for air capability. They agitated for action by the military, and also helped to raise funds and provide volunteer or reserve pilots and extra aircraft for requisition in wartime.[148] The popular press, such as Alfred Harmsworth's papers in Britain, found that the sensationalization of aeronautical feats sold copies while at the same time putting pressure on governments to pay for military aviation.[149] A continual driving force, as with all armaments in the period, was the fear that foreign rivals would gain the upper hand with a new technology.

By 1911 the air race was still the only serious competition in progress between most of the European armies despite the confrontation over Bosnia and Herzegovina. The crisis did not involve the serious threat of a great-power war, precisely because the balance of military power was so lopsidedly against Russia. Germany and Austria-Hungary triumphed in the crisis by leaving the decision up to this military imbalance, since the outcome of a resolution on the diplomatic level would probably have gone against them. In this way the balance of military power did determine the course of international confrontation in 1909, even without a war, both by making war impossible through deterrence and by forcing the militarily weaker side to give way irrespective of any negotiation. The imbalance, and the prospect of its disappearance, gave Austria-Hungary for the first time a real incentive for fighting an actual war against Serbia and Montenegro, which lay at its mercy. The notion of a preventive war gained a firm foothold in the consciousness of the decision makers.

At that point the strict logic of military power ceased to dictate events in 1909. Not only did Germany and Austria-Hungary never seriously contemplate actually attacking Russia while it was weak simply because it would presumably regain its power later. The Vienna government also renounced the idea of a preventive war against Serbia and Montenegro. The emperor and his government still assumed that a peaceful settlement was preferable to a war, even a victorious one, as long as they could secure a satisfactory result without fighting. The prospect of an inevitable future conflagration was already present in the minds of statesmen and generals in Vienna and Berlin, but it did not yet dominate them except in the case of Conrad. It was still possible to imagine a course of events that would not necessarily bring about a three-front war for the Dual Monarchy or a two-front war for the Reich.

The crisis had the most dramatic results in Russia and, to a much lesser degree, the South Slav states and Italy. For these countries, Germany's and Austria-Hungary's reliance on military superiority during the confrontation had drawn attention to their armies' inferiority, and they became determined to do something about it. Consequently, even without building up their own armies significantly, Germany and Austria-Hungary had provoked their potential adversaries into competitive military expansion against them. To an even greater degree than in the first Moroccan crisis, the German decision to use the threat of force as a bluff touched off reactions on the other side that were designed to make it harder for the threateners to threaten again. The next time they tried it, the balance of military power looked very different.

Chapter 5

THE SECOND MOROCCAN CRISIS
AND THE BEGINNING OF GERMAN PANIC,
1911–1912

IN NOVEMBER 1911 the German government and army high command decided to begin a program of military development that they knew would lead to a land armaments race between the great powers. The kaiser, his ministers, and his generals agreed to place a vast new army bill before the Reichstag, in preparation for what they regarded as an inevitable European war, and it became law six months later. Six months before their decision they had not contemplated either the military increase or an imminent war. What brought about thoughts of both was the second Moroccan crisis, between June and early November of 1911. During the confrontation itself it was not likely that Germany and the Entente powers would actually fight, but afterward, as a result of it, the likelihood that they eventually would increased dramatically.

The crisis threw into relief a change in the political and military balance between the European powers. In the confrontation, it became clear that for the first time Germany would face a two-front war if it fought one of its European adversaries. At last Russia's military recovery was complete enough so that Russian intervention on the side of France could not be discounted. Indeed, it seemed virtually certain in any general war in the future, due to Russia's humiliation over the Bosnian annexation. This new prospect instilled fear in the German leadership and prompted them to drop their previous inhibitions against army expansion. They decided to arm as quickly as possible in order to gain an advantage in a coming conflict, regardless of the risk of spurring the other powers to do the same.

In this transformation, the balance of military power played a major part. It did little to cause the 1911 crisis directly, since neither side entered expecting a trial of military strength, but it had a crucial effect on the outcome. Germany's capitulation and humiliation were in large part the result of its perception that it would have to fight if it wished to prevail, and that it would probably have to fight Britain and Russia as well as France if it wished to fight at all. This was partly a political calculation, but it rested on the facts of military power. After the crisis, contemplating the implications of what had just happened, the German leadership decided to react with military preparations. The army law of May 1912, the first step in an outright land-armaments race, was the result of a transformation in the perceived balance of military power.

The second Moroccan crisis began as the personal scheme of the pugnacious new state secretary of the Foreign Office in Berlin, Alfred von Kiderlen-Wächter. He hoped to win a diplomatic success against France over its renewed attempts to consolidate the hold on Morocco that it had gained in 1906.[1] Kiderlen-Wächter did not plan to fight a war. He merely sought to score a coup in world politics that would efface what he regarded as Germany's earlier humiliations. At the same time he stood to strengthen the establishment parties against the Social Democrats in the 1912 Reichstag elections. The French gave him his opportunity in the spring of 1911 when they began advertising their intention to send troops to Fez in Morocco, ostensibly to protect their nationals in the city from a growing indigenous movement against the colonists' inroads. The Sultan of Morocco, Mulai Hafid, had in fact appealed to Paris for aid against the insurgents, but the Germans could see as plainly as anyone that the French would hardly be likely to withdraw once they had established such a military presence. Kiderlen proposed to challenge the move and either keep the French out or appropriate a corresponding slice of the country as "compensation" to Germany. Either way, Berlin would assert its power and make sure that France did not continue its colonial expansion without Germany. Kiderlen's plan was to let the French go ahead with their military mission to Fez at first and then, once they were there, to assert his demands by taking as hostages two ports on the Atlantic coast of Morocco where Germans claimed interests: Mogador and Agadir. The French would have to choose between giving up Fez or allowing the Germans to keep the western part of the country. Paris would receive no help from its allies, Kiderlen calculated, since Britain's concern for Morocco did not extend outside the Mediterranean seaboard, while Russia would naturally be as reluctant as ever to take risks for the sake of French colonial claims. The basis for the German demands was to be the Algeciras treaty of 1906, which stipulated that no European power could take action infringing the independence of Morocco without consulting the other signatories and compensating those with "interests" in the country.[2]

Kiderlen's action went as planned at first, but then turned into a fiasco when the Entente powers chose to stand behind France. The Wilhelmstraße craftily refrained from warning Paris of its demands until after French troops had occupied Fez on 21 May 1911. Then Germany presented its objections and backed them up by sending a cruiser, the *Panther*, to anchor in Agadir harbor and give threatening substance to Berlin's claims on 1 July. This brought Joseph Caillaux's government in haste to the negotiating table, but there matters stuck. The two powers quickly reached an impasse on the compensations to be granted to Germany. On 21 July the British government threw its weight behind France when David Lloyd George, the chancellor of the exchequer and until then a well-known advocate of a moderate position toward Germany in the Liberal cabinet, gave a speech at the Lord Mayor of London's banquet at Mansion House, asserting that Britain should be ready to fight to defend its interests rather than sacrifice its position as a great power.[3] Lloyd George did not mention Germany or Morocco specifically, but his meaning was clear: the British government did not intend to allow Berlin to dictate affairs on the continent or to make threats with warships. Kiderlen, like Bülow in 1905, had gravely miscalculated in thinking that the British would be glad enough to see France's colonial aspirations cut down to size as long as it did not happen on the route to India. If a conference were held, Germany might well be outvoted again. If it came to a war, the Germans would have to face a France backed by Britain and, as it turned out, possibly by Russia as well.

In the end Berlin gave way. The kaiser enjoined Kiderlen against any more threats after July, while France stood firm. In his negotiations with the French ambassador in Berlin, Jules Cambon, Kiderlen had to agree to a de facto French protectorate over Morocco on 4 November, in return for the cession of tracts of the French Congo to add to Germany's West African possessions. The deal utterly failed to save face for Germany, since Kiderlen had engaged in bullying talk and colluded with nationalist associations to heat up emotions over compensations, while the press throughout Europe had blazed with bellicose headlines for four months. A bitterly hostile Reichstag vented its disappointment on the chancellor when it convened to hear him defend his Morocco policy in November 1911.

The balance of military power played little part in the origins of the second Moroccan crisis, except on a very general level. Kiderlen-Wächter's desire to isolate France and assert German power had some basis in the perception that Berlin was facing an increasingly hostile coalition across the gulf of a naval race and past diplomatic confrontations. In a general way, he presumably expected to overawe France with German power, but he made no reference whatever to the military situation when he laid out his plans to challenge the move on Fez.[4] In his detailed scenarios describing the alternatives France would face, he did not include the possibility of threatening France with a war, let alone of fighting one. He discounted Britain's interests in the country and made no mention at all of Russia. The dispatch of *Panther* to Agadir was partly for dramatic effect as an assertion of German world power. The Reich government had been painfully aware of its inability to engage in this kind of gunboat diplomacy before the construction of its battlefleet. Kiderlen did not consult the army high command first, or even Tirpitz, who was on holiday at the time and considered the move rash when he found out about it.[5] The only military operations Kiderlen foresaw were deployments allegedly in support of German citizens at the ports, and perhaps later to extend German influence in western Morocco. The French, for their part, had no thoughts of a European war when they prepared to march on Fez.[6]

On the course and outcome of the resulting crisis, however, the balance of military power had a substantial effect. In the first place, it led to a diplomatic resolution because the chances in a war looked bad for both sides, with the risk of an unfavorable outcome and the virtual certainty of disproportionate sacrifices whatever the result. The few official threats of a recourse to arms during the crisis were decidedly veiled.[7] In the second place, the balance of military power helped to ensure Germany's ultimate capitulation. Berlin was outvoted diplomatically and could not menace its opponents with war as in 1905 and 1909 because for the first time this would have entailed the risk of a conflict with France, Britain, and Russia all together. This was a wholly new situation, which deprived Berlin of the military ascendancy it had grown accustomed to exploiting. All France had to do was call the bluff, and this time its hollowness would be exposed.

THE BALANCE OF MILITARY POWER IN THE CRISIS

War looked like a bad prospect for anyone in 1911. On the Entente side, the balance of military power compelled France to at least a certain level of transigence. From the point of view of Paris the chances in a war over Morocco did not seem promising. Both the government and the army were in phases of traumatic transition when the crisis erupted. On the same day that the French military mission occupied Fez, an aeroplane crashed into the spectators' area at an aerial display at Issy-les-Moulineaux, killing the well-respected war minister, Maurice Berteaux, and gravely injuring Ernest Monis, the prime minister.[8] Another cabinet, led by Joseph Caillaux, took office just as the *Panther* dropped anchor at Agadir.

The new war minister, Adolphe-Marie Messimy, found his army debating what to do about its inferiority to the Germans in heavy artillery. The French had given 155mm quick-firing howitzers to their army commands by 1909, but everybody knew that the Germans would have far more large-caliber guns. The French had only the 120 pieces they had constructed, none of their other heavy artillery being both quick-firing and mobile for field operations. The Germans had approximately 380 heavy field howitzers by 1911, of 150mm caliber and also quick-firing: a superiority of three to one. They also assigned a varying array of even more powerful mobile quick-firing field guns to each army depending on its task: 105mm and 137mm long-range cannon and 210mm mortars.[9] All of this still left out the siege artillery, where the Germans were introducing far more modern and powerful types. The Germans trained heavy field artillery units together with other arms in maneuvers for use on the battlefield and integrated them into corps commands. The French did not. During the crisis the Conseil Supérieur de la Guerre occupied itself with the problems of procuring comparable weapons, as well as light howitzers, of which France had none and Germany a substantial proportion in its field artillery.[10] France's advantage even in medium field guns rested on a very slim margin of superior training and tactics now that the Germans had fully reequipped with the 77mm quick-firing gun that had essentially the same characteristics as the French 75. The Germans would have a crushing superiority in heavy artillery, as well as the advantage of possessing light howitzers. In field guns and light howitzers alone, German active corps outnumbered French ones by 144 to 120. The prime minister took account of this unequal balance in his consideration of France's situation during the crisis.[11]

Messimy also had to deal with a great upheaval in the army leadership over military organization and command authority just as he entered office. Since early in 1911, the president of the Conseil Supérieur de la Guerre and wartime commander in chief, General Paul-Henry Michel, had been pressing for a plan to transform the army's composition and mobilization. His ideas represented a step toward those of Jean Jaurès and the political left, who wanted the state to rely heavily on citizen reservists in an army designed for national defense. Michel submitted his proposal formally to the Conseil Supérieur on 19 July 1911, just as the negotiations over Morocco were nearing a deadlock in Berlin.[12] He wanted to make massive use of reserves in order to counter Germany's numerical strength. According to his plan, the reservists would mobilize alongside the regulars, and form reserve regiments that would be paired with regular ones to constitute "demi-brigades" from the outset of operations. This would double the forces available for use in the opening battles, and give France enough forces for a much broader deployment that Michel proposed, extending all along the frontier to prevent any outflanking move by way of Belgium. Everyone on the Conseil Supérieur de la Guerre was against the idea. The generals argued that the scheme would slow down mobilization and give the Germans several days' head start in which to attack the French army while it was unprepared. The reserve units, they also maintained, would be insufficiently trained and would bloat each corps into an unwieldy mass as big as an army, with completely insufficient artillery and support services. They considered such a force totally inadequate for the kind of offensive operations that all of them, including Michel, regarded as essential to victory.[13]

Messimy dealt the *coup de grâce* to Michel's plan in the council, and sacked the general for good measure. To help prevent such disputes in the future, Messimy dissolved the bicephalous structure of the French high command at the same time. Henceforward there would no longer be a chief of staff alongside a designated commander in chief who would lead the army in war and meanwhile preside over the Conseil Supérieur. Instead, all functions would be in the hands of a single chief of the general staff, who would make the war plans, head the council, and command the main field army on mobilization. At the end of July 1911, in the midst of the Agadir crisis, the war minister chose for this post General Joseph-Jacques-Césaire Joffre.

Joffre took office radiating confidence and pugnacity, but in fact did little to improve the French army's chances for a war over Morocco in the summer of 1911. He at once set about changing the established war plan. Plan XVI, designed for an initial defensive, was to become "Plan XVI, Variant No. 1." The left wing would now extend as far north as Mézières, and the main body would be ready for an early offensive into Lorraine between Metz and Strassburg.[14] This was an expedient that Joffre adopted until he could lay more ambitious plans for a full-scale offensive deployment. But even the interim scheme did not officially take effect until September 1911 after feverish staff work, so during the Moroccan crisis the French army was engaged in changing its war plans as well as its leaders and command structure. It remained distinctly inferior to the German army in numbers. Although confidence in French national spirit and the great morale boost of an air service far more spectacular than Germany's led many newspapers to trumpet the nation's readiness to fight over Morocco, official estimates were more sober.[15] Joffre was perplexed as to whether the Germans would make their main effort on the Franco-German frontier or in Belgium, opposite which the Deuxième Bureau continued to report that the Germans were building suspiciously numerous railways and enormous detraining platforms.[16] In August 1911, he gave the government the decisive evaluation of the military situation and the reaction was perfectly plain. Joffre recalled in his memoirs the interview with Caillaux and President Fallières: "The President of the Council asked me point-blank: 'General, it is said that Napoleon did not give battle except when he thought his chances of success were 70 out of 100. Do we have a 70 in 100 chance of victory if the situation forces us into war?' I was in some difficulty as to how to reply. In the end I said: 'No, I do not consider that we have.'—'Very well,' replied Caillaux, 'in that case we will negotiate.'"[17]

What worried Caillaux and the French military planners even more than the readiness of their own army was the reliability of their allies. Both the Russians and the British transmitted ambiguous signals about their willingness to join in a war over Morocco. Naturally some of this hesitancy arose from the desire to leave an escape route open in case France acted as the aggressor and therefore nullified the undertakings of mutual defense. But some of it was due to genuine doubt about the capabilities of the Entente armies, and the French themselves were far from confident of either the willingness or the ability of Britain and Russia to help them in time.

The Russians were ambiguous in their promises of support. In part this was a reflection of their fear of being dragged into a war over French colonial claims in which St. Petersburg had no interest.[18] Izvolsky, at that time ambassador in Paris, was fond of reminding the French of their cautionary advice in 1908–9 about starting a war over a matter that would not seem important to the French public. He warned the French foreign minister, Justin de Selves, to find a diplomatic solution, since "Russia of course remains faithful to its alliance, but it would have difficulty making its public opinion accept a war over Morocco."[19] Explicit declarations of support alternated with evasions. In August 1911, for example, after a phase of hesitation, Izvolsky informed de Selves that "he was officially charged with telling me that, if as a result of the failure of our current negotiations we were to end up in a conflict with Germany, Russia would give us not only diplomatic but also military assistance against it."[20] Later in the same month, the acting foreign minister in St. Petersburg retreated from this promise temporarily.[21] The chief of the general staff, General Iakov Zhilinski, then reassured his French counterpart in their annual talk at the end of August that the tsar's government desired "scrupulously to fulfill the obligations that the Convention imposes upon it."[22]

The Russians equivocated partly because their army was not ready. Izvolsky pointed out to Caillaux in July that military weakness would make intervention hazardous: "We would in any case be all the more prevented by the fact that we are in no state to participate in a European war. We still need at least two years to reorganize our forces before we will be ready to face such a struggle."[23] The Russians persistently urged caution in Paris for this reason, even when professing their loyalty to the alliance. The tsar told the French ambassador in St. Petersburg that "if all else failed he would honor his signature, but that Russia was not ready, that we must be prudent and try to reach an accommodation with Germany."[24] In the August staff talks, General Zhilinski declared that he could mount an attack with at least the active forces as soon as they were deployed on the fifteenth day of mobilization, and pin down five to six German corps.[25] At the same time, however, he cautioned that the supply services for these formations would not be ready yet and the reserves would take longer to arrive. Furthermore, the distribution of heavy field artillery, machine guns, and modern rifle ammunition would not be complete for years, and the need to fight Austria-Hungary would make the situation more difficult. Zhilinski concluded: "Under these conditions Russia does not seem to be in a state to sustain a war against Germany with the certainty of success for at least two years. It would surely be capable of warding off blows, but perhaps less so of delivering any."

Such caution merely confirmed what the French thought of Russian military capabilities. In spite of Zhilinski's assertions, the standard estimate in the Deuxième Bureau and the general staff in Paris was that the Russians could only make their presence felt by about the thirtieth day of mobilization, more than two weeks after the main clash on the western front was expected.[26] British intelligence estimated that thirty days was the minimum time it would take for the Russians to mount an offensive.[27] Caillaux collected information on the Russian army which convinced him that he could not count on its playing any effective role.[28] He also received a note from Messimy reporting that the chief of the general staff's visit to Russia had yielded the impression that the army there would require two to four more years of reorganization, which was essentially what the Russians themselves estimated.

If they were unsure of what they could count on from Russia, the French were a little more certain of British aid, but not convinced that it would make much difference in the short run if it came to a war over Morocco. Even after Lloyd George's Mansion House speech, the Foreign Office remained careful to keep its options open. It warned the French that they must not be the aggressors in any war—always a hazardous point of judgment—and that the final decision about any eventual British intervention would have to rest with Parliament and public opinion in Britain. In his desire to give assurances to France, Grey always trod a precarious path in the Liberal cabinet between supporters and opponents of a continental policy.[29] Prime minister Herbert Henry Asquith forbade Grey to authorize regular staff talks between British and French planners, lest Paris come to expect assistance as a matter of course. "The French ought not to be encouraged in present circumstances to make their plans on any assumptions of this kind," Asquith wrote as late as September 1911, at the height of confrontations.[30]

Nor did the French and British have plans for joint operations ready before the crisis. Grey did not pay any serious attention to the progress of Britain's own military arrangements after authorizing them in 1906.[31] When General Wilson became Director of Military Operations in 1910, he found only theoretical schemes in existence for the employment of British forces on the continent, left over from the 1905 crisis. In the meantime Haldane had organized the army to furnish the four- or six-division British Expeditionary Force, but there were still no detailed plans ready for its mobilization, the requisition of horses, and rail and sea transport to France.[32] Wilson's vigorous cultivation of contacts with the Foreign Office and French military leaders, pressing for attention to contingency plans, resulted in no concrete preparations.[33] In 1910 General Foch replied to Wilson's first queries as DMO by saying that it did not matter how many soldiers the British sent to France: one alone would do, so long as he was killed, in order to bring Britain in on France's side.[34] The remark expressed the French view that British aid would be useful primarily as a deterrent or for naval assistance in the event of a long war. Considerable doubt remained about how much Britain's few divisions could contribute to the French campaign on land, even assuming they could arrive in time. General Michel, shortly before the Moroccan crisis, made no provision for them in his plans to expand the French army and deploy a cordon of divisions along all of the eastern frontier, including what later became the British sector opposite Belgium.[35]

When joint war plans did materialize, they did not take effect before the crisis was over. Only in July, after the *Panther*'s arrival at Agadir, did Wilson obtain permission to go to Paris and confer with Messimy and the chief of staff, General Auguste Dubail, about British war plans. This resulted in an agreement, signed by Wilson and Dubail on 20 July, promising a British Expeditionary Force in the event of a land intervention. It was to consist of six divisions—150,000 men—deployed somewhere in the Arras-Cambrai–St. Quentin sector. However, Wilson was still unable to tell his own superiors just how long mobilization would take.[36] Joffre later assured the British that he could furnish rail transport for their forces in France, but they did not have their own arrangements in order. Any military move would have been largely an improvisation. In August 1911, with Britain diplomatically committed to supporting France, the Foreign Office began to take a more active interest in the military options.[37] At Wilson's urging, Haldane asked him and the Chief of the Imperial General Staff, Sir William Nicholson, to prepare a detailed study of Britain's situation in the event of a European war for presentation to the Committee of Imperial Defence. These deliberations got under way slowly in London, and Joffre did not even meet the British military attaché in Paris until 24 August, a month after becoming chief of staff.[38] The French kept their war plan secret from their allies until after the crisis was over, in November 1911, when Wilson saw it on a visit to Paris to meet Joffre for the first time.[39]

The British government received a discouraging impression of its armed services' war plans when the Committee of Imperial Defence met on 23 August to consider what to do if a war broke out.[40] The session lasted all day, and mostly consisted of a debate over which of two plans would best suit Britain's needs in case it had to help France in a European war: the army's or the navy's. General Wilson made the case for a land operation alongside the French, showing by ingenious calculation that Britain's six divisions might tip the balance between Germanys' eighty-four and France's sixty-six if they intervened soon enough in the crucial Verdun-Maubeuge sector. The First Sea Lord, Admiral Sir Arthur Wilson, presented the navy's rather ineffectual plan for amphibious operations against ports and islands on the northern coast of Germany, with the army diverted away from any operations in France. Asquith and Grey preferred the army's proposal for direct intervention to save the French, but had to watch the spectacle of the service chiefs wrangling over conflicting plans and establishing that the navy had made no provisions for transporting an expeditionary force across the Channel. The meeting adjourned without a decision on which of the two strategies to adopt. The army had made a much better impression, and it secured the navy's serious cooperation with transport plans for the expeditionary force after Lord Haldane threatened to resign if no such measures were taken.[41] However, the army and navy staffs did not actually hammer out the full arrangements until January 1912, long after the Moroccan crisis was over.[42]

As far as the politicians were concerned, the CID meeting showed that a war would be ruinous and risky, whichever strategy Britain followed. Neither the army nor the navy promised a quick victory, even if their plans worked. The naval scheme suggested nothing to stop the Germans from marching into Paris, but the army did not exactly offer a glowing prognosis either.[43] The generals discounted the Russians, who would mobilize too late and with only forty divisions at the outset. The French, they thought, would lose if the British did not help.[44] If Britain did intervene immediately, Nicholson considered that "the numbers of the opposing forces at the decisive point would be so nearly equal during the opening and early actions of the war that it is possible for the allies to win some initial successes which might prove invaluable." He expected British participation to raise French morale and provide naval leverage in a long war. The chief of staff's conclusion was essentially a negative one:

> It seems, therefore, that in a war between Germany and France in which England takes active part with the French the result in the opening moves

might be doubtful, but the longer the war lasted the greater the strain would be on Germany. . . . Our navy is powerful, while our expeditionary force is very small if measured in terms of European armies, but these two in alliance with France might prove a formidable obstacle to German victory; whereas if we once allow Germany to defeat France our expeditionary force would be valueless and the duration of our naval predominance could be measured in years.

Winston Churchill, at that time Home Secretary, forecast a long war of attrition, in which the Entente powers would compensate in staying power for the German army's initial impact.[45] "If the French army has not been squandered by precipitate or desperate action," Churchill wrote in his own memorandum to the committee, the Entente could eventually attempt a counteroffensive. Meanwhile, he warned, "Such a policy demands heavy and hard sacrifices from France, who must, with great constancy, expose herself to invasion, to having her provinces occupied by the enemy, and to the investment of Paris, and whose armies may be committed to retrograde or defensive operations." Indeed, the CID meeting devoted considerable time to debating what a British expeditionary force ought to do if the French retreated as they had done in 1870. In the end, Churchill argued in his memorandum, Britain would prevail, assuming that it helped France, but he made the possibilities sound chilling in his conclusion: "The steady augmentation of British military strength during the progress of the war would, however, put us in a position by the end of the twelfth month to secure or re-establish British interests outside Europe, even if through the defeat or desertion of allies we were forced to continue the war alone."

All of these were fairly bloodcurdling prospects for the civilian ministers to contemplate. It was one thing for military men to say that British intervention could save France from catastrophe and give the Entente a fair chance of victory after initial defeats. To a strategist facing war, this was a reasonable calculation of advantage. To a diplomat in peacetime, however, this looked like a terrible prospect. A war without British intervention would mean the defeat of France followed by German hegemony on the continent. A war involving Britain would begin with retreats and heavy sacrifices, and probably end in ultimate victory—if the generals were right. All of this assumed that plans and preparations were ready, which they were not, and that the British mobilized on the same day as the French, an eventuality the government was certainly not prepared to guarantee. In the face of the military prospects as put forward by either the army or the navy, it is not surprising that Asquith and Grey preferred to solve the Moroccan question by negotiation. No unequivocal assurances went out to France, and the Quai d'Orsay took its cue in negotiations with the Germans.

Although the military situation looked hazardous for France and Britain, it held its risks for Germany too. The balance of military power made a war appear dangerous enough for the Germans so that they could not push the threat of it far in negotiations for fear of provoking a genuine conflict. Part of the reason for the government's unease about war was the unreadiness of the public to engage in a European struggle over Morocco or stretches of the Congo. Germany did not have a powerful diplomatic case for taking the law into its own hands in the face of opposition from the Entente, and would almost certainly have to act as the aggressor since France had produced a fait accompli at Fez and could not be dislodged without the Germans breaking off negotiations and starting a war. Politically, the wisest course was to negotiate for whatever Germany could get. The diplomatic circumstances affected the military outlook as well. France by itself was not too formidable an enemy, but supported by Britain it was strong enough at sea to make the Germans think twice before attacking it. More importantly, aggression against France would give the *casus belli* for a Russian intervention against Germany. This created a wholly new military balance, of a kind that had not arisen in the 1905–6 and 1908–9 crises, when Russia had been crippled. By 1911 it was no longer clear that Russia would stay out of a European war, due to its military recovery. This forced the Germans to tread carefully.

Against France itself, the odds for Germany did not look bad, although there were reasons to suppose that a campaign would not be easy either. The Germans outnumbered the French as ever, and by 1911 had more reserve corps equipped for use in the front line than in 1905. They possessed ten Krupp 305mm mortars and two 420mm ones with which to demolish the Belgian Meuse forts.[46] The Germans successfully disguised the existence of these siege pieces from foreign intelligence by designating them as "heavy coastal mortars." The shells from the 305 could pierce the thickest armored cupolas of the Liège and Namur defenses even if a surprise assault during mobilization did not succeed in seizing the first fortress. This meant that the Germans could deploy their forces on both sides of the Meuse and gain room for a massive outflanking move through Belgium, almost as broad as that envisioned by Schlieffen.[47] Both the French and the German armies were at comparable stages of equipment with machine guns and motor vehicles. The one area that could give the Germans some cause for concern was the overwhelming French superiority in aviation. There were twenty-two dirigibles operational in Germany by the end of 1911, nine of them owned by the army, compared to France's two civilian and two military airships. But the French army owned sixty-five aeroplanes and had one hundred and twenty trained officer pilots, against only twenty planes and pilots in the German army. Counting civilian owners as well in the total available for mobilization, France had four hundred and fifty aeroplanes and five hundred aviators, while in Germany there were only one hundred fifty and one hundred thirty-five, respectively, displaying a great disparity in the two countries' potential resources as well as first-line strength.[48] Nevertheless, the German high command did not subscribe to the more enthusiastic theories of the French press about the aeroplane as a war-winning weapon, and Major Winterfeldt continued to send confident assessments back from Paris throughout the second Moroccan crisis.[49]

The French ceased to look like such an easy target once their allies were added. The Royal Navy still enjoyed a crushing superiority over the German fleet, and one reason for Kaiser Wilhelm's urging caution upon Kiderlen in the crisis after the Mansion House speech may have been the fear of losing his new navy in a war before it was ready to challenge the British.[50] Admiral Tirpitz was against any premature sacrifice of the fleet.[51] General von Wandel in the war ministry thought it would be hard to win a long war against Britain, even though victory on land in France was reasonably certain.[52] The real difficulty, however, lay on the Russian side. Although the foreign ministry in St. Petersburg made it clear that it did not want a war with Germany over Morocco, there were no more reports saying that Russia could under no circumstances mobilize for a European campaign.[53] Russian tactics still looked cautious and ragged to German and Austro-Hungarian observers, and much equipment remained to be completed, especially in the heavy field artillery. Nevertheless by early 1911, intelligence reports had begun to assume that mobilization would take place if necessary.[54] After the crisis was over, Wandel wrote that he had never believed Germany should "take on a European war against France and England and presumably also Russia," on account of Morocco.[55] In 1911 Moltke warned: "It is possible to assume with certainty that the next war will be one on two fronts."[56]

Throughout the crisis the military leadership in Germany urged caution. The whole enterprise had been Kiderlen-Wächter's idea, and he had not consulted the army before undertaking it, evidently not expecting a military confrontation. General von Wandel wrote in mid-August 1911:

In this case too, as so often before, the dispatch of our warships ("Panther," then "Berlin") seems to have been a matter not of a carefully evaluated decision with all its consequences considered, but rather of a sudden impulse. There was no understanding whatsoever of what might arise from it and of how all these possibilities were to be dealt with; the order is said to have taken shape in a few hours one afternoon, without precise knowledge of local conditions, the anchorage and the like. It is hardly surprising that we now find ourselves more or less at a loss in the face of the resulting political difficulties. . . . But it is characteristic of our circumstances of government that neither the War Minister nor the Chief of the Army General Staff is in any way informed of how things stand.[57]

Heeringen, Kiderlen, Bethmann Hollweg, and the kaiser all agreed that the army ought to refrain from actions that could be construed as military preparations.[58] They remained ready to fight if German "honor" seemed to be at stake, but in all other cases they were resolved not to go to war. If a conflict broke out, they realized, Germany must not appear to be the aggressor lest Russia be drawn in by its alliance with France.

A war that broke out over the Agadir crisis would not have been nearly so localized or so predictable in its outcome as one over the first Moroccan crisis or the annexation of Bosnia and Herzegovina. It might in many ways have resembled what happened in 1914: a general European war started by the Germans on the model of the Schlieffen plan. They would have deployed some twenty-three active and nine reserve corps against France's eighteen to twenty-two corps, leaving three active and three and a half reserve corps to watch East Prussia.[59] The assault would probably have spilled over to the left bank of the Meuse as in 1914, with heavy mortars demolishing the Liège and Namur forts. The French would have reacted by deploying in their Plan XVI positions for defense between Belfort and Vouziers, allowing the Germans a clear path through Belgium and northern France. To what degree the French attempted a simultaneous blow into Lorraine, and whether they had the full twenty-two corps in line extending north to Mézières, would have depended upon when the war broke out, since Joffre only implemented the dispositions for this in September 1911. The British Expeditionary Force would have arrived at least several days later, due to the lack of plans for its transport. This would have constituted a weakness for the Entente. A compensating strength would have been the far better aerial reconnaissance available to the French, which probably would have aided them in responding to the German attack while the Germans developed a far less detailed view of their enemies' movements.

Russian intervention would have been slow and less effective than it was in 1914, which could have made the difference to German success on the western front. The army still suffered from the aftereffects of the Manchurian war, and its deployment scheme was new. More importantly, the Russian army would have undertaken a far less bold offensive than it did in 1914, confining itself instead, as General Zhilinski had implied to the French, to limited operations under Plan 19 with its unready army in a war over French colonies rather than the Balkans.[60] In particular, the Russians would probably have had to defend themselves against a powerful Austro-Hungarian offensive into Poland, in greater strength than that which materialized in 1914 when Conrad had already committed a large part of his forces to the Balkans. Austria-Hungary's alliance with Germany would probably have brought it in against Russia when Russia declared war on Germany. Italy would have remained neutral at the outset, having avoided commitments to either side during the Moroccan crisis and not being prepared at the time for a war on the Alps. It would have been all the more likely to stand aside as the army shifted its attention to the invasion of Libya, which took place that September, in the later phase of the Moroccan crisis. A European war would certainly have been risky for all participants, and would have had little chance of remaining localized. The worst-case scenarios of the planners in all countries had some justification. Most importantly, the French could not be certain that Russia would intervene, while the Germans could not be certain that Russia would stay out.

THE GERMAN REACTION TO THE CRISIS: THE 1912 ARMY LAW

The balance of military power dominated the aftermath of the second Moroccan crisis. As a result of the confrontation, Germany's political and military leaders completely reassessed the domestic as well as the international situation, and embarked on a massive program of army expansion. This began as a new military law in 1912, whose originators were quite conscious that it would trigger competition from the Reich's potential enemies. They took the step for three principal reasons, all of which arose nearly simultaneously and reinforced each other. One of these had little to do with the military balance on land, but much to do with the general military-diplomatic confrontation and the naval race. This was the Reich chancellor's effort to introduce an army bill for the purpose of heading off a new naval increase that threatened to wreck his policy of repairing relations with Britain after the crisis. The other two sources of the 1912 military law were immediate results of perceptions of the balance of military power. On the one hand, members of the public and especially the national parties in the Reichstag expressed disappointment and alarm at Germany's capitulation over Morocco. They sought reasons for it in military weakness and redress for it in military revival. On the other hand, the army leaders themselves reevaluated Germany's strategic position as a result of what had happened in the summer of 1911. They suddenly began to take a serious view of the prospect of a general European war that would pit Germany against a formidable array of opponents. All three of these impulses resulted in a move to increase the army without regard for the dangers, in an atmosphere where the domestic political situation favored it and the international environment seemed to demand it. None of the three influences would have been decisive on its own. The military law of 1912 was a result of the interpenetration of perceived political, diplomatic, and military imperatives that brought about a full-scale land armaments race in Europe in the years immediately before 1914. The framers of the resulting bill designed it partly as a political weapon, but mostly as a military one. They regarded it as both a deterrent to war and a means of preparing for one.

The influence least related to the balance of military power was Bethmann Hollweg's search for a means of preempting any new naval law in 1912.[61] Tirpitz exploited the Moroccan crisis to call for a supplementary battleship-construction bill, or *Novelle*, while the confrontation was still in progress. Britain's stern response to the German challenge at Agadir, and the wave of Anglophobic chauvinism this raised among Reich nationalists, gave the naval secretary an opportunity to demand a Novelle that would keep Germany building capital ships at a high rate even after the current program lapsed. Bethmann was alarmed, knowing that a big new naval bill would torpedo his chances of securing any kind of rapprochement with Britain, a relationship he desired all the more after the hostile stance the British had taken in the crisis. Tirpitz's scheme would also ruin the Reich chancellor's domestic policy. Bethmann hoped to ease back on the immense naval spending pressures that made it so hard to maintain simultaneously a semblance of fiscal stability, a party grouping in the Reichstag that embraced the right and center of the political spectrum, and the nonprogressive and uneconomical tax structure upon which the conservative political consensus depended. Adolf Wermuth, the treasury secretary, firmly opposed naval spending increases in his efforts to enforce fiscal responsibility while avoiding tax increases. The kaiser, however, began to favor Tirpitz's plan in September 1911, and Bethmann cast about for some means of talking him out of it.

During the last phase of the Moroccan negotiations, he hit upon the idea of introducing an army expansion bill that would serve as an alternative and take up all the available funds. The prospect of a new military law suited the requirements of the government as well as the soldiers, and developed in a series of conversations between Wermuth, Bethmann Hollweg, and Heeringen in late September and October 1911.[62] With some prompting from the chancellor, the war minister declared in a conversation on 9 October that "the changed political situation" made an army increase desirable.[63] Heeringen's statement was cautious and conditional, however, as well as highly secret. Even the General War Department of his ministry knew nothing of it at first, and as late as January 1912 they were still uncertain what would be decided.[64] It was enough for Bethmann to work with, however, during long- and short-range budget planning consultations with Wermuth and the kaiser in the fall of 1912.[65] He convinced the emperor, who had in any case for some years been in favor of strengthening the army, that a costly increase in the military budget would be necessary in 1912, breaking with the Quinquennat to introduce a new, raised, five-year plan of expansion. Bethmann's strategy backfired catastrophically, however. The army law went through, but did not stop the navy's Novelle from passing as well. This saddled the government with all the disadvantages of both: astronomical new financial burdens, a consequent political crisis over how to fund the increase through taxes, and continued antagonism toward England alongside a more aggressive posture on land.

What allowed the government to make its case for the army law in the first place was a transformation in public perceptions of military power during the Moroccan crisis. A call for action arose in the Reichstag and in the patriotic and naval leagues that had grown strong during the Bülow years. Kiderlen-Wächter bore considerable responsibility for this movement. In the first place, his combative policy and public utterances during the crisis heightened the sense of confrontation and chauvinism surrounding German *Weltpolitik*. In addition, by ostentatiously nailing the Reich's colors to the mast over the Moroccan question, he made the subsequent treaty in November seem like a colossal forfeit of the country's honor and prowess as he had defined it. Finally, he conspired explicitly with nationalist leaders, most importantly Heinrich Claß, leader of the Pan-German League, to launch a publicity campaign for extravagant claims against France. This produced extensive results especially when reinforced by Tirpitz's similar collaboration with the Navy League to agitate against Britain's obstruction of German world-political aspirations.[66] The movement, added to Kiderlen's policies, provoked reactions in the press throughout Europe, especially in France and Britain.

In the military sphere this manifested itself particularly in praise for French triumphs in aviation, and in a wave of criticism directed against the German army. These attempts to portray Germany as militarily inferior had a highly partisan, journalistic cast to them, but they were persistent enough to stimulate genuine debate in German public and political circles about the army's readiness. This controversy turned into an uproar when the government retreated over the Moroccan issue in an atmosphere of military confrontation. The feats of French aviators had enjoyed prominence for some time, but in 1911 they soared to almost legendary altitudes. Military observers had long criticized the German army for inflexible and outmoded tactics. The issue exploded in the

public realm, however, when the London *Times* published a series of
articles in October 1911 by its acclaimed military correspondent, the
retired Lieutenant-Colonel Charles à Court Repington, expounding a
devastating critique of the September *Kaisermanöver*.[67] At every level
from generalship to small-unit tactics, Repington reported on rigid, predictable, obsolete practices, and stung German pride with his overall
verdict: "The German Army, apart from its numbers, confidence in itself, and high state of organization, does not present any signs of superiority over the best foreign models, and in some ways does not rise above
the level of the second rate."[68]

The combined effect was an outraged reaction in the Reichstag when
the crisis was over. Bethmann tried to defend the government's Morocco policy in the chamber debates on the treaty in November, but
met with a storm of abuse.[69] Only the Social Democratic Party, ironi-
cally enough, defended the government's moderation in the final settlement. All other parties, from the Conservatives to the Center and National Liberals, and even the Independents, denounced Bethmann's and
Kiderlen's policy of engaging Germany's prestige and then giving way at
the last moment. The main speakers of all the bourgeois parties denounced Britain in particular for its hostility toward Germany. Ernst
Bassermann, chairman of the National Liberals, led the call for a policy
of rearmament to deter future trespassing against Germany's "honor."
He demanded a naval bill primarily, but intimations came from all sides,
notably from the normally cautious agrarian-conservative leader, Ernst
von Heydebrand und der Lasa, that military preparations of all kinds
must be on the agenda. The non-Socialist parties other than the Independents all hailed the emergence of nationalistic sentiments as the only
positive result of the crisis. Such emotions only grew stronger in the
wake of the Reichstag debate, gaining intensity as the government pub-
licized its plans for naval and military bills.

The movement for a new armament effort on land reached its climax
in January 1912, when a retired general, August Keim, formed the
Deutscher Wehrverein, a national Army League, expressly to agitate for
military increases.[70] At the same moment the renowned military expert,
General Friedrich von Bernhardi, published *Germany and the Next War*,
written in 1911 under the influence of the Moroccan crisis.[71] In this
two-volume work, Bernhardi articulated an ultramilitarist doctrine of
the "biological necessity" of warfare, arguing that a Germany increasingly surrounded by hostile powers must one day embark on an offensive war to smash France forever in a climactic fight for existence.
"World power or extinction" was his slogan. He adopted a vulgarized
Darwinist world view and ruthless concern with armament and military
efficiency, even at the cost of disrupting the hierarchic social structure

upon which Germany's military and political elite depended. His arguments were typical of the Wehrverein's program as a whole and of the right-radical militarist movement that burst into prominence in the wake of the second Moroccan crisis. The war ministry and the government had no hand in the foundation of the Wehrverein or in the formulation of its call for rearmament, and indeed reacted to its pressure with little enthusiasm.[72]

The final element in the genesis of the 1912 army law was a profound reassessment of the balance of military power by the army leaders themselves in Germany. The diplomatic events of the Moroccan crisis, combined with the realization that the military power of potential enemy armies had grown, prompted them to take a far grimmer and more urgent view of the strategic situation. The transformation of attitudes in the civilian leadership as well as in the Reichstag presented the military command with both the opportunity and the imperative to devote new resources to the army. During the crisis General von Heeringen had confined himself to authorizing Moltke to carry out further long-term improvements in the equipment and encadrement of reserve brigades and corps.[73] Even afterward, the war minister temporized for more than a month while Bethmann toyed with the idea of a new military bill. It was probably not a coincidence that Heeringen finally presented the chancellor with a concrete and extensive demand for an army law on 19 November 1911, a week after the Reichstag's Morocco debate and just after he learned that the kaiser would approve Tirpitz's Novelle.[74] The cautious-minded war ministry took its cue to some extent from Bethmann's urgings and from the Reichstag's agitation, having always paid close attention to what was attainable in parliament, and to protecting the army's public image.[75] But when the generals did demand a budget increase, they showed that there had also been strong military reasons for their reserve, and that their subsequent conversion was far more than merely a reluctant submission to politics.

General von Heeringen's memorandum to Bethmann calling for a new army law on 19 November 1911 was the manifesto for a complete reappraisal of the likelihood of war.[76] It represented a decision in favor of massive rearmament. The war ministry had always warned the government that this would be the prelude to a major conflict, and a step to be taken only if such a struggle seemed inevitable and imminent.[77] In the aftermath of the Moroccan crisis, Heeringen made up his mind on this dilemma. If a navy law were to pass, he decided, the army would have to be strengthened simultaneously in preparation for a war that must almost certainly follow. The navy's persistent defiance of Britain was growing risky with Tirpitz's latest Novelle, Heeringen argued, and the Agadir crisis had heated up the atmosphere to the point where

Germany's enemies might take anything as an excuse to start a war. "The introduction of a German naval bill might provide such a cause," he wrote, "especially if the hypothesis is correct that England's finances no longer permit it to outbid the armaments of other powers at sea." Since naval expenditure took so long to translate itself into battleships afloat, Germany would be vulnerable if it provoked the Entente without a suitable deterrent on land: "Under these circumstances the War Minister and the Chief of the Army General Staff consider it imperative that a strengthening of German armed power not be carried out unilaterally in favor of the navy, but rather that a reinforcement of the army in a measure calculated to insure peace must take place at the same time. If both cannot be done simultaneously, then the army must be expanded first. . . . Under its protection, so to speak, the reinforcement of the navy can take place."[78]

Heeringen argued that a war seemed all the more possible as long as the army did not inspire the kind of fear that had deterred adversaries in the past. He himself considered the forces adequate, at least for the time being, but the uproar over the crisis had persuaded him that not everyone thought the same way. "The War Minister and the Chief of the Army General Staff," he wrote, "are convinced that the German army is still equal to its opponents." The war ministry was in the habit of discounting French fanfares about aircraft as premature since aeroplanes were not yet ready to win a war.[79] Repington's criticisms of the German army maneuvers were a public embarrassment, but they did not set off undue alarm in the German high command itself since they contained the usual catalogue of indictments, were obviously designed as a partisan blow in the crisis, and were written about a set of maneuvers that everyone, including the Germans themselves, had agreed were exceptionally poor compared to other years.[80] The French canceled their grand maneuvers in 1911 due to the crisis and replaced them with a smaller exercise.[81] Heeringen asserted, however, that a certain danger lay in the growing tendency of the public to think that the German army was weak, regardless of the real state of affairs. The army might be strong enough for the present, he wrote; "But it is already certain today that the German field army no longer commands so much respect in the eyes of our enemies as to deter a test of arms with it. . . . As a result we will certainly have to reckon with a war—as far as this can be said about such questions at all—if any particular provocation to it is given." The German army had to expand as long as it did not present the appearance of strength sufficient to intimidate all potential opponents.

Just over a week later, the war ministry laid out the shape that a new law should take, together with a more specific exposition of the military situation that demanded it. This came in a memorandum on 29 November from General von Wandel in the General War Department, who would be responsible for drafting the bill.[82] Wandel began by contrasting the situation that had yielded the prevailing moderate Quinquennat with the circumstances after the Moroccan crisis:

> The information that has newly become public concerning the course of political events last summer makes Germany's military position appear in a substantially different light from when the last peacetime strength law was introduced. At that time we expected only France as a definite enemy. Although Russia was allied to it, one could nevertheless assume after the Potsdam agreement of autumn '10 and in view of the military weakness of Russia at the time, that it would take part only half-heartedly, if at all, in a Franco-German war. The Entente with England appeared to be based more on its moral support than on actual cooperation by its army and fleet.

However, this state of affairs was beginning to erode, Wandel wrote. Germany still enjoyed a strong military position and its rivals had not yet completed their rearmament, but the relative strengths of the alliance blocs were changing:

> Today this point of view is still basically correct. But now we know that the number of our likely enemies has grown, while that of our allies has decreased. England will be on France's side under all circumstances, and will support it not only with diplomatic notes, but with strong land and sea power. It seems beyond doubt that Russia is working with gigantic financial resources on the reconstruction of its army and, now that it is no longer hampered by the worry of complications in the far east, will be inclined to give vent to the ever-growing anti-German mood through active participation in war.

Furthermore, the Germans could no longer even remotely hope that Italy would honor its Triple Alliance commitment to put pressure on France since for two months the Italians had been growing ever more deeply involved in the conquest of Libya from the Ottoman Empire. Belgium and Holland would tie down more German troops in the future, and France might receive reinforcements from Africa.

To Wandel, the Moroccan crisis had shown above all that a war might now occur at any time. The unexpected military confrontation arising from Kiderlen's Agadir gambit had shaken the army leadership out of the conviction that it would have ample warning before any conflict. Wandel reasoned, much as Heeringen did, that "we must draw still another lesson from the past: that we are never safe from a war, but rather that our enemies will force one upon us without fear of consequences that will affect the entire world, whether by a direct declaration of war or by some form of challenge that Germany's honor makes it impossible to tolerate." The Germans, no longer the only ones confident of their power, could no longer expect to be the only ones to wield the threat of war as a bluff in international politics. In particular, Wandel pointed to the new offensive doctrine that Joffre and others were bringing to the French army, which meant that an attack might be expected from the west now, rather than merely a reaction to a Schlieffen-style offensive.

The Moroccan crisis had also furnished an unprecedented political opportunity for reinforcing the army to meet these new dangers. Wandel urged presenting a military bill while the Reichstag was prepared to vote for it. He observed: "The ground is favorably prepared for this as scarcely ever before. At present few Germans would deny that we are surrounded by enemies, that a war with them is scarcely to be avoided, and that Germany's position in the world is therefore at stake. In recognition of this, numerous voices have already spoken out loudly from various parties for a strengthening of the army; people are generally resolved for such a proposition." The war ministry's two constant objections to an army increase had suddenly fallen away in 1911: the strategic situation had turned from calm to threatening, and parliamentary opposition had turned to support.

General von Wandel's plan was to complete the 1911 "technical Quinquennat" in one year instead of five, and supplement it with a large new military bill that would greatly expand the forces overall. The peacetime strength would rise, though still not above the limit of 1 percent of the population set by the constitution. The continual buffeting of the army's budgets in the Reichstag had kept the numbers well below this proportion—to the outrage of general staff officers who watched the French squeeze more than 1.2 percent of their much smaller population into uniform to create an army nearly as big. Wandel proposed replacing reservists in many units with regulars. This reinforcement would have the side effect of pouring more trained men into the reserves every year for recall in wartime. It was also the moment, Wandel proposed, to establish two new army corps in peacetime. The two "Kriegskorps" of spare regular units, which were to have been improvised on mobilization, would now receive standard recruitment districts and higher command elements from peacetime, raising the regular strength from twenty-three corps to twenty-five. Finally, the technical units that the army had stitched together with personnel transferred from regular formations must receive full permanent establishments and command structures. There must be a standard machine gun company for every regiment ("the foreign armies are numerically superior to us in this arm"), as well as searchlight units, a new telegraph battalion, a permanent aviation branch, and perhaps another railway battalion.

The war ministry's new attitude was welcome to the war planners of the general staff, who had long pressed for more money and soldiers, and who had likewise been shocked into a new sense of emergency by the events of 1911. On 2 December General von Moltke responded to a request from Heeringen by sending the Reich chancellor a rambling seventeen-page exposition of his strategic views.[83] The chief of the general staff predicted a war, stemming from French aggression or a collision of British and German interests. He saw no possibility of fighting either France or Britain by itself. The British would certainly back the French, and Germany would have to invade France in the case of a war with Britain. Above all, Moltke feared that Russia would now intervene in such a conflict. The balance in any European war seemed to be tilting heavily against Germany. The experience of 1911 had put aside all doubt, he wrote: "The political grouping of Europe today will make an isolated war between France and Germany as far as can be foreseen impossible. If it comes to a military clash between the two states, the remaining great powers will be drawn in as well in such a way as to force active intervention upon them." Besides the British army now being ready to put 130,000 to 150,000 men on the continent, Moltke warned: "It is not true to assert that Russia is still incapable of engaging in a European war for some time." He pointed to the improvement of the reserve system and to increases in the number of corps consequently ready for front-line service. The redistribution of garrisons and improvement of rail lines, he alleged, had cut mobilization time in half compared to five years earlier. The field artillery had been rearmed, some heavy field guns procured, and new siege artillery ordered. The Russians had improved their fortifications and rejuvenated the high command. In a European war Germany would still throw almost everything into the Schlieffen offensive against France first, leaving a minimum of troops opposite Russia. But now the entire army could not face westward as in 1905, and in the European balance as a whole the numbers had begun to weigh against Germany and Austria-Hungary. "For a number of years now," the chief of staff wrote, "the situation in this respect has shifted substantially to the detriment of the allied Monarchies."

Moltke portrayed Germany and Austria-Hungary as encircled by hostile powers. Even Belgium and Holland were discussing military increases for security after the Moroccan crisis. Italy had virtually defected from the Triple Alliance, and might draw Austro-Hungarian forces away from the Russian front. The Italians' war against the Ottomans in Libya decreased the chances that the Turks would help Berlin and Vienna in a great-power conflict. "Everyone is preparing for the great war," wrote Moltke, "which they all expect sooner or later." Only Austria-Hungary was paralyzed by its intractable legislature, while Germany, "surrounded by enemies, . . . leaves thousands of its able-bodied men untrained every year, and consequently useless for national defense." Moltke concluded with an ominous call for preparedness that began to sound like the military-Darwinistic rhetoric of Conrad or, more recently, Bernhardi and the Wehrverein:

> The political relations of Europe today are such that its future configuration will probably be decided only by a war of the opposing blocs against one another.
>
> But it always remains the duty of every state not only to look the future calmly in the eye, but also to prepare itself for the day of decision that will judge whether its inner strength gives it the right to further claims on life or not.
>
> Germany must arm for this decision. I consider both a further development of its fleet and a greater drawing upon its able-bodied manpower, that is to say a raising of the peacetime strength, as an imperative of self-preservation. Both must go hand in hand.

Moltke's was only the most extreme statement of one of the three main influences that converged to produce the army law of 1912. None of it might have happened without Tirpitz's efforts to pass a new naval bill which heated up the situation so much that Bethmann was prepared to resort to an army increase to forestall it. The proposals for naval as well as military laws would probably have led nowhere if the Moroccan politics had not caused outrage in the Reichstag and nationalist circles and produced a parliamentary mandate of the kind that emerged in the autumn of 1911. And finally the particular notion of a massive military bill, intruding upon the Quinquennat, seemed justified to the generals only as a consequence of a reevaluation of the dangers facing Germany and a belief that war might be imminent. The army leaders had no special desire to stamp out Tirpitz's naval bill as Bethmann did, and their secret memoranda to the chancellor revealed motivations that went far beyond any mere bowing to the pressure of the Reichstag and militaristic agitators like Keim and Bernhardi.[84] The acceptance of the idea of a future war was a major component of all these ways of thinking, with the possible exception of Bethmann's. It was a new feature of discussions in 1911, despite previous diplomatic bluffs with threats of war. Much of this was due to the changed perception of the balance of military power that the outcome of the Moroccan crisis forced upon the public and the generals. It did not yet result in a call for preventive war, but many of the components of such a calculation were already in place at the highest levels in Germany when the military bill took shape.

The German army increase passed in the Reichstag with the support of all the bourgeois parties at the same time as Tirpitz's supplementary naval law, in May 1912.[85] It essentially fulfilled the outline proposed by Wandel in November. The provisions of the 1911 Quinquennat were accelerated for completion by 31 October 1912. Thereafter the peace-time strength was to increase by two new permanent corps, and over the course of the next four years more regulars, permanent technical forma-tions, and machine gun units would all be added. In effect, the prevail-ing Quinquennat was simply enlarged by some 188.2 million marks and 28,890 men. The bill survived an acrimonious dispute between the war ministry and Wermuth, who refused to accept the enormous financial strain of the naval and military laws at once without a corresponding property tax that would draw upon the major potential sources of reve-nue in the Reich.[86] Bethmann found it impossible, as ever, to reconcile the right-wing parties of the largest property owners to this notion, and refused to sacrifice their interests to the center and left. The chancellor had even less room for maneuver than usual after the Social Democrats, enemies of all military expansion, became the largest party in the Reich-stag in the January 1912 elections. Wermuth resigned in March when the kaiser and Bethmann insisted on proposing the bills irrespective of financial difficulties. The atmosphere of conflict also extended to the in-ternational sphere. The failure of negotiations with Britain for slowing the pace of naval armament, most notably with the maladroit reception of Lord Haldane's mission to Berlin for special talks in February 1912, contributed to the impetus for passage of the fleet and army measures. Bethmann managed to keep the military and naval chiefs from explicitly directing the increases against particular foreign powers, but he could not prevent many of the nationalist party leaders from calling for the vote with chauvinistic speeches denouncing the enemies that were alleg-edly encircling the Reich.[87]

In other countries the reactions to the second Moroccan crisis were not so extreme, but they were nevertheless notable. France and Britain had won, which prompted less self-examination. The unilateral German move at Agadir and Kiderlen's bellicose posture in negotiations led to ever more suspicion of Germany at all levels. In France a note of tri-umphalism brought the election of a nationalistic Chamber of Deputies in January 1912, which installed Raymond Poincaré, the dynamic evan-gelist of a *réveil national,* as prime minister. The military and naval staffs in London and Paris also completed their plans for the prompt delivery of a British Expeditionary Force to the continent.[88] The Italians took the opportunity of the northern powers' involvement in the confronta-

tion over Morocco to launch their invasion of Tripolitania and Cyrenaica, at a time when none of the European colonial powers was in a
position to alienate Rome by vetoing the move. Operations soon
bogged down in a guerrilla war over a largely desert land, with the Ottoman Empire keeping resistance in Libya alive against the Italians, who
found their expeditionary force rapidly expanding to over a hundred
thousand men in 1912 without any appreciable progress.[89] The first intimations of Italy's entanglement in Libya in turn prompted Conrad to
call on Aehrenthal and Franz Joseph to unleash a preventive war across
the Alps while the enemy was distracted.[90] This was finally too much for
Aehrenthal and for the emperor too, who sacked Conrad after an outburst of wrath at Schönbrunn Palace in November 1911.[91]

The most significant military consequence of the second Moroccan
crisis remained the German decision to embark on an extraordinary program of land armament in the expectation of a future war. Kiderlen-
Wächter had begun the confrontation with no such thought in mind, as
an effort to play the game of diplomatic bluff. The military situation did
not look favorable to either side in the crisis. There was no overwhelming imbalance of forces as in 1909, or even a substantial one as there had
been in 1905. The result, however, was a defeat and a traumatic realization for the Germans. The military leaders in Berlin decided they would
probably have to fight a war, and fight it against Russia and the western
powers together. To this perception on the part of the soldiers was
added the public alarm that resulted from giving way in the crisis under
the shadow of widespread debates about military effectiveness, and of
martial posturing and agitation orchestrated by elements of the leadership as well as by outsiders. These impulses brought forth the strange
conjunction of Tirpitz's *Novelle,* Bethmann's plan to steer across its
bows with an army bill, and the call for a military effort. The resulting
German army law started an international spiral of land-armaments construction. The Germans regarded themselves as responding to a threat
from all sides, but at the same time they took the plunge in full expectation that their rivals would react, and that war would only be a matter of
time. In due course, the prophecy fulfilled itself.

Chapter 6

THE BALKAN WARS AND
THE SPIRAL OF ARMAMENTS, 1912–1913

ON 8 OCTOBER 1912, the First Balkan War broke out when Montenegro declared war on the Ottoman Empire. Serbia, Bulgaria, and Greece joined in nine days later. Linked by a series of alliances concluded in the past year, the Balkan states flung themselves into a struggle to conquer all the lands the Ottoman Empire still controlled in the Balkans (see Map 3).[1] With the Turks weakened by their continuing campaign to hold Libya against the Italians, the autumn of 1912 presented an opportunity for the Balkan states to claim their shares of European Turkey. The Porte hastily concluded its protracted negotiations with the Italian government, signed away its sovereignty over Tripolitania and Cyrenaica, and turned all of its strength to the defense of its possessions in Europe. The Ottoman lands there were the key to the defense of Istanbul and the straits, as well as the empire's assurance of a continuing role in European affairs. But the war was a disaster for the Turks. On 24 October the Serbs smashed one Ottoman force in Macedonia at Kumanovo, while the Bulgarians won a simultaneous victory at Kirk Kilise. Within a month of the opening of hostilities the Greek army had occupied Salonika, and the Turks had lost all of their European possessions: Albania, Epirus, Macedonia, and Thrace. They retreated to Chatalja, the last defensive position before Istanbul. There, with the rumble of shellfire audible in the capital, they finally held the Bulgarians, fighting them to a standstill until peace negotiations opened in December. There was a renewed outbreak of combat that winter, and a second Balkan war in the summer of 1913 as the victors fought among themselves over the distribution of the territorial spoils. The Ottomans managed to regain eastern Thrace as far as Edirne (Adrianople), but their expulsion from the rest of Europe was final.

The defeat swung the strategic balance in Europe heavily against the German/Austro-Hungarian alliance and arrived just in time to bring a fresh burst of urgency to an armaments race that was fast developing among the great powers. Quite apart from the diplomatic crisis caused by the prospect of intervention, particularly on the part of Austria-Hungary, the wars eliminated the Ottoman Empire as a counterweight to the Balkan states in southeastern Europe and replaced it with a greatly strengthened array of Balkan powers fielding expanded and battle-hardened armies. Most importantly, Serbia and Montenegro posed a wholly new threat to Austria-Hungary. No longer a pair of tiny principalities with feeble armed forces, they were now certain to be dangerous enemies of the Dual Monarchy in any European conflict.[2] The result of the Balkan Wars gave new urgency to German and Austro-Hungarian preparations for such a general conflagration, spurring on a race to arms that had already begun with the 1912 army law in Germany. It brought forth another, even larger German army bill and ensured that the momentum generated by the Agadir crisis would continue. The result contributed to a perception in Berlin and Vienna that the military situation was growing ever more threatening and must eventually lead to a war for survival. In the absence of successful efforts to find a political route out of the dilemma, this change in the strategic balance helped induce a mentality that made statesmen, above all in Austria-Hungary, prepared to accept the risk of war in 1914 as they had not been in previous crises.

REACTIONS TO THE GERMAN ARMY LAW AND THE BALKAN WARS

Before the outbreak of the First Balkan War, a land armaments race between the European powers was already under way in 1912. The separate governments carried out military expansions and strategic collaboration in explicit reaction to perceived threats from their rivals, and a reciprocal dynamic of military increases ensued. The process repeated what had taken place between the navies of the great powers in preceding decades, though with greater urgency for most countries because armies represented a more vital threat among continental states than fleets did. The competition in land armaments in 1912 eclipsed naval construction. It arose above all from the German army law of that year, and consisted mainly of reactions on the part of the Entente. The French recognized that the German move had been prompted by fear as a result of the second Moroccan crisis and the alignment of Entente power it had revealed.[3] This realization, however, did not make the German expansion appear any less threatening. The army law was a direct challenge, and the response was not slow in coming.

In France it was greatly facilitated by the nationalist revival that followed the Agadir crisis.[4] This outpouring of patriotic emotion was partly a product of the confrontation itself, during which the press had portrayed France's reputation and greatness as being at stake. It was also the result of Raymond Poincaré's effort to break the dominance of the Radical party in French politics by brandishing the banner of nationalism to distract attention from issues of social egalitarianism and relations between church and state. For a strong foreign policy in the face of the apparent German menace, he could gather support from a wide variety of parties and assemble a shifting majority that no longer depended invariably upon the Radicals and their domestic program.[5] The Germans gave Poincaré his opportunity with Agadir and the 1912 army law. The protagonist of his muscular external policy was the French army, which the nationalists took every opportunity to exalt. Public military displays, like the reinstitution of the *retraite* played by military bands in the streets of Paris, became increasingly conspicuous, and the officer corps regained social prestige.[6]

All of the Entente powers strengthened their armies. In the course of 1912 the French war ministry succeeded in pushing two more *lois des cadres* through the Chamber of Deputies, this time to buttress the infantry and cavalry. These laws reorganized units and reassigned officers in order to increase the readiness of the regular formations and prepare more reserve units to mobilize alongside them.[7] Aeroplanes, which continued to inspire vast enthusiasm, found their military worth confirmed when the Italian command in Tripoli began to rely heavily on them for reconnaissance in the Libyan desert from late 1911 onward.[8] The French still had the largest and most advanced air service in the world, while by dint of sheer spending the Russians reached second place in numbers of aircraft available by 1912.[9] In that year the French and British armies began organizing their aircraft into regular squadrons with fixed establishments, assigned to ground units or fortresses.[10] The Russian army increased its annual recruit contingent by a law of July 1912, which was to take effect with the class called up in 1913. It eliminated a host of special dispensations that had exempted a large proportion of the able-bodied men from military service.[11] The annual call-up increased by 20,000, to over 450,000 per year. Test mobilizations continued and reserve training increased. New war plans went into effect, less defensive and designed to send attacks westward sooner.[12]

The Entente powers above all took extensive and often ostentatious measures to cement their joint strategy in 1912. In the summer the French reached naval agreements with both Russia and Britain. The latter was by far the more important. It moved the principal wartime base of the French fleet from Brest to Toulon, where it would deploy mostly in the Mediterranean in the event of war and leave the Royal Navy to concentrate on operating in the North Sea and protecting the Channel and Atlantic coasts of France.[13] This effective distribution of labor meant that the German fleet would face the undivided attention of its most formidable opponent at sea. To improve the strategic situation on land, Poincaré made a celebrated visit to Russia in August. He talked to the tsar, to Kokovtsev who was now prime minister, and to the new foreign minister Sergei Sazonov, urging all of them to improve the strategic railway network in the west.[14] Most prominently of all, the French grand maneuvers in September boasted two leading Entente military figures as guests of honor. Sir Henry Wilson was invited from Britain and invested with the Legion of Honor. Also at Joffre's side was the Grand Duke Nicholas Nikolaevich, the tsar's uncle and designated commander of the field army in wartime, with a large retinue of senior Russian officers. The Entente commanders cut a conspicuous figure on the maneuver field (not least because both Wilson and the Grand Duke stood over six feet tall) and made rousing speeches of solidarity at numerous banquets.[15] Afterward Nicholas toured fortresses and camps in Lorraine with Joffre and the war minister, Aléxandre Millerand, receiving lavish military honors. His wife, the Grand Duchess Anastasia, won popular adulation by gathering up a handful of soil from Lorraine to bring back to Russia, and the visit of the imperial couple to Paris was a sensational social and public relations success.

In more discreet diplomatic circles, the French managed by November 1912 to extract a commitment from Sir Edward Grey to consult on joint military plans if war threatened. The Foreign Office still carefully avoided anything that explicitly bound Britain to join France in a war against Germany, but the letters exchanged between Grey and the French ambassador, Paul Cambon, contained a formula that went beyond anything previously conceded: "If either Government had grave reason to expect an unprovoked attack by a third Power, or something that threatened the general peace, it should immediately discuss with the other, whether both Governments should act together to prevent aggression and to preserve peace, and if so what measures they would be prepared to take in common. If these measures involved common action, the plans of the General Staffs would at once be taken into consideration, and the Governments would then decide what effect should be given to them."[16] The combination of the Grey-Cambon letters, the Anglo-French naval agreement, and Sir Henry Wilson's vigorous war planning with the French created momentum for actual support of France in the event of a conflict, to the alarm of many cabinet members who were against any sort of commitment.[17]

Even in Austria-Hungary with its deadlocked legislature, the general armament of 1912 produced enough unease to stimulate a military increase. Conrad's successor as chief of staff, General Blasius Schemua, had views on strategy that scarcely differed from Conrad's own, advocating a violent, expansionist foreign policy aimed chiefly at dominating the Balkans. He wrote to Franz Joseph in February 1912 that international affairs were in a "critical period," characterized by "social unrest, armaments fever, economic collapse. We are already in the midst of war;

only the decisive final action is still to come."[18] Schemua called on the government to join in the general "competition" with armament measures of its own. The changed mood of the joint council of ministers became apparent in the debate over new military spending in July.[19] Berchtold, now the foreign minister, warned of the prospect of Anglo-German or Austro-Russian tension in any of several areas causing a general war: "Each of these instances could at any moment place us in the necessity of having to grasp at the *ultima ratio.*" This was quite different from the reassuring language that Aehrenthal had always used with his ministerial colleagues. Indeed, Berchtold argued, "the situation was quite different from a year earlier." The war minister, General Moritz von Auffenberg, feared having to fight both Italy and Russia at once over a Balkan conflict. He warned that "if a war were forced upon us, he would not be able to put our chances in it at more than 2:3." For once, both the minister-president and the finance minister of the Austrian part of the monarchy expressed themselves prepared to accept the financial and political cost of more military credits "under the pressure of the external situation." The Hungarian ministers still insisted that there was no money for new weaponry, although for a change they did agree to a substantial increase in the peacetime strength. The most important convert was István Tisza, by then the leading moderate in Hungary. In June Tisza convinced the parliament in Budapest that the army was in grave enough straits to require implementation of the two-year service law that the high command had sought for years.[20] In return for the introduction of artillery in the Landwehr and Honvédség the Delegations voted for more men in the common army, serving for a shorter time but bringing units up closer to strength and permitting the long-postponed reorganization of the field artillery. The confident declarations of the preceding years had evaporated and the prospect of a future general war had begun to stimulate measures that the powers had not taken either in 1909 or during the second Moroccan crisis.

The result of the First Balkan War at the end of 1912, however, had an even more galvanizing effect. The new balance of power that the war brought about, as well as the large-scale fighting it involved, transformed the atmosphere of tension into one of emergency. Above all it came as a blow to Austria-Hungary, and consequently to its German ally as well. After grappling with the prospect of intervention by the Dual Monarchy to stop the South Slav victory before it became overwhelming, Berlin and Vienna turned to a fatalistic policy of preparing even more urgently for a general European settling of accounts. The Balkan War came at a moment when the Entente was feeling its strength. On 2 September, as the crisis approached, the French general staff had answered an inquiry of Poincaré's with a report estimating that if Austria-

Hungary entangled itself in a Balkan conflict it would not have enough strength left over to distract Russia seriously from Germany in a European war. Circumstances would be even more favorable if Britain joined in: "Under these conditions, the Triple Entente would have the greatest chances of success and could achieve a victory permitting it to remake the map of Europe."[21] Poincaré passed this news on to the Russians, and told Izvolsky on 10 October, after Montenegro declared war, that France would support Russian action in defense of the South Slavs against an Austro-Hungarian intervention. Sukhomlinov confidently invited the French military representatives in St. Petersburg in December to "tell them in Paris that they can rest assured, everything is ready here, without fuss; you will see."[22]

The war electrified Vienna. As it became clear that a conflict was about to break out in the Balkans, the joint council of ministers dropped its opposition to new spending on armaments and voted for the six-year increase of 250 million crowns for artillery and fortress construction which the Hungarians had blocked that summer.[23] "The situation today was indeed a different one from that in July," admitted the minister-president of Hungary. Berchtold described the state of affairs as "very serious." General von Auffenberg "considered a war with Russia in the next few years to be very likely." The general staff called for intervention at once, to attack Serbia while it was engaged to the south and before it grew too strong. First Schemua and then Conrad, after the latter was reinstated as chief of staff on 7 December 1912, argued repeatedly that the opportunity had come to crush Serbia while this was still possible.[24] Following Kirk Kilise and Kumanovo, Schemua gloomily calculated that after the war, with completed equipment and vast acquisitions of population and territory, Serbia and Montenegro would be able to marshal 400,000 men against Austria-Hungary, whereas at present the total would be only 185,000, a number the Dual Monarchy could hold off even if it mounted its main campaign against a Russian intervention. "*In the future,*" he wrote to the emperor, "*our forces will no longer be sufficient for both.*"[25]

The Vienna government wavered, however, and finally shied away from intervention throughout the Balkan Wars. It was clear to everyone that Russia might well join in and cause a general European conflict. The Hungarians, besides, were reluctant to embark even on a victorious campaign, since it would mean annexing more Slavic lands and diluting the Magyar predominance in the east.[26] Rather than intervening in either of the Balkan Wars and precipitating a European conflagration, the Dual Monarchy carried out military measures on the sidelines. Beginning in November 1912, the army called up reservists and raised the strength of units along the southern frontier and in Galicia.[27] These measures produced a half-armed standoff with Russia when the latter responded by retaining its departing class with the colors through the winter rather than sending them home in the autumn, as was customary when the new recruit contingent arrived for training.[28] This meant that there were four annual contingents under arms in Russia instead of the usual three, increasing the standing strength by a third and eliminating the period of vulnerability that afflicted most armies as they trained their new recruits each winter. During the Balkan Wars the Dual Monarchy passed a series of extraordinary military bills.[29] The joint finance minister washed his hands of responsibility for the fiscal consequences by declaring that, "as long as it was desired to maintain the Monarchy as a great power, these expenses must be borne. It would be necessary to give up Eastern Galicia, Tyrol, and Bosnia in order perhaps to buy some peace; but then of course that very great power which we wish to uphold would cease. . . . A war would perhaps be cheaper than the present state of affairs. It was useless to say we have no money. We must pay until a change comes about and we no longer have almost all of Europe against us."[30] The war ministry announced that the August 1913 increase was necessary "on the one hand due to technical innovations and on the other hand in view of the political situation that has changed drastically to the Monarchy's disadvantage."[31] Proclamations of military necessity and the inevitability of future war began to make themselves heard in the wider political debate, instead of being confined to the sulfurous secret memoranda of the chief of the general staff.[32]

In Berlin too, the Balkan conflict elicited talk of a general war. When Schemua visited in November, Moltke and Kaiser Wilhelm assured him that they would fight if Russia did.[33] The Prussian chief of staff expressed no qualms about a European war, in which, as he repeated, Germany would have to beat France before turning its main forces eastward. At the same time, Moltke began expressing the view that, since a general war was inevitable, it would be better to fight it at once rather than later, since the military balance was tilting steadily against Germany and Austria-Hungary. He made his first and frankest statement of this view at an emergency council with Tirpitz and two other senior naval commanders called by the kaiser, the so-called "War Council" of 8 December 1912.[34] The emperor raised the prospect of a European war being unleashed by Austro-Hungarian action against Serbia.[35] The chief of the general staff announced: "I consider a war to be inevitable, and the sooner the better." Tirpitz preferred to wait until the navy was stronger, to which Moltke retorted that the fleet would not be ready even years later, "and that the army would get into a steadily worse situation since our opponents armed faster than we did because we were very constrained by costs." Little came of these declarations at the time, made as they were among an ad hoc convocation of military leaders. Nevertheless, they clearly indicated the increasing tendency of some policy makers to think in apocalyptic terms as a result of the changing political and military situation. Later in the crisis, in February 1913, Moltke told the Austro-Hungarian military attaché that "the start of a world war was probably to be considered," though as often as not his declarations of this kind had a chastening effect on Vienna.[36] Bethmann suggested less enthusiasm for Austro-Hungarian intervention, unlike the firm mandate that Bülow had offered during the Bosnian crisis when Russian mobilization could be ruled out. No blank check was yet on offer to Vienna, nor were the Austrians quite ready to cash one.

The German Reaction to the Balkan Wars: The 1913 Army Law

The German reaction to the Balkan Wars was a fresh round of army expansion. The question of actually fighting was one that had to be decided in Vienna, and Moltke's declaration that sooner would be better for a European conflict did not determine the Reich's foreign policy. The chief of the general staff had uttered it at a meeting that included only himself, the kaiser, and the naval high command. The war minister, chancellor, and foreign secretary did not take part, and there is no evidence that they were aware of the proceedings, let alone directly influenced by them in their policy. What the Reich government did certainly reflected the expectation of a future war and the fear of rising military rivals, but it took the form of military increases rather than a drive for immediate war. It was a continuation, with greater urgency and on a larger scale, of the course taken with the 1912 army law.

The fears that had led to the 1912 expansion never really abated, but the Balkan Wars lent them added force. Outside of government, pressure came from the Wehrverein, the right-radical militarists in general, and Heinrich Claß, the Pan-German leader whose turgid manifesto for social and military transformation of the state appeared in his book *If I Were the Kaiser* in the spring of 1912.[37] None of these publicistic elements ceased their agitation when the 1912 law passed. Instead they called for a total commitment to military efficiency and the use of all the nation's able-bodied manpower for the armed forces. The outbreak of the First Balkan War raised the level of excitement and added fresh fuel to the ultranationalist agitation. The kaiser, ever a champion of military readiness, first proposed another army bill on 13 October 1912, at the very beginning of the Balkan conflict. He summoned Bethmann, Kiderlen-Wächter, Heeringen, and von Moltke to a meeting, together with the chief of his military cabinet, in the imperial hunting lodge at Huber-tusstock.[38] He proposed introducing a new army law as the Austro-Hungarian government had just done, and later suggested that both the army and the navy take advantage of the public's present willingness to make sacrifices for the armed forces.[39]

The Balkan Wars persuaded the military leaders that the future would demand such an increase, and provided them with a public justification for it. At the October meeting, Heeringen and Moltke denied the need for any further expansion and argued that it would be impractical.[40] In the course of the next month and a half, however, they changed their minds. As the devastating news of the campaign in the Balkans unfolded, Moltke, Heeringen, and even Bethmann began to agree that they needed to strengthen the army more rapidly than ever.[41] Even before the "War Council" of the kaiser and his military chiefs on 8 December, the movement for a new army law was well afoot. Moltke acted partly under the influence of the energetic Colonel Erich Ludendorff, who had just risen to an influential position on the general staff, determined to transform Germany into an efficient nation in arms somewhat as Keim and Bernhardi envisioned it. Initially the generals pretended that their demands arose from the danger of a "sudden attack" on the Reich by Russia and France.[42] They played upon the public alarm aroused by the Balkan conflict, Russia's retention of the outgoing recruit class under arms, and news of Joffre's preparations to take the offensive in a future war under Plan XVII. In fact an overall increase in the peacetime strength, of the kind they proposed, would have done little to avert any present danger, against which the German army took no preventive measures at all.

The real purpose of the plan was to meet a change in the military balance that the high command foresaw as a result of the current crisis. In a clarification to Heeringen on 2 December, Moltke admitted that the situation was not unduly threatening for the time being, and that the real danger lay in the future:

> For the moment we can face a war with confidence, since Russia is not ready, while France is on the one hand heavily engaged in Morocco and on the other hand menaced by Italy's alignment with Austria and Germany. The military-political situation is therefore a favorable one for us at present. But it can change. In two or three years Russia will have gained strength, France may be unburdened in Africa, and the latent antagonism may be revived between Italy and Austria, which in turn may be challenged by the militarily strengthened Balkan states. Then Germany must be strong enough to rely on its own power, and can therefore not undertake the development of its military strength soon enough.[43]

Heeringen repeated much the same thing to Bethmann in a meeting later that month.[44] The war minister also expressed his usual concern for the army's public image, complaining that he could not ignore the rising demand from the Wehrverein, the Pan-Germans, and others for broader military service as long as the necessary manpower was available in the population. At the same time the question of an army increase had arisen in the Reichstag when the National Liberal leader Ernst Basserman proposed a move to universal service and bigger financial sacrifices during debates on the Reich military budget at the beginning of December.[45] The kaiser was likewise pushing Heeringen to take action, and Bethmann had to admonish the war minister and Admiral Tirpitz against making ambitious spending plans with the emperor behind the government's back.[46]

The changing military balance also became the public justification for the new military law when the government put it before the Reichstag at the beginning of 1913. Bethmann painted a pessimistic picture of Germany's strategic situation when he wrote to secure the consent of the federal governments of the Reich states on 8 February.[47] The 1912 army law, he maintained, had been comparatively modest:

> In the meantime the political relations of Europe have substantially changed. The Balkan crisis that has held all Europe in tension for months still continues and has created a series of potential conflicts for us and our allies. . . . Whether the German army at its present establishment will suffice to meet all the challenges seems doubtful. A major part of the forces of our Italian ally is for the moment immobilized by its engagement in Tripoli; the Austrian armed forces too are limited in their capability by the extensive military deployment that has become necessary on the southern frontier of the empire.

This weakened Germany's position, as did the continued strengthening of the French and Russian armies, Bethmann argued. The government published its fears openly with the imperial proclamation introducing the law laid before the legislature in February, which began: "As a result of the events that are unfolding in the Balkans, the relationship of power in Europe has been altered."[48]

When Heeringen went before a closed committee session of the Reichstag party leaders in April 1913 to convince them of the necessity of the army law, he expounded the full array of strategic dangers.[49] Italy had most of its forces disorganized by detachments for the war in Libya, and in any case had little chance of making any impression on the French by an attack through the easily defensible Alpine passes. France had strengthened its army with the cadre laws, and made progress with fortifications, aircraft, and machine guns. Austria-Hungary would now have to leave six of its sixteen army corps against Serbia alone as a result of the Balkan Wars, and had dangerously low effectives in its units. "The situation had changed the most in Russia," according to the war minister; "we were surprised that development had gone so fast." Vast expenses there had improved equipment and were in the process of creating four new corps, two for the European frontier: "The situation of Germany in comparison with 1912 had become much more difficult. Today it was still tenable by virtue of our faith in the excellence of our troops; but in the future these troops would no longer be sufficient. Russia was not yet ready for war, the Balkan states too would only come into the calculation in the future. But in a few years this would be different. Russia had enough men and money and a willing parliament. Already today it had 400,000 more men than in 1912."[50] The war minister told the commission that France and Russia together had 827,000 more soldiers than Germany and Austria-Hungary. If Serbia, Belgium, and Bulgaria were added to the array of enemies, the superiority rose to 1.2 million; 1.45 million if reserves counted. All of this left out Britain. This kind of totaling of available forces, however tendentious its results could sometimes be, was largely a new feature of military administrations in 1912 and 1913. At that point, though, the practice became common as a means of justifying military increases, as well as more plausible due to the obvious coalescence of military alliance groups.

The army's arguments had their effect upon parliament and government. Heeringen's listeners in the Reichstag commission largely shared his alarm. August Bebel, the Socialist leader, argued that the balance was, if anything, even less favorable than the war minister said, and that a military law would not solve the problem. Matthias Erzberger, the Catholic Center Party chairman, declared, "The principal cause of the present danger lay in the changed situation of the army in Russia; against this there was no other means than the bill." He seconded Bebel's opinion that the next war would be a world war. When Bethmann answered a summons to testify, he agreed that France and Russia would definitely fight together in any conflict, probably joined by Britain. There was no "guarantee" against war, the chancellor warned, and it would certainly be a war on two fronts for Germany: "It was regrettable but there was no way around it. It would be a struggle for existence. Should we face it with less armament than we could afford?" Both army and civilian leaders had embraced the prospect of all-out preparation for a coming war of fearsome proportions.

As the army law of 1913 took shape under the shadow of the Balkan Wars, an impassioned debate unfolded within the high command over what form the expansion should take.[51] The war ministry and the general staff agreed about the problem of a European war, but disagreed about the solution. With the arrival of immense new funds and manpower, the perennial divergence between the two authorities over expansion policy became a more contentious issue than it had been since 1892. With the admixture of war-preparedness thinking and right-wing militarist pressure in the public, the old struggle over limited development versus broad expansion took on the dimensions of a new debate in Germany about military organization in society. Throughout the imperial period the army had served the social status quo effectively, while financial limits and the political institution of the Quinquennat had guaranteed that the war ministry would prevail in a conservative attitude toward the social and military consequences of sudden expansion. The general staff called in vain, especially under Schlieffen, for massive infusions of men and money with which to realize ambitious war plans. In 1912 the general staff saw a chance to change all this. It proposed a profound shift, to a new interpretation of what the nation in arms meant. Moltke, prompted by Ludendorff, strove to make the 1913 army law a blueprint for the full exploitation of Germany's considerable reserve of manpower. The effort showed with peculiar irony how the demands of mass warfare could expose contradictions between the values of militarism so often associated with reaction on the one hand, and the revolutionary vision of the army as a democratizing people in arms on the other.

The general staff demanded the institution of universal military service. As it was, Germany did not call up every able-bodied man of military age. All males were liable to conscription, but the constitution limited the army's size in peacetime to 1 percent of the population. This had been part of Bismarck's original deal with the federal states and the parliament to secure unification and three-year military service. The war ministry adhered to the limit without protest since the restriction allowed the army to set very high standards of physical fitness, as well as to leave out potential troublemakers and antimilitarists. In 1911 Moltke had acquiesced in the war ministry's insistence on maintaining the existing system even while instituting the 1912 military law.[52] With the next bill, Moltke called for a change. The driving force behind the demand was Ludendorff, who drafted or rewrote most of the chief's memoranda on the subject and inscribed the war minister's replies with acid marginalia. In the first general staff proposal for the 1913 law, which Ludendorff composed on Moltke's behalf on 25 November 1912, the program emerged clearly.[53] Not only would fortresses and existing units have to be reinforced: "We must in my opinion go still further and give our entire army the strength that alone can ensure success in the next war, that we will fight together with allies but nevertheless largely with our own forces, for Germany's greatness. We must be resolved at least to use the whole of our human resources. We must become once again the people in arms into which we were once made in a great era by great men. In this, Germany must not go backward; it can only go forward." Moltke called for manpower increases, "if at all possible extending to the full implementation of universal service." The demand reappeared in every general staff opinion on the proposed military law, often contrasting Germany's efforts with those of France and emphasizing the advantages of a younger army, as in the voluminous memorandum sent to Bethmann on 21 December 1912:

> France inducts 82 percent of its eligible men into the army; Germany some 52 to 54 percent! If we use our manpower to the same extent as France, with universal service we easily arrive at a raising of the recruit contingent by 150,000 men and of our peacetime strength by 300,000. An increased drawing upon the younger cohorts is nothing less than a social duty. With it we would take the burden off of the older cohorts, in which there are many fathers of families, and postpone their use in the face of the enemy. It would remove the need for a large part of the Landwehr men who are at present assigned to reserve formations to go into the field immediately while thousands of young people stay at home because they are not trained.[54]

With this colossal influx of manpower, the general staff hoped to create more and stronger units for its war plans. The increased demands placed on the German army by the Balkan Wars and the expansion of French and Russian power made it all the more necessary to mobilize rapidly—which would be easier with strong peacetime units needing fewer reservists—and to have very large forces available for operations. The general staff proposed to use an enlarged army to raise the peacetime establishment of most formations, to add numerous cavalry and technical units, to increase reserve cadres, and, with more funds, to modernize fortresses and procure arms and equipment. Most controversially, Moltke wanted to add three more army corps to the permanent organization.[55] This would account for the bulk of the expansion and place more resources at the disposal of strategic planning for a two-front war.

The war ministry was against it. Heeringen and the General War Department of the ministry planned instead for a much smaller army bill. While it would still be far larger than the 1912 law, with most of the features proposed by the general staff, it would call for far less of an increase in manpower, raising unit strengths by less and dispensing with the three new corps and the notion of universal service. Like the general staff's plan, it called for a further addition to the original 1911 Quinquennat, with its provisions to be completed by 1916. But it would strengthen the existing system rather than create a new one. In hoping to add 300,000 men to the peacetime army, Moltke was proposing to enlarge it by nearly 50 percent. The war ministry proposed an increase only about a third of this size, which, although ambitious, would add only about one-sixth to the army's existing strength. Behind the war ministry's reluctance to undertake a program as vast as Moltke wanted were not only a long-established mentality that resisted radical upheaval in a venerated organization, but also urgent questions of military expediency. The political motive for the ministry's policy was to maintain the army as a reliable servant of the monarchy and aristocracy without disturbing the political status quo through vast expenditures and consequently progressive taxation. The military consideration was preserving the combat effectiveness that came from thorough discipline, training, and equipment.

The political imperative for the war ministry's caution in 1913 came from a long Prussian military tradition of social exclusivity. The monarchy had always depended upon this for maintaining political reliability, from the *Junker*-officered army of Frederick the Great and the suppression of bourgeois influence over the Landwehr after the Napoleonic Wars, to the exclusion of Jews and anyone without establishment credentials from the officer corps in the Kaiserreich.[56] Officer selection, as delegated to cadet schools and regimental commands, rejected Jewish candidates and gave preference to aristocrats, especially in elite regiments and the highest ranks. Bourgeois officers had become an increasing presence throughout the nineteenth century in the absence of sufficient aristocratic applicants, but they were expected to display what Kaiser Wilhelm called "nobility of temperament" by embracing the traditionalistic and monarchical ethic of the officer corps. The law forbade officers from participating in politics. The army imposed rigid discipline among the troops, watched the men for signs of Socialist or antimilitarist inclinations, and preferred obedient recruits from the farms to potentially politicized urban youths. The general staff issued regulations for street fighting in insurgent towns in case the army might have to put down strikes (which it often did) or a revolution (which the ruling classes often feared). All of these practices helped make the army a central support for the social and political establishment in the Prusso-German state.

The Germans were not the only ones to run their army with such reactionary methods, which often contributed to military effectiveness as well as political stability, although the Prussian army enjoyed a reputation for being the most obsessive in their application. Anti-Semitism, which certainly had a negative effect on efficiency, was endemic to officer selection and promotion to one degree or another in all European armies, with the general exception of the Austro-Hungarian. The Dreyfus affair was only the most famous instance of its consequences. All the principal armies also gave preference to aristocratic birth in these matters, except to some degree in France, where the strange battles of church and state, republicanism, Bonapartism, and various strands of monarchism in the governing classes confused the politics of the officer corps and made a career in it more than usually open to candidates from the lower bourgeoisie or the ranks. In the Russian army, to take an extreme example of the opposite, only 48 percent of the officers were nonaristocratic by the outbreak of the First World War, while in Germany the proportion in 1913 was 70 percent.[57] No officers in Europe liked the prospect of Socialist or antimilitarist agitation in the barrack room, and all watched their men closely for symptoms. All also preferred to have farm boys rather than city workers in the ranks. This was not only because of the presumed political consequences but also because rural recruits were more likely than urban ones to be healthy and accustomed to hard outdoor work. Besides, men used to riding or caring for horses were always at a premium in armies that depended essentially upon animal power for movement in the field, and which contained a large proportion of mounted units. All the European armies routinely operated against their own populations, breaking strikes, performing police duty, and suppressing civil unrest. It was not normally popular work with officers or men, but the Germans did not have anything like a monopoly on it. In the measure that the German army did prove more effective than its counterparts in ensuring thorough training, political reliability, high esprit de corps, the absence of mutinies, tight discipline, and a high proportion of strong rural youths in the ranks, foreign observers tended to admire it more often than they regarded it as obsolete. The techniques of social control ensured good performance as much as they protected the social status quo.

An attitude of pure political reaction played a small part in the war ministry's resistance to a massive expansion of the army in 1913. The general staff's proposal for increasing the forces by half in less than three years threatened the social and political system, and the war ministry's resistance to a shift to universal service in 1913 corresponded perfectly with the general attitude of a high command opposed to change and worried about drawing new and dubious elements into the army. On one occasion, General von Heeringen made this argument explicitly. In a memorandum to Moltke on 20 January 1913, the war minister warned that even his own more limited proposal would endanger current officer selection criteria:

> I regard the expansion of the Prussian army by nearly a sixth of its establishment to be such a far-reaching measure that one must carefully consider whether its internal cohesion—especially where officers and noncommissioned officers are concerned—will suffer substantially from it. Without reaching into circles little suited for additions to the officer corps—which, quite apart from other dangers, would as a result be exposed to democratization—and without a lowering of standards, we will not be able to meet the extraordinarily increased requirement in both categories [i.e., officers and NCOs].[58]

The remark expressed stark cynicism and echoed a similar statement von Einem had made in 1904.[59] Such political considerations, however, took up only a fraction of the war ministry's attention in 1913. The eventual shortage of politically reliable officer candidates was only one of a great many reasons Heeringen gave within the same memorandum (which was three printed pages long) for favoring a smaller army bill. No other written reference to this preoccupation appeared in the voluminous and secret surviving correspondence concerning the 1913 law. Outside of the high command, serving officers do not seem to have been predominantly concerned with the social objections to an expansion of the army any more than the war ministry was, since they formed an important component of membership in the Wehrverein, whose entire program was based on the call for broad military service.[60]

Technical military obstacles constituted the war ministry's chief objection to a total overhaul of national service. Conscripting 50 percent more men, as the general staff demanded, obviously posed colossal difficulties. The war minister foresaw the problem of training them up to the standards of the German army. Here the question of officers and noncommissioned officers became crucial, as he had put it to Moltke in December 1912: "In my opinion there are limits to the possibility of raising establishments, set by considerations of the training of the individual soldier, which only takes place thoroughly and endures reliably in the reserves when the peacetime strength of the units during active service still allows the commander of a company etc. to give attention to each individual. Consequently the creation of extensive new formations is prevented by the impossibility of procuring officers and noncommissioned officers in sufficient numbers."[61] Attracting and training enough officers and NCOs, from any background whatever, would be difficult and would take time in a profession where careful instruction and long experience were at a premium. Even for the war ministry's smaller proposal, the army would have to find 3,975 new officers, 14,849 NCOs, 116,915 private soldiers, and 27,624 horses within three years.[62] Officers were already in short supply, and it would take years to produce enough experienced NCOs by raising service incentives. The increased recruit contingent would take up all the available able-bodied men, and the new horses would be very difficult to procure. "After all of this," declared Heeringen, "I am convinced that the army bill currently under consideration in itself already imposes a difficult task on the army. An even greater burden would substantially damage its inner quality." The kaiser agreed "that the increased need for officers, noncommissioned officers and men resulting from the War Ministry's plans was already so great that the army could not bear an even larger expansion for the moment."[63]

The war ministry also worried about organizing and equipping a sudden influx of troops, particularly at a time when the 1912 law was already imposing pressure. General von Wandel, who would be responsible for implementing many of the changes, noted with exasperation in his diary that even Heeringen's plan would be hard to carry out:

> in the interests of the army it would be imperative not to bring in another military increase so soon. We are short of over 1,300 lieutenants; the cadres are weakened & will be all the more so due to the establishment of the machine gun companies in 1913; in the field artillery effectives have been going down for years; everywhere uniform issue and accommodation are not up to the proper levels. If new organizational changes are undertaken now or in the next months, they will increase the disarray and confusion & exacerbate the already excessive nervousness even further.

Upon learning of Moltke's proposals for universal service and new corps formations, Wandel wrote that the general staff had obviously thrown all organizational considerations to the winds: "They apparently do not even question the feasibility of providing the gigantic resulting wartime strengths with ammunition and supplies."[64] He told a general staff delegation, which included Ludendorff, that it would be impossible to recruit, encadre, train, and equip three new corps in any reasonable time, or to provide rail lines for their mobilization.[65] Heeringen concluded his 20 January memorandum to Moltke with a similar warning: "And finally it must not be forgotten that in spite of years of effort we have still not succeeded in outfitting the existing formations with all types of war material as completely as would be urgently desirable. The raising of new corps, whose needs demanded attention first, would postpone the conclusion of the measures for the other corps as well until an unforeseeable future, since in the end the financial capacity of the Reich too has a limit."[66]

The war ministry's political doubts mostly concerned the budget in the Reichstag. In first proposing his own more limited army law in December 1912, Heeringen acknowledged to Bethmann that he could not see how the money even for such a bill was to be raised in the legislature.[67] "Where the millions for it will come from, I do not know," wrote Wandel.[68] Heeringen also knew that the Reichstag would object to the absence of a constitutional basis for universal service. He correctly pointed out that after the 1912 law the German army already amounted to nearly the statutory 1 percent of the Reich's population, and that the total armed forces including the navy actually came to 1.2 percent.[69] The minister had to answer charges of this kind in the Reichstag; the chief of staff did not. Heeringen did not object in principle to a larger army since he eventually consented to the idea of introducing the three new corps with the next Quinquennat once the current changes were in place.[70] His concerns were more for the rapidity, dislocation, and cost of the general staff's proposals. The kaiser looked forward to adding more corps when it became feasible.[71] The war ministry's concerns about sudden expansion were mostly bureaucratic, but the German army depended upon an efficient bureaucracy. The world war later showed, as the wars of unification already had, how important these matters of organization were in an age of industrialized mass warfare.[72]

Even as it was, the resulting army law of 1913 was a gigantic measure with major political consequences. The kaiser and Bethmann backed the war ministry's plan, and Ludendorff was silenced by a transfer to a regimental command. The result was the biggest army law in German history, loaded on top of the 1911 Quinquennat and its 1912 expansion. The forces increased by approximately one-sixth, at a cost of 884 million marks plus an annual addition of 183 million to the budget. Moltke was at least right in predicting in December 1912 that the Reichstag would be willing to pass a large measure in the wake of the Balkan upheavals. All of the bourgeois parties voted in favor of the bill in July 1913, with loud proclamations of national danger and sacrifice.[73] The news of military increases impending in France and Russia in reaction to the German measures only increased the readiness of the Reichstag to vote for the bill.[74]

The law was a full capitulation to the notion of a land armaments race in Europe. The government threw out Tirpitz's plan for a parallel naval increase, and the fleet effectively no longer competed with Britain's. To fund the 1913 army law, Bethmann broke with the Reich government's hitherto sacrosanct policy of preserving the economic interests of the landowning classes.[75] The Reich chancellor grasped the nettle and designed a limited tax on the increase of property. This did not come close to covering the deficit caused by military spending, but the government's traditional constituency on the right felt betrayed and outraged. To pass the tax, Bethmann actually resorted to the support of the parliamentary left in an unprecedented *volte-face*. He employed the stratagem of separating the army law from its funding bill. A coalition of the center and right voted for the former for the sake of nationalist aspirations, while a coalition of the center and left, including the Social Democrats, voted for the latter to secure the principle of direct taxation of wealth by the Reichstag. By the standards of the antiprogressive Reich leadership, it was an act of desperation that showed how much the military crisis had traumatized the government. The prospect of actually starting a preventive war was still confined to Moltke's single ineffectual outburst in the December 1912 meeting with the kaiser, and German policy was to continue the armaments race. Nevertheless, the Reich leadership sacrificed many of its policies to this competition on the grounds that war might be imminent. The step from believing in the likelihood of war to accepting its necessity was not to be a long one.[76]

The Reaction of the Entente: The French Three-Year Law and Russian Army Increases

The other European powers responded to the German army law by accelerating their own rearmament. The German expansion was the principal reason for French and Russian measures in 1913 and 1914. With their reactions the Entente powers helped to ensure that the Reichstag would pass the law, which in turn galvanized parliamentary support for armament bills in other countries. It was a classic arms-race dynamic, unfettered by any significant negotiation between the powers for a halt. Statesmen did not undertake even the type of vain attempts they had made to negotiate agreements against naval construction. As the notion of an inevitable war increasingly prevailed, governments reacted with attempts to avoid it—or at least to make its circumstances more favorable—through diplomacy, but they also fatalistically prepared for the great conflict. From 1909 to 1911 Moltke and the retired Schlieffen had still written of forming a formidable Austro-German bloc that continental powers would be reluctant to attack. By 1912 armaments in all countries were accompanied by no significant talk of deterrence.

The Entente powers understood perfectly well what the Germans were doing with the 1913 law, and took their own measures in full consciousness of the competition that was under way. In the winter of 1912–13 it became clear that the Reich government was preparing a new army increase, and in Paris and St. Petersburg it was quite obvious why this should be so. Sukhomlinov told General de Laguiche, the French military attaché: "Germany is in a very critical position. It is encircled by enemy forces: to the west France, to the east Russia—and it fears them."[77] The Russian war minister's understanding of the situation scarcely differed from that of the German high command. Britain, as

Sukhomlinov pointed out to Laguiche, was now a certain enemy of Germany, while the Austro-Hungarian army was losing its value in the face of strengthening Balkan states. "It is therefore up to Germany to play a large role on its own; I can understand its worry, and as a result the measures it is taking seem natural to me." Jules Cambon wrote a similar assessment from Berlin at the same time.[78] He concluded, however, that the reasons for the German increase were less important than the consequences for France: the German army would become younger and more numerous. "Whatever the case," he wrote, "it is certain that as of now the German military proposal obliges us to seek by what means France might make up for the disproportion of forces that will result for it from the establishment of universal military service in Germany."

The answer the French hit upon was a return to three-year military service.[79] The idea had been in the air for some time before the army officially proposed it. The French military attaché in Berlin, as well as Cambon, repeatedly stressed that France would have to match the German increase somehow.[80] Since the French army already used essentially all able-bodied men of military age in the country under the provisions of the 1905 two-year service law, the only way to increase the number of troops under arms at any given time was to make them serve for longer. This would not raise the number of trained men in the population, but it would yield more regulars, and therefore more units in peacetime that could be filled up with reservists on mobilization. It would also give the reserves more hope of being effective when called up, since they would have been trained more thoroughly while on active duty. And finally, the quality of the army would presumably rise if larger proportions of the mobilized units were regular soldiers, two-thirds of whom would have received more than a year's training at any given time. This would respond to the appeals of the French military attaché in Berlin for an enhancement in quality to offset Germany's steadily increasing advantage over France in quantity.[81] Professional military men in France were eager for a return to what they regarded as serious soldiering with three-year service, and Joffre was a ready proponent of the idea. He introduced a plan for it to the Conseil Supérieur de la Guerre on 4 March 1913, as the German military law was being publicly prepared, and he obtained a unanimous vote for it.[82]

In the public and secret debates that followed, the army tried any argument that would make the three-year law sound like the necessary response to Germany's military increases. The technical rationales offered for it varied widely, and its political appeal rested upon impulses that had little or no basis in military reasoning. When Jean Jaurès and a wide array of progressive politicians mounted a determined attack on the proposal, the divergent reasons that military men had for supporting the law made the project look extremely problematic. In front of the parliamentary army commission in March 1913, the war minister, Eugène Etienne, initially made a disastrous showing with one of the arguments Joffre had used in the Conseil Supérieur and which seemed to convey the kind of obvious urgency that would capture civilians' attention. The proposed German military law, Etienne argued, was about to transform the German army into a force capable of attacking France with twenty-five corps without even waiting for reservists to come to the colors.[83] The commission demolished this theory as totally implausible, and Jaurès pointed out that if it were true then the army's proposal would be a totally inadequate response since it was only to bring five instead of the current three frontier-based corps up to near-ready strength and raise the establishments of the rest.[84]

Joffre fared better a week later by arguing that the real point was that the German army would in future possess a higher proportion of active troops, making its units more effective and quicker to mobilize since they would require fewer reservists.[85] He proposed that the French create the same situation on their own side to keep pace. As it was, he said, the frontier corps did not have the two-hundred-man infantry companies in peacetime they would need if they were to mobilize fast enough. At the same time, companies in the rest of the army were well below one hundred men, which would mean that incorporating the necessary reservists to bring them up to the war strength of two hundred fifty would take three or four weeks. By that time, he remarked, "the affair will already have been settled." Joffre's deputy, General Legrand-Girarde, testified to the need also to raise the number of technical units of all kinds: "We are in this respect—I am forced to admit—notably inferior to our possible opponents."

In the broader political public, where the technical argument about unit establishments had less appeal, the war-scare mentality functioned effectively to rally support across a wide spectrum, very much as in Germany. Poincaré was elected president in February 1913, and he appointed a cabinet packed with supporters of the *loi des trois ans,* under Louis Barthou. The government deliberately presented the new service law as a response to the threat of an immediate German attack.[86] It counted on a wave of alarm and patriotic chauvinism to make it hard to vote against the bill, even though the law was really designed to increase strength in the long run rather than the short term. The issue was not decided until the Radicals, still powerful under Caillaux, made up their minds. The bill would reverse their program for a short-service citizen army of national defense, but to vote against it risked damaging the party's popularity in an increasingly ultranationalist environment. The government finally tempted them on board by proposing to finance the army increase with a progressive property tax that the egalitarian Radicals were eager to obtain.[87] The tactic, which came as a bitter blow to the center and right, bore an uncanny resemblance to Bethmann Hollweg's maneuver at the same time to lure the left of the Reichstag into financing the 1913 army law at the expense of the agrarian-industrial bloc. The *loi des trois ans* passed in the Chamber two weeks after the German army bill, on 19 July 1913, a triumph for Poincaré's national politics and for Joffre. The peacetime strength rose by about one-sixth, to over 700,000 men. The metropolitan army received a 22nd corps; the number of corps at near-readiness strength for *couverture* on the frontier rose to five, and unit effectives throughout the army increased dramatically.

Joffre acquired the manpower he wanted for a new offensive war plan. Plan XVII had been maturing ever since he became chief of staff, but in 1913 he was at last able to unveil it to the Conseil Supérieur de la Guerre. Instead of deploying cautiously to absorb the shock of an initial German invasion, the whole army would now mobilize well forward, close against the eastern frontier between Belfort and Hirson, leaving the Italian border virtually denuded and no major forces in the rear to protect Paris or embody reserve formations.[88] Even the reserve divisions, with their improved cadres, would now deploy in the main army sector, ready to support an early offensive northeastward into Germany. The strengthened *couverture* made this forward deployment safer, as did recent improvements in the railway network that reduced mobilization time by a day between 1912 and 1913.[89] Here again, the perceived shift in the balance of military power influenced planning, as the operations office observed in its introduction to the project: "The events in the East, the reconstitution of the Russian forces, the maritime rivalry of England and Germany, all combine to make the balance of forces tilt to the side of the Triple Entente."[90]

The three-year law and Plan XVII also had an international dimension aimed at the Russian alliance, a consideration that added urgency to efforts from the start. In March 1913 Delcassé, who was now the French ambassador in St. Petersburg, reported that the tsar and his government were preparing to react to the German law with a military expansion of their own.[91] When Sazonov spoke to Delcassé about the measures in view, the French ambassador replied by impressing upon him "the magnitude of our own effort and how indispensable it is, in order to obtain the desired effect, that the French effort and the Russian effort should be coordinated and simultaneous."[92] To his own government, Delcassé continued, "There is no need for me to emphasize the importance of the resolutions that M. Sazonov has just announced to me and how much they respond to our concerns. I might add that, from the tone in which he asked me: 'will the projects proposed in France become a reality?,' it is easy to measure the interest the imperial government attaches to them." The tsar pointedly praised the French three-year law plan to Delcassé and noted Russia's interest in it.[93] The French perceived the passage of the three-year law not only as a reinforcement of their own strength but also as a signal of their resolve and a consequent encouragement to Russian emulation.[94] In much the same way, Joffre held up the prospect of a powerful French offensive under Plan XVII at the 1913 staff talks in Russia as a bid for Zhilinski to promise an early attack from the east to match it.[95]

The Balkan Wars and the German 1913 law inspired the Russians with an earnest desire to accelerate their own armaments, but the sheer inefficiency of government and command made the proposed plans slow to take effect. In the autumn of 1912 the Balkan conflict already prompted the tsar to order the prime minister and finance minister, Kokovtsev, to spare no expense in meeting Sukhomlinov's demands for funds, which resulted in large expenditures for the semi-mobilization that took place during the winter.[96] In March 1913, when the German army law came into the open, the tsar called his ministers together at Tsarskoe Selo and aired Sukhomlinov's plan for a vast new military expansion in response. It was the foundation for what later became known as the "Great Program" of rearmament. Sazonov and the tsar triumphantly reported to the French that a vast increase was impending, and Berlin and Vienna soon picked up the news. It was not, however, altogether clear what the Russian plan consisted of. The French heard various predictions of long- and short-term effects of the project, including a raising of the peacetime strength ranging from 75,000 to 260,000 men; increases in the service term; the addition of between two and four new corps; wildly varying cost estimates; and durations ranging from the immediate to four years.

The reason for these conflicting reports was that the Russian leadership itself had not agreed on what to do. A naval bill, passed in 1912 at the tsar's instigation to rebuild the fleet that had been sunk at Port Arthur and Tsushima, already consumed a prodigious share of funds.[97] At the same time, a bitter personal and professional enmity between Sukhomlinov and Kokovtsev ensured that the army and the civil authorities never cooperated with one another's plans and obstructed progress at every step. This divisiveness was characteristic of Russia's autocratic system of government, which lacked a deliberative cabinet and relied instead on the competing independent jurisdictions of ministers responsible only to the sovereign.[98] When Sukhomlinov laid his Great Program before the imperial council in March 1913, Kokovtsev had never seen it or heard of it.[99] His first reaction was an angry denunciation of the war

ministry for wasting the vast sums placed at its disposal in the past, much
of which he claimed went unspent due to the inefficiency of the army
and its procurement base. Kokovtsev had often made such accusations
before.[100] At the council the prime minister went on to say that there
was indeed money available—some 400 million roubles, which was even
more than the war ministry requested—but that the spending plan
placed before him was riddled with omissions and miscalculations and
would have to be totally rewritten before it could be presented to the
Duma. This was not surprising, he noted, since the finance ministry had
not once been consulted in the preparation of the document. But instead of offering to cooperate in its redesign, he said the war ministry
should rewrite the plan and present it again when it was ready. As a result, a more or less complete budget proposal did not reach the Duma
until 1914. Meanwhile, Sukhomlinov, Sazonov, and the tsar came away
from the meeting imagining that Kokovtsev had approved the funds,
while the prime minister believed he had rid himself of the matter for the
time being.

The result was a series of partial measures in 1913 that sufficed to
alarm the Germans and Austro-Hungarians while keeping the French
confident that the Russian army was gaining value. By the end of June
the Duma had passed only the ordinary military budget as arranged in
1912—already a substantial increase in the annual recruit contingent
but nothing like what had been promised to the French in March
1913.[101] The parliament debated aspects of Sukhomlinov's proposals
beginning that summer. The increases remained in suspense, however,
as the Duma discussed them, took its 1913 recess, and did not vote on
them until June 1914.[102] In the interim, the army continued to retain its
outgoing class under arms during the winter while the new recruits were
being trained. This perpetuated the practice instituted during the Balkan Wars, insuring that the army always had three experienced classes
under arms and a standing strength 30 percent greater while the in-
coming men were still being turned into soldiers. It greatly preoccupied
military men in Berlin and Vienna.[103]

There was much talk of improving Russia's strategic rail network, but
scarcely any practical progress. Joffre, Poincaré, and Delcassé all prevailed upon the Russian government and general staff to build more
lines in order to speed mobilization.[104] The French foreign ministry and
financial authorities approved a program of loans to St. Petersburg on
the condition that "the railway works whose necessity the French and
Russian Chiefs of Staff recognized in the conferences in August 1913
will be undertaken as soon as possible, so as to be completed within four
years."[105] The Russian generals had no objection to the French helping
them obtain more funds, but Kokovtsev resented being told how he

could spend the money he borrowed at considerable cost. He protested to the French that it would contribute far more to Russia's overall power if the resources went to lines of commercial use, which would in any case serve mobilization as well, rather than to purely military lines that would produce no revenue.[106] The Russians continued to do next to nothing for their strategic railways in the west, and the French knew it. Zhilinski himself admitted to Laguiche that the Duma preferred to put the funds into commercial routes and road construction. "I am not completely unhappy with this," the Russian chief of staff conceded, "since it is always a development of the country's wealth and power, but from the purely military point of view this does not make a difference to you."[107] In November the French assistant military attaché in St. Petersburg noted that the vast transportation budget for 1914 was mostly for civilian lines, roads, and waterways.[108] Virtually all that remained for strategic railways was earmarked for the far east, where the long trans-Siberian and Amur River routes still called for huge investments. Major Wehrlin reported, "It seems difficult to foresee the execution of major strategic works in Europe for another two years."

Whatever the realities of the situation, the spectacle of Franco-Russian military cooperation against Germany in 1913 looked impressive. The French three-year law gave a dramatic sign of the victory of Poincaré and the national slogan over the Radicals' policies of military restraint. Nobody knew quite what the Russians were achieving because they were not sure themselves, but the steady stream of proclamations and rumors about contingent and budget increases and new army corps were hard for foreign observers to discount. Parliaments noisily debated military expansions while French cooperation with Russia was more conspicuous than ever. Its supreme symbol was Joffre's triumphal visit to the Russian imperial maneuvers of 1913 with a retinue including five generals. Gone were the secretive journeys that the French and Russian chiefs of staff had made each year to meetings in the past. Joffre spoke with the tsar and the military leaders, and cemented his growing personal friendship with Grand Duke Nicholas. He made extravagant speeches in praise of "the most powerful army in the world," inspected units, and cut an imposing figure at military exercises with his walrus mustache and solid *embonpoint* astride a magnificent gray horse.[109]

The crisis over the Balkan Wars perpetuated the arms race that Germany had provoked after 1911. It did so as a direct result of changing perceptions of the balance of military power. The competition in armaments had begun as a result of a conscious effort by Germany to redress what appeared to be a growing preponderance on the side of the Entente in the wake of the Agadir crisis by means of the 1912 army law. The Balkan

Wars tilted the likely balance of forces for a future war more heavily against Germany and Austria-Hungary by virtually eliminating their Ottoman ally from the European scene and replacing it with a strengthened array of Balkan states threatening the Dual Monarchy. This prompted Berlin and Vienna to accelerate the pace of their armaments irrespective of the strategic dangers and the domestic financial and political sacrifices that the increases entailed. The Entente powers' reaction to the military increases of their rivals included a series of army increases and increasingly ostentatious joint war planning. These activities constituted a reciprocal dynamic of military competition that was unlike anything that had occurred before 1911. It contributed to rising chauvinism and fears of insecurity on both sides. Not only did the pace and the rationale of military increases change, but attitudes toward the prospect of war itself took on a new character. In public as well as in the secret communications of military and civilian leaders, alarmist rhetoric about armaments and the likelihood of a general conflagration became prevalent as it had not been before 1911. The notions of "preventive" and "inevitable" war gained ground in the mentality of military leaders and even some statesmen in Austria-Hungary and Germany. Some of the inflammatory talk consisted of conscious exaggerations designed to muster support for military increases, and often generals invoked present emergencies as justifications for spending increases that were actually designed to secure resources for the longer term. This did not make the rhetoric any less destabilizing or any less of a departure from the previous tone of discourse. It profoundly affected the assumptions with which statesmen faced the next great international crisis.

Chapter 7

THE EUROPEAN ARMIES AND
THE OUTBREAK OF THE FIRST WORLD WAR

IN THE SUMMER OF 1914 one more diplomatic crisis erupted in the midst of the armaments race between the European powers. On 28 June a Serb nationalist shot Archduke Franz Ferdinand and his wife at Sarajevo in Bosnia, where the Habsburg heir apparent was conducting a tour of inspection. Throughout July the representatives of the great powers negotiated in an effort to resolve the conflict that the assassination raised. In many respects, the interests at stake were not significantly greater than those in the other European crises of the preceding decade. The dispute revolved around Austria-Hungary's desire to exact a heavy retribution from Serbia for its involvement in the plot, in the hope of convincing Belgrade that it must cease its efforts to foment separatism in the South Slav regions of the Dual Monarchy. Russia, backed by France, objected to extreme penalties or violations of sovereignty being inflicted on Serbia, while Berlin supported the Dual Monarchy in its intention to take the opportunity for dealing a lasting blow against the South Slavs. Efforts to convene an international conference on the matter failed. Vienna issued an ultimatum for Serbia's compliance with demands for stiff guarantees of cooperation in an investigation of the assassination plot, and Belgrade refused the harshest of these conditions. Preparatory military mobilizations began in Serbia, Austria-Hungary, and then Russia, amid a flurry of attempts in the European capitals to reach a last-minute compromise. These failed, and all the major powers except Italy declared war against each other in the first days of August.

The shifting balance of military power in Europe and the new sense of urgent competition in land armaments strongly influenced the great powers' decision to go to war. Above all, these developments prompted statesmen to think pessimistically about the future. The growth in the military strength of the Entente and Balkan armies made them appear to leaders in Berlin and Vienna as if they would become a major danger in a few more years, and yet there still seemed to be a reasonable chance of defeating them in a present war. The speed of the escalating armaments race, as well as the mentality it engendered, made the decision to mobilize a far more likely choice than it had been in previous confrontations. The conviction among a widening circle of decision makers that a general war was inevitable contributed to this attitude. So did the growing acceptance of the notion of fighting a preventive war to forestall a worse situation in the future. For the Entente powers, the military balance looked more favorable than it had in most crises, and both France and Russia perceived a need to demonstrate willingness to act in behalf of each other and of the South Slavs in order to preserve the strong alliance they had achieved. In Paris and St. Petersburg, too, the escalating armaments competition and the chauvinistic rhetoric that accompanied it made war seem less remote, as well as making Germany in particular appear more dangerously aggressive than ever before.

THE BALANCE OF MILITARY POWER IN 1914

When the Archduke and his wife were assassinated in 1914, the balance of military power in Europe was not very different from that in the last major crisis, in the summer of 1911. On the one hand, Germany had reaped much more benefit from the army expansions of 1912 and 1913 than the Entente powers had, and Austria-Hungary had made significant progress. The Germans had succeeded in significantly expanding an army that was already powerful, while the Austro-Hungarians had broken some of the parliamentary constraints on their own resources. On the other hand, the Entente had drawn closer together, become ready for war in a measure that it was not in 1911, and grown more willing to fight if necessary. The French had gained confidence and ensured that their alliances could and would function together, in the case of both Britain and Russia. The passage of a few years had brought the Russian army from a state of doubtful readiness to a condition where fighting a war seemed quite feasible even if not yet optimal. The desirability of defending its newly valuable Balkan allies made the imperative for war seem far more compelling to St. Petersburg than it had done in the 1911 confrontation over Morocco.

With the army increases, Germany had made very great progress by 1914. Two new army corps were firmly established from peacetime and the war ministry had set up virtually all of the 1913 law's new formations.[1] The recruit contingent size had risen in 1912 and 1913, but was limited enough so that the efficient internal organization of the German army could not absorb the new manpower and transform it into battle-ready units. The 1913 project would not be complete until 1916, especially where new weaponry was concerned, but the stage reached by 1914 was one of strength. The second of the very large 1913-size recruit classes was still due to be incorporated in the fall of 1914, so the manpower increase foreseen by the 1913 law was only half complete, but the

1911 and 1912 laws had been more than fulfilled. This meant strengthened cadres for both the active army and the reserves, speeding mobilization and making the resulting formations well trained and vigorous. The new corps made a corresponding number of reserve divisions available for use in operations. The existing reserve corps and some new ones had begun to receive additional equipment and command structures. The strengthening of the engineers, railway troops, and other technical formations had increased Germany's lead over all other armies in this realm.

The two years since the second Moroccan crisis had led to some vital technical improvements in other areas as well. The provision of machine gun companies for infantry regiments had been fully carried out, so that a section of two guns would be available for each battalion as in other European armies. By 1914 all troops wore the field-gray service uniform in the field and sufficient stocks were on hand for the reserves. The air service was at last catching up with the French, so that the field commands would now have at their disposal a strong array of well over two hundred aeroplanes, organized into squadrons to provide reconnaissance ahead of the armies.[2] A sufficient number of very heavy mobile siege mortars was available by 1914 to destroy the Liège and Namur forts quickly and make way for the right flank's swing through Belgium on both banks of the Meuse. There were twelve 305mm mortars, which was two more than in 1911, and since then Krupp had produced an additional five of the much more powerful 420mm "Short Naval Cannon," of which only two had existed at the time of the Agadir crisis.[3] The latter weapons threw a shell that weighed nearly as much as an entire field gun, to a range of over 13 kilometers, delivering more than twice the weight of explosive of the 305 over half again as far. A new generation of heavy field guns was also just becoming available during the July crisis. The heavy siege mortars remained the only significant military secret in Europe that was successfully kept in the period, but even from other points of view observers generally acknowledged the technical equipment of the German army as the best in the world in both quantity and quality.[4] Only in aeroplanes were the French universally judged superior. Nobody reproached the morale or endurance of German soldiers, although their tactics remained subject to censure for rigidity, predictability, and insufficient dispersal under fire.[5]

In Austria-Hungary, 1912 and 1913 had brought expansion without dislocation too, though on a much more modest scale.[6] Under the influence of the Balkan crises and deals struck with Vienna on matters such as artillery for the Honvédség, the Hungarians stopped obstructing the prompt call-up of the annual recruit class. The increased contingent also helped raise establishments in peacetime. This brought few major new units but meant a reorganization of the artillery, more regular and thorough training, and the prospect of quicker mobilization. It also permitted the regular establishment of machine gun detachments at a rate of two guns per infantry battalion. The pike-gray field uniform was standard except in the cavalry for some time before 1914. A major addition to the forces' heavy firepower had come about with the production at the Škoda works of a powerful 305mm siege mortar, which the army ordered in 1911 and distributed to a few batteries by 1914.[7] Conrad and a series of war ministers had pressed for such a weapon since 1906 to smash Italian fortresses in the Alps, but only the influx of funds from 1912 onward made it possible to acquire the piece, along with heavy tractors for towing it. In other technical realms, however, the 1912–13 increases brought no substantial progress. The 80mm 1905/08 gun remained the only modern weapon in the field artillery, the light and heavy howitzers still lacking quick-firing mountings.[8] There were not enough motor vehicles available, and the air service had only about eighty-four operational planes and thirty-five for training. Foreign observers continued to rate the tactical performance of the forces as solid, due to the good order and endurance of the infantry and to the artillery's general use of covered firing positions. The higher command, however, continued to rank as uninspired.

In France, on the other hand, it is doubtful whether the expansions after 1912 brought an overall improvement in fighting power. The *lois des cadres* for the infantry and cavalry that passed after the Moroccan crisis certainly strengthened the existing units, but the three-year law was still causing more dislocation than anything else by the time the July crisis arrived. The army called up two enlarged annual contingents of recruits in rapid succession in the autumn of 1913. This was the only way to obtain the raised strength at once rather than phasing it in over six years, since the classes under arms had rioted at the rumor that they might be ordered to remain for a third year. At first the result was nothing but overcrowded barracks and insufficient uniforms and equipment. Once the outgoing class went home, the army was left in the absurd situation of having only one trained class under arms alongside two larger untrained classes during the winter of 1913–14. The law produced recruits so much faster than officers and NCOs to instruct them that training sank to perilously low levels.[9] Although the problem of weak unit establishments receded, the hoped-for consequence of quicker mobilization and greater unit cohesion due to higher peacetime strengths could not be expected for about three years. The French increase had the disadvantage of being far more sudden and disruptive than the German, confirming one of the Prussian war ministry's doubts about rapid expansion. The French army was in any case less well equipped than the German to absorb such training demands since it had a somewhat smaller proportion of officers to men, and far fewer of the all-important NCOs. A German infantry company normally possessed eighteen to twenty long-service noncommissioned officers in peacetime; a French company had only eight or nine, besides some recruits promoted in their second year of service.[10] Another major obstacle lay in the shortage of large training camps in France. With larger armies, longer-ranged weapons, and dispersed tactics, the availability of very spacious training areas gained importance. In France there were already fewer than in Germany—eight compared to twenty-two large camps— and money to acquire more was lacking. Despite frequent efforts, the war ministry did not secure any new ones by 1914.[11]

The army improvements from 1912 onward did not solve the French army's technical armament problems, and in this respect it fell significantly behind Germany, although it remained superior to the other European armies. The Germans caught up with the French, for practical purposes, in the areas where France had enjoyed a margin of superiority. Equipment with machine guns, of which the French had started with more, became approximately equal at two per battalion, although French reserve units had more than German ones. Both armies deployed substantially the same number of aeroplanes by the summer of 1914, although the French arguably still enjoyed an advantage in quality. The French 75mm field gun remained excellent and was organized into strong four-gun batteries from peacetime, whereas the Germans would mobilize more cumbersome six-gun batteries like the other European armies and trained with a less realistic proportion of men and ammunition caissons per gun in peacetime.[12]

In heavy field artillery the French made no practical progress despite the great influx of funds and preoccupation with the matter from 1911 onward. They lost considerable time debating the adoption of a light field howitzer like the Germans', only to drop the idea as unnecessary. One argument against it was that the powerful 75mm shell of the regular field gun could be fitted with a special aerodynamic base-plate, the infamous *plaquette Malandrin,* to give it a curved trajectory for plunging fire. In practice this proved to be a dangerously unreliable expedient. In 1911 Joffre and Messimy realized the importance of procuring additional heavy field guns, despite the weight and ammunition supply problems they would add to marching columns. But delays in designing, testing, and producing suitable weapons meant that in three years almost nothing reached the units. Joffre adopted an interim solution for the implementation of Plan XVII in April 1914: the army could field more than three hundred heavy guns if it supplemented the existing 155mm howitzers with surplus batteries, formed from coastal-defense artillery personnel and employing wheel-mounted versions of obsolete 120mm cannon and howitzers. In the autumn the army expected to replace these with a promising new 105mm long gun that was in production. In practice, however, the only quick-firing heavy field guns in service in July 1914 were still the Rimailho 155mm howitzers, numbering a little over a hundred, and the rest were of no use for supporting an army in mobile operations. The Germans had approximately four hundred comparable 150mm howitzers at corps level by then, as well as 100mm cannon, 210mm mortars, assorted other calibers, and far superior siege artillery. Joffre was engaged in a program to strip the French fortresses of heavy guns and improvise siege trains from them as a complement to the mostly obsolete array the army possessed.[13]

Most notoriously, the French failed to resolve the problem of a modern field uniform at the same time as their rivals. The other European armies completed the transition from bold to neutral-colored uniforms with the influx in 1912–13 of funds and new recruits to be clothed. As war minister, Messimy had succeeded in having a green uniform tested in three regiments at the French 1911 maneuvers, but patriotic sentiment was against it especially at the time of the *réveil national*. Later the proposal of a shade of blue, the blue-gray "*bleu horizon,*" with its French national overtones, helped to make the prospect more palatable, and finally a law passed for a uniform of this color—on 9 July 1914.[14] Naturally no stocks arrived until the war was under way, and the army went to the front in blue coats and red trousers. The problem extended to other types of equipment at a low level as well, from telephones and field kitchens to binoculars and range-finders, where the French army lost ground to the Germans as the latter put their new funds and efficient industry to work. The French were excellently equipped by most European standards, but had the misfortune to confront the most thoroughly outfitted army in the world by 1914. If France was to counter quantity with quality, the military attaché in Berlin observed, it had a long way to go where equipment was concerned.[15] In tactics, the French still received better reports than other armies, with more or less good use of terrain and normally flexible and dispersed formations, although there were major lapses. If the individual training of the soldiers was universally recognized as being far below German standards, foreign observers as always rated the men as enthusiastic and the officers and staff work as highly professional.[16]

Most of the practical results of military expansion for Russia still lay in the future by the time of the July crisis. Important changes had taken

place, however. First of all, in the three years since the second Moroccan crisis the slow reforms of the Sukhomlinov program had begun to
take effect. Reserves had been trained, and the army had gained confidence after its uncertain stance in 1911. Secondly, the contingent increases that accompanied the Balkan crises produced a larger army with
stronger peacetime establishments, even though the number of units did
not rise significantly. In the third place, the extension of the service term
to allow for the retention of the outgoing class during the training of
new recruits eliminated what was normally a vulnerable period of the
year for European armies in the winter. Finally, there was some progress
in the procurement of modern armaments as programs at last yielded
results. Their funding also improved with the Balkan crises, some years
of good harvests and exports, and Kokovtsev's relatively able management of the economy. The infantry received modern sharp-nosed small
arms ammunition like that of the west European armies. An air service
built up an impressive number of aeroplanes, though its dependence on
foreign types and training caused it to be taken less seriously than its
western counterparts. Most importantly, the artillery made important
strides in catching up with the Germans'. The light howitzer batteries
completed their rearmament with quick-firing Krupp 120mm pieces,
and the heavy field artillery at last received Schneider-Creusot 150mm
quick-firing howitzers to substitute for about half of its 555 obsolete
weapons. The remainder were in the process of being replaced by the
delivery of Schneider 107mm quick-firing cannon in 1914. A few modern howitzers even reached the outdated siege and fortress artillery, although most of this remained virtually useless for operations and the
heaviest new type, a Schneider 280mm mortar, proved to be a failure.[17]
This left the Russian artillery still far behind the Germans, but in a far
better position than in 1911, when only the field gun had been remotely
modern.

The main change in Russia, however, the "Great Program" of rearmament proposed by Sukhomlinov, did not pass in the Duma until
June 1914. This set of reforms was due to increase the standing army
by 400,000 men (or a quarter of Russia's 1913 strength; half of Germany's) by 1917. Two new corps would form in the west, unit strengths
would increase, and twenty-six new cavalry regiments would be raised.
The artillery would receive 132 field guns per corps instead of the existing 108. It would switch to batteries of four guns like the French, rather
than the existing unwieldy eight-gun formations.[18] But all of this was
still only a law in parliament, after first having been formulated a year
earlier. Automobiles and trucks remained far rarer than in other European armies, while hardly any of the country's considerable extension of
its railroads had been in a direction that would quicken mobilization.

Foreign observers noted little improvement in the training and tactical performance of the army. As ever, the troops appeared solid and patient but without initiative or good NCOs. The officers seemed excessively dependent on orders from above, which in turn were overelaborate, and all units moved sluggishly, with poor reconnaissance and slow reaction times. The artillery fired exclusively from defiladed positions, but gave the impression of exaggerated caution, all of which observers ascribed to the traumatic experience of the Manchurian campaign.[19]

Of the Entente armies, the British experienced the least change of all after 1912. The budget remained stable and scarcely any new units or manpower appeared. The expeditionary force for France already possessed its full organization, as well as two machine guns per infantry battalion and a complement of quick-firing medium and heavy field artillery. The only significant change was the addition of an air service, the Royal Flying Corps, in 1912, which built five of its seven proposed squadrons by 1914 to accompany the expeditionary force. Stimulated by the example of the continental powers, Britain went from having virtually no serviceable air capability in 1911 to possessing a well-equipped and rationally organized aerial reconnaissance force of ninety-five frontline aircraft by 1914.[20] From the point of view of its performance in the field, the British army continued to look competent and effective. The infantry moved in good order and was well trained at the individual level. All arms made good use of cover, and the artillery functioned smoothly, although the cavalry appeared to lack the spirit or the training for effective shock action. The higher commands continued to experience difficulty in the unaccustomed task of handling large forces when corps-sized formations assembled for maneuvers.[21]

The Italian army, wavering between the two European alliance groupings, went through a dramatic cycle of loss and partial recovery of effectiveness between 1911 and 1914, due to its campaign in Libya. The engagement of over 100,000 men in North Africa drew off nearly half of the Italian army's peacetime strength. Although the government called up reservists and more recruits to fill out the home forces and furnish replacements, this was no substitute for experienced regulars with proper cadres. Training in the metropolitan army fell to disastrous levels and the expeditionary corps used up the mobilization stores. Most funds and equipment, including virtually all of the army's machine guns, went to the operations in Tripolitania and Cyrenaica.[22] When the indigenous population carried on the struggle after the Ottoman capitulation in October 1912, the deployment in North Africa had to continue with only gradual reductions. This wrecked the Pollio-Spingardi program of army reform. Money still went to the fortress system on the northeastern frontier as previously allocated, largely completing the works there by 1914, and attempts at artillery procurement continued. However, there was nothing to be had for actual increases of the forces to match those of powers to the north. Machine guns, in particular, were much more scarce than in the other armies, at fewer than two per regiment even in the official establishment. In 1913 the war minister appealed in vain to Giolitti for a bill that would at least bring the existing forces up to modern levels of equipment and training without even attempting an expansion.[23] By July 1914 the Deport quick-firing 75mm field guns were finally beginning to arrive from the manufacturers to replace the most obsolete pieces in the inventory, and the army possessed Krupp 149mm howitzers for its heavy field artillery.[24] But all it had gained from its entanglement in Libya was experience—not much of it encouraging—and a reasonably effective air service. The forces were beginning to recover by 1914, but reorganization would take time. The Italian army held no annual maneuvers after 1911, having its hands full in North Africa, but the performance of the army there did not impress foreign observers.[25] The commanders were cautious, moving only when they enjoyed crushing superiority, and the troops showed scarce initiative in action. The slow campaign of holding outposts against guerrilla attacks, with occasional limited advances to fresh positions, seemed to promise little for the kind of fast-moving war of mass and maneuver that soldiers were expecting on the European battlefronts.

However, another force that might face Austria-Hungary, the Balkan armies, grew dramatically. The South Slav forces gained experience, equipment, and new recruiting territory in the Balkan Wars. The army intelligence bureau in Vienna reported with dismay in February 1914: "All states—especially the victorious ones—are enlarging and reorganizing their armies: Greece is tripling, Serbia doubling, Rumania and finally even Bulgaria and Montenegro are strengthening their armies by significant amounts. . . . In the place of the three army corps and three independent divisions (i.e., a total of twelve divisions) which are disappearing from what used to be European Turkey, in the near future at least five to seven Serbian, ten Greek, one Bulgarian, and two Montenegrin divisions are appearing."[26] It was far from clear whether Bulgaria or Rumania, let alone Greece, would fight against the Dual Monarchy in a future war, of course, and the combined Serb and Montenegrin peacetime forces would still not amount to much more than 100,000 men. Their equipment, too, was exiguous by north European standards, most notably in machine guns and artillery. But the Balkan Wars had shown that the forces could fight and would not hesitate to mobilize very large numbers of reservists. The Austro-Hungarian estimate of the war strength of Serbia in 1914 was 420,000; of Montenegro 50,000.[27] The likely Ottoman ally in the Balkans had been replaced by a dangerous military power grouping.

While the German and Austro-Hungarian armies together gained the most from the military increases of 1912–13, the Entente made more progress in the realm of alliances and cooperation. In this latter respect the situation of Germany and Austria-Hungary changed little. The two states continued to enjoy very close relations, which saw no radical alteration except with respect to the rivals they faced. A certain change had come over the Triple Alliance as a whole with the weakening of Italy and its consequent détente with the Dual Monarchy. The general staffs had even revived some joint military planning for the improbable contingency of Italian forces traveling by way of Austria to fight alongside the German army in Lorraine.[28] But the Entente had made dramatic strides toward military cooperation, both in secret and in public. The Grey-Cambon letters, the Anglo-French naval agreement, and French military and naval conversations with Russia all provided important new assurances of mutual support in a European war. In 1913 and early 1914 the French and British general staffs actually concluded the full arrangements for the transport of the British Expeditionary Force to its deployment areas in France, completing the preparations they had begun during the Moroccan crises.[29] In the public realm, prominent state and staff visits to governments and military events had done much to create an expectation of cooperation in war. On 20–23 July 1914, at the height of the crisis, the French prime minister René Viviani and President Poincaré visited St. Petersburg to talk to the tsar and his ministers. The bellicose atmosphere in the Entente states had greatly increased with the *réveil national* and three-year law debates in France, and with Pan-Slav excitement in Russia over the Balkan crises.

Moltke recognized this in February 1913 in his comments on the feasibility of the Schlieffen plan.[30] At the end of 1912 the retired Schlieffen had died, dictating on his deathbed a final amendment to his plan for throwing all of the German army against France. Moltke noted, however, that his renowned predecessor had thought only in terms of a war started by France, in which Russia might wait to see what the result in the west would be. But this took no account either of the prospect of war breaking out with Russia first, or of the new strength of the Franco-Russian alliance. "As matters stand now," Moltke wrote, "it is impossible for a situation to arise where either France or Russia initially stands by as a passive spectator. Rather, both will simultaneously mobilize and enter as enemies of Germany. That Russia might somehow hesitate to march into East Prussia if no troops are left there to defend it is out of the question under the present political treaties and conditions." In any war, Germany would have to divide its forces. Just as Moltke acknowledged the impossibility of fighting only France, in April 1913 he gave concrete expression to his growing conviction that France would never stay out of a Russo-German war. He canceled all further work on the *Großer Ostaufmarsch*, the contingency plan for an initial attack against Russia rather than France.[31] A major map exercise by the general staff the month before had confirmed what he had always suspected: an offensive to the east would peter out in the vast spaces of Poland and western Russia without securing a decisive success against the opposing army of the kind he hoped for in France.[32]

These transformations contributed strongly to the judgment in Berlin and Vienna by 1914 that it would be better to fight a general war sooner rather than later. Conrad, Franz Ferdinand, and von Moltke had ventured the idea in the Bosnian crisis, and Moltke had expressed it openly, at least for a moment, in the 1912 Balkan confrontation. But by 1914 the notion had gained a wider currency among statesmen as well as soldiers, largely due to the changing military balance. The tangible results of the German and Austro-Hungarian military increases gave them a temporarily improved material position. Although this had been counterbalanced by the increased cohesion of the Entente, the real problem seemed to be that the latter also possessed great latent material strength that could make itself felt in the future. When the French three-year law and the Russian Great Program took their full effect, by about 1917, they would add an overwhelming numerical advantage to the Entente.[33] Meanwhile, the Germans would presumably be primarily confined to completing the 1911–16 Quinquennat and supplementary laws, a large part of whose provisions were already in place in 1914. There was little prospect of Austria-Hungary obtaining major new resources for its armed forces, and when Italy did recover its strength it could be expected to resume its antagonistic attitude toward the Dual Monarchy. Even the Belgian army overcame a long period of stasis in 1913 in reaction to the perceived threat from Germany, and secured a bill to increase its forces from 180,000 to 250,000.[34] The alignment of states might get worse for Germany and Austria-Hungary in the future; the balance of forces available to both sides seemed almost certain to. The temporary tractability of Italy and the dislocation resulting from the early stages of massive army renewals in France and Russia made the 1914–15 period into a window of reasonable military opportunity for Berlin and Vienna. The situation had been better before, but by 1914 it looked as if it would get far worse in the future. Without the influence of an armaments race and its rhetoric, such a purely military consideration might have had little effect on international relations. In the tense atmosphere of Europe after the 1912–13 scramble for armaments, it could hardly go unnoticed.

THE BALANCE OF MILITARY POWER AND
THE DECISION FOR WAR

All the great powers spent the July crisis of 1914 primarily engaged in trying to avoid a general European war.[35] Although their failure was due to a wide range of events and forces, military considerations strongly influenced their preferences. To call the outbreak of the First World War in 1914 purely a preventive war by either group of powers would be an exaggeration. However, the changed military balance and the prospect of future change did mean that statesmen as well as generals approached the situation with attitudes toward the use of armed force substantially different from those they had held in the crises of the previous decade. This made war a more likely result. In the first place, the majority of the leadership in Vienna had become convinced that a war, or at least an act of force, against Serbia was vital to the preservation of the Dual Monarchy, even if it involved the risk of a general European conflict. Secondly, the German government was determined to see Austria-Hungary take military action against Serbia, and was far less convinced than before of the efficacy of a diplomatic victory. At the same time, the Germans too believed that the risk of a European war was an acceptable price to pay. Their main concern was to avoid accepting the blame for such a conflict, in the hope of securing a better constellation of allies and domestic support. The Russians, for their part, regarded war as a possibility as never before, because their army was in an unprecedented state of readiness and because they refused to contemplate the loss of prestige and power that they feared from a capitulation in the Balkans such as the one the military balance had forced on them in 1909. The French offered their support on the principle that a European war would be preferable to watching their strongest ally be destroyed, or to risking the loss of Russia's military support in the future. The British were the least interested in taking advantage of the opportunity to fight a European war under conditions perceived to be favorable, but preserving a balance of military power in Europe was a fundamental motive of the Foreign Office for urging intervention to prevent German hegemony on the continent. Italy's abstention in 1914 was enforced by its military weakness, even if guided by other considerations as well. All sides would have preferred to deter a general conflagration, but were prepared to accept one if necessary.

In Austria-Hungary all of the principal decision makers came to desire a forceful settlement with Serbia, even with the acknowledged risk of a war against Russia. Conrad, of course, had held this view for a long time. Even before the Sarajevo assassination, his calls for an invasion of Serbia were accompanied by a consideration of the consequences. In a conference with the principal ministers of the monarchy in October 1913, he argued: "if R. declares war (& now it must come to a war with R. sooner or later) then the present moment is no less favorable than perhaps another time."[36] He freely referred to the coming "fight for existence," the "great decision," in which the Dual Monarchy would inevitably have to participate. With this prospect in view, he preferred either to knock out the Balkan threat beforehand or else to bring on the general struggle at once.[37] More importantly, other leading figures in Vienna who had previously been against war even with Serbia came increasingly to contemplate it. At the October 1913 meeting on what to do about the Serbs, all of the joint ministers agreed on firm measures.[38] Berchtold merely feared that the Triple Alliance provisions would not take effect if Austria-Hungary attacked Serbia without sufficient pretext, and that Russia might intervene against an isolated Dual Monarchy. István Tisza, who had become minister-president of Hungary, did not want an outright conquest of Serbia because of the problems that more Slavs in the monarchy would cause for Budapest, but he was fully in favor of "a humiliation, reduction" and "financial, economic & military restriction" of Serbia. The minister-president in Vienna, Joseph Count Stürgkh, agreed with him. In March 1914 Tisza sent Franz Joseph a memorandum pressing for a strengthening of alliances to thwart what he regarded as Russian and French efforts to start a "world war" once they had forged "an iron ring around us" in the Balkans.[39] "It is my firm conviction," Tisza wrote, "that Germany's two neighbors are carefully proceeding with military preparations, but will not start the war so long as they have not attained a grouping of the Balkan states against us that confronts the monarchy with an attack from three sides and pins down the majority of our forces on our eastern and southern frontier." His agenda was still for diplomatic steps, but his language and assumptions took on an apocalyptic tone.

When Franz Ferdinand was assassinated and Germany offered its support against Russia in the event of an Austro-Serbian conflict, all the principal figures in the monarchy came around to the idea of war. Conrad naturally wanted to take the opportunity of the assassination for striking against Serbia immediately.[40] Franz Joseph was ready to move as long as he was sure of Germany's support.[41] Once Szögyény reported from Berlin that the German government would stand behind Austria-

Hungary, Berchtold overcame his initial fears and convened a council of ministers on 7 July to propose "rendering Serbia harmless for ever by an act of force."[42] The foreign minister "was quite aware that a passage of arms with Serbia could bring about a war with Russia." However, he thought that St. Petersburg's apparent policy of gathering a Balkan alliance against the Dual Monarchy was a threat that must be forestalled:

> He was of the opinion that we must take into account that in the face of such a policy our situation must steadily deteriorate, all the more so as a passive toleration would certainly be taken by our South Slavs and by Rumania as a sign of weakness and would enhance the attractive power of both bordering states.
>
> The logical consequence of what had been said would be to preempt our adversaries and to arrest the process of development—which was already in full progress—by means of a prompt reckoning with Serbia, which it would not be possible to do later.

This was a long way from Aehrenthal's policy of securing victory without war in 1909, and showed obvious concern with a changing strategic balance. This time the war minister, General Alexander von Krobatin, was for a war rather than a diplomatic success, which would be "worthless" in his opinion. "From the military point of view," he said, "he was obliged to emphasize that it would be more favorable to start the war at once rather than at a later time, since the relationship of power would shift disproportionately against us in the future." He proposed mobilizing only against Serbia first but being ready for a general mobilization if Russia intervened. Stürgkh urged quick action since the Germans advised and supported it. The joint finance minister, Leon Ritter von Bilínski, was also for war, and he expressed "the conviction that the decisive struggle was inevitable sooner or later," and that internal problems in Bosnia and Herzegovina could not be solved either without destroying Serbian power. At the conference the only opponent of military action was Tisza, who insisted on first issuing an ultimatum with which Serbia might comply. The Hungarian minister-president dropped his opposition when Belgrade rejected a few of the resulting demands and presented the Dual Monarchy with a diplomatic pretext for war.[43]

In Berlin the Reich leadership backed Austria-Hungary from the beginning of the crisis, although there was more concern than in Vienna for the prevention of a general European war. Moltke had by this time more than once expressed his opinion that a world war would be better sooner than later, most recently when Conrad had come to meet him while he was taking a cure for bronchitis at Karlsbad in Bohemia in May 1914.[44] The German chief of staff had told his colleague "that all postponement meant a lessening of our chances; we could not compete with

Russia in masses." Kaiser Wilhelm too was given to proclamations about the "inevitable" war of the Germanic powers against their adversaries, often phrased in terms of an apocalyptic racial struggle of "Slavs and Teutons." When he met Berchtold in Vienna in October 1913 he assured him "that I stand behind you and am ready to draw my sword whenever your actions make it necessary."[45] When the crisis over the Sarajevo assassination broke out, the kaiser reassured Vienna through Szögyény that Austria-Hungary enjoyed Germany's absolute support for action against Serbia, even if Russia were to intervene. The statesmen in Berlin, however, assumed at the outset that Russia would not fight over Serbia, and that the pattern of 1909 would repeat itself.[46] On 24 July Pourtalès delivered Bethmann's stiff admonition to St. Petersburg that any war must remain "localized" between Serbia and Austria-Hungary.[47] If not, the German government warned, a general war would follow. Bethmann also rejected a British proposal for a conference of the powers to adjudicate the Austro-Serbian dispute, just as Bülow had vetoed such efforts in 1908 and 1909.

There were some major differences in the German position in 1914, however, which made war more likely than it had been in the Bosnian crisis. In the first place, Moltke had become devoted to the belief that even a general European war would be preferable to a negotiated settlement that left Vienna less than triumphant and the Serbs still powerful.[48] He realized later in the crisis that an Austro-Hungarian mobilization must bring about a Russian one and hence a general war, as he explained in a memorandum to Bethmann on 29 July.[49] He proposed no alternative but to back Vienna absolutely and "prepare to wage war on two fronts." In the second place, unlike the situation in 1908–9, there was no steady stream of reports from St. Petersburg reassuring Berlin that Russia was incapable of mobilizing and that the leadership was declaring its impotence in the face of the Austro-Hungarian move. On the contrary, there were increasing indications in the course of July that the Russians would stand firm. Bethmann and his colleagues could not count on Russian neutrality. Instead, they had to gamble on it. Likewise, the French and British did not exclude the possibility of supporting Russia if it acted. Altogether, the elements of risk in the German calculation were far higher than in previous crises, and accompanied by a fatalistic acceptance of whatever course Russia decided to thrust upon the Austro-German alliance. Finally, unlike in the Bosnian crisis, Berlin actively urged its ally to invade Serbia, and to do so quickly. This was mostly in the hope of presenting the powers with a fait accompli and avoiding a general war, but the element of risk was present as not in Bülow's calculations of 1909. From early on in the crisis Bethmann was deeply pessimistic, speaking to his intimates of an ever more likely war against the powers he believed were steadily surrounding Germany and Austria-Hungary. "The future belongs to Russia," he mused to his private secretary, "as it grows and grows and weighs upon us like an ever-deepening nightmare."[50] He hoped that an uncompromising stance might deter the French from supporting their allies, breaking up the Entente, or else that a war with Austria-Hungary fully engaged might hold fair prospects of victory.[51] "In a few years," the chancellor believed, Russia could "no longer be stopped," unless a dramatic change came about in the European alliance system.[52] At least in this measure the intention to bring about a preventive war had taken hold of the German leaders.

Russia's decision to declare war on Austria-Hungary was mostly reactive and based upon political considerations, but the military balance was nevertheless important in making intervention an option at all. The main reasons for the tsar's and Sazonov's decision to mobilize against Austria-Hungary when it marched against Serbia were that another capitulation as in 1909 would sacrifice all of Russia's credibility as protector of the South Slavs, and that this time the French offered their support as they had not over Bosnia and Herzegovina.[53] However, none of this would have made much difference if the Russian army had been as unready in 1914 as it was in 1909. Rearmament still had a long way to go, but no military man continued to regard mobilization as impossible. When Tsar Nicholas convened crown councils at Krasnoe Selo on 24 and 25 July at which Sazonov put the case for opposing Austria-Hungary with the threat of war, the army leaders did not demur.[54] The Grand Duke Nicholas, who had had the opportunity to confer with the tsar beforehand, said nothing. Sukhomlinov denounced the proposal for a partial mobilization, against Austria-Hungary only, for which no plan existed. He also pointed out that as long as the rearmament program was not complete there was no guarantee of superiority over an Austro-German alliance. But together with the navy minister he declared "nevertheless that hesitation was no longer appropriate as far as the Imperial Government was concerned. They saw no objection to a display of greater firmness in our negotiations."[55] Sukhomlinov later wrote: "It would have been altogether different if in 1914 I had been in the same position as Rediger in 1909." As it was, however, the war minister presided over a largely transformed instrument and could be sure of French and British intervention as not before.[56] Even as a professional matter, it would simply have been difficult for the generals to declare themselves once again unable to do anything. They had pleaded powerlessness for an embarrassingly long time already, and in 1914 there still seemed to be a reasonable chance of deterring war by a resolute stand over Serbia.[57] If Russia failed to take it, the next crisis might not again offer the chance of firm Entente support over a matter of immediate interest to

St. Petersburg. On the domestic front, the same wave of patriotic enthusiasm that had propelled the political classes into broad support for rearmament and an active pro-Slav policy in the immediately preceding years now meant that the Duma also expected decisive action. The autocracy was in no position to risk losing the confidence of the main parties that still supported it.[58]

The French decision to back Russia was more or less automatic, but it had some basis in calculations of relative military power. By the end of July the Quai d'Orsay was transmitting affirmations of support through its ambassador in St. Petersburg, Maurice Paléologue, who was an ardent proponent of the Franco-Russian alliance and invariably presented Paris with an appealing impression of Sazonov's policy.[59] In any case, with the *réveil national*, the presidency of Poincaré, and the confident military leadership of Joffre, it was not likely that France would leave its ally in the lurch in any major confrontation with Germany. A crucial military consideration was the recovery of the Russian army. There was no talk as there had been in the Bosnian crisis of the Russians being unable to help themselves. From a strategic point of view, it seemed opportune for the French to fight when a Balkan coalition would take part, rather than later when it might already have been wiped out. It also appeared better to do so when Russia was certain to mobilize promptly, which would always be a doubtful matter when only French interests were at stake. The politicians left no evidence of consulting the military extensively on the actual chances for a war as they had done in previous crises. Instead they conferred often with the generals about mobilization measures and the famous order to keep all troops away from the immediate frontier so as to demonstrate emphatically to the British that the French would not be acting as the aggressors. Joffre recalled in his memoirs that Messimy summoned him on 24 July and told him that a conflict was likely:

> The habit of continually concerning myself with preparing for war made me consider this formidable prospect without surprise. So I simply replied: "Very well! *Monsieur le Ministre*, we will fight if we need to." My attitude must have had the effect of reassuring the minister, for he came over to me, without disguising his emotion, energetically shook my hand, and said to me: "Bravo!" Then, together, we examined as calmly as ever the measures that needed to be taken first if the threat of war materialized.[60]

Apart from this perfunctory exchange, the government displayed less anxiety about the opinions of its military experts than about the willingness of Britain to enter a war against Germany.

The British delayed until the very end, but in their case the final decision rested on immediate political and long-term strategic concerns rather than on fine calculations of the military balance. Sir Edward Grey first tried to keep the peace on the continent by telling both sides that they could not count on Britain, and when that failed he worked to secure a mandate from the cabinet and the public for the policy of supporting France. His principal advisors urged intervention on the grounds that to stand aside would be to face the *fait accompli* of a German invasion of France.[61] The undersecretary for European affairs, Sir Eyre Crowe, also argued many points of prestige and justice and ended by saying that Britain's actual capacity to fight was not the essential matter. The armed forces were certainly ready, he asserted: "The question at issue is not whether we are capable of taking part in a war, but whether we should go into the present war. That is a question firstly of right or wrong, and secondly of political expediency." Grey's own decision rested partly on a military consideration, but not a momentary one: the need to prevent German domination of the continent and consequently the isolation of Great Britain.[62] His most persuasive argument in the cabinet was naval rather than military. The fleet was pledged to defend the northern coasts of France, which would be open to German attack if Britain remained neutral.[63] The joint war planning between the two general staffs and the British Directorate of Military Operations, despite its explicitly noncommittal character, had also created a considerable expectation of aid from Britain in both popular and official circles in France, a point that Grey stressed in his arguments to the government and the House of Commons. The Liberal dissenters in the cabinet eventually supported him partly as a result of Grey's and Asquith's threats to resign if their policy were not adopted; partly because Conservative leaders in Parliament signaled that they would favor intervention even if the government did not; and partly due to the prospect of public outrage at the German violation of Belgian neutrality.[64]

Italy's policy in the July crisis stood under stronger military imperatives than any other country's. Even if Antonio Salandra's government had wanted to intervene, it had practically no army to put into the field in July 1914. Salandra and the foreign minister, Antonino Di San Giuliano, in any case preferred to help try to avert a European war in which Italy had little to gain. Italy would have been a very junior partner in whichever alliance it joined, and its subsequent intervention was almost completely opportunistic. But one of the main reasons why the opportunity did not come sooner was because Italy could not have mobilized in 1914, and Salandra knew it.[65] From the moment he took office in March 1914, the prime minister had received reports from the general staff and war ministry on the catastrophic shortages of trained men and equipment that the Libyan war had caused.[66] At the height of the July crisis the new chief of the general staff, Luigi Cadorna, presented King Victor Emanuel with an exhaustive memorandum explaining at length the deficiencies of the army's plans and armament for war.[67] His wrong-headed assumption that the campaign would be against France cannot have inspired any greater confidence. On 2 August Cadorna reported that mobilization itself would take a month, and indeed would be desirable at once in order to have the army ready for use at a later date. The forces would need much preliminary reorganization once they had been called up, "given the state of the cadres, the lack of training, the state of matériel, the shortage of both animal and motor transport . . . [and the need] above all to reconstitute that moral cohesion which the vicissitudes of recent times have, as Your Excellency is aware, so gravely compromised, not to say destroyed."[68] The army was short of 350,000 uniforms, vast quantities of boots, half of the 26,000 officers necessary for the war strength, and small arms. Infantry companies would need to mobilize with 80 percent of their strength composed of reservists. Only the active army could be armed with the modern 1891 rifle; the second-line units would have to receive an obsolete type. There were not even enough machine guns to give a section to each regiment. Since only three artillery regiments had received the new Deport 75mm field guns by August 1914, the existing Krupp 1906 semi-quick-firers had to be hastily redistributed among the whole of the field artillery as the non-quick-firing types were retired and batteries reduced from six to four guns. This change yielded only sixty-four pieces per corps instead of the planned ninety-six, as well as many crews unfamiliar with their equipment.[69] It would cost the Italian army a tremendous effort, lasting until the following spring, to reconstitute itself for a campaign after its total hollowing out in the Libyan war, which still dragged on in 1914. During the July crisis there was no question of Italy's contributing a deterrent against Austro-Hungarian action.

By the time of the July assassination in 1914, the main participants had changed their hierarchy of preferences for the outcome since previous confrontations, in a way that made war seem to them like a much less unthinkable option than before. This was chiefly due to perceived changes in the balance of military power, particularly as the decision makers predicted it for the future. The current equilibrium in 1914 was not extremely different from that in 1911, the increases in the military strength of the two sides having largely canceled each other out in the intervening armaments race. Changes, however, looked as if they were going to continue, and this prospect made the future appear ominous to both sides for different reasons.[70] The situation was paradoxical, but the fears none the less vivid.

For Germany and Austria-Hungary, the obvious problem was that they had grown nearly as far as they could in the immediate term, while the Entente powers appeared to have considerable increases still ahead. The Austro-German alliance had moved from a position of ascendancy over its possible opponents in the 1904 to 1910 period, to a situation of being scarcely able to face the coalition against it with reasonable hopes of success in the confrontations of 1911 to 1914. As Conrad put it during the July crisis: "In 1908–9 it would have been a foregone conclusion, in 1912–13 it would have been a game with decent chances, *now* we play *va banque*."[71] In future, the balance seemed likely to grow still less favorable. While Germany had the prospect of continuing to make some gains, most of its benefits from the 1912 and 1913 laws were already in place, and Austria-Hungary appeared to have few fresh resources available. Political crises seemed destined to weaken the Dual Monarchy in the future. The Entente powers, on the other hand, appeared to have most of their military growth still to come. France would in due course reap its gains from three-year service, and above all Russia seemed to be standing on the brink of almost unlimited expansion. This left Berlin and Vienna facing the possibility of being forced into a position of powerlessness against the Entente. The window of military superiority seemed to be closing, which suddenly made the opportunity more tempting. Statesmen in Berlin had acquired the habit at least since 1905 of being able to hold their own in military confrontations with rival powers over matters in any way touching their interests. The prospect of losing this capability in the atmosphere of 1914 was a disquieting one.[72]

For the Entente too, however, the future looked sinister if the July crisis did not turn out favorably. The main risk was that the Entente might fall apart if it did not stand together this time. Under the conditions of 1914, this seemed to promise a future confrontation, or series of confrontations, of isolated powers against an invincible Austro-German coalition free from its Balkan distractions. Statesmen in Paris and St. Petersburg regarded the July crisis as a vital test of the Entente's cohesion, and believed there were good chances that failing such a test would convince the participants that the alliance was not worthwhile. From a military standpoint, the Entente's chances in a present war seemed viable by 1914, even though they were not as good as they were likely to become after several more years of peace. If given the choice, the Entente leaders would have preferred to wait and fight a war later if necessary, but the crisis over Serbia forced them to decide at once. Both sides were therefore gambling against military eclipse in 1914.

The prospect of military weakness would not have seemed nearly so dangerous if it had not been for the polarization and militarization of international relations since 1911, which caused statesmen to make decisions based to a much greater extent on the strategic position than they had in the preceding years. Attitudes toward war had changed profoundly with the armaments race. Even where generals did not press for immediate military action as they did in Vienna, and even though the decision for war always rested ultimately with civilian leaders, many of these statesmen had themselves appropriated the strategic assumptions of the soldiers.[73] On all sides, war had come to seem like a less disastrous option than diplomatic defeat, and a politician like Bethmann could contemplate the "leap into the darkness" with a kind of resigned fascination.[74]

A general European war was not the preferred outcome for any of the participants, of course. Diplomatic victory was. In fact, the powers generally hoped that diplomatic victory might make a future war unnecessary. For Germany and Austria-Hungary, success in the July crisis would have meant a negotiated settlement that gave Vienna a free hand against the Serbs. The result they desired was a breaking up of the Entente due to French and British reluctance to be drawn into war for the sake of Russian interests in the Balkans, and to Russia's disgust at not being supported by its western partners. There was also the hope of eliminating the South Slav threat to the internal stability of the Dual Monarchy, probably by an invasion and partition of Serbia, or perhaps merely by severe punitive measures that would chasten Belgrade. Either way, statesmen in Vienna hoped that a success of this kind would stamp out the aspirations of the separatists at the same time as it unified the population in loyalty to the throne. For the Entente powers, diplomatic victory would have meant the preservation of the coalition against Austro-German expansionism, and ultimately the development of a military grouping so strong that it would deter Berlin and Vienna from war in the future, and presumably from further aggressive policies. For both sides in the July crisis, the preferred outcome of a diplomatic victory would have made a big war between the European powers unnecessary, at least in the near term.

As a consequence of these strategic calculations, the great powers entered the 1914 crisis with a hierarchy of preferences in which a European war was no longer at the bottom of the list. The best option on both sides was a diplomatic victory, which offered the possibility that a war might not have to be fought at all. The worst prospect was diplomatic defeat, which all sides regarded as unacceptably disastrous, and conducive to a future war under worse conditions. Somewhere in between these outcomes lay the possibility of fighting it out in 1914 with reasonable hopes of success, subject to the chances of war. Given that the preferred outcome was impossible because the aims of the two sides were mutually exclusive, the second choice—war—became the most likely result. Here lay the crucial difference between 1914 and previous crises, where one side or the other had always accepted diplomatic defeat rather than risk war, which at the time had been a practically unthinkable prospect. The turbulent military events of the years between 1911 and 1914 had wrought a profound change in the attitudes of the decision makers.

EPILOGUE: THE EUROPEAN ARMIES IN THE WORLD WAR

The European armies marched in 1914 partly due to the spiraling armaments race, which might have continued if they had not gone to war. It was, of course, possible that diplomatic changes such as an Anglo-German rapprochement could have slowed the rush to arms, or that financial considerations or domestic upheaval in any of the countries involved could have interrupted the cycle. As it was, however, the European powers in 1914 were nearer to the beginning than to the end of the military revolutions their leaders had planned. The French three-year service law was only due to have its full effect from 1916 onward. The Russian Great Program had just passed through the Duma when the war broke out, but it was designed to increase the standing army to nearly two million men by 1917, along with massive procurement of artillery and other armaments.[75] In Germany, a major transformation of the basis of military service was in sight by 1914. In August 1913 the new Prussian war minister, General Erich von Falkenhayn, had proposed implementing truly universal service, disregarding the 1 percent population threshold entirely, and incorporating all able-bodied men into the armed services as in France. In June and July of 1914, he worked out a plan with Bethmann and the kaiser to adopt universal service with the 1916 Quinquennat and implement it in a ten-year program lasting until 1926.[76] In Austria-Hungary, Conrad was developing a scheme for a "reserve army" system to keep pace with Russian and Balkan expansion. Since 1913 he had been proposing a plan to use reserves in a new fashion for the Dual Monarchy: not only to complete regular units on mobilization and take up rear-area duties, but to constitute entire divisions and mountain brigades of their own for use in the first line. In a ten-year program Conrad hoped to put the organization in place in both the common army and the Landwehr and Honvédség, increasing the forces by more than 50 percent. The Ersatzreserve and Landsturm would take over line-of-communication and interior duties.[77]

On the other hand there was no shortage of indications that the powers might be unable to carry out such ambitious plans. In France in 1914 the Radicals were on their way back to power while the Socialists gathered strength in the April elections. The three-year law might soon have been seriously attenuated even though its immediate repeal would have been virtually impossible.[78] In Russia the Duma had accepted the Great Program, but the ponderous pace of all preceding reform in the army promised that its implementation would be slow and erratic even if the state finances could support it. In Germany too, financing would have been an obstacle to still larger military plans of the kind Falkenhayn planned, even if he had managed to keep the fleet off the agenda. Approval in the Reichstag for universal service was in any case far from assured as the extremes of left and right grew stronger with almost every election. Austria-Hungary's reserve army was still only a proposal of Conrad's by 1914, and the financially straitjacketed and politically deadlocked legislature of the Dual Monarchy would hardly have been more receptive to it than to earlier military expansions. The Italians would eventually have come around to an army reform after the war against the Ottoman Empire. However, the recovery would have been gradual, due to lingering military involvement in North Africa (which in the event lasted until 1931) as well as the slow pace of armament transformations in Italy.

When the European armies did mobilize in August 1914 the numerical weight of land forces lay on the side of the Triple Entente, but the Central Powers enjoyed some qualitative superiority due to the high state of development of the German army. In the crudest terms, Russia deployed some 28 two-division army corps in the west; France deployed 22 plus the equivalent of a further 6 in independent reserve divisions. Great Britain sent two to France. Germany entered the war with 26 active and 13 reserve corps, and Austria-Hungary with 16 corps (although each of these contained a third division of the Landwehr or Honvédség). Counting Belgium and Serbia, the Entente fielded the equivalent of approximately 58 corps to the Central Powers' 54. German corps, however, possessed more artillery than any others: 144 field guns and light howitzers, in addition to modern heavy field artillery, which in other armies was mostly obsolete and too scarce to assign down to corps level. The German reserve corps had exactly half as many field guns as the active corps, and no heavy artillery. French corps had 120 field guns, although with superior four-gun battery organization. Russian corps had 108, and Austro-Hungarian only 96 despite their excess of infantry. The armies of all the great powers fighting in 1914 had approximately two machine guns per battalion of infantry. Germany was the richest in technical equipment in general, as measured for example by its mobilization of 202 engineer companies altogether in the active corps, compared to 168 for Russia, 95 for France, 64 for Austria-Hungary, and 12 with the British Expeditionary Force.

Although these proportions counted in the opening battles, they and the prewar calculations that had been based on them were soon swept away in the titanic struggle of national resources that lasted until 1918. The scale and duration of the war itself owed much to the military development of the decade that preceded it. The European armies of 1914 were very different from those of 1904. There had been some organizational changes, such as the increasing reliance upon reservists in both active units and their own formations, which prefigured the war of masses. More importantly, all armies had acquired the weapons that helped to make maneuver nearly impossible on the west European fronts from late 1914 onward. Quick-firing artillery and machine guns cut down troops that exposed themselves in order to advance. Reconnaissance by aircraft made it difficult to achieve surprise on any significant scale. Telephones linked defensive systems together, but the absence of portable radios meant that an attack quickly outran its means of communication. The protracted contest of material that these armaments helped to bring about had the effect of calling forth in turn new technologies from the industrial societies that had produced them, such as poison gas, armored fighting vehicles, and aerial bombardment. The European armies had taken up the lethal machinery of the twentieth century in the decade before the war without the changes in organization, communication, and transport that could overcome the deadlock they created.[79]

Nothing in the armaments race before 1914 had done much to affect the way in which either military or civilian leaders employed these instruments, so the strategic paralysis of the world war is hard to attribute to any particular development of the armies in the preceding decade. The problems of long-term supply and war production, which became decisive as the struggle proceeded, had been deliberately avoided by those who had prepared the most for the conflict. This was partly the result of an expectation that the war would be short and decisive with so many resources deployed in the first shock; and partly the consequence of military men recoiling from the awful prospect of what such preparations might imply. The tactical development of all the European armies during the preceding decade effectively went out the window in 1914. The sheer masses of reservists called up allowed only relatively schematic and improvised movements on the battlefield, which had little to do with the hotly debated and more or less carefully rehearsed assault drills of the maneuver grounds. On the operational level, some mentalities endured, such as the German inclination to commit their forces to predictable, heavy blows as at the Marne and Ypres. But on the ground itself there was often little to choose between the "*souple*" skirmishing of the French infantry and the orderly double-time bounds of the Germans. Herds of hastily recalled reservists with officers and NCOs from wherever they could be found were not capable of carrying out either tactical scheme very precisely in the confusion of combat, and both withered away with nearly equal bloodiness under shrapnel and small arms fire. The cavalry that all the European armies, and especially the Russian, had built up with such expense and care in enormous quantities proved useless for shock action, and functioned only in a limited role in reconnaissance and screening during the opening campaigns and in some operations on the eastern front. In many cases the troopers eventually took up rifles and helmets and went into the trenches with the rest.

Many characteristics of the individual European armies and their preparations for war did, however, affect their performance on the battlefields of 1914–18. The cohesion and thorough training of the German army proved unexpectedly to be a particular asset for mobilizing and encadring reserves and new recruits in a prolonged war of masses. Its relatively high level of technical equipment gave it a head start in the contest of material, and its unique complement of heavy artillery was a great advantage in trench warfare. Large-caliber shells proved vital for caving in entrenchments and dugouts or smashing enemy batteries at long range. The French army's reserves and training system produced less effective formations to follow the initial field army, although the vaunted morale, traditions, and modern field artillery of the active forces carried them through the opening campaigns in spite of tremendous losses. The heavy artillery found itself resorting to a series of inadequate expedients to improvise guns to compete with the Germans'.[80] The Russian army, as ever, suffered disastrously from lack of advanced training, cadres, and equipment, which allowed the Germans in particular to outmaneuver it repeatedly with inferior forces. The revolutions of 1917 stemmed in large part from the disastrous defeats that ensued. Austria-Hungary continued more or less successfully to fend off the vicissitudes of national and linguistic diversity within the army until the last campaign of the war, but lacked the material resources to sustain a long struggle, just as it had lagged in the competition to modernize before 1914. The British army performed with professional cohesion in the initial battles, but the small size that had so often led observers to discount it before the war meant that the available formations disappeared with frightening speed. The high command was not able to raise and train a really large force for action until 1916, and even then entrusted it only with comparatively primitive tactics. Nevertheless, the industrial resources that had made Britain so formidable before the war

CONCLUSION

BETWEEN 1904 and 1914 a major change came about in the way European statesmen perceived military power, and that change made war a more likely outcome of the 1914 crisis than of those in the preceding decade. The military environment in Europe went from a state of gradual peacetime development, relatively little heeded by civilian leaders, to one of intense competitive army increases explicitly directed against rival powers and constituting a major object of political concern. This transformation arose not only because of the land armaments race between 1912 and 1914, but also because of perceptions throughout the decade that the balance of military power among the states was changing. The policies that flowed from these perceptions, interacting with diplomatic alignments and crises, brought about the transformation by the time of the Sarajevo assassination in 1914.

The most acutely perceived feature of the military situation during this period was the incapacitation of the Russian army in the aftermath of its collapse in the war with Japan and the 1905 revolution. The complete prostration of the largest military force in Europe came at a time when Germany's policy of assertiveness as a world power was leading that country into nearly irreconcilable naval rivalry with Britain and periodic colonial conflicts with France. This meant that Germany had a variety of individual rivals, over which it enjoyed a period of appreciable military superiority. As a result, statesmen in Berlin succumbed to the temptation to use the threat of war as a tool of coercion in international crises that they would otherwise have resolved purely by diplomacy. The process accelerated with the development of a "preventive war" mentality in the increasingly turbulent Austro-Hungarian monarchy. This attitude in Vienna was itself a product of the belief that the strategic situation was currently favorable and might not remain so if Italy or Russia became stronger. These perceptions of the balance of military power conditioned the policy of all the European states in the first Moroccan crisis and in the Bosnia and Herzegovina annexation crisis.

The bellicosity of Germany under these circumstances prompted closer military cooperation between the Entente governments in an effort to redress the balance, leading to joint war planning and slightly increased preparation of their armies for a land war in Europe. This, combined with the beginnings of the Russian army's recovery, created the impression in Berlin that the balance of military power was in the process of changing to the disadvantage of Germany and Austria-Hungary. This impression crystallized into a sense of potential inferiority and strategic emergency in the aftermath of the second Moroccan crisis. In response, Germany started a general land armaments race in 1912, in the hope of either retaining the ability to intimidate its adversaries or else being prepared for victory in a general war.

The arms race and the rhetoric that accompanied it quickly created a new attitude toward the use of military force in Europe. Commentators routinely compared the strength of armies in public, statesmen explicitly directed military spending bills against the armaments of specific foreign powers, and public movements in favor of military preparedness gained importance. In Vienna and Berlin the notion of fighting a preventive war before the Entente coalition became invincible gained a degree of acceptance among vital decision makers that would have been unthinkable a few years earlier. As a consequence, the main powers entered the July crisis of 1914 with a fatally changed order of preferences for the outcome. For virtually all of them, war was no longer the worst option. It was not the optimal result for any of them: each preferred a diplomatic success without war. But by 1914 a war, with reasonably good perceived chances of victory, seemed to a significant proportion of statesmen like a better prospect than a diplomatic defeat. The latter, they believed, for different reasons in each case, would bring about virtually certain eclipse, probably in the form of a future war under far worse circumstances. The Germans and Austro-Hungarians, in particular, calculated that a diplomatic victory in 1914 might actually make a future war unnecessary by breaking up the coalition they faced. With this changed attitude, quite different from the aversion to war shown in previous confrontations, the powers were more disposed to allow a crisis to escalate into a general conflict by 1914.

Such a comparison of the various states' preferences over the course of several crises spanning the decade before the war helps to explain why 1914 was different. Simply to anatomize the events of July and the first days of August in that year is to confront a complex series of decisions by individual statesmen. This in itself can explain a great deal, but certain choices remain difficult to account for. To step back, however, and compare the prevailing attitudes toward war and military power with those held by statesmen in preceding crises shows critical differences that make the result easier to understand. In particular the degree of fatalism that seemed to overcome Bethmann Hollweg in the final days, when peace could theoretically have been saved by Germany restraining Austria-Hungary from a full-scale invasion of Serbia, is less mystifying.

All of this obviously depended heavily on developments in international politics. Without the polarization of alliance groupings and the failure of any rapprochement between Berlin or Vienna and their rivals, the changing military balance would have gone almost unnoticed outside of professional circles. Without a series of diplomatic crises, statesmen's attitudes toward military power would have remained untested. Under the circumstances, political developments made military strength important, but at the same time they were themselves influenced by changing perceptions of the military situation. The relationship between international politics and relative military power was one of interdependence.

In none of the diplomatic crises between 1905 and 1914 did statesmen enter confrontations with the intent to provoke a war, or even to threaten their adversaries with one. Once the crises came to a head, however, the principal decision makers often did menace their opponents with war and almost invariably took the balance of military power into consideration. This did not mean that the strategic situation dictated the outcome of all crises. It was crucial to Germany's successful bluff in the first phase of the 1905 Moroccan crisis, but did not affect the outcome of the second phase, when the actual will to fight over the issues at hand was decisive. In the Bosnian crisis it permitted Berlin and Vienna to force Russia into capitulation, but did not persuade Austria-Hungary to take full advantage of the situation by invading Serbia, an action that the Russians could have done nothing to prevent. In the second Moroccan crisis it helped persuade Germany to retreat, but the balance of forces looked risky to all participants, and the outcome was not strictly a matter of a military preponderance on one side. In 1914, however, perceptions of military strength did have a strong influence on the decisions for war. This was partly because statesmen perceived that windows of opportunity were closing, and partly because the armaments competition of the preceding two years had forced even civilian leaders to think extensively about military power long before the crisis itself made war an immediate prospect.

The circumstances of 1914 in turn suggest why states do not necessarily contemplate starting a war whenever they enjoy a military advantage over their rivals. The mere existence of a window of opportunity is not enough to prompt a preemptive strike, even if some strategic thinkers do propose it, as Conrad did from 1906 onward and Moltke after 1911. If it were, then Germany ought to have attacked France in 1905 or Russia in 1909, disposing of rivals while they were weak. Instead, thoughts of preemptive war came only later to the principal statesmen, when the window of opportunity actually appeared to be closing. This circumstance made preemption seem more urgent. On the other hand, the change in the balance by itself would probably not have been enough to convince statesmen that war was preferable to retreat in the July crisis. The changed atmosphere brought about by the armaments race and its accompanying rhetoric added a crucial difference.

In this sense, the arms race did precipitate the First World War. It had many of the destabilizing effects that theorists predict for such competitions. Armament measures in one country created the impression of aggressive intent toward others. Shifts in the balance of military strength accelerated and appeared more threatening. As a result, windows of opportunity for victorious wars seemed to be in the process of closing. As states spent more on armaments, they began to worry about how long their resources would last in such a contest against their adversaries'. Simultaneously, the mobilization of more manpower, funds, and equipment demanded the engagement of popular chauvinism, a sense of national emergency, and the risk of domestic reaction against the new sacrifices, all of which made war seem to statesmen like a more acceptable option in a crisis. All of these influences helped the notion of a preventive war, based on calculations of relative military capability, to migrate from the minds of a few generals into the thoughts of civilian leaders. It had always been possible to find soldiers who routinely weighed the possible results of a war, like Conrad, Sir Henry Wilson, and later von Moltke. Such assessments were part of the job of these technicians. It was quite a different matter when this way of thinking began to affect the policy of civilians who had characteristically paid little attention to the military balance except in isolated moments of crisis, like Berchtold and Bethmann Hollweg.

The causes of the arms race itself are consequently a matter of considerable significance. The most striking thing about them is that they lay essentially in the international rather than the domestic realm. There is no evidence that lobbying by armaments manufacturers for large new contracts for, say, artillery or fortress construction played an influential part in the actual spiral of armaments increases. In any case the army laws of the last prewar years relied heavily on new call-ups of manpower rather than capital-intensive renewals of machinery. Most people still regarded superiority in land warfare primarily as a matter of procuring and training more men as more effective soldiers, a process that relied only in part on sophisticated new weaponry. Nor did the army increases in any country arise primarily from domestic political coalitions independent of the strategic situation. Chauvinism in right-wing and center parties eager to prove their patriotic credentials certainly played their part in passing the Russian budgets in the Duma, the German supplementary bills of 1912 and 1913, and the three-year law in France. But whether any of these would have gained momentum without the international armaments dynamic is extremely doubtful. None were part of long-standing strategies of political stabilization like the naval construction *Sammlung* engineered by Miquel, Tirpitz, and Bülow. Statesmen and publicists mustered the support for them in an ad hoc fashion, rather than as a means of promoting the interests of any particular social, economic, or political group. The German and French army laws of 1912 and 1913 in fact embodied considerable sacrifices of the traditional interests of the dominant political classes in order to secure funding and approval, again in contrast to the reactionary character of the various naval bills in Germany.

Instead, the army increases came about as a direct response to a transformed strategic environment. Their more or less simultaneous birth in parliaments, governments, and high commands occurred immediately after the perception of a military threat from abroad, and the secret as well as public rationales for them were phrased entirely in these terms. This is perhaps not too surprising in view of the vital role that armies played in the national security of the continental powers in contrast to the navies, which acted more as accessories to global expansion. Fleets could function as political tools and symbols, and statesmen could allow naval races to gather considerable steam without causing wars. The development of armies, on the other hand, was more closely connected with the real likelihood of conflict.

The significance of the military dynamic does not reduce the importance of other explanations for the origins of the First World War. The process just described depended upon a multitude of circumstances. It unfolded in an age of nationalist and militarist ideology, conditioned by social-Darwinist assumptions and by the results of the relatively limited European wars of the nineteenth century with their decisive outcomes and definite gains for the victors. These wars had been effective in militarily crippling the defeated side for a certain time, quite apart from any actual territorial gains, and therefore they offered a model for fighting offensive wars even in the absence of specific goals of conquest. The July crisis could likewise only have come about in the form that it did in a world dominated by alliance groupings which confronted each other periodically over points of territorial, colonial, or naval contention. The system was particularly unstable since it contained a flagging Austro-Hungarian empire prepared to lash out at its antagonists, and a rising Germany determined to assert itself in a position of world power. Domestic considerations propelled these ambitions in both states, and gave varying incentives elsewhere too for aggressive state policy as a means of buttressing the social and political status quo at home. The whole situation was particularly volatile due to the prevalence of offensive-minded tactical and strategic thinking in armies, which were bound to each other by the interlocking hair-trigger mobilization and attack plans of hostile alliances, dependent upon railroad timetables and head starts measured in days.

All of these combustible elements, however, had been constantly present on the European scene for some time by 1914. The main things that had actually changed in the near term were perceptions of military power, transformed by the interaction of the strategic balance and international politics. There had been plenty of diplomatic crises before 1914, just as the domestic tensions in several of the European states in that year had their precedents as well. The crisis in the military realm, bringing its incentive to fight a war before it was too late, represented the most significant difference between the July crisis and those that had come before it. Had the assassination occurred ten years earlier, or even as late as 1911, it is hard to imagine that it would have resulted in a general European war. The nonstrategic interests at stake for the powers in 1914 were not much greater than those in other crises. The armaments race on land and the speculation about imminent or preventive wars were new.

Throughout the decade before 1914 the European armies contended with the problems of modernization and predictions about the shape of a future war in a time of rapidly changing technology. On the one hand, they met these challenges with lamentable inadequacy. They failed to ready the plans, equipment, and type of forces suitable for a long war of material. They prepared to rush headlong into ruinous offensives, relying on firepower to increase the strength of the attack, while shrinking from contemplation of what the new weapons would do for the defensive, or of what would happen if the initial onslaughts failed to produce a decision. On the other hand, the generals were far less resistant to new technology than conventional portrayals suggest. Their offensive tactical schemes did take modern firepower into account, even though their biases in favor of the attack made them dedicate most of their thought to how the new weapons would make it easier, rather than harder, to get forward. The generals were eager enough to adopt quick-firing artillery, machine guns, and the other hardware of twentieth-century war, but constantly had to balance the desirability of these against the expenditure and manpower they required during a period when scarcely expanding military budgets virtually ruled out increases.

Critics of the prewar high commands also ignore the difficulties presented by the sheer proliferation of new inventions that overworked technical staffs had to evaluate. The less practical innovations included dirigibles, bicycles for mass transport, mobile armor plates to shield attacking infantry, clusters of darts to be dropped from aircraft over enemy formations, range-finders for use in infantry firing lines, light machine guns to be carried by individual soldiers (which proved simply too complex to be reliable in the decade before the war), heliographs for communication, and even in a few instances the camouflage painting of horses. All of these and many others were considered, laboriously tested, and eventually discarded or used in marginal roles by most of the European armies at some point in the decade before 1914. Not everything that was new was useful, and it took a considerable effort to refine practical military equipment from the profusion of novelties thrown up by industrial society. Some inventions that later proved important, most notably poison gas and tanks, did not attract any significant attention in official circles before the war, but arguably their subsequent development in wartime owed much to the development of articulated technical testing branches in the European general staffs in the period before the war. The existence of experienced personnel and a bureaucratic structure, created to absorb the inventions of the turn of the century, permitted the continuing and rapid introduction of the means of machine warfare even as the conflict was in progress. Most previous wars had been fought to the end with approximately the same technology that had existed at the outset.

Within these limitations, the pre-1914 Prussian-German army proved far more effective in preparing for war than many modern authors have argued. It generally had sound military reasons for decisions that have often been ascribed primarily to social-reactionary motives, and foreign observers at the time certainly did not discount its accomplishments. Contemporaries greatly overrated the improvement of the Russian army after 1909, perhaps eager not to leave anything to chance. However, the significance of what the Russians did achieve, in simply becoming capable of waging a European war again, was enormous. The French army enjoyed a high reputation among foreign observers as well as at home for its enthusiasm and readiness with the newest technologies, though the ordeal of the First World War subjected its failings in more traditional realms to a terrible test. The Austro-Hungarian army functioned and retained a remarkably high level of cohesion in spite of the national conflicts in the Dual Monarchy, but lagged badly in the technical domain. The Italian army performed by far the worst of all the European forces before the war, and its engagement in the conquest of Libya nullified the incipient reforms that might have made it a more dangerous opponent—or even a deterrent to Austro-Hungarian action in the Balkans—by 1914. The British army had the easiest task in training and modernization due to its small size, but for the same reason appeared to weigh little in the strategic balance. Its transformation in the course of total war between 1914 and 1918, although it would have been impossible without the sacrifice of major continental allies, was in the end a formidable one.

PEACETIME STRENGTH OF
THE EUROPEAN ARMIES, 1904–1913

THE TABLE BELOW cannot give an exact representation of the number of officers and men under arms in Europe, for the reasons discussed in Chapter 1. It is intended only to present a very general sense of the orders of magnitude involved in the relative peacetime strengths of the powers. The figures are based on those given in the German annual, *Von Löbells Jahresberichte über die Veränderungen und Fortschritte im Militärwesen,* the publication that gave the most consistent comparative tabulations for the prewar years. The various statistical publications of the governments, when they existed at all, used such divergent criteria for computation—often varying or ceasing from year to year even within the same series—that they are not a good source for international comparisons. The "von Löbell" reports, compiled in this period by the retired General Gerhard von Pelet-Narbonne and a staff of experts, constituted a major source for professional military men throughout Europe and are therefore a suitable reference point for a study of contemporary perceptions. They ceased their publication of comparative statistics when the war broke out, which meant that no figures were available for peacetime strengths in 1914—a calculation that had generally been made toward the end of each year.

The numbers given here refer to both officers and enlisted men, not including gendarmerie and generally excluding colonial forces (with the most important exception of Britain). Nevertheless, even within the von Löbell reports, methods of tabulation varied from one country to another, and even from one year to the next due to changes in organization of the forces or in editorial policy by governments as well as by the publishers of the *Jahresberichte.* The figures grew particularly unreliable with the army increases of 1912–13, as strengths changed rapidly and nobody was quite sure which of the new measures were taking effect and what the actual consequences were for the size of recruit contingents in a particular year. Matters did not have time to stabilize enough for an accurate count before the war broke out and mobilization submerged the call-ups projected for the autumn of 1914.

Only the figures for Germany and Austria-Hungary should be taken as reasonably accurate. Those for Russia were mostly a rough guess, as

TABLE A.1

Peacetime Effectives of the Powers (Officers and Enlisted Men)

	Russia[a]	Germany	France	Austria-Hungary	Italy	Great Britain
1904	1,900,000+	606,866	575,000	361,770	221,085	209,460
1905	1,900,000−	609,552	595,000	361,770	220,834	213,780
1906	1,000,000	614,353	590,000	362,398	249,816	196,600
1907	1,000,000	616,838	602,492	366,578	249,917	179,209
1908	1,000,000	619,006	610,923	365,742	~247,000	183,280
1909	1,209,000	610,196	567,484	369,203	~247,000	181,900
1910	1,303,000	610,083	574,342	370,510	238,617	182,350
1911	1,345,000	612,557	593,556	353,017	253,786	182,700
1912	1,332,000	646,321	611,709	391,297	256,000	192,590
1913	1,300,000	782,344	~700,000	n.a.	256,000	192,144

Source: Based on Gerhard von Pelet-Narbonne, ed., *Von Löbells Jahresberichte über die Veränderungen und Fortschritte im Militärwesen*, Berlin, 1904–13. The numbers listed as approximate for France and Italy in 1908, 1909, and 1913 are interpolations made when the *Jahresberichte* do not list the number of officers for the year. Since the bulk of the forces were enlisted and the number of officers did not fluctuate very much, the variation is not likely to be significant.

[a] The figures for the Russian army between 1904 and 1908 cover only troops stationed in European Russia and the Caucasus; thereafter the entire empire is included.

indicated, for example, by the roundness of the numbers. The arbitrary decision whether to include only troops based in "European" Russia, or those in the Caucasus and the rest of the empire as well, obviously complicated matters, and the editors' decision to change their policy concerning this in 1909 does not make it any easier to measure change over time. The French, like the Italians, reported various figures depending on whether the strength was the budgeted one, the official size of the units assuming full peacetime establishments, or the number of men actually with the colors. The latter number in any case fluctuated enormously in the course of the year as various categories were called up and discharged. Italy experienced the wildest variations from late 1911 onward, due to the deployment of over 100,000 men in Libya (which the von Löbell tabulations claim not to include) and the continual transfer of men to and from North Africa, accompanied by the call-up of additional recruits and reservists as replacements. The high strengths given for Britain reflect the absence of a division between the colonial and home forces: both are included here, with the obvious exception of the separate Indian Army. A large proportion of the forces shown were therefore stationed in the colonies and not immediately available for European service. Throughout the period, the size of the Expeditionary

Force to be dispatched to the continent remained fixed at 100,000 to 150,000. The initial decline in the strength of the British army shown here reflects the continuing demobilization of forces from South Africa as well as the experiment with a shorter service term. Taking all of these things into account, the most remarkable features of the resulting numbers for all the powers are the comparative stability throughout the period until 1912 and the fairly constant relative strength of all the armies.

ARMY EXPENDITURES OF
THE EUROPEAN POWERS, 1904–1914

THE TABLE given here should not be regarded as an exact compilation of the amounts the European governments spent on their armies, for the reasons discussed in Chapter 1. It is presented in order to show very approximately the relationship between the expenditures of the powers in the period, and different official and scholarly publications will report substantially varying amounts depending on their criteria of inclusion and the purposes for which they were designed. Here in each case the source has been used that appears most likely to approximate a consistent tabulation over the entire period, for the most part excluding costs for gendarmerie, pensions, war expenditures, and colonial forces (the latter with the notable exception of Britain).

It must be stressed that the armies undoubtedly made considerably greater expenditures than those shown here, concealed under various budget headings and accounting devices, and there is no guarantee whatsoever of consistency in reporting. The problems of tabulation became particularly acute with the army increases of 1912–13, when legislation designated sums for future as well as current expenditure, and at all times various forms of supplementary credits might or might not have been included in the regular figures. The amounts voted for 1914 have been given here in cases where the annual budget had been passed by the time war broke out, but it must be borne in mind that these were only preliminary projections.

The British and Italian state budgets ran on fiscal rather than calendar years. The British expenditures are comparatively large because they include the forces stationed in the colonies (apart, of course, from the Indian Army), since the budget made no distinction for the funds allocated to the maintenance of the fraction of the forces that would actually be sent to France on the outbreak of war. The comparatively higher pay of Britain's professional army should also be kept in mind, along with the costs of maintaining forces overseas. The initial decline in expenditures was primarily due to the absorption of remaining costs from the South African war and the continuing withdrawal of troops from the occupation force there.

TABLE B.1
Annual Army Expenditures of the Powers (Pounds Sterling)

	Russia[a]	Germany[b]	France[c]	Austria-Hungary[d]	Italy[f]	Great Britain[f]
1904	38,135,105	31,655,076	26,811,890	17,568,152	8,165,153	40,292,214
1905	38,800,726	34,544,958	27,149,037	17,005,860	11,337,958	32,227,365
1906	39,841,721	36,369,819	28,491,214	16,903,416	11,496,531	29,806,589
1907	41,093,773	39,171,776	30,921,155	18,381,998	11,853,320	29,077,038
1908	50,440,315	41,897,734	30,916,754	18,303,948	11,837,463	27,403,495
1909	56,956,710	39,820,279	31,709,611	19,446,159	11,948,464	27,024,192
1910	56,101,091	39,558,815	34,574,847	19,958,399	12,958,149	27,256,162
1911	56,161,071	39,955,932	37,191,744	21,060,797	14,147,445	27,579,826
1912	59,504,479	47,302,090	36,491,522	22,394,923	16,751,706	28,033,305
1913	67,751,868	80,938,522	37,194,227	24,130,138	n.a.	28,242,320
1914	n.a.	68,534,435	47,716,936	n.a.	n.a.	28,532,992

Note: Amounts converted to sterling according to exchange rates listed in the *Statesman's Yearbook*, London, 1904–14. These did not fluctuate significantly in the period.

[a] "Nouvelles Militaires," *Revue militaire des armées étrangères*, Paris, 1904–14.

[b] "Einnahmen und Ausgaben des Deutschen Reiches," *Statistisches Jahrbuch für das Deutsche Reich*, Berlin, 1904–16.

[c] Assemblée Nationale, *Journal officiel de la République Française: Lois et Décrets*, Paris, 1903–July 1914. Supplementary credits voted during each year have been included.

[d] Pelet-Narbonne, *Von Löbells Jahresberichte über die Veränderungen und Fortschritte im Militärwesen*, Berlin, 1904–13.

[e] Ibid., 1904–13. Expenditures voted by fiscal rather than calendar year (e.g., 1903–4).

[f] PRO WO33/536, 550, 554, 586, 631, War Office, *Reports on the Account of Army Expenditure*, London, 1904–14. Expenditures voted by fiscal rather than calendar year.

Overall, the stability in the relative size of the powers' expenditures is remarkable throughout the period until 1912. The table reflects notable expansions in Russian expenditures in 1908–9 and 1912–13. There are also substantial increases in Germany in 1912–14, Austria-Hungary in 1913, and France in 1914.

NOTES

INTRODUCTION

1. Fritz Stern, *The Politics of Cultural Despair: A Study in the Rise of the Germanic Ideology* (Berkeley, 1961); James Joll, *1914: The Unspoken Assumptions* (London, 1968); Roland N. Stromberg, *Redemption by War: The Intellectuals in 1914* (Lawrence, Kans., 1982); Paul Kennedy and Anthony Nicholls, eds., *Nationalist and Racialist Movements in Britain and Germany before 1914* (Oxford, 1981); Jost Dülffer and Karl Holl, eds., *Bereit zum Krieg: Kriegsmentalität im Wilhelminischen Deutschland 1890–1914* (Göttingen, 1986).

2. Luigi Albertini, *The Origins of the War of 1914*, 2 vols., trans. Isabella M. Massey (London, 1957); Fritz Fischer, *Germany's Aims in the First World War* (New York, 1967); idem, *War of Illusions: German Policies from 1911 to 1914*, trans. Marian Jackson (London, 1975); Imanuel Geiss, *Julikrise und Kriegsausbruch 1914*, 2 vols. (Hannover, 1963); Hans-Ulrich Wehler, *The German Empire, 1871–1918* (Dover, N.H., 1985).

3. A. J. P. Taylor, *The Struggle for Mastery in Europe, 1848–1918* (Oxford, 1954), esp. xxii–xxxi; Ludwig Dehio, *The Precarious Balance: Four Centuries of the European Power Struggle*, trans. Charles Fullman (New York, 1962); Gordon A. Craig and Alexander L. George, *Force and Statecraft: Diplomatic Problems of Our Time* (Oxford, 1983); Nazli Choucri and Robert C. North, *Nations in Conflict: National Growth and International Violence* (San Francisco, 1975), 26–43; Lancelot L. Farrar Jr., *Arrogance and Anxiety: The Ambivalence of German Power, 1848–1914* (Iowa City, 1981); Richard Langhorne, *The Collapse of the Concert of Europe: International Politics, 1890–1914* (New York, 1981); Paul M. Kennedy, "The First World War and the International Power System," in *Military Strategy and the Origins of the First World War*, ed. Steven E. Miller (Princeton, 1985), 7–40.

4. Arthur J. Marder, *The Anatomy of British Sea Power: A History of British Naval Policy in the Pre-Dreadnought Era, 1880–1905* (Hamden, Conn., 1964); idem, *From the Dreadnought to Scapa Flow: The Royal Navy in the Fisher Era*, vol. 1 (Oxford, 1961); Jonathan Steinberg, *Yesterday's Deterrent: Tirpitz and the Birth of the German Battle Fleet* (New York, 1965); Volker R. Berghahn, *Der Tirpitz-Plan: Genesis und Verfall einer innenpolitischen Krisenstrategie unter Wilhelm II* (Düsseldorf, 1971); idem, *Germany and the Approach of War in 1914* (New York, 1973); Paul M. Kennedy, *The Rise of the Anglo-German Antagonism, 1860–1914* (Boston, 1984); Ivo Nikolai Lambi, *The Navy and German Power Politics, 1862–1914* (Boston, 1984); Michael Epkenhans, "Großindustrie und Schlachtflottenbau 1897–1914," *Militärgeschichtliche Mitteilungen* 43, no. 1 (1988): 65–141.

5. Gerhard Ritter, *The Schlieffen Plan: Critique of a Myth*, trans. Andrew Wil-

son and Eva Wilson (New York, 1958); Samuel R. Williamson, *The Politics of Grand Strategy: Britain and France Prepare for War, 1904–1914* (Cambridge, Mass., 1969); Paul M. Kennedy, ed., *The War Plans of the Great Powers, 1880–1914* (London, 1979); David French, *British Economic and Strategic Planning, 1905–1915* (London, 1982); Jack Snyder, *The Ideology of the Offensive: Military Decision Making and the Disasters of 1914* (Ithaca, N.Y., 1984); Miller, *Military Strategy and the Origins of the First World War*; Scott D. Sagan, "1914 Revisited: Allies, Offense, and Instability," *International Security* 11, no. 2 (Fall 1986): 151–173.

6. Dieter Senghaas, *Rüstung und Militarismus* (Frankfurt am Main, 1972); Samuel P. Huntington, "Arms Races: Prerequisites and Results," in *Power, Action and Interaction: Readings on International Politics*, ed. George H. Quester (Boston, 1974), 499–541; Raoul Naroll, *Military Deterrence in History* (Albany, N.Y., 1974); Choucri and North, *Nations in Conflict*; Michael Wallace, "Arms Races and Escalation: Some New Evidence," *Journal of Conflict Resolution* 23, no. 1 (March 1979): 3–16; Bruce M. Russett, *The Prisoners of Insecurity: Nuclear Deterrence, the Arms Race, and Arms Control* (San Francisco, 1983); Richard Ned Lebow, "Windows of Opportunity: Do States Jump Through Them?" and Steven Van Evera, "The Cult of the Offensive and the Origins of the First World War," both in Miller, *Military Strategy and the Origins of the First World War*, 147–186, 58–107.

7. George W. F. Hallgarten, *Das Wettrüsten: Seine Geschichte bis zur Gegenwart* (Frankfurt am Main, 1967); Kennedy, "Arms Races and the Causes of War, 1850–1945," in *Strategy and Diplomacy 1870–1945: Eight Studies*, 163–177 (London, 1983); Michael Geyer, *Deutsche Rüstungspolitik, 1860–1980* (Frankfurt am Main, 1984).

CHAPTER 1

1. Standard surveys include Bernard Brodie, *Sea Power in the Machine Age* (New York, 1969); John Gooch, *Armies in Europe* (London, 1980); Michael E. Howard, *War in European History* (Oxford, 1976); William H. McNeill, *The Pursuit of Power: Technology, Armed Force, and Society since A.D. 1000* (Chicago, 1982); Dennis E. Showalter, *Railroads and Rifles: Soldiers, Technology, and the Unification of Germany* (Hamden, Conn., 1975); and Hew Strachan, *European Armies and the Conduct of War* (London, 1983).

2. Reichsarchiv, *Der Weltkrieg 1914 bis 1918*, vol. 1, *Kriegsrüstung und Kriegswirtschaft* (Berlin, 1930), 251.

3. Martin Van Creveld, *Supplying War: Logistics from Wallenstein to Patton* (Cambridge, 1980), 75–141.

4. John Kininmont Dunlop, *The Development of the British Army, 1899–1914* (London, 1938), 153.

5. The approximate peacetime strength of the European armies from year to year in this period is given in the table in Appendix A.

6. Approximate figures for the official military budgets of the European powers in the period are given in Appendix B.

7. Choucri and North, *Nations in Conflict*, 114–117.

8. Assemblée Nationale, *Journal officiel de la République Française: Lois et Décrets*, January 1904–July 1914.

9. Examples of efforts to assess the part played by military spending in individual European economies of the period can be found in Peter-Christian Witt, *Die Finanzpolitik des deutschen Reiches von 1903 bis 1913* (Lübeck, 1970); and Francesco A. Répaci, *La finanza pubblica italiana nel secolo 1860–1960* (Bologna, 1962).

10. Choucri and North, *Nations in Conflict*, Appendix A, pp. 294–299.

11. François-Léon-Emile Rimailho, *L'artillerie de campagne* (Paris, 1924), 23–64; Bruce I. Gudmundsson, *On Artillery* (Westport, Conn., 1993), 4–7.

12. Reichsarchiv, *Kriegsrüstung*, 1:232–236; Karl von Einem, *Erinnerungen eines Soldaten* (Leipzig, 1933), 85–87.

13. Generalstab, Evidenzbüro, *Veränderungen im Heerwesen Russlands im Jahre 1903*, January 1904, KA MKSM 1904 18–32/2; Generalstab, Evidenzbüro, *Veränderungen im Heerwesen Russlands 1904*, April 1905, KA MKSM 1905 18–4/1.

14. Capt. Girodou (French military attaché in Vienna) to Ministère de la Guerre, 12 January, 27 May 1905, SHAT 7N 1129/4 nos. 67, 93.

15. Maj. Messier de St. James (French military attaché in Rome) to Min. Guerre, 20 February 1905, SHAT 7N 1368/2 no. 301.

16. Dunlop, *British Army*, 154–155.

17. "La question des canons de campagne dans les armées étrangères," *Revue militaire des armées étrangères* 64, no. 922 (September 1904): 208.

18. Cf. John Ellis, *The Social History of the Machine Gun* (New York, 1975), 47–71.

19. Hans Meier-Welcker and Wolfgang von Groote, eds., *Handbuch der deutschen Militärgeschichte 1648–1939*, 5 vols. (Munich, 1979), 5:165.

20. Conseil Supérieur de la Guerre, *Procès-verbal*, 7 June 1905, SHAT 1N 9/11 pp. 116–119.

21. Generalstab, Evidenzbüro, *Veränderungen im Heerwesen Russlands im Jahre 1903*, January 1904, KA MKSM 1904 18–3/2.

22. Girodou to Min. Guerre, 10 May 1905, SHAT 7N 1129/4 no. 91.

23. Generalstab, Evidenzbüro, *Veränderungen im Heerwesen Italiens im Jahre 1904*, 24 February 1905, KA MKSM 1905 18–2/1.

24. Col. d'Amade (French military attaché in London) to Min. Guerre, 29 September 1904, SHAT 7N 1221/2 no. 313; Capt. von Heydebreck, Großer Generalstab, *Unternehmungen Englands gegen Deutschland zu Lande*, 2 January 1905, BA-MA RM5/1605 nos. 35–52.

25. Lt.-Col. Gastaldella (Italian military attaché in Berlin), *Relazione sulle manovre imperiali tedesche dell'anno 1904*, 20 November 1904, AUSSME G-22/16 no. 112.

26. "Les manoeuvres impériales allemandes en 1904" (Part 2), *Revue militaire des armées étrangères* 65, no. 926 (January 1905): 27; Generalstab, Evidenzbüro, *Veränderungen im Heerwesen Russlands 1904*, April 1905, KA MKSM 1905 18–4/1.

27. Azar Gat, *The Development of Military Thought: The Nineteenth Century* (Oxford, 1992), 137–138.

28. Jay Luvaas, *The Military Legacy of the Civil War: The European Inheritance* (Chicago, 1959), 226–233.

29. Karl von Clausewitz, *On War*, trans. and ed. by Michael Howard and Peter Paret (1976; reprint, Princeton, 1984).

30. Charles Jean Jacques Joseph Ardant du Picq, *Études sur le combat: combat antique et combat moderne*, 6th ed. (Paris, 1904).

31. Colmar von der Goltz, *Das Volk in Waffen* (Berlin, 1883), 274–297.

32. Stromberg, *Redemption by War*.

33. Azar Gat, *The Origins of Military Thought: From the Enlightenment to Clausewitz* (Oxford, 1989).

34. Hippolyte Langlois, *Enseignements de deux guerres récentes: Guerres Turco-Russe et Anglo-Boer* (Paris, ca. 1904), 28; Ferdinand Foch, *Des principes de la guerre: Conférences faites à l'École Supérieure de la Guerre par F. Foch* (Paris, 1903), 302–330; Georges Gilbert, *La Guerre Sud-Africaine* (Paris, 1902), 565–566; von der Goltz, *Das Volk in Waffen*, 340–341; George Francis Robert Henderson, *The Science of War: A Collection of Essays and Lectures 1892–1903* (London, 1905), 78–79; Michael E. Howard, "Men against Fire: The Doctrine of the Offensive in 1914," in *Makers of Modern Strategy from Machiavelli to the Nuclear Age*, ed. Peter Paret (Princeton, 1986), 510–526; and Bruce I. Gudmundsson, *Stormtroop Tactics: Innovation in the German Army, 1914–1918* (New York, 1989), 8, 21–22.

35. E.g., Min. Guerre, *Décret du 3 Décembre 1904 portant règlement sur les manoeuvres de l'infanterie* (Paris, 1904), 39, 55.

36. Foch, *principes de la guerre*, 328; Bonnal, *Récente guerre Sud-Africaine*, 39–42; Langlois, *Enseignements de deux guerres récentes*, 161–163; Gilbert, *Guerre Sud-Africaine*, 576–579; and Henderson, *Science of War* , 55–57, 62, 163–164.

37. Jean de Bloch, *La guerre*, 6 vols. (reprint; New York, 1973).

38. Langlois, *Enseignements de deux guerres récentes*, 210.

39. Ibid., 215.

40. Von der Goltz, *Das Volk in Waffen*, 334–335.

41. Thomas Pakenham, *The Boer War* (London, 1979), 136–138, 195–196, 204–206, 227–233, 293–295.

42. Bonnal, *Récente guerre Sud-Africaine*, 13–35, 54–63; Gilbert, *Guerre Sud-Africaine*, 519–533; Langlois, *Enseignements de deux guerres récentes*, 111–173.

43. Deuxième Bureau, *Enseignements de la guerre russo-japonaise. Note n° 16.—Les Enseignements*, March 1907, SHAT 7N 670.

44. Deuxième Bureau, *Enseignements de la guerre russo-japonaise. Note n° 12. Tactique d'Artillerie (choix des positions et exécution des feux)*, March 1906, SHAT 7N 670.

45. Deuxième Bureau, *Enseignements de la guerre russo-japonaise. Note n° 10.—Matériel d'Artillerie*, February 1906, SHAT 7N 670.

46. Generalstab, *Die russische und japanische Artillerie im Feldkriege* (sent by Schlieffen to Wandel), 28 July 1905, BA-MA N564 (Nachlaß Wandel)/6 no. 2.

47. Capt. Soloviev, "Le combat de l'infanterie dans la guerre russo-japonaise," *Revue militaire des armées étrangères* 67, no. 938 (January 1906): 26.

48. François Oscar de Négrier, "Le moral des troupes," *Revue des deux mondes* 25, no. 1 (1 February 1905), 495–498; Hermann von Kuhl, *Der deutsche Generalstab in Vorbereitung und Durchführung des Weltkrieges* (Berlin, 1920), 7.

49. Foch, *Des principes de la guerre*.

50. Ibid., 265.

51. Ibid., 274–275.

52. Von der Goltz, *Das Volk in Waffen*, 493–500.

53. Bloch, *La guerre*, 4:1–268, 6:140–144.

54. Guglielmo Ferrero, *Il militarismo: dieci conferenze* (Milan, 1898); Norman Angell, *The Great Illusion* (London, 1910).

55. Kuhl, *Der deutsche Generalstab*, 142–160; Wolfgang Foerster, *Aus der Gedankenwerkstatt des Deutschen Generalstabes* (Berlin, 1931), 26–31; Günther E. Rothenberg, "Moltke, Schlieffen and the Doctrine of Strategic Envelopment," in *Makers of Modern Strategy*, ed. Peter Paret, 296–325; Lancelot L. Farrar, *The Short-War Illusion: German Strategy and Domestic Affairs, August–December 1914* (Santa Barbara, Calif., 1973), 4–11.

56. France, *Journal officiel de la République Française: Débats, Assemblée Nationale*, esp. 1904, vol. 2, sessions of 24 May to 7 June; France, *Journal officiel de la République Française: Documents parlementaires—Chambre* no. 50 (1/1904), 141–162.

57. Col. de La Panouse, "L'organisation militaire," *Revue des deux mondes* 21, no. 2 (May 1904): 318–352; Négrier, "Le moral des troupes," 482–494; Conseil Supérieur de la Guerre, *Procès-verbal*, 27 September 1907, SHAT 1N 9/11 pp. 190–216.

58. These laws were not actually passed until 1909 for the artillery and 1912 for the infantry and cavalry, too late to compensate for the discharge of the last three-year service class in 1908. See Großer Generalstab, 3. Abteilung, *Zusammenstellung der wichtigsten Veränderungen im Heerwesen Frankreichs 1908*, 15 February 1909, BA-MA RM5/1234 nos. 3–55; idem, *Heerwesen Frankreichs 1909*, 15 February 1910, BA-MA RM5/1234 nos. 150–186.

59. Sergei Dobrorolski, *Die Mobilmachung der russischen Armee 1914* (Berlin, 1922), 14–15.

60. Schlieffen to Bülow, 18 August 1905, PAAA R10449 no. 8353z; Allan K. Wildman, *The End of the Russian Imperial Army*, vol. 1, *The Old Army and the Soldiers' Revolt (March-April 1917)* (Princeton, 1980), 44–45; Pertti Luntinen, *French Information on the Russian War Plans, 1880–1914* (Helsinki, 1984), 98–100; William Charles Fuller, *Strategy and Power in Russia, 1600–1914* (New York, 1992), 404.

61. Gen. Beck, *Denkschrift 1904*, 28 December 1904, KA MKSM 1905 24–2/1.

62. Denis and Peggy Warner, *The Tide at Sunrise: A History of the Russo-Japanese War, 1904–1905* (New York, 1974); Richard M. Connaughton, *The War of the Rising Sun and Tumbling Bear: A Military History of the Russo-Japanese War* (New York, 1988); Bruce W. Menning, *Bayonets before Bullets: The Imperial Russian Army, 1861–1914* (Bloomington, Ind., 1992), 155–199.

63. William Charles Fuller, *Civil-Military Conflict in Imperial Russia, 1885–1914* (Princeton, 1985), 131–149.

64. Edward Viscount Grey of Fallodon, *Twenty-Five Years, 1892–1916* (London, 1925), 1:48–49; Paul M. Kennedy, *The Rise and Fall of British Naval Mastery* (London, 1983), 214–223; Samuel R. Williamson, *The Politics of Grand Strategy: Britain and France Prepare for War, 1904–1914* (Cambridge, Mass., 1969), 1–15; Keith M. Wilson, *The Policy of the Entente: Essays in the Determinants of British Foreign Policy 1904–1914* (Cambridge, 1985), 3–16, 59–120.

65. Dunlop, *British Army*, 69–118.

66. Ibid., 130–227.

67. John Gooch, *The Plans of War: The General Staff and British Military Strategy c. 1900–1916* (London, 1974), 176–190.

68. Peter-Christian Witt, *Die Finanzpolitik des deutschen Reiches von 1903 bis 1913* (Lübeck, 1970), 1–94; Eckart Kehr, *Battleship Building and Party Politics in Germany, 1894–1901*, trans. Pauline R. Anderson and Eugene N. Anderson (Chicago, 1973), 306–358; Berghahn, *Der Tirpitz-Plan*.

69. Reichsarchiv, *Kriegsrüstung*, 1:74.

70. Günther E. Rothenberg, *The Army of Francis Joseph* (West Lafayette, Ind., 1976), 131.

71. Girodou to Min. Guerre, 12 January 1905, SHAT 7N 1129/4 no. 67.

72. Rothenberg, *Army of Francis Joseph*, 134.

73. Tisza *Vortrag* to Franz Joseph, 21 February 1904, KA MKSM 1904 12–3/4 nos. 1, 21; *Ministerrath für Gemeinsame Angelegenheiten, Protokoll*, 16 April 1904, HHStA PA XL/302 no. 19, 5 May 1904, HHStA PA XL/303 no. 24.

74. *Ministerrath für gemeinsame Angelegenheiten. Protokoll*, 28 November 1904, HHStA PA XL/303 no. 46; Gen. Beck, *Denkschrift 1904*, 28 December 1904, KA MKSM 1905 25–2/1; Michael Behnen, *Rüstung, Bündnis, Sicherheit: Dreibund und informeller Imperialismus 1900–1908* (Tübingen, 1985), 100–109, 113–118.

75. Messier to Min. Guerre, 13 June, 10 December 1904, SHAT 7N 1368/1 nos. 234, 278.

76. Lt.-Col. Lombardi, Ufficio del Capo di Stato Maggiore, *La mobilitazione e la radunata dell'esercito alla frontiera N.E.*, 22 August 1904, AUSSME F-4/11.

77. Giorgio Rochat and Giulio Massobrio, *Breve storia dell'esercito italiano dal 1861 al 1943* (Turin, 1978), 150–152; Massimo Mazzetti, "L'Esercito nel periodo Giolittiano (1900–1908)," in *L'Esercito italiano dall'Unità alla Grande Guerra (1861–1918)*, Ufficio Storico, Corpo di Stato Maggiore dell'Esercito, Italy (Rome, 1980), 248.

CHAPTER 2

1. Albertini, *Origins of the War of 1914*, 1:153–174.

2. Christopher M. Andrew, *Théophile Delcassé and the Making of the Entente Cordiale: A Reappraisal of French Foreign Policy 1898–1905* (London and New York, 1968).

3. Norman Rich, *Friedrich von Holstein: Politics and Diplomacy in the Era of Wilhelm II*, 2 vols. (Cambridge, 1965), 2:678–745.

4. Cf. Gerhard Ritter, *The Schlieffen Plan: Critique of a Myth*, trans. Andrew and Eva Wilson (New York, 1958), 112–124; Albrecht Moritz, *Das Problem des Präventivkrieges in der deutschen Politik während der ersten Marokkokrise* (Frankfurt, 1974); Rich, *Friedrich von Holstein*, 696–702.

5. Bülow to Wilhelm II, 26 March 1905, GP XX/1 no. 6576 pp. 273–277.

6. Memorandum by Holstein, 3 June 1904, GP XX/1 no. 6521 pp. 207–209; Ritter, *Schlieffen Plan*, 112–113; Rich, *Friedrich von Holstein*, 684–694.

7. Albertini, *Origins of the War of 1914*, 1:153; Bülow to Radolin, 4 May 1905, GP XX/2 no. 6650 pp. 365–366.

8. Bülow to Wilhelm II, 26 March 1905, GP XX/1 no. 6756 p. 275.

9. Barrère to Delcassé, 4 June 1905, DDF 2/VI no. 491 p. 585.

10. Albertini, *Origins of the War of 1914*, 1:157.

11. Radolin to Bülow, 27 April 1905, GP XX/2 no. 6635 p. 345; Radolin to Bülow, 8 May 1905, GP XX/2 no. 6657 p. 373.

12. Bülow to Holstein, 6 May 1905, GP XX/2 no. 6653 p. 370.

13. Bülow to Radolin, 4 May 1905, GP XX/2 no. 6650; Radolin to Auswärtiges Amt, 3 June 1905, GP XX/2 no. 6680 pp. 402–403.

14. Moulin to Min. Guerre, 14 July 1904, SHAT 7N 1476/7 no. 2311; Moulin to Min. Guerre, 10 and 23 September 1904, SHAT 7N 1476/8 nos. 2337, 2342.

15. Moulin to Min. Guerre, 27 June 1905, SHAT 7N 1477 no. 2455.

16. Lichnowsky (Auswärtiges Amt) to Reichskanzlei, 19 April 1904, PAAA R10449 no. 525; Schlieffen to Bülow, 20 April 1904, PAAA R10449 no. 280/04g.

17. Bülow to Schlieffen, 4 June 1905, PAAA R10449 no. 664.

18. Schlieffen to Bülow, 10 June 1905, PAAA R10449 no. 471.

19. Bülow to Radolin, 4 May 1905, GP XX/2 no. 6650 pp. 365–366.

20. Bompard to Delcassé, 5 May 1905, DDF 2.VI no. 401 p. 475.

21. Radolin to Bülow, 8 May 1905, GP XX/2 no. 6657 p. 373.

22. Sir Francis Bertie (British ambassador in Paris) to Delcassé, 24 April 1905, DDF 2.VI no. 347 pp. 414–415.

23. Lansdowne to Cambon (French ambassador in London), 25 May 1905, DDF 2.VI no. 465 *Annexe* pp. 558–559; see also Cambon to Delcassé, 18 May 1905, DDF 2.VI no. 443 pp. 522–523; Samuel R. Williamson, *The Politics of Grand Strategy: Britain and France Prepare for War, 1904–1914* (Cambridge, Mass., 1969), 36–38.

24. Radolin to Auswärtiges Amt, 27 April 1905, GP XX/2 no. 6635 p. 345.

25. Field-Marshal Prince Arthur, Duke of Connaught, *Annual Report of the Inspector-General of the Forces for 1904*, 1 November 1904, PRO WO 163/10 no. 212; idem, Appendix 2, Arthur to Army Council, 23 May 1905.

26. Deuxième Bureau, *Note sur l'armée anglaise*, 1904, SHAT 7N 670/4.

27. Capt. von Heydebreck, Großer Generalstab, *Unternehmungen Englands gegen Deutschland zu Lande*, 2 January 1905, BA-MA RM5/1605 nos. 35–52.

28. Balfour, *A Note on Army Reform and the Military Needs of Empire* (discussed and approved by the Committee of Imperial Defence), 22 June 1904, PRO CAB 4/1 no. 26B.

29. Maj. Huguet (French military attaché in London) to Etienne (war minis-

ter), 21 December 1905, DDF 2.VIII no. 256 pp. 352–353; Maj.-Gen. J. M. Grierson to Lord Sanderson (Foreign Office), 11 January 1906, BD III no. 211 pp. 172–173; John Ecclesfield Tyler, *The British Army and the Continent, 1904–1914* (London, 1938), 18; Duncan Stewart Macdiarmid, *The Life of Lieut. General Sir James Moncrieff Grierson* (London, 1923), 212; Williamson, *Politics of Grand Strategy*, 46–47.

30. Adm. C. L. Ottley to First Sea Lord, 13 January 1906, BD III no. 221(a) pp. 185–186.

31. Capt. von Heydebreck, *Unternehmungen Englands gegen Deutschland zu Lande*, 2 January 1905, BA-MA RM5/1605 nos. 35–52.

32. Lieut.-Col. Huguet to Min. Guerre, 18 November 1905, SHAT 7N 1222/1 no. 72.

33. Bülow to Holstein, 6 May 1905, GP XX/2 no. 6653 p. 370.

34. See Appendix A.

35. Reichsarchiv, *Kriegsrüstung*, 1.i:61–66, 87.

36. Min. Guerre, *Les Armées françaises dans la Grande Guerre*, vol. 1 *La guerre de mouvement* (Paris, 1922), 26–29.

37. Ibid., 1.i: Carte No. 2.

38. Reichsarchiv, *Kriegsrüstung*, 1:61–71, 1 Anl.: Tabelle 11.

39. A sketch map of this plan, based on material from the Reichsarchiv lost during the Second World War and showing the number of divisions assigned to each sector, is published in Friedrich von Boetticher, "Der Lehrmeister des neuzeitlichen Krieges," in *Von Scharnhorst zu Schlieffen 1806–1906: Hundert Jahre preußisch-deutscher Generalstab*, ed. Friedrich von Cochenhausen (Berlin, 1933), 267. For the availability of German reserve formations, see Reichsarchiv, *Kriegsrüstung*, 1 Anl.: Tabellen 11, 13.

40. Reichsarchiv, *Kriegsrüstung*, 1 Anl.: Tabelle 11.

41. *Renseignement fourni par le Chef d'État-major de l'Armée, le 11 November 1904* ("vu par le Ministre 23 Mai 05"), MAE CP Allemagne NS 29 no. 93.

42. Maurice Paléologue, "Un prélude à l'invasion de la Belgique (1904)," *Revue des deux mondes* 102, no. 11 (1 October 1932): 514.

43. Négrier's inspection report (excerpt), 31 July 1904, DDF 2.VI *Annexe* II p. 604; see also pp. 604–607, subsequent army documents, July 1904–February 1905.

44. François Oscar de Négrier, "Le moral des troupes," *Revue des deux mondes* 25, no. 1 (1 February 1905): 481–505; Conseil Supérieur de la Guerre, *Procès-verbal*, 18 February 1905, SHAT 1N 9/11, pp. 77–97.

45. Deuxième Bureau, *Note sur l'artillerie de campagne allemande*, 20 March 1905, SHAT 7N 670/1.

46. Reichsarchiv, *Kriegsrüstung*, 1:236.

47. "La question du canon de campagne dans les armées étrangères," *Revue militaire des armées étrangères* 64, no. 922 (September 1904): 208; Deuxième Bureau to Brugère, *Note sur l'artillerie allemande*, 19 December 1904, SHAT 7N 670/1 no. 93bis; Pendezec to Delcassé, 26 May 1905, MAE CP Allemagne NS 29 nos. 108–109.

48. Troisième Bureau, *Note pour le Conseil Supérieur de la Guerre*, January 1904, SHAT 7N 48/2.

49. Von Einem to Generalkommandos und Inspektionen der Fuß- und Feldartillerie, 2 July 1904, HStAS-KA M1/9 Bd. I vol. II nos. 100–102; Deuxième Bureau to Brugère, *Note sur l'artillerie allemande*, 19 December 1904, SHAT 7N 670/1 no. 93bis.

50. Min. Guerre, *Grande Guerre*, 1:29–30, 1.i: Carte No. 2.

51. Troisième Bureau, *Hypothèse de concentration des armées du nord-est*, April 1901, SHAT 7N 1754/2; Luntinen, *French Information on the Russian War Plans*, 78–81.

52. Troisième Bureau, *Post scriptum* to 1901 *Hypothèse de concentration*, March 1906, SHAT 7N 1754/2.

53. Troisième Bureau, *Note sur des renseignements récents relatifs à la concentration des armées allemandes*, 13 August 1904, SHAT 7N 1756/3 no. 1; Jan Karl Tannenbaum, "French Estimates of Germany's Operational Plans," in *Knowing One's Enemies: Intelligence Assessments before the Two World Wars*, ed. Ernest R. May (Princeton, 1984), 151–152; Paléologue, "Invasion de la Belgique," 487–488, 507, 509; Wolfgang Foerster, "Ist der deutsche Aufmarsch 1904 an die Franzosen verraten worden?" *Berliner Monatshefte* 10, no. 11 (November 1932): 1053–1067.

54. Paléologue, "Un prélude à l'invasion de la Belgique," 487, 495–496, 509–510, 513–514; Maurice Paléologue, "La démission de M. Delcassé en 1905," *Revue des deux mondes* 101, no. 3 (15 June 1931): 766; Tannenbaum, "French Estimates of Germany's Operational Plans," 153–155.

55. Conseil Supérieur de la Guerre, *Procès-verbal*, 18 February 1905, SHAT 1N 9/11 pp. 77–97.

56. Paléologue, "Invasion de la Belgique," 513–514; Tannenbaum, "French Estimates of Germany's Operational Plans," 155–156; Christopher Andrew, "France and the German Menace," in *Knowing One's Enemies*, ed. Ernest R. May, 140–141.

57. Paléologue, "Invasion de la Belgique," 507.

58. Boetticher, "Der Lehrmeister des neuzeitlichen Krieges," 267. The Prussian general staff's 1905–6 deployment plan (which was effective from 1 April 1905 to 1 April 1906) should not be confused with the well-known documents prepared by Schlieffen in December of 1905, which have been published by Ritter and may be seen in Schlieffen, *Krieg gegen Frankreich*, Dec, 1905, PRO CAB 20/1 no. 1, nos. 79–98, and the accompanying maps in PRO CAB 20/4. These appear to have been Schlieffen's design for a future scheme of operations, left as a kind of testament during the final days before his replacement by Moltke as chief of staff. They called for the use of a number of reserve and replacement formations that were not ready at the time. See Reichsarchiv, *Der Weltkrieg 1914 bis 1918: Die militärischen Operationen zu Lande*, vol. 1, *Die Grenzschlachten im Westen* (Berlin, 1925), 55; Reichsarchiv, *Kriegsrüstung*, 1 Anl.: Tabellen 11, 13.

59. Ritter, *Schlieffen Plan*, 41–45.

60. Ibid., 38–47; Kuhl, *Der deutsche Generalstab*, 156–159; Foerster, *Aus der Gedankenwerkstatt des Deutschen Generalstabes*, 29–30.

61. Schlieffen, *Krieg gegen Frankreich*, December 1905, PRO CAB 20/1 no. 1 nos. 79–98.

62. Kuhl, *Der deutsche Generalstab*, 155–160; Foerster, *Aus der Gedanken-werkstatt des Deutschen Generalstabes*, 26–31; Ritter, *Schlieffen Plan*, 21–37.

63. Reichsarchiv, *Kriegsrüstung*, 1:252.

64. Von Einem, *Erinnerungen*, 111. Nothing exists to show that Schlieffen would have objected to a war in 1905 either. See Ritter, *Schlieffen Plan*, 104–111; Gordon A. Craig, *The Politics of the Prussian Army, 1640–1945* (New York, 1955), 283–286; L. C. F. Turner, "The Significance of the Schlieffen Plan," in *The War Plans of the Great Powers, 1880–1914*, ed. Paul M. Kennedy (London, 1985), 209–210; Ivo Nikolai Lambi, *The Navy and German Power Politics, 1862–1914* (Boston, 1984), 259–260; Moritz, *Problem des Präventivkrieges*, 216–224.

65. Paléologue, "La démission de M. Delcassé," 764, 769–771.

66. Joseph Chaumié (Minister of Justice), *Note sur le Conseil des Ministres où M. Delcassé a donné sa démission*, 6 June 1905, DDF 2.VI *Annexe* I p. 602.

67. Bihourd to Delcassé, 28 April 1905, DDF 2.VI no. 369 pp. 431–432.

68. Cambon to Delcassé, 4 June 1905, DDF 2.VI no. 416 p. 586; Barrère to Delcassé, 8 May 1905, DDF 2.VI no. 491; Paléologue, "La démission de M. Delcassé," 764.

69. Andrew, *Delcassé and the Making of the Entente Cordiale*; Albertini, *Origins of the War of 1914*, 1:154–155; Paléologue, "La démission de M. Delcassé," 764.

70. Radolin to Bülow, 8 May 1905, GP XX/2 no. 6658 pp. 375–376.

71. Joseph Chaumié, *Note sur le Conseil des Ministres où M. Delcassé a donné sa démission*, 6 June 1905, DDF 2.VI *Annexe* I p. 601.

72. Ibid., 601–604.

73. Radolin to Auswärtiges Amt, 27 April 1905, GP XX/2 no. 6635 pp. 344–345; Bülow to Radolin, 4 May 1905, GP XX/2 no. 6650 pp. 364–367; Radolin to Bülow, 8 May 1905, GP XX/2 no. 6658 pp. 375–376.

74. Metternich to Bülow, January 1906, GP XX/1 no. 6923 pp. 45–51; Grey to Sir Frank Lascelles (British ambassador in Berlin), 9 January 1906, BD III no. 229 pp. 209–211; Memorandum by Grey, 20 February 1906, PRO FO 800/92 nos. 26–29; Charles Hardinge (Foreign Office), *Notes* to the foregoing, 23 February 1906, PRO FO 800/92 nos. 30–31.

75. Moltke to Bülow, 23 January 1906, GP XX/1 no. 6942 pp. 74–76.

76. Min. Guerre, *Grande Guerre*, 1.i:29–33.

77. Troisième Bureau, *Post scriptum* to 1901 *Hyopothèse de concentration*, March 1906, SHAT 7N 1754/2.

78. Brig.-Gen. Moulin to Min. Guerre, 27 January 1906, SHAT 7N 1477 no. 2523.

79. Dunlop, *Development of the British Army*, 236–240, 322–323; Grey, *Twenty-Five Years, 1892–1916* (London, 1925), 1:72–75; Tyler, *British Army and the Continent*, 25–51; Williamson, *Politics of Grand Strategy*, 61–84.

80. Macdiarmid, *General Grierson*, 215–217.

81. Dunlop, *Development of the British Army*, 236–246.

82. Maj. Huguet to Min. Guerre, 18 November 1905, SHAT 7N 1222/1 no. 72; Col. Huguet to Min. Guerre, 26 January 1906, DDF 2.IX no. 68 pp. 103–104.

83. Committee of Imperial Defence, *Minutes of 82nd Meeting*, 24 November 1905, PRO CAB 2/1 nos. 161–162.

84. Wilhelm to Bülow, 31 December 1905, "Neue Briefe aus der Kaiserzeit," *Berliner Tageblatt* 57, no. 487; Col. von Gebsattel (Bavarian military representative in Berlin) to Gen. von Horn (Bavarian war minister), 22 December 1905, BHStA-KA M.Kr. 42 no. 2791; Gebsattel to Horn, 30 March 1906, BHStA-KA M.Kr. 42 no. 885.

85. Lambi, *German Navy and Power Politics*, 251–257.

86. Senator d'Estournelles de Constant to Rouvier, 19 January 1906, DDF 2.IX no. 22 pp. 31–39; Bülow to Moltke, 24 January 1906, GP XXI/1 no. 6943 pp. 77–79; Ritter, *Schlieffen Plan*, 120.

87. Bernhard von Bülow, *Denkwürdigkeiten*, 4 vols., ed. by Franz von Stockhammern (Berlin, 1930–31), 2:122–123; von Einem, *Erinnerungen*, 113.

88. Wilhelm to Bülow, 29 December 1905, GP XX/2 no. 6887 pp. 690–696.

89. Carl E. Schorske, *German Social Democracy, 1905–1917: The Development of the Great Schism* (1955; reprint, Cambridge, Mass., 1983), 36–47.

90. Stig Förster, *Der doppelte Militarismus: Die deutsche Heeresrüstungspolitik zwischen Status-quo-Sicherung und Aggression 1890–1913* (Stuttgart, 1985), 147.

91. Wilhelm to Bülow, 31 December 1905, "Neue Briefe aus der Kaiserzeit," *Berliner Tageblatt* 57, no. 487.

92. Bülow, *Denkwürdigkeiten*, 2:198; von Einem, *Erinnerungen*, 114–115.

93. John Gooch, *The Plans of War: The General Staff and British Military Strategy c. 1900–1916* (London, 1974), 191; Williamson, *Politics of Grand Strategy*, 89–114.

CHAPTER 3

1. Conseil Supérieur de la Guerre, *Procès-verbaux* 28 September and 7 October 1907, SHAT 1N 9/11 pp. 217–239 and 1N 10/12 pp. 1–18; Joseph Reinach, Commission de l'Armée, *Note du Rapporteur de la Sous-Commission, Question de l'Artillerie*, 1908/9, SHAT 7N 49/1.

2. Brig.-Gen. Moulin to Min. Guerre, 27 January 1906, SHAT 7N 1477 no. 2523; Rouvier to Bompard (French ambassador in St. Petersburg), 14 February 1906, MAE CP Russie NS 38 pp. 26–28; Bompard to Rouvier, 10 March 1906, MAE CP Russie NS 38 pp. 46–47.

3. *Procès-verbal de l'entretien du 8/21 Avril 1906 entre les chefs d'état-majors généraux des armées russe et française*, 21 April 1906, MAE CP Russie NS 38 pp. 61–64, 18 July 1907, 11 September 1908, MAE CP Russie NS 39 pp. 284–285, 103–108; Youri Danilov, *La Russie dans la Guerre Mondiale (1914–1917)* (Paris, 1927), 113–118; Fuller, *Strategy and Power*, 415.

4. Moulin to Min. Guerre, 9 July 1907, MAE CP Russie NS 38 pp. 267–270.

5. Moulin to Min. Guerre, 25 November 1906, SHAT 7N 1477 no. 2608; Deuxième Bureau, *Concentration russe: Enregistrement des principaux ren-*

seignements, 1907–1909, SHAT 7N 1537/6; Menning, *Bayonets before Bullets*, 239.

6. Moulin to Min. Guerre, 27 January 1906, SHAT 7N 1477 no. 2523; see also Moulin to Min. Guerre, 21 February 1906, SHAT 7N 1477 no. A-1906.

7. Moulin to Min. Guerre, 25 November 1906, SHAT 7N 1477 no. 2608.

8. Moulin to Min. Guerre, 6 March 1906, SHAT 7N 1477 no. B-1906.

9. Moulin to Min. Guerre, 27 January 1906, SHAT 7N 1477 no. 2523.

10. Moltke to Bülow, 7 March, 31 May, 9 August 1906, PAAA R10449 nos. 574, 616, and 634.

11. Posadowsky-Wehner to Kriegsministerium, 11 March 1908, PAAA R10424 no. 12; Großer Generalstab, 1. Abteilung, *Jahresbericht 1907*, 1908, BHStA-KA Generalstab 207 no. 22.

12. Conrad, *Denkschrift 1906*, 31 December 1906, KA MKSM 1907 25-1/1; Conrad, *Denkschrift 1907*, 14 January 1908, KA MKSM 1908 25-1/1.

13. Danilov, *La Russie dans la Guerre Mondiale*, 58; Risto Ropponen, *Die Kraft Rußlands. Wie beurteilte die politische Führung der europäischen Grossmächte in der Zeit von 1904 bis 1914 die Kraft Russlands?* (Helsinki, 1968), 213–235; William C. Wohlforth, "The Perception of Power: Russia in the Pre-1914 Balance," *World Politics* 39, no. 3 (April 1987): 355–368.

14. Moltke to Bülow, 9 August 1906, PAAA R10449 no. 634.

15. Posadowsky-Wehner to Kriegsministerium, 22 March 1906, PAAA R10421 no. 33.

16. Moulin to Min. Guerre, 27 January 1906, SHAT 7N1477 no. 2525; Sir Arthur Nicolson (British ambassador in St. Petersburg) to Grey, 2 January 1907, PRO FO 881/8864.

17. Posadowsky-Wehner to Kriegsministerium, 28 June 1906, PAAA R10422 no. 82; Moulin to Min. Guerre, 28 June 1906, SHAT 7N 1477 no. 2550; Moltke to Bülow, 9 August 1906, PAAA R10449 no. 634.

18. Generalstab, Evidenzbüro, *Veränderungen im Heerwesen Russlands im Jahre 1908*, 23 April 1909, KA MKSM 1909 18-2/2.

19. Moltke to Bülow, 9 August 1906, PAAA R10449 no. 634; Moulin to Min. Guerre, 10 July, 25 November, and 12 December 1906, SHAT 7N 1477 nos. 2554, 2610, and 2622; Generalstab, Evidenzbüro, *Veränderungen im Heerwesen Russlands im Jahre 1906*, February 1907, KA MKSM 1907 18-3/1; idem, *Heerwesen Russlands 1907*, 30 May 1908, KA MKSM 1908 18-4/1; idem, *Heerwesen Russlands 1908*, 23 April 1909, KA MKSM 1909 18-2/2; Fuller, *Civil-Military Conflict in Imperial Russia*, 129–161.

20. Posadowsky-Wehner to Kriegsministerium, 11 March 1908, PAAA R10424 no. 12; Danilov, *La Russie dans la Guerre Mondiale*, 58; Dietrich Geyer, *Russian Imperialism: The Interaction of Domestic and Foreign Policy 1860–1914*, trans. Bruce Little (New York, 1987), 255–256.

21. Michael Perrins, "The Council for State Defence, 1905–1909: A Study in Russian Bureaucratic Politics," *Slavonic and East European Review* 58, no. 3 (July 1980): 370–398; Danilov, *La Russie dans la Guerre Mondiale*, 59–61; Wladimir Aleksandrowitsch Suchomlinow, *Erinnerungen* (Berlin, 1924), 195–204; Fuller, *Strategy and Power*, 409–412.

22. Danilov, *La Russie dans la Guerre Mondiale*, 76–79.

23. Generalstab, Evidenzbüro, *Veränderungen im Heerwesen Russlands im Jahre 1908*, 23 April 1909, KA MKSM 1909 18–2/2.

24. Generalstab, Evidenzbüro, *Veränderungen im Heerwesen Russlands im Jahre 1907*, 30 May 1908, KA MKSM 18–4/1.

25. Geyer, *Russian Imperialism*, 264–272.

26. Posadowsky-Wehner to Kriegsministerium, 19 December 1906, PAAA R10422 no. 151; Posadowsky-Wehner to Kriegsministerium, 4 April, 25 May, 25 July, and 14 August 1907, PAAA R10423 nos. 19, 27, 37, and 39.

27. Moulin to Min. Guerre, 10 December 1906, SHAT 7N 1477 no. 2620; Großer Generalstab, 1. Abteilung, *Jahresbericht 1907*, 1908, BHStA-KA Generalstab 207 no. 22.

28. Marder, *Anatomy of British Sea Power*, 515–545.

29. Arthur J. Marder, *From the Dreadnought to Scapa Flow: The Royal Navy in the Fisher Era* (Oxford, 1961), 1:135–185; Holger H. Herwig, *"Luxury" Fleet: The Imperial German Navy 1898–1918* (London, 1980), 56–65; Berghahn, *Germany and the Approach of War*, 61–84.

30. Dunlop, *Development of the British Army*, 232–235.

31. War Office, *Report on the Account of Army Expenditure for 1911–1912*, 1913, PRO WO 33/631 p. 8.

32. Dunlop, *Development of the British Army*, 241–290; Tyler, *British Army and the Continent*, 66–77.

33. War Office, *Army Re-Organization: Comparison of the Proposed Organization of the Military Forces of the United Kingdom with their Present Organization*, January 1907, PRO CAB 37/86 no. 9.

34. Deuxième Bureau, *Réorganisation de l'Armée Anglaise*, September 1906, SHAT 7N 670/4.

35. Witt, *Die Finanzpolitik des deutschen Reiches*, 95–132, 152–199.

36. Moltke to von Einem, 7 April 1906, 88, 1 Anl. no. 28 pp. 94–95; von Einem to Moltke, 6 June 1906, 1 Anl. no. 30, pp. 96–98, Moltke to von Einem, 2 October 1906, 1 Anl. no. 32, pp. 104–105; Moltke to von Einem, 12 April 1907, 1 Anl. no. 33, p. 106, all in Reichsarchiv, *Der Weltkrieg 1914 bis 1918*, vol. 1, *Kriegsrüstung und Kriegswirtschaft* (Berlin, 1930); Moltke to Tschirschky (state secretary in foreign ministry), 9 October 1906, PAAA R794 no. 649.

37. Moltke to von Einem, 6 June, 4 September 1906, BHStA-KA M. Kr. 990 no. 20265; Großer Generalstab, 4. Abteilung, *Der augenblickliche Stand u. die voraussichtliche Weiterentwicklung des Festungsbaus in Frankreich*, 30 August 1906, BHStA-KA Generalstab 489 no. 259; Großer Generalstab, 4. Abteilung, *Die belgischen und holländischen Befestigungen und die Grundsätze ihrer Verteidigung*, 1908, BHStA-KA Generalstab 224.

38. Reichsarchiv, *Kriegsrüstung*, 1:252–253.

39. Gerhard Ritter, *The Sword and the Sceptre*, trans. Heinz Norden (Munich, 1959), 206–216.

40. Gebsattel (Bavarian military representative in Berlin) to Bavarian war minister, 1 March, 17 November 1907, BHStA-KA M.Kr. 42 no. 581 and M.

Kr. 5562 no. 21092; von Einem diary entry, 1905, BA-MA N324(Einem)/3 p. 4; von Einem, *Erinnerungen,* 59–65.

41. Von Einem to Bülow, 18 June 1906, PAAA R794 no. 1367/06.

42. Reichsarchiv, *Kriegsrüstung,* 1:236.

43. Von Einem to Bülow, 18 June 1906, PAAA R794 no. 1367/06.

44. Ibid.

45. Deuxième Bureau, *Enseignements de la guerre russo-japonaise. Note nº 2. Mitrailleuses,* December 1905, SHAT 7N 670.

46. Ibid.; Generalstab, Evidenzbüro, *Veränderungen im Heerwesen Rußlands im Jahre 1905,* March 1906, KA MKSM 1906 18–3/1.

47. Moulin to Min. Guerre, 15 September 1906, SHAT 7N 1477 no. 2571.

48. Deuxième Bureau, *Note sur les détachements de Mitrailleuses: Empire Allemand,* 16 May 1905, SHAT 7N 670/1 no. 265; Conseil Supérieur de la Guerre, *Procès-verbal,* 7 June 1905, SHAT 1N 9/11 pp. 116–119.

49. Moltke to Tschirschky, 9 October 1906, PAAA R794 no. 649.

50. Conseil Supérieur de la Guerre, *Procès-verbal,* 27 September 1907, SHAT 1N 9/11 pp. 190–216.

51. Girodou to Min. Guerre, 23 February 1907, SHAT 7N 1130/1 no. 208.

52. Consiglio dell'Esercito, *Seduta del 26 Marzo 1908,* 26 March 1908, AUSSME F-4; Commissione d'Inchiesta sull'Esercito, *Relazione N. II,* 23 June 1908, ACS PCM 362/1/3 no. 432.

53. Moulin to Min. Guerre, 30 November 1904, SHAT 7N 1476/8 no. 2394; Conseil Supérieur de la Guerre, *Procès-verbaux,* 7 June 1905, 31 March 1906, SHAT 1N 9/11 pp. 116–119, 135–140; Moulin to Min. Guerre, 23 March 1906, SHAT 7N 1477 no. 2540; Laguiche to Min. Guerre, 12 November 1907, SHAT 7N 1108/3 no. 399; Großer Generalstab, 3. Abteilung, *Zusammenstellung der wichtigsten Veränderungen im Heerwesen Frankreichs 1908,* 15 February 1909, BA-MA RM5/1234 nos. 3–55; Reichsarchiv, *Kriegsrüstung,* 1:229–231.

54. Deuxième Bureau, *Notes sur les manoeuvres d'automne du XIVᵉ corps allemand,* 5 November 1904, SHAT 7N 670/1 no. 107; Col. d'Amade (French military attaché in London) to Min. Guerre, 29 September 1904, SHAT 7N 1221/2 no. 313; Deuxième Bureau, *Note sur les détachements de Mitrailleuses. Empire Allemand,* 16 May 1905, SHAT 7N 670/1 no. 265; Laguiche to Min. Guerre, 1 December 1906, 7N 1108/2 no. 314; Messier to Min. Guerre, 10 February 1907, SHAT 7N 1369/1 no. 518; Laguiche to Min. Guerre, 10 October 1907, SHAT 7N 1108/3 no. 398. Machine guns appeared in German Imperial maneuvers from 1901 and were used with the infantry there from 1907. The French first deployed them at their grand maneuvers in 1902; the Italians in 1906, and the Austro-Hungarian army in 1907.

55. Deuxième Bureau, *Enseignements de la guerre russo-japonaise. Note nº 7.—Habillement,* January 1906, SHAT 7N 670; Generalstab, Evidenzbüro, *Veränderungen im Heerwesen Russlands 1904,* April 1905, KA MKSM 1905 18–4/1.

56. D'Amade to Min. Guerre, 29 September 1904, SHAT 7N 1221/2 no. 313; Graf von Schulenburg (German military attaché in London) to Reichs-

kriegsministerium, 24 August 1905, BHStA-KA Generalstab 146 no. 509; Großer Generalstab, *Die Taktik der englischen Armee*, 1907, BHStA-KA Generalstab 146 no. 6001.

57. Bonnal, *Récente guerre Sud-Africaine*, 45.

58. Von Einem, *Erinnerungen*, 89.

59. Von Einem to Bülow, 18 June 1906, PAAA R794 no. 1367/06; Laguiche to Min. Guerre, 17 February 1909, SHAT 7N 1109/1 no. 531.

60. Capt. Asinari Di San Marzano (Italian military attaché in Vienna) to Stato Maggiore, 27 September 1907, AUSSME G-22/10 no. 81.

61. Girodou to Min. Guerre, 11 January 1908, SHAT 7N 1130/2 no. 260.

62. Messier to Min. Guerre, 20 January, 10 September 1907, SHAT 7N 1369/1 nos. 507, 581; Consiglio dell'Esercito, *Seduta del 21 Novembre 1908*, 21 November 1908, AUSSME F-4.

63. Generalstab, Evidenzbüro, *Veränderungen im Heerwesen Russlands im Jahre 1908*, 23 April 1909, KA MKSM 1909 18–2/2.

64. Moulin to Min. Guerre, 6 April 1904, SHAT 7N 1476/7 no. 2268; Deuxième Bureau, *Enseignements de la guerre russo-japonaise. Note n° 4. Appareils collectifs de cuisine*, December 1905, SHAT 7N 670.

65. Deuxième Bureau, *Enseignements de la guerre russo-japonaise. Note n° 5.—Établissement des liaisons su le champ de bataille (Emploi du télégraphe et du téléphone)*, December 1905, SHAT 7N 670.

66. Von Mutius to Kriegsministerium, 7 January 1907, BA-MA PH 9V/142 no. 128.

67. Generalstab, Evidenzbüro, *Veränderungen im Heerwesen Russlands im Jahre 1906*, February 1907, KA MKSM 1907 18–3/1.

68. Laguiche to Min. Guerre, 12 February 1907, SHAT 7N 1108/2 no. 340; Moltke to Kriegsministerium, 4 December 1907, BA-MA PH 9V/142 nos. 386–387; Girodou to Min. Guerre, 9 September 1907, SHAT 7N 1130/1n. 248.

69. Girodou to Min. Guerre, 11 February 1906, SHAT 1129/5 no. 134; Deuxième Bureau, *Les automobiles en essai dans l'Armée allemande*, 18 February 1907, SHAT 7N 672/1.

70. Generalstab, Evidenzbüro, *Veränderungen im Heerwesen Italiens im Jahre 1905*, March 1906, KA MKSM 1906 18–2/1; von Einem to Bülow, 18 June 1906, PAAA R794 no. 1367/06; Moltke to Tschirschky, 9 October 1906, PAAA R794 no. 649.

71. Moltke to Tschirschky, 9 October 1906, PAAA R794 no. 649.

72. Großer Generalstab, 4. Abteilung, *Motorluftschiffahrt in Frankreich*, 14 March 1907, BA-MA PH 9V/142 no. 157.

73. Radolin (German ambassador in Paris) to Bülow, 23 July 1907, PAAA R6749 no. 493.

74. Jules Cambon to Pichon, 27 July 1907, MAE CP Allemagne NS 103 no. 292.

75. Laguiche to Min. Guerre, 2 August 1908; Reichsarchiv, *Kriegsrüstung*, 1:268–269, SHAT 7N 1108/4 no. 481.

76. Militärgeschichtliches Forschungsamt, ed., *Die Militärluftfahrt bis zum*

Beginn des Weltkrieges 1914, 3 vols. (Freiburg im Breisgau, 1965–66), 1:35–73.

77. Laguiche to Min. Guerre, 24 June 1908, SHAT 7N 1108/4 no. 422.

78. Below (Prussian ambassador in Stuttgart) to Bülow, 4 July 1908, PAAA R782 no. 51.

79. Laguiche to Min. Guerre, 2 August 1908, SHAT 7N 1108/4 no. 481; Peter Fritzsche, *A Nation of Fliers: German Aviation and the Popular Imagination* (Cambridge, Mass., 1992), 9–43.

80. Militärgeschichtliches Forschungsamt, *Militärluftfahrt*, 1:65.

81. Pradère-Niquet (French consul in Mannheim) to Ministère des Affaires Etrangères, 6 August 1908, MAE CP Allemagne NS 104 nos. 21–22.

82. Wilhelm II to interior ministry (copy), 8 August 1908, BA-MA R43F/1335 no. 71.

83. Frhr. von Lyncker (Inspektor der Verkehrtruppen) to Kriegsministerium, 24 August 1908, PAAA R782 no. 1745/08.

84. Militärgeschichtliches Forschungsamt, *Militärluftfahrt*, 1:68–69.

85. Lieut. Aderholt to Abteilung I of Artillerie Prüfungs-Kommission, 20 September 1907, BA-MA PH 9V/142 nos. 363–364; Ostertag (German attaché in London) to Kriegsministerium, 30 December 1907, BA-MA PH 9V/142 nos. 436–437; Alfred Gollin, *No Longer an Island: Britain and the Wright Brothers, 1902–1909* (Stanford, 1984).

86. Generalstab, Evidenzbüro, *Veränderungen im Heerwesen Italiens im Jahre 1908*, 10 March 1909, KA MKSM 1909 18–1/2.

87. Col. Wyndham (British military attaché in St. Petersburg), *Memorandum on the Military Policy and Armament of Russia, 1908*, 30 January 1909, PRO FO 881/9425 no. 20.

88. KA MKSM 1908 25–1/1, Conrad, *Denkschrift 1907*, 14 January 1908.

89. Großer Generalstab, 3. Abteilung, *Zusammenstellung der wichtigsten Veränderungen im Heerwesen Frankreichs 1908*, 15 February 1909, BA-MA RM5/1234 nos. 3–55.

90. Laguiche to Min. Guerre, 25 December 1908, SHAT 7N 1108/4 no. 511; Militärgeschichtliches Forschungsamt, *Militärluftfahrt*, 1:57–58.

91. Maj. Herberstein (Austro-Hungarian military attaché in Paris) to Kriegsministerium, *Manöver-Bericht 1904*, 18 October 1904, KA Generalstab 1904 25–3/42.

92. Gen. Lacroix, *Impressions recueillies par M. le Général de Lacroix, Gouverneur militaire de Lyon, sur la valeur et les procédés de combat de la cavalerie allemande*, 23 January 1906, SHAT 7N 670/1 no. F. 121.

93. Von Mutius to Kriegsministerium, 9 October 1907, BHStA-KA M. Kr. 990 no. 89.

94. Min. Guerre, *Décret du 3 Décembre 1904 portant règlement sur les manoeuvres de l'infanterie* (Paris, 1904), pp. 38–41, 52, 68–73.

95. E.g., War Office General Staff, *The Military Resources of France*, 1905, PRO WO 33/363.

96. Deuxième Bureau, *Enseignements de la guerre russo-japonaise. Note n° 16.—Les Enseignements*, March 1907, SHAT 7N 670.

97. Laguiche to Min. Guerre, 15 October 1908, SHAT 7N 1108/4 no. 488.

98. Von Mutius to Kriegsministerium, 9 October 1907, BHStA-KA M. Kr. 990 no. 89.

99. Von Mutius to Kriegsministerium, 29 April 1906, PAAA R6748 no. 12.

100. Von Mutius to Kriegsministerium, 9 October 1907, BHStA-KA M. Kr. 990 no. 89.

101. Maj. Zaccone, *Relazione sulle grandi manovre francesi del 1908*, October 1908, AUSSME G-23/18.

102. Von Mutius to Kriegsministerium, 9 October 1907, BHStA-KA M. Kr. 990 no. 89.

103. War Office General Staff, *The Military Resources of France*, 1905, PRO WO 33/363; von Mutius to Kriegsministerium, 9 October 1907, BHStA-KA M. Kr. 990 no. 89; Maj. Zaccone, *Relazione delle grandi manovre francesi del 1908*, October 1908, AUSSME G-23/18; Laguiche to Min. Guerre, 15 October 1908, SHAT 7N 1108/4 no. 488; Großer Generalstab, 3. Abteilung, *Zusammenstellung der wichtigsten Veränderungen im Heerwesen Frankreichs 1908*, 15 February 1909, BA-MA RM5/1234 nos. 3–55.

104. Von Mutius to Kriegsministerium, 29 April 1906, PAAA R6748 no. 12.

105. Von Mutius to Kriegsministerium, 29 June 1907, PAAA R6749 no. 17.

106. François Oscar de Négrier, "Le moral des troupes," *Revue des deux mondes* 25, no. 1 (1 February 1905): 481–505; Col. de La Panouse, "L'organisation militaire," *Revue des deux mondes* 21, no. 2 (May 1904): 346.

107. War Office General Staff, *The Military Resources of France*, 1905, PRO WO 33/363.

108. Posadowsky-Wehner to Kriegsministerium, 25 November 1908, PAAA R6750 no. 52.

109. Von Mutius to Kriegsministerium, 24 April 1908, PAAA R6749 no. 11.

110. Von Mutius to Kriegsministerium, 29 April 1906, PAAA R6748 no. 12.

111. Laguiche to Min. Guerre, 15 October 1908, SHAT 7N 1108/4 no. 488.

112. Deuxième Bureau, *Note sur les manoeuvres d'automne du XIVe corps allemand*, 5 November 1904, SHAT 7N 670/1 no. 107; "Les maneouvres impériales allemandes en 1904" (Part 2), *Revue militaire des armées étrangères* 65, no. 926 (January 1905): 17; "Les maneouvres impériales allemandes en 1905," *Revue militaire des armées étrangères* 67, no. 940 (March 1906): 234; "Les maneouvres impériales allemandes en 1906," *Revue militaire des armées étrangères* 69, no. 953 (April 1907): 329; Laguiche to Min. Guerre, 1 December 1906, SHAT 7N 1108/2 no. 314; Comando del Corpo di Stato Maggiore, Riparto Operazioni, Ufficio Scacchiere Orientale, *Relazione sulle manovre tedesche del 1908*, June 1909, AUSSME G-22/50 no. 473.

113. Laguiche to Min. Guerre, 15 October 1908 (extracts reported from 1904), SHAT 7N 1108/4 no. 488.

114. Field Marshal Prince Arthur, Duke of Connaught, *Annual Report of the Inspector-General of the Forces, 1906,* 1 October 1906, PRO WO 163/12 Appendix pp. 3–74.

115. Gen. Lacroix, *Impressions recueillies par M. le Général de Lacroix, Gouverneur militaire de Lyon, sur la valeur et les procédés de combat de la cavalerie allemande,* 23 January 1906, SHAT 7N670/1 no. F. 121; see also Laguiche to Min. Guerre, 10 July 1908, SHAT 7N 1108/4 no. 423.

116. Laguiche to Min. Guerre, 12 February 1907, SHAT 7N 1108/2 no. 340.

117. Laguiche to Min. Guerre, 15 October 1908, SHAT 7N 1108/4 no. 488.

118. Lt.-Col. Gastaldella (Italian military attaché in Berlin), *Relazione sulle manovre imperiali tedesche del 1904,* 20 November 1904, AUSSME G-22/16 no. 112; "Les manoeuvres impériales allemandes en 1905" (Part 2), *Revue militaire des armées étrangères* 67, no. 940 (March 1906): 227–231; idem, "Les manoeuvres impériales allemandes en 1908," *Revue militaire des armées étrangères* 73 no. 976 (March 1909): 212–213; Gen. Lacroix, *Impressions recueillies par M. le Général de Lacroix, Gouverneur militaire de Lyon, sur la valeur et les procédés de combat de la cavalerie allemande,* 23 January 1906, SHAT 7N 670/1 no. F. 121; and Gudmundsson, *Stormtroop Tactics,* 18.

119. Laguiche to Min. Guerre, 1 December 1906, SHAT 7N 1108/2 no. 314.

120. Gastaldella, *Relazione sulle manovre imperiali tedesche dell'anno 1904,* 20 November 1904, AUSSME G-22/16 no. 112.

121. Moulin to Min. Guerre, 20 November, 10 December 1907, MAE CP Allemagne NS 103 nos. 308, 312–314.

122. "Les manoeuvres impériales allemandes en 1904" (Part 2), *Revue militaire des armées étrangères* 65, no. 926 (January 1905): 18.

123. Gastaldella, *Relazione sulle manovre imperiali tedesche del 1904,* 20 November 1904, AUSSME G-22/16 no. 112; "Les manoeuvres impériales allemandes en 1905" (Part 2), *Revue militaire des armées étrangères* 67, no. 940 (March 1906): 231–233.

124. Gebsattel to Bavarian war ministry, 13 June 1905, BHStA-KA M. Kr. 43 no. 10392; and Gudmundsson, *Stormtroop Tactics,* 20–21.

125. Von Dorrer (Württemberg military representative in Berlin) to Württemberg war ministry, 14 September 1907, HStAS-KA M 1/3 bd. 670 no. 1763.

126. Schlieffen to Gen. von Wandel (Allgemeines Kriegsdepartement), enclosing a report by Majors Etzel and Bronsart von Schellendorf and Capt. Hoffmann, Generalstab, 23 June 1905, BA-MA N564(Wandel)/6 no. 1.

127. Comando del Corpo di Stato Maggiore, Riparto Operazioni, Ufficio Scacchiere Orientale, *Relazione sulle manovre imperiali tedesche del 1906,* 30 April 1907, AUSSME G-22/49 no. 471; idem, *Relazione 1908,* June 1909, AUSSME G-22/50 no. 473; "Les manoeuvres impériales allemandes en 1908" (Part 2), *Revue militaire des armées étrangères* 73, no. 976 (March 1909): 214–215.

128. Comando del Corpo di Stato Maggiore, Riparto Operazioni, Scac-

chiere Orientale, *Relazione sulle manovre imperiali tedesche del 1907*, 30 April 1908, AUSSME G-22/49 no. 472.

129. Deuxième Bureau, *Le règlement d'exercices pour l'infanterie allemande du 29 Mai 1906*, September 1906, SHAT 7N 760/1 no. 7920; "Les procédés de combat et les méthodes d'instruction dans l'infanterie allemande de 1870 à la fin de 1906" (Part 2): "Le règlement sur les exercices et manoeuvres du 29 Mai 1906," *Revue militaire des armées étrangères* 69, no. 950 (January 1907): 44–45; "Le nouveau service en campagne de l'armée allemande"(Part 2), *Revue militaire des armées étrangères* 72, no. 972 (November 1908): 449–450.

130. Gebsattel to Bavarian war ministry, 4 May 1907, BHStA-KA M. Kr. 990 no. 1244.

131. Moltke to Wandel, enclosing a 12 April report by Col. Lauenstein, 30 April 1906, BA-MA N564(Wandel)/6 no. 7.

132. Von Dorrer to Württemberg war ministry, *Bericht über die Kaisermanöver 1908*, 14 September 1908, HStAS-KA M 1/3 bd. 671.

133. Laguiche to Min. Guerre, 15 October 1908, SHAT 7N 1108/4 no. 488.

134. "Idées allemandes sur le rôle et l'emploi de la cavalerie"(1 and 2), *Revue militaire des armées étrangères* 63, no. 917 (April 1904): 298–303, and vol. 63, no. 918 (May 1904): 416–430; Gastaldella, *Relazione sulle manovre imperiali tedesche dell'anno 1904*, 20 November 1904, AUSSME G-22/16 no. 12.

135. Gen. Lacroix, *Impressions recueillies par M. le Général de Lacroix, Gouverneur militaire de Lyon, sur la valeur et les procédés de combat de la cavalerie allemande*, 23 January 1906, SHAT 7N 670/1 F. 121.

136. Ibid.; Laguiche to Min. Guerre, 1 December 1906, SHAT 7N 1108/2 no. 314; "Les manoeuvres impériales allemandes en 1905" (Part 2), *Revue militaire des armées étrangères* 67, no. 940 (March 1906): 234–235; Comando del Corpo di Stato Maggiore, Riparto Operazioni, Scacchiere Orientale, *Relazione sulle manovre imperiali tedesche del 1907*, 30 April 1908, AUSSME G-22/ 49 no. 472.

137. Laguiche to Min. Guerre, 10 July 1908, SHAT 7N 1108/4 no. 423.

138. Laguiche to Min. Guerre, 1 and 11 December 1906, SHAT 7N 1108/ 2 nos. 314, 318.

139. Gastaldella, *Relazione sulle manovre imperiali tedesche dell'anno 1904*, 20 November 1904, AUSSME G-22/16 no. 112.

140. Großer Generalstab, *Die Feldbefestigung im russisch-japanischen Kriege*, 15 August 1905, BA-MA N564(Wandel)/6 no. 3; see also Deuxième Bureau, *Enseignements de la guerre russo-japonaise. Note n° 3. Outils*, December 1905, SHAT 7N 670.

141. "Les manoeuvres impériales allemandes en 1906" (Part 2), *Revue militaire des armées étrangères* 69, no. 953 (April 1907): 329; Laguiche to Min. Guerre, 1 and 8 December 1906, SHAT 7N 1108/2 nos. 314, 315; Comando del Corpo di Stato Maggiore, Riparto Operazioni, Scacchiere Orientale, *Relazione sulle grandi manovre tedesche del 1906*, 30 April 1907, AUSSME G-22/49 no. 471; Laguiche to Min. Guerre, 15 October 1908, SHAT 7N 1108/4 no. 488.

142. Laguiche to Min. Guerre, 17 February 1909, SHAT 7N 1109/1 no. 531.

143. Laguiche to Min. Guerre, 15 October 1908, SHAT 7N 1108/4 no. 488.

144. Gudmundsson, *On Artillery*, 31–35.

145. Reichsarchiv, *Kriegsrüstung*, 1:246.

146. Von Einem to Generalkommandos und Inspektionen der Fuß- und Feldartillerie, 2 July 1904, HStAS-KA M1/9 Bd. 1 v. ii nos. 100–102.

147. Gen. André, *Note de présentation N° 2 pour la question du renforcement de l'artillerie de campagne*, 28 January 1904, SHAT 7N 48/2; Conseil Supérieur de la Guerre, *Procès-verbal* 30 January 1904, SHAT 1N 9/11 pp. 49–60.

148. "L'artillerie lourde de campagne en allemagne," *Revue militaire des armées étrangères* 69, no. 954 (May 1907): 446.

149. Troisième Direction (Artillerie), *Note pour l'Etat-Major de l'Armée (3e Bureau)*, 29 February 1904, SHAT 9N 30; Troisième Direction, *Note pour le Cabinet du Ministre: Etat actuel de la fabrication du matériel de 155c M^{le} 1904 T.R.*, 17 December 1908, SHAT 7N 49/7 no. 2797.

150. Deuxième Bureau, *Note sur l'artillerie allemande*, 19 December 1904, SHAT 670/1 no. 93bis; Deuxième Bureau, *Rapport sur les manoeuvres impériales allemandes en 1904*, 1 November 1904, SHAT 7N 670/1 no. 93; Laguiche to Min. Guerre, 10 June 1906, SHAT 7N 1108/2 no. 229 pp. 19–20; Comando del Corpo di Stato Maggiore, Riparto Operazioni, Scacchiere Orientale, *Relazione sulle manovre imperiali tedesche del 1907*, 30 April 1908, AUSSME G-22/49 no. 472.

151. Deuxième Bureau, *Les enseignements de la guerre russo-japonaise. Note n° 10.—Matériel d'Artillerie*, February 1906, SHAT 7N 670.

152. Großer Generalstab, *Die russische und Japanische Artillerie im Feldkriege*, 28 July 1905, BA-MA N564(Wandel)/6 no. 2.

153. Großer Generalstab, *Die Feldbefestigung im russisch-japanischen Kriege*, 15 August 1905, BA-MA N564(Wandel)/6 no. 3.

154. Moltke to Tschirschky, 9 October 1906, PAAA R794 no. 649.

155. Moulin to Min. Guerre, 18 December 1906, SHAT 7N 1477 no. 2639.

156. Report by Lt.-Col. Lauenstein, Großer Generalstab, 10 December 1905, BA-MA N564(Wandel)/6 no. 6.

157. Moulin to Min. Guerre, 22 November 1906, SHAT 7N 1477 no. 2601.

158. Moulin to Min. Guerre, 20 August 1906, SHAT 7N 1477 no. 2564.

159. Generalstab, Evidenzbüro, *Veränderungen im Heerwesen Russlands im Jahre 1907*, 30 May 1908, KA MKSM 1908 18–4/1.

160. War Office General Staff, *The Military Resources of the Russian Empire*, 1907, PRO WO 33/419.

161. Beck, *Denkschrift 1904*, 28 December 1904, KA MKSM 1905 25–2/1.

162. Report by Lt.-Col. Lauenstein, Großer Generalstab, 10 December 1905, BA-MA N564(Wandel)/6 no. 6.

163. Großer Generalstab, 1. Abteilung, *Zusammenstellung der wichtigsten Veränderungen im Heerwesen Rußlands im Jahre 1905*, 1905–6, BHStA-KA

Generalstab 207 no. 23; Generalstab, Evidenzbüro, *Veränderungen im Heerwesen Russlands im Jahre 1906*, February 1907, KA MKSM 1907 18–3/1.

164. Col. Wyndham, *Memorandum on the Military Policy and Armament of Russia, 1908*, 30 January 1909, PRO FO 881/9425 no. 20.

165. Moulin to Min. Guerre, 20 August 1906, SHAT 7N 1477 no. 2564.

166. Ibid.; Moulin to Min. Guerre, 6 March 1906, SHAT 7N 1477 no. B-1906.

167. Col. Pierre, Ecole Supérieure de la Guerre, *Conférence sur l'Armée Russe*, 1907, SHAT 7N 1535.

168. Moulin to Min. Guerre, 20 August 1906, SHAT 7N 1477 no. 2564.

169. Großer Generalstab, 1. Abteilung, *Zusammenstellung der wichtigsten Veränderungen im Heerwesen Rußlands im Jahre 1906*, 1906–7, BHStA-KA Generalstab 207 no. 13.

170. Generalstab, Evidenzbüro, *Veränderungen im Heerwesen Rußlands im Jahre 1905*, March 1906, KA MKSM 1906 18–3/1.

171. Moulin to Min. Guerre, 22 November 1906, SHAT 7N 1477 no. 2601.

172. Col. d'Amade to Min. Guerre, 29 September 1904, SHAT 7N 1221/2 no. 313.

173. Großer Generalstab, *Die Taktik der englischen Armee*, 1907, BHStA-KA, Generalstab 146 no. 6001.

174. Huguet to Min. Guerre, 23 September 1906, SHAT 7N 1222/3 no. 143.

175. Capt. von Heydebreck, Großer Generalstab, *Unternehmungen Englands gegen Deutschland zu Lande*, 2 January 1905, BA-MA RM5/1605 nos. 35–52.

176. Huguet to Min. Guerre, 3 July 1907, SHAT 7N 1223/1 no. 215.

177. D'Amade to Min. Guerre, 29 September 1904, SHAT 7N 1221/2 no. 313.

178. Großer Generalstab, *Die Taktik der englischen Armee*, 1907, BHStA-KA Generalstab 146 no. 6001.

179. Arthur, *Annual Report of the Inspector-General of the Forces, 1906*, 1 October 1906, PRO WO 163/12 Appendix, pp. 3–74.

180. Gen. Michel, *Rapport du Général Michel sur le séjour de la mission française en Angleterre, du 24 au 28 Juin 1907*, 28 June 1907, SHAT 7N 672/4 dossier AB.

181. Huguet to Min. Guerre, 18 November 1905, SHAT 7N 1222/1 no. 72.

182. Heydebreck, *Unternehmungen Englands gegen Deutschland zu Lande*, 2 January 1905, BA-MA RM5/1605 nos. 35–52; Schulenburg to Kriegsministerium, 24 August 1905, BHStA-KA Generalstab 146 no. 509; Großer Generalstab, 3. Abteilung, *England. Auszug aus dem Orientierungsheft*, 1 May 1906, BHStA-KA Generalstab 146.

183. Großer Generalstab, 3. Abteilung, *Auszug aus dem Orientierungsheft für England*, 24 December 1907, BHStA-KA Generalstab 146.

184. Beck, *Denkschrift 1905*, 27 December 1905, KA MKSM 1906 25–1/1.

185. Conrad, *Denkschrift 1907*, 14 January 1908, KA MKSM 1908 25–1/1.

186. Girodou to Min. Guerre, 9 January 1906, SHAT 1129/5 no. 129.

187. Girodou to Min. Guerre, 11 January 1908, SHAT 7N 1130/2 no. 260.

188. San Marzano, *L'esercito austro-ungarico alla fine del 1908*, January 1909, AUSSME G-24 Austria 14/4 no. 23.

189. Girodou to Min. Guerre, 9 January 1906, SHAT 7N 1129/5 no. 129; see also idem, 11 January 1908, SHAT 7N 1130/2 no. 260.

190. István Deák, *Beyond Nationalism: A Social and Political History of the Habsburg Officer Corps, 1848–1918* (Oxford, 1990).

191. Girodou to Min. Guerre, 29 May 1904, SHAT 7N 1129/3 no. 26; see also idem, 9 January 1906, SHAT 7N 1129/5 no. 12.

192. Girodou to Min. Guerre, 9 September 1907, SHAT 7N 1130/1 no. 248.

193. San Marzano, *Rapporto confidenziale sulle grandi manovre austro-ungariche svoltesi in Carinzia dal 2 al 7 settembre 1907*, undated, AUSSME G-22/10.

194. Girodou to Min. Guerre, 20 September 1905, SHAT 7N 1129/4 no. 102; San Marzano to Stato Maggiore, 17 September 1906, AUSSME G-29 Austria 13/3 no. 44/iv.

195. Girodou to Min. Guerre, 9 September 1907, SHAT 7N 1130/1 no. 248; San Marzano to Stato Maggiore, 27 September 1907, AUSSME G-22/10 no. 81.

196. Girodou to Min. Guerre, 23 February 1907, SHAT 7N 1130/1 no. 208.

197. San Marzano to Stato Maggiore, 27 September 1907, AUSSME G-22/10 no. 81.

198. Girodou to Min. Guerre, 10 January 1909, SHAT 7N 1130/3 no. 333.

199. Girodou to Min. Guerre, 10 May 1905, SHAT 7N 1129/4 no. 91.

200. Girodou to Min. Guerre, 23 February 1907, SHAT 7N 1130/1 no. 208.

201. Frhr. von Hammerstein-Equord to Kriegsministerium, 11 September 1905, PAAA R7804 no. 274.

202. Saletta, *Relazione delle Grandi Manovre nella Campania del 1905*, undated, AUSSME F-4/58.

203. Saletta, *Relazione delle Grandi Manovre nell'Alto Novarese del 1907*, undated, AUSSME F-4/49.

204. Messier to Min. Guerre, 10 September 1907, SHAT 7N 1369/1 no. 581.

205. Messier to Min. Guerre, 30 December 1904, SHAT 7N 1368/1 no. 288; see also idem, 10 February 1907, SHAT 7N 1369/1 no. 518.

206. Messier to Min. Guerre, 10 September 1907, SHAT 7N 1369/1 no. 581.

207. Saletta, *Relazione delle Grandi Manovre nella Campania del 1905*, undated, AUSSME F-4/58; Saletta, *Relazione delle Grandi Manovre nell'Alto Novarese del 1907*, undated, AUSSME F-4/49.

208. Ufficio del Capo di Stato Maggiore dell'Esercito, *Confronto tra il presumibile grado d'istruzione del nostro esercito e quello degli Stati confinanti*, 9 December 1905, AUSSME F-4/11.

209. Domenico De Napoli, "Il caso Ranzi ed il modernismo militare" in *L'Esercito italiano dall'Unità alla Grande Guerra (1861–1918)*, Ufficio Storico, Corpo di Stato Maggiore dell'Esercito, Italy (Rome, 1980), 221–244.

210. Messier to Min. Guerre, 30 December 1906, SHAT 7N 1368/3 no. 497.

211. Generalstab, Evidenzbüro, *Veränderungen im Heerwesen Italiens im Jahre 1907*, 15 March 1908, KA MKSM 1908 18–1/1; see also idem, *Heerwesen Italiens 1904*, 24 February 1905, KA MKSM 1905 18–2/1.

212. Messier to Min. Guerre, 10 September 1907, SHAT 7N 1369/1 no. 581.

213. Messier to Min. Guerre, 10 March 1906, SHAT 7N 1368/3 no. 421.

214. *Veränderungen im Heerwesen Italiens im Jahre 1907*, 15 March 1908, KA MKSM 1908 18–1/1.

215. Messier to Min. Guerre, 30 January 1905, SHAT 7N 1368/2 no. 295; see also idem, 20 November 1904, SHAT 7N 1368/1 no. 267.

216. Hammerstein-Equord to Kriegsministerium, 11 September 1905, PAAA R7804 no. 274.

217. Messier to Min. Guerre, 10 March 1906, SHAT 7N 1368/3 no. 421.

218. Generalstab, Evidenzbüro, *Veränderungen im Heerwesen Italiens im Jahre 1905*, March 1906, KA MKSM 1906 18–2/1.

219. Generalstab, Evidenzbüro, *Veränderungen im Heerwesen Italiens im Jahre 1904*, 24 February 1905, KA MKSM 1905 18–2/1.

220. Messier to Min. Guerre, 20 September 1906, SHAT 7N 1368/3 no. 459; see also idem, 10 February 1907, SHAT 7N 1369/1 no. 518.

221. Saletta, *Relazione delle Grandi Manovre nella Campania del 1905*, undated, AUSSME F-4/58.

222. Jullian to Min. Guerre, 6 March 1908, SHAT 7N 1369/2 no. 48.

223. Hammerstein-Equord to Kriegsministerium, 7 December 1908, PAAA R7807 no. 364.

224. Szögyeny (Austro-Hungarian ambassador in Berlin) to Ministerium des Äußern, 8 April 1906, and Szögyeny to Goluchowski (Austro-Hungarian foreign minister), 10 April 1906, HHStA PA I/477 no. 38.

225. Comando del Corpo di Stato Maggiore, Riparto Intendenza, Ufficio Trasporti, *Relazione intorno al progetto di mobilitazione e radunata verso la frontiera nord est in data luglio 1906*, 15 March 1907, AUSSME F-4/64 no. 1; Massimo Mazzetti, "I piani di guerra contro l'Austria dal 1866 alla Prima Guerra Mondiale," in *L'Esercito italiano dall'Unità alla Grande Guerra (1861–1918)*, Ufficio Storico, Corpo di Stato Maggiore dell'Esercito, Italy (Rome, 1980), 161–177.

226. Gen. Pitreich (Austro-Hungarian war minister) to ministers-president of Austria and Hungary, 28 March 1904.

227. Beck, *Denkschrift 1904*, 28 December 1904, KA MKSM 1905 25–2/1.

228. Conrad, *Denkschrift II: Hinsichtlich des Kriegsfalles gegen Rußland und Italien*, 17 April 1908, KA Generalstab, Operationsbüro 742 nos. 406–411.

229. Ufficio del Capo di Stato Maggiore dell'Esercito, *La mobilitazione e radunata dell'esercito alla frontiera N.E.*, 22 August 1904, AUSSME F-4/11; Mazzetti "I piani di guerra contro l'Austria."

230. Comando del Corpo di Stato Maggiore, Riparto Operazioni, Ufficio Scacchiere Orientale, *Attività militare dell'Austria-Ungheria in genere ed alla frontiera italiana in ispecie*, November 1906, AUSSME G-22/50 no. 26; idem, *Attività militare*, March 1908, ACS PCM 1908/367 categoria 6, fasc. 4; Commissione Suprema Mista per la Difesa dello Stato, *Verbale della 3ª Seduta (11 Maggio 1908)*, 11 May 1908, AUSSME F-9/1bis/1 pp. 26–41.

231. Mazzetti, "L'Esercito nel periodo Giolittiano," 247–256; Michael Behnen, *Rüstung, Bündnis, Sicherheit. Dreibund und informeller Imperialismus* (Tübingen, 1985), 183–195.

232. Generalstab, Evidenzbüro, *Veränderungen im Heerwesen Italiens im Jahre 1906*, 19 February 1907, KA MKSM 1907 18–1/1–2; idem, *Heerwesen Italiens 1907*, 15 March 1908, KA MKSM 1908 18–1/1; Commissione Suprema Mista per la Difesa dello Stato, *Verbale della 2ª Seduta (8 Maggio 1908)*, 8 May 1908, AUSSME F-9/1bis/1 pp. 13–25; Barrère to Min. des Affaires Etrangères, 9 and 14 June 1908, MAE CP Italie NS 44, nos. 25, 31; Commissione d'Inchiesta per l'Esercito, *Relazione Nº II*, 23 June 1908, ACS PCM 362/1/3 no. 432; Generalstab, Evidenzbüro, *Veränderungen im Heerwesen Italiens im Jahre 1908*, 10 March 1909, KA MKSM 1909 18–1/2; Felice De Chaurand de Saint-Eustache, *Come l'esercito italiano entrò in guerra* (Milan, 1929), 106–114.

233. Consiglio dell'Esercito, *Seduta del 23 Marzo*, 23 March 1908, AUSSME F-4.

234. Mazzetti, "L'Esercito nel periodo Giolittiano," 251–256; AUSSME F-9/1bis/1 pp. 1–11, Commissione Suprema Mista per la Difesa dello Stato, *Verbale della 1ª Seduta (6 Maggio 1908)*, 6 May 1908.

235. Rothenberg, *Army of Francis Joseph*, 139–152; Behnen, *Rüstung, Bündnis, Sicherheit*, 124–145.

236. Girodou to Min. Guerre, 23 February 1907, SHAT 7N 1130/1 no. 208; Schönaich (Austro-Hungarian war minister) to Bolfras (Chief of His Majesty's Military Chancellery), 18 March 1907, KA MKSM 1907 4–3/2.

237. Beck, *Transport von Belagerungsartilleriematerial auf nicht fahrbaren Kommunikationen*, 12 May 1906, KA Generalstab 1906 44–8/3; Girodou to Min. Guerre, 11 October 1906, SHAT 7N 1129/5 no. 184.

238. Kriegsministerium, Abteilung 2, to Militärkanzlei Seiner Majestät, 3 February 1906, KA MKSM 1906 33–1/10; Maj. von Bülow (German military attaché in Vienna) to Kriegsministerium, 19 February 1906, PAAA R8616 no. 8.

239. Beck, *Denkschrift 1904*, 28 December 1904, KA MKSM 1905 25–2/1.

240. Conrad, *Denkschrift 1906*, 31 December 1906, KA MKSM 1907 25–1/1; Franz Conrad von Hötzendorf, *Aus meiner Dienstzeit*, 4 vols. (Vienna, 1921–25), 1:13–38, 39–73; Rothenberg, *The Army of Francis Joseph*, 144–145, 150–152; Behnen, *Rüstung, Bündnis, Sicherheit*, 145–152, 159–164.

241. Conrad to Militärkanzlei Seiner Majestät, *Denkschrift*, 6 April 1907, KA MKSM 1907 25–1/3 nos. 1–17.

242. Conrad to to Militärkanzlei Seiner Majestät, *Nachtrag* to 6 April *Denkschrift*, 13 April 1907, KA MKSM 1907 25–1/3 nos. 19–25.

243. Conrad to Militärkanzlei Seiner Majestät, *Denkschrift*, 6 April 1907, KA MKSM 1907 25–1/3 nos. 1–17.

244. Rothenberg, *The Army of Francis Joseph*, 141–142.

245. Aehrenthal to Militärkanzlei Seiner Majestät, 18 April 1907, KA MKSM 1907 25–1/3 nos. 3–10.

246. Conrad to Franz Joseph, 14 January 1908 and Conrad, *Denkschrift 1907*, 14 January 1908, KA MKSM 1908 25–1/1.

247. Stato Maggiore correspondence to Giolitti, March-April 1904, ACS PCM 1904/316 categoria 7, fasc. 5/1; correspondence between Stato Maggiore and Ufficio Diplomatico del Ministero degli Affari Esteri, March-April 1906, ASMAE P 505, esp. nos. 2285, 18777, and 19366.

248. Giuseppe Avarna di Gualtieri to Guicciardini (foreign ministry), 22 April 1906, ASMAE P 505 no. 29907; see also Lt.-Col. Del Mastro (Italian military attaché in Vienna) to Avarna, 1 March 1905, AUSSME G-29 Austria 13/1 no. 31; Avarna to Tittoni, 6 March 1907, ASMAE P 506 no. 17772.

249. Albertini, *Origins of the War of 1914*, 1:180–184; Aehrenthal, *Aufzeichnung über eine zwischen Freiherrn von Aehrenthal un dem italienischen Minister des Äußern Herrn Tittoni am 15. Juli 1907 zu Desio stattgehabte Unterredung*, undated, HHStA PA I/489 nos. 251–271.

250. Giovanni Giolitti, *Memorie della mia vita*, 2 vols. (Milan, 1922), 1:260.

251. Wedel (German ambassador in Vienna) to Bülow, 15 May 1904, PAAA R8615 no. 204; Monts (German ambassador in Rome) to Bülow, 21 May 1904, PAAA R7803 no. 149; Hammerstein-Equord to Kriegsministerium, 20 March 1906, PAAA R7804 no. 160.

CHAPTER 4

1. Quoted in William Gleason, "Alexander Guchkov and the End of the Russian Empire," *Proceedings of the American Philosophical Society* 73, part 3, 1983 (Philadelphia, 1983), 34–35.

2. Ibid., 1–35.

3. E.g., Posadowsky-Wehner to Kriegsministerium, 16 June, 3 July 1908, PAAA R10425 nos. 35, 38; Generalstab, Evidenzbüro, *Veränderungen im Heerwesen Russlands im Jahre 1908*, 23 April 1909, KA MKSM 1909 18–2/2.

4. Albertini, *Origins of the War of 1914*, 1:190–297; Momčilo Ninčić, *La crise bosniaque (1908–1909) et les puissances européennes*, 2 vols. (Paris, 1937); Bernadotte E. Schmitt, *The Annexation of Bosnia* (Cambridge, 1937; reprint, New York, 1970).

5. *Aufzeichnung über eine Besprechung der gemeinsamen Minister, die am ersten Dezember 1907 bei dem Herrn Minister des Aeussern Freiherr von Aehrenthal über die Gegenwärtige Situation in B. u. der H. stattfand*, 11 December 1907, HHStA PA XL/306.

6. *Ministerrath für gemeinsame Angelegenheiten, Protokoll*, 19 August, 10 September 1908, HHStA PA XL/307 nos. 34, 42.

7. Conrad, *Besprechung bei Ex. Aehrenthal—18.11.1907* (notes), KA B/1450:45 no. 26; see also Conrad to Aehrenthal, 19 November, 18 December

1907, Conrad, *Aus meiner Dienstzeit* 1:80, 368; KA B/1450:45 nos. 28, 44; Conrad, *Unterredung mit dem Minister des Äusseren am 17./12. 07.* (notes), KA B/1450:45 no. 38.

8. Conrad to Franz Joseph, 14 January 1908, KA MKSM 1908 25–1/1; Conrad, *Denkschrift 1907*, 4 January 1908, KA MKSM 1908 25–1/1; Conrad, *Denkschrift I*, 17 April 1908, KA Generalstab, Operationsbüro 742 nos. 402–405; Conrad, *Grundlagen für die Concreten Kriegs-Vorbereitungs-Arbeiten 1909*, 22 October 1908, KA B/1450:47 no. 94; Conrad, *Aus meiner Dienstzeit*, 1:72–79.

9. *Ministerrath für gemeinsame Angelegenheiten, Protokoll*, 19 August 1908, HHStA PA XL 307 no. 34.

10. Generalstab, Evidenzbüro, *Veränderungen im Heerwesen Russlands im Jahre 1907*, 30 May 1908, KA MKSM 1908 18–4/1; idem, *Heerwesen Russlands 1908*, 23 April 1909, KA MKSM 1909 18–2/2.

11. Aehrenthal to Berchtold, 27 June 1908, HHStA PA X 133/2 nos. 88–91.

12. Aehrenthal to Bülow, 12 June 1908, PAAA Österreich 95, Bd. 15; Berchtold to Aehrenthal, 23 April 1908, HHStA PA X 133/3 nos. 9–18.

13. Maj. Posadowsky-Wehner to Kriegsministerium, 11 March 1908, PAAA R10424 no. 12.

14. Aehrenthal, *Aufzeichnung der Unterredung Seiner Exzellenz des Herrn Ministers, Freiherrn von Aehrenthal mit Herrn Izwolski zu Buchlau am 16. September 1908*, 16 September 1908, HHStA PA I/483 nos. 316–331.

15. Bülow to Wilhelm II, 5 October 1908, GP XXVI/1 no. 8939 pp. 50–51.

16. Bülow to Tschirschky (German ambassador in Vienna), 13 October 1908, GP XXVI/1 no. 9033 p. 161.

17. Szögyény to Aehrenthal, 16 December 1908, HHStA PA I/484 nos. 179–194.

18. Posadowsky-Wehner to Kriegsministerium, 10 December 1908, PAAA R10425 no. 56; see also Pourtalès to Bülow, 1 November 1908, PAAA R11091 no. A.18347; Capt. (naval) von Hintze (German military plenipotentiary in St. Petersburg) to Kriegsministerium, 24 February 1909, GP XXVI/2 pp. 621–622 (cited in footnote to no. 9390, Kageneck to Kriegsministerium, 23 February 1909).

19. Posadowsky-Wehner to Kriegsministerium, 10 December 1908, PAAA R10425 no. 56.

20. Pourtalès to Bülow, 11 December 1908, GP XXVI/1 no. 9152 p. 335; Pourtalès to Bülow, 20 and 24 February 1909, GP XXVI/2 nos. 9387, 9403 pp. 617, 633–635.

21. Nicholas II to Wilhelm II, 28 December 1908, GP XXVI/2 no. 9187 pp. 387–388; Wilhelm II to Franz Joseph, 26 January 1909, GP XXVI/2 no. 9193 pp. 401–402; Nicholas II to Wilhelm II, 25 January 1909, GP XXVI/2 no. 9194 pp. 402–404.

22. Szögyény to Ministerium des Äußern, 30 November 1908, Ö-UA I no. 678 p. 530; Kiderlen personal letter, recipient not identified, 7 March 1909, in

Ernst Jäckh, *Kiderlen-Wächter, der Staatsmann und Mensch: Briefwechsel und Nachlaß*, 2 vols. (Berlin and Leipzig, 1924), 2:25.

23. Metternich to Bülow, 7 January 1909, GP XXVI/2 no. 9190 pp. 393–396.

24. Nicolson to Grey, *Russia: Annual Report 1908*, 8 February 1909, enclosing Wyndham, *Memorandum on the Military Policy and Armament of Russia, 1908*, 30 January 1908, PRO FO 881/9425; Pourtalès to Bülow, 24 January 1909, PAAA R10425 no. 34.

25. Pichon (French foreign minister) to French ambassador in St. Petersburg, 23 January 1909, MAE CP Russie NS 58 nos. 44–46; Szögyény to Ministerium des Äußern, 16 December 1908, Ö-UA I no. 752 pp. 607–608.

26. Moulin to Min. Guerre, 2 September 1908, MAE CP Russie NS 39 nos. 97–101; Deuxième Bureau, *Concentration russe*, 28 October 1908, SHAT 7N 1537/6; Deuxième Bureau, *Note sur une action militaire éventuelle de la Russie en Europe*, 2 March 1909, SHAT 7N 1537/7.

27. Bülow to Wilhelm II, 29 January 1909, GP XXVI/2 no. 9197 pp. 409–410; see also Bülow to Wilhelm II, 22 February 1909, GP XXVI/2 no. 9388 pp. 618–620; note by Schoen (state secretary of the German foreign office), 28 February 1909, GP XXVI/2 no. 9409 p. 639.

28. *Unterredung des Chefs mit B^r Aehrenthal* (notes dictated by Conrad to his adjutant), 18 February 1909, KA B/1450:48 no. 19; see also Conrad, *Besprechung mit Ex. von Aehrenthal. Wien. 7 Dec. 1908* (notes), KA B/1450:47 no. 106.

29. Aehrenthal to Bülow, 20 February 1909, HHStA PA I/484 nos. 227–249.

30. Conrad, *Besprechung mit Ex. von Aehrenthal. Wien. 7 Dec. 1908* (notes), KA B/1450:47 no. 106; Tschirschky to Bülow, 17 Dec. 1908, GP XXVI/1 no. 9160 p. 343.

31. Aehrenthal to Conrad, 15 July 1908, KA B/1450:47 no. 56; Conrad, *Aus meiner Dienstzeit*, 1:80, 94–98.

32. Conrad, *Besprechung mit Ex. von Aehrenthal. Wien. 7 Dec. 1908* (notes), KA B/1450:47 no. 106; Aehrenthal to Bülow, 8 Dec. 1908, HHStA PA I/484 nos. 141–165.

33. Szögyény to Aehrenthal, 16 December 1908, HHStA PA I/484 nos. 179–194.

34. The texts are reprinted in Conrad, *Aus meiner Dienstzeit*, 1:379–406, 631–634; see also Norman Stone, "Moltke-Conrad: Relations between the Austro-Hungarian and German General Staffs, 1909–1914," *Historical Journal* 9, no. 2 (1966): 201–228.

35. Moltke to Conrad, 21 January 1909, Conrad, *Aus meiner Dienstzeit*, 1:380–381.

36. Conrad, *Vortrag bei S. Majestät am 23. Dec. 1908. Schönbrunn* (notes), KA B/1450:47 no. 109.

37. Conrad's unaddressed notes, 16 October 1908, KA B/1450:47; Conrad to Franz Joseph, 17 October 1908, KA Generalstab 1908 63–25/3; Conrad, *Grundlagen für die Concreten Kriegs-Vorbereitungs-Arbeiten 1909*, 22 October

1908, KA B/1450:47 no. 94; Conrad, *Kriegsfall gegen Serbien und Montenegro*, 8 March 1909, Conrad, *Aus meiner Dienstzeit* 1:640–655.

38. Conrad, *Grundlagen für die Concreten Kriegs-Vorbereitungs-Arbeiten 1909*, 22 October 1908, KA B/1450:47 no. 94.

39. Maj. Kageneck (German military attaché in Vienna) to Kriegsministerium, 23 February 1909, GP XXVI/2 no. 9390 p. 621.

40. Posadowsky-Wehner to Kriegsministerium, 10 December 1908, PAAA R10425 no. 56.

41. Ibid. (end note by Wilhelm II).

42. See Appendix A, above, and Generalstab, Evidenzbüro, *Veränderungen im Heerwesen der Balkanstaaten im Jahre 1907*, 25 May 1908, KA MKSM 1908 18–3/2.

43. Conrad's unaddressed notes, 16 October 1908, KA B/1450: 47; Conrad, *Aus meiner Dienstzeit*, 1:117–118.

44. Conrad, *Kriegsfall gegen Serbien und Montenegro*, 8 March 1909, Conrad, *Aus meiner Dienstzeit*, 1:640–655.

45. Crozier (French ambassador in Vienna) to Pichon, 4 November 1908, MAE CP Autriche-Hongrie NS 53 no. 185; Girodou to Min. Guerre, 1 and 22 December 1908, SHAT 7N 1130/2 nos. 327, 331; idem, 10 January 1909, SHAT 7N 1130/3 no. 333; Kageneck to Kriegsministerium, 18 March 1909, PAAA R8619 no. 23.

46. Girodou to Min. Guerre, 28 June and 5 October 1908, SHAT 7N 1130/2 nos. 299, 315; Kriegsministerium, *Reihenfolge der Umbewaffnung der Feldartillerie*, 3 November 1908, KA MKSM 1908 33–1/62–3; Comando del Corpo di Stato Maggiore, Riparto Operazioni, Scacchiere Orientale, *Notizie sull'Artiglieria austro-ungarica*, 24 January 1909, AUSSME G-22/5; Conrad, *Denkschrift für das Jahr 1909*, 21 February 1910, KA MKSM 1910 25–1/2.

47. Schönaich to Franz Joseph, 31 October 1908, KA MKSM 1908 4–3/9; Kriegsministerium to all Militärterritorialkommandos, 16 January 1909, KA MKSM 1909 4–3/2.

48. Conrad, *Aus meiner Dienstzeit*, 1:144–157.

49. See the Austro-Hungarian annual intelligence reports, 1904–1908, in Generalstab, Evidenzbüro, *Veränderungen im Heerwesen der Balkanstaaten*, KA MKSM 1904 18–6/1, 1905 18–5/1, 1906 18–5/1, 1907 18–2/1, 1908 18–3/2.

50. Generalstab, Evidenzbüro, *Veränderungen im Heerwesen der Balkanstaaten im Jahre 1907*, 25 May 1908, KA MKSM 1908 18–3/2.

51. *Veränderungen im Heerwesen der Balkanstaaten im Jahre 1905*, May 1906, KA MKSM 1906 18–5/1.

52. Conrad's unaddressed notes, 16 October 1908, KA B/1450:47; Conrad, *Kriegsfall gegen Serbien und Montenegro*, 8 March 1909, Conrad, *Aus meiner Dienstzeit*, 1:117–118, 640–655.

53. Conrad, *Aus meiner Dienstzeit*, 1:141, 162.

54. Conrad, *Besprechung bei Ex. Ährenthal—18.11.1907* (notes), KA B/1450:45 no. 26; Conrad to Aehrenthal, 19 November 1907, KA B/1450:45 no. 28; Conrad, *Unterredung mit dem Minister des Äusseren am 17./12. 07* (notes), KA B/1450:45 no. 38.

55. Capt. Putz (Conrad's adjutant), *Besprechung des Chefs mit B^r Aehrenthal*, 29 January 1909, KA B/1450:48 no. 11.

56. Aehrenthal to Bülow, 8 December 1908, HHStA PA I/484 nos. 141–165; see also Aehrenthal to Bülow, 20 February 1909, HHStA PA I/484 nos. 227–249.

57. Count Ulrich von Brockdorff-Rantzau, file note, 17 March 1909, GP XXVI/2 no. 9453, p. 687.

58. Szögyény to Aehrenthal, 16 December 1908, HHStA PA I/484 nos. 179–194; see also idem, 16 December 1908, Ö-UA I no. 752 pp. 606–611.

59. Moltke to Conrad, 21 January 1909, Conrad, *Aus meiner Dienstzeit*, 1:380.

60. Franz Joseph to Wilhelm II, 18 January 1909, GP XXVI/2 no. 9192 p. 401; Wilhelm II to Franz Joseph, 26 January 1909, GP XXVI/2 no. 9193 pp. 401–402.

61. Kageneck to Kriegsministerium, 18 March 1909, PAAA R8619 no. 23; see also Pourtalès to Auswärtiges Amt, 17 March 1909 (end note by Wilhelm II), GP XXVI/2 no. 9451 p. 683.

62. Diary entry by Kiderlen, 20 March 1909, Jäckh, *Kiderlen-Wächter*, 2:26.

63. Bülow to Pourtalès, 21 March 1909, GP XXVI/2 no. 9460 pp. 693–695.

64. Lt.-Col. Matton (French military attaché in St. Petersburg) to Min. Guerre, 6 March 1909, SHAT 7N 1535 no. 13.

65. Fuller, *Strategy and Power*, 421.

66. Posadowsky-Wehner to Kriegsministerium, 10 March 1909, PAAA R10425 no. 11; Hintze to Wilhelm II, 13 March 1909, PAAA R11093.

67. Cited in Hintze to Wilhelm II, 13 March 1908, PAAA R11093; see also Gleason, *Alexander Guchkov*, 38–29.

68. Hintze to Wilhelm II, 13 March 1908, PAAA R11093.

69. Pourtalès to Auswärtiges Amt, 17 March 1909, GP XXVI/2 no. 9451 p. 683; see also Pourtalès to Bülow, 18 March 1909, GP XXVI/2 no. 9452 pp. 683–685.

70. Aehrenthal, *Aufzeichnung über das am 15. Mai 1909 zwischen Seiner Majestät Kaiser Wilhelm und Baron Aehrenthal stattgehabte Gespräch*, HHStA PA I/489 nos. 336–341; Aehrenthal to Franz Joseph, Franz Ferdinand, Schönaich and Conrad, *Promemoria*, 15 August 1909, HHStA PA I/488 nos. 403–444.

71. Conrad to Franz Joseph, 3 April 1909, HHStA PA I/488 nos. 376–389.

72. Conrad, *Aus meiner Dienstzeit*, 1:162–163.

73. Capt. Putz, *Unterredung des Chefs mit B^r Aehrenthal*, 17 January, 18 February 1909, KA B/1450:48 nos. 6, 19; Conrad, *Aus meiner Dienstzeit*, 1:138.

74. Conrad to Franz Joseph, 3 April 1909, HHStA PAI/488 nos. 376–389.

75. Ibid.; Conrad memorandum to staff bureaux, 6 June 1909, KA Generalstab Operationsbüro 742 nos. 412–423; Conrad to Aehrenthal, 2 July 1909, HHStA PA I/488 nos. 392–399.

76. Conrad to Moltke, 10 April 1909, Conrad, *Aus meiner Dienstzeit*, 1:405.

77. Stone, "Moltke-Conrad," 211–214.

78. Moltke to Conrad, 14 September 1909, Conrad, *Aus meiner Dienstzeit*, 1:165.

79. Alfred von Schlieffen, "Der Krieg in der Gegenwart," *Deutsche Revue* 34, no. 1 (January 1909): 13–24.

80. Jäckh, *Kiderlen-Wächter*, 2:20–21.

81. Pourtalès to Bülow, 16 January 1909, GP XXVI/2 no. 9191 p. 398.

82. Hintze to Schoen, 24 October 1908, PAAA R11091; see also Hintze to Wilhelm II, 13 March 1909, PAAA R11093; Albertini, *Origins of the War of 1914*, 1:293–294.

83. Cited in Gleason, *Alexander Guchkov*, 38–39; see also Posadowsky-Wehner to Kriegsministerium, 10 March 1909, PAAA R10425 no. 11; Pourtalès to Bülow, 22 April, 6 May 1909, GP XXVI/2 nos. 9530, 9532 pp. 777–781, 783–786; Hintze to Wilhelm II, 29 May 1909, GP XXVI/2 no. 9545 pp. 804–808; Norman Stone, *The Eastern Front, 1914–1917* (London and New York, 1975), 28–29.

84. Berchtold (Austro-Hungarian ambassador in St. Petersburg) to Aehrenthal, 4 April 1909, HHStA PA X/134 nos. 68–73.

85. Gleason, *Alexander Guchkov*, 39; Stone, *Eastern Front*, 24–30; Fuller, *Civil-Military Conflict in Imperial Russia*, 237–244.

86. Fuller, *Strategy and Power*, 423–430.

87. Stone, *Eastern Front*, 30–33; Großer Generalstab, 7. Abteilung, *Jahresbericht 1909*, 30 November 1909, BHStA-KA Generalstab 208 no. 50; Matton to Min. Guerre, 6 July 1910, SHAT 7N 1535 no. 145; Großer Generalstab, 7. Abteilung, *Jahresbericht 1911*, 12 February 1912, BHStA-KA Generalstab 489 no. 87.12; Vladimir Nikolayevich Kokovtsov, *Out of My Past*, trans. Laura Matveev (Stanford, 1935), 253–255; Danilov, *La Russie dans la Guerre Mondiale*, 69–76; Fuller, *Strategy and Power*, 427, 432–433.

88. Großer Generalstab, 1. Abteilung, *Zusammenstellung der wichtigsten Veränderungen im Heerwesen Russlands im Jahre 1910*; idem, *Heerwesen Russlands 1911*, 21 February 1911, 18 March 1912, BA-MA RM5/1486 nos. 190–216, 220–241; Generalstab, Evidenzbüro, *Jahresbericht über die russische Wehrmacht 1911*, 15 April 1912, KA MKSM 1912 18–2/3; Wladimir Aleksandrowitsch Suchomlinow, *Erinnerungen* (Berlin, 1924), 330–350.

89. Deuxième Bureau, *Armée russe: notice*, November 1909, SHAT 7N 1537/5; Suchomlinow, *Erinnerungen*, 339.

90. Posadowsky-Wehner to Kriegsministerium, 27 August 1910, PAAA R10247 no. 34; Großer Generalstab, *Jahresbericht 1910. I. Kurzer Überblick über die Entwicklung der Befestigungen, der Festungs- und schweren Artillerie sowie des Jngeneurwesens der östlichen Staaten 1910*, 30 November 1910, BHStA-KA, Generalstab 208 no. 58.

91. Schneider-Creusot, *Note sur le réarmement de l'artillerie russe en 1909 et 1910 (commandes à Krupp et au Creusot)*, 25 October 1910, SHAT 7N 15939/A₃; Maj.-Gen. von Lauenstein (German military plenipotentiary in St. Petersburg) to Wilhelm II, 23 March 1911, PAAA R11092 no. A5763[11]; Lauenstein to Kriegsministerium, 31 March 1911, PAAA R10428 no. 11.

92. Aehrenthal, *Aufzeichnung über die in Berlin mit Seiner Majestät Kaiser Wilhelm und dem Reichskanzler Herrn von Bethmann Hollweg geführten Gespräche: 22.-25. Februar 1910*, 6 March 1910, HHStA PA I/488 nos. 252–261.

93. Aehrenthal, *Aufzeichnung über Unterredungen mit dem deutschen Staatssekretär Herrn von Kiderlen-Wächter in Marienbad*, 1 August 1910, HHStA PA I/488 nos. 323–334.

94. Posadowsky-Wehner to Kriegsministerium, 12 March 1910, PAAA R10427 no. 11.

95. Großer Generalstab, 1. Abteilung, *Die wichtigsten Veränderungen im Heerwesen Russlands im Jahre 1910*, 21 February 1911, BA-MA RM5/1468 nos. 190–216.

96. Cf. Posadowsky-Wehner to Kriegsministerium, 22 April, 6 May 1909, PAAA R10426 nos. A.7168, 21; Moltke to Bülow, 29 May 1909, enclosing Großer Generalstab report, *Geplante Zurückverlegung des russischen Aufmarsches*, PAAA R10450.

97. Großer Generalstab, *Die Reorganisation des russischen Heeres*, 14 November 1910, PAAA R10450; see also Großer Generalstab, *Die Reorganisation der russischen Armee*, August 1910, PAAA R10450.

98. Heeringen to Bethmann, 13 August 1910, BA R43F/1252 nos. 116–117; Posadowsky-Wehner to Kriegsministerium (Wilhelm II's notations), 27 August 1910, PAAA R10247 no. 34.

99. Generalstab, Evidenzbüro, *Jahresbericht über die russische Wehrmacht 1910*, 1 May 1911, KA MKSM 1911 18-2/4-2.

100. Kageneck to Kriegsministerium, 30 July 1910, PAAA R8621 no. 45.

101. Deuxième Bureau, *Résumé des conclusions de l'étude de Juin 1909 relative aux nouveaux projets de Mobilisation et de Concentration Russes*, June 1909, SHAT 7N 1537/3; Deuxième Bureau, *Note au sujet du voyage du Chef d'Etat-Major Général Russe, Général Mychlaevski*, September 1909, SHAT 7N 1537/3; Deuxième Bureau, Section d'Orient, *Note au sujet des projets russes*, 10 February 1910, SHAT 7N 1537/3; Gen. Laffon de Ladébat, *Note au sujet de l'exécution de la Concentration Franco-Russe*, 22 March 1910, SHAT 7N 1538; Jules Cambon to Pichon, 30 May 1910, and Georges Louis (French ambassador in St. Petersburg) to Ministère des Affaires Etrangères, 16 June 1910, MAE CP Russie NS 40 nos. 10–11, 21; Fuller, *Strategy and Power*, 433.

102. Brun to Pichon, 14 December 1910, MAE CP Russie NS 40 nos. 81–82; see also Matton to Min. Guerre, 6 July 1910, SHAT 7N 1535 no. 145; Capt. Gros, Ecole Supérieure de la Guerre, *Conférence sur l'Armée russe*, 1911, SHAT 7N 1535.

103. Wyndham, *Memorandum on the Military Policy and Armament of Russia, 1910*, 1911, PRO FO 881/9856.

104. Nicolson to Grey, *Russia: Annual Report, 1909*, 30 December 1909, PRO FO 881/9583.

105. Witt, *Die Finanzpolitik des deutschen Reiches*, 318–320, 323; Förster, *Der doppelte Militarismus*, 190–194; correspondence of Bethmann, Wermuth, Heeringen et al., April-November 1910, BA R43F/1252; Wandel, *Tagebuch II*, 30 June 1910, 9 June 1911, BA-MA N564(Wandel)/4.

106. Reichsarchiv, *Kriegsrüstung*, 1:89–97; Einem to Moltke, 23 July 1909, *Kriegsrüstung*, 1:114–116; Ludwig Rüdt von Collenberg, *Die deutsche Armee von 1871 bis 1914* (Berlin, 1922), 70–87.

107. Director of Military Operations, *The Value to a Foreign Power of an Alliance with the British Empire*, 8 March 1909, PRO WO 106/45 no. 1; Committee of Imperial Defence, *Report of the Sub-Committee of the Committee of Imperial Defence on the Military Needs of the Empire*, 24 July 1909, PRO CAB 4/3 no. 109-B; Tyler, *British Army and the Continent*, 66–103; Charles E. Callwell, *Field Marshal Sir Henry Wilson: His Life and Diaries*, 2 vols. (London, 1927), 1:88–94; Williamson, *Politics of Grand Strategy*, 89, 111–112, 141.

108. Pollio to Spingardi, 18 March 1909, AUSSME F-4/75 no. 32; Hammerstein-Equord to Kriegsministerium, 3 April 1909, PAAA R7807 no. 175; Mietzenyi (Austro-Hungarian military attaché in Rome) to Conrad, 3 April 1909, KA Generalstab 1909 25–4/20.

109. Commissione d'inchiesta per l'esercito, *Ottava Relazione*, 30 June 1910, ACS PCM 1910 400/14 no. 376; De Chaurand de Saint-Eustache, *Come l'esercito italiano entrò in guerra*, 68–78; Rinaldo Cruccu, "L'esercito nel periodo Giolittiano (1909–1914)," in *L'Esercito italiano dall'Unità alla Grande Guerra (1861–1918)*, Ufficio Storico, Corpo di Stato Maggiore dell'Esercito, Italy (Rome, 1980), 260–261; Behnen, *Rüstung, Bündnis, Sicherheit*, 200–202.

110. Spingardi, *Memoria sui bisogni dell'amministrazione della guerra e sulla situazione del suo bilancio*, December 1909, AUSSME F-4/74 no. 11.

111. Jullian to Min. Guerre, 30 October 1910, SHAT 7N 1369/3 no. 324; Hammerstein-Equord to Kriegsministerium, 11 February, 12 March 1911, PAAA R7809 nos. 109, 125; Jagow (German ambassador in Rome) to Auswärtiges Amt, 30 March 1912, and Kleist (German military attaché in Rome) to Kriegsministerium, 30 March 1912, PAAA R7810.

112. Comando del Corpo di Stato Maggiore, Riparto Intendenza, Ufficio Trasporti, *Relazione sul progetto dei trasporti in vigore per la mobilitazione e radunata N.E.*, 30 May 1910, AUSSME F-4/64 no. 487; Mazzetti, "I piani di guerra contro l'Austria," 174.

113. Pellé to Min. Guerre, 9 October 1909, SHAT 7N 1109/2 no. 29.

114. Großer Generalstab, 3. Abteilung, *Die französischen Armeemanöver 1909*, 10 December 1909, BA-MA RM5/1234 nos. 125–141.

115. Großer Generalstab, 3. Abteilung, *Zusammenstellung der wichtigsten Veränderungen im Heerwesen Frankreichs 1909*, 15 February 1910, BA-MA RM5/1234 nos. 150–186.

116. Generalstab, Evidenzbüro, *Veränderungen im Heerwesen Russlands im Jahre 1908*, 23 April 1909, KA MKSM 1909 18–2/2; Wyndham, *Memorandum on the Military Policy and Armament of Russia, 1908*, 30 January 1909, PRO FO 881/9425 no. 20; Generalstab, Evidenzbüro, *Veränderungen im Heerwesen Italiens im Jahre 1908*, 10 March 1909, KA MKSM 1909 18–1/2; Capt. Levesque (French military attaché in Vienna) to Min. Guerre, 18 October 1909, SHAT 7N 1130/3 no. 52; idem, 5 February 1910, SHAT 1130/5 no. 131.

117. Deuxième Bureau, *Progrès de la flotte aérienne allemande*, 25 May 1909, SHAT 7N 672/1; Pellé to Min. Guerre, 3 September 1909, SHAT 7N 1109/1 no. 23.

118. Generalinspektion der Verkehrstruppen, section of report: *B. Auf dem Gebiete der Flugmaschinen*, 1909, BA-MA PH 9V/160 nos. 29–31; Militärgeschichtliches Forschungsamt, ed., *Die Militärluftfahrt bis zum Beginn des Weltkrieges 1914*, 3 vols. (Freiburg im Breisgau, 1965–1966), 1:118, 3:22–25.

119. Winterfeldt to Kriegsministerium, 4 September 1909, BA-MA PH 9V/144 nos. 387–388; see also idem, 31 December 1909, PAAA R6751 no. 48.

120. Generalinspektion der Verkehrstruppen, *B. Auf dem Gebiete der Flugmaschinen*, 1909, BA-MA PH9V/160 nos. 29–31.

121. Winterfeldt to Kriegsministerium, 15 May 1910, PAAA R6751 no. 9.

122. Generalinspektion der Verkehrstruppen, *B. Auf dem Gebiete der Flugmaschinen*, 1909, BA-MA PH 9V/160 nos. 29–31.

123. Winterfeldt to Kriegsministerium, 4 September 1909, BA-MA PH 9V/144 nos. 378–388.

124. Generalinspektion der Verkehrstruppen, *B. Auf dem Gebiete der Flugmaschinen*, 1909, BA-MA PH 9V/160 nos. 29–31; Winterfeldt to Kriegsministerium, 15 May 1910, PAAA R6751 no. 9.

125. Generalinspektion der Verkehrstruppen, *B. Auf dem Gebiete der Flugmaschinen*, 1909, BA-MA PH 9V/160 nos. 29–31.

126. Militärgeschichtliches Forschungsamt, *Militärluftfahrt*, 1:118, 3:13.

127. Ibid., 3:18–21.

128. Deutsche Flugplatz-Gesellschaft to Heeringen, 31 August 1909, BA R43F/1535 no. 197.

129. Pellé to Min. Guerre, 4 October 1909, SHAT 7N 1109/1 no. 28.

130. Wandel, *Tagebuch II*, 1 October 1909; also 7 July 1910, BA-MA N564(Wandel)/4.

131. Deutsche Flugplatz-Gesellschaft to Heeringen, 31 August 1909, and Heeringen to Wahnschaffe (Unterstaatssekretär der Reichskanzlei), 30 September 1909, BA R43F/1335 nos. 197, 223; Deuxième Bureau, *L'Aéronautique: situation à la fin de 1909 dans les principales armées étrangères*, 1 December 1909, SHAT 1N 17/5 no. 1.

132. Pellé to Min. Guerre, 15 May 1910, SHAT 7N1109/2 no. 121; idem, 12 November 1910, SHAT 7N 1109/3 no. 189.

133. Generalinspektion der Verkehrstruppen, *B. Auf dem Gebiete der Flugmaschinen*, 1909, BA-MA PH 9V/160 nos. 29–31; Pellé to Min. Guerre, 28 October 1911, SHAT 7N 1110/2 no. 376.

134. Pellé to Min. Guerre, 12 November 1910, SHAT 7N 1109/3 no. 189.

135. Ibid.; see also Pellé to Min. Guerre, 7 August 1911, SHAT 7N1110/2 no. 327.

136. Winterfeldt to Kriegsministerium, 30 November 1910, BA-MA PH 9V/160 nos. 21–28.

137. Pellé to Min. Guerre, 12 May 1910, SHAT 7N 1109/2 no. 120.

138. Pellé to Min. Guerre, 21 April 1911, SHAT 7N 1110/1 no. 279.

139. Pellé to Min. Guerre, 28 October 1911, SHAT 7N 1110/2 no. 376.

140. Ibid.; Chef des Generalstabes der Armee, *Die französischen Armeemanöver 1911*, 16 January 1912, BA-MA RM5/1234 nos. 310–330.

141. Pellé to Min. Guerre, 26 August 1909, SHAT 7N 1109/1 no. 19; idem, 9 October 1909, SHAT 7N 1109/2 no. 29; Großer Generalstab, 3. Ab-

teilung, *Die französischen Armeemanöver 1909*, 10 December 1909, BA-MA RM5/1234 nos. 125–141.

142. Committee of Imperial Defence, *Aerial Navigation: Report of a Sub-Committee of the Committee of Imperial Defence Appointed by the Prime Minister*, 28 January 1909, PRO CAB 4/3 no. 106-B.

143. Großer Generalstab, 3. Abteilung, *Die französischen Armeemanöver 1910*, January 1911, BA-MA RM5/1234 nos. 189–221; Maj. Pennella, *Relazione sulle grandi manovre francesi 1910*, October 1910, AUSSME G-23/18.

144. Committee of Imperial Defence, *Minutes of the 101st Meeting*, 25 February 1909, PRO CAB 2/2 nos. 48–49; Guillemin (French chargé d'affaires in Vienna) to Pichon, 24 June 1909, MAE CP Autriche-Hongrie NS 53 no. 241; Deuxième Bureau, *Matériel de navigation aérienne de l'armée austro-hongroise*, 6 October 1909, SHAT 7N 1141/6 no. 4466; Jullian to Min. Guerre, 25 October 1909, SHAT 7N 1369/2 no. 205; Deuxième Bureau, *L'Aéronautique: situation à la fin de 1909 dans les principales armées étrangères*, 1 December 1909, SHAT 1N 17/5 no. 1.

145. Levesque to Min. Guerre, 25 September 1910, SHAT 7N 1130/5 no. 235; Esher to Committee of Imperial Defence, *Aerial Navigation*, 6 October 1910, PRO CAB 4/3 no. 119-B; Generalstab, Evidenzbüro, *Jahresbericht über die russische Wehrmacht 1910*, 1 May 1911, KA MKSM 1911 18-2/4–2; Huguet to Min. Guerre, 14 February 1911, SHAT 7N 1226/3 no. 536; Generalstab, Evidenzbüro, *Jahresbericht über die Wehrmacht Italiens 1910*, 11 March 1910, KA MKSM 1911 18-2/1–2.

146. Generalstab, Evidenzbüro, *Die italienischen Königsmanöver 1911*, 1911, KA MKSM 1911 33-5/10; Generalstab, Evidenzbüro, *Jahresbericht über die russische Wehrmacht 1911*, 15 April 1912, KA MKSM 1912 18-2/3.

147. Levesque to Min. Guerre, 28 September 1911, SHAT 7N 1131/1 no. 335.

148. Winterfeldt to Kriegsministerium, 14 June 1910, PAAA R6751 no. 14; Großer Generalstab, *Allgemeiner Stand der Frage Ende Dezember 1911*, 1912, HStAS-KA M1/3 Bd. 651 nos. 15–16.

149. Gollin, *No Longer an Island*, 192–216, 353–468.

CHAPTER 5

1. Albertini, *Origins of the War of 1914*, 1:327–333; Fischer, *War of Illusions*, 71–94; Emily Oncken, *Panthersprung nach Agadir: Die deutsche Politik während der Zweiten Marokkokrise 1911* (Düsseldorf, 1981).

2. Note by Kiderlen, 3 May 1911, GP XXIX no. 10549 pp. 101–108.

3. *The Times*, "Extract from a Speech of Mr. Lloyd George on July 21, 1911, at Mansion House," 22 July 1911, BD VII no. 412 pp. 391–392.

4. Note by Kiderlen, 3 May 1911, GP XXIX no. 10549 pp. 101–108.

5. Alfred von Tirpitz, *Erinnerungen* (Leipzig, 1919), 181; Wandel, *Tagebuch II*, 16 August 1911, BA-MA N564(Wandel)/4.

6. Albertini, *Origins of the War of 1914*, 1:327–328.

7. *The Times*, "Extract from a speech of Mr. Lloyd George on July 21, 1911, at Mansion House," 22 July 1911, BD VII no. 412 p. 391; Grey to Goschen

(British ambassador in Berlin), 25 July 1911, BD VII no. 419 p. 398; Kiderlen to Metternich, 25 July 1911, GP XXIX no. 10625 p. 212; and Metternich to Auswärtiges Amt, 25 July 1911, GP XXIX no. 10626 pp. 213–214; Cambon telegrams to Paris, June-November 1911, MAE Papiers Jules Cambon 12/4, 12/5.

8. Adolphe-Marie Messimy, *Mes souvenirs* (Paris, 1937).

9. Deuxième Bureau, *Renseignements sur l'Artillerie à pied Allemande*, 3 December 1910, SHAT 7N 1117/1; Reichsarchiv, *Der Weltkrieg 1914 bis 1918*, vol. 1, *Kriegsrüstung und Kriegswirtschaft* (Berlin, 1930), 246–251, 1 Anl.: 327–398 and Tabelle 13; Douglas Porch, *The March to the Marne: The French Army, 1871–1914* (Cambridge, 1981), 232–245.

10. Conseil Supérieur de la Guerre, *Procès-verbal*, 19 July 1911, SHAT 1N 10/12 p. 184–215; Gudmundsson, *On Artillery*, 29–34.

11. Joseph Caillaux, *Agadir: Ma politique extérieure* (Paris 1919), 146.

12. Min. Guerre, *Grande Guerre*, 1.i:137–139, 1.i:Carte Nº 5; Michel to Berteaux, *Concentration et plan d'opérations*, February 1911, ibid. 1.i:Annexes 7–11; Conseil Supérieur de la Guerre, *Procès-Verbal*, 19 July 1911, SHAT 1N 10/12 pp. 184–215; Joseph-Jacques-Césaire Joffre, *Mémoires du Maréchal Joffre 1910–1917*, 2 vols. (Paris, 1932), 1:7–9.

13. Conseil Supérieur de la Guerre, *Procès-Verbal*, 19 July 1911, SHAT 1N 10/12 pp. 184–215; Michel to Berteaux, *Concentration et plan d'opérations*, February 1911, Min. Guerre, *Grande Guerre* 1.i:Annexes, 7–11; Porch, *March to the Marne*, 169–212; Snyder, *Ideology of the Offensive*, 41–56.

14. Min. Guerre, *Grande Guerre*, 1.i:39–43; Joffre to Troisième and Quatrième Bureaux, 6 September 1911, 1.i Annexes 17–18; Joffre, *Mémoires*, 1:23–26; Samuel R. Williamson, "Joffre Reshapes French Strategy, 1911–1913," in *The War Plans of the Great Powers, 1880–1914*, ed. Paul M. Kennedy (London, 1985), 133–154; Col. Fairholme (British military attaché in Paris) to Sir Francis Bertie (British ambassador in Paris), 24 August 1911, PRO FO 800/100 nos. 258–259.

15. Caillaux, *Agadir*, 146; Winterfeldt to Kriegsministerium, 7 August 1911, GP XXIX no. 10705 pp. 323–325; Bertie to Grey, 21 August 1911, BD VII no. 488 p. 461.

16. Fairholme to Bertie, 24 August 1911, PRO FO 800/100 nos. 258–259; Deuxième Bureau, *Note sur les chemins de fer allemands à la fin de 1910*, December 1910, SHAT 7N 672/1.

17. Joffre, *Mémoires*, 1:15–16.

18. Caillaux, *Agadir*, 143.

19. Justin de Selves (French foreign minister) to Georges Louis (French ambassador in St. Petersburg), 21 August 1911, DDF II.14 no. 200 pp. 255–256; see also Louis to de Selves, 1 September 1911, DDF II.14 no. 234 pp. 305–307.

20. De Selves to ambassadors in Berlin, St. Petersburg and London, 14 August 1911, DDF II.14 no. 172 p. 207.

21. Louis to de Selves, 25 and 31 August, 1 September 1911, DDF II.14 no. 215 p. 274, no. 225 p. 292, and no. 236 pp. 308–309.

22. Louis to de Selves, 1 September 1911, DDF II.14 no. 235 pp. 307–308;

see also Dubail to Min. Guerre, 1 September 1911, and Louis to de Selves, 2 September 1911, DDF II.14 nos. 239, 241 pp. 310–314.

23. Caillaux, *Agadir*, 143.

24. Ibid., 143; see also Louis to de Selves, 22 August 1911, MAE CP Russie NS 40 no. 204.

25. Dubail and Zhilinski, *Procès-verbal de l'entretien du 18/31 Août 1911, entre les chefs d'État-Major des armées française et russe*, 31 August 1911, DDF II.14 no. 232 pp. 298–305.

26. Deuxième Bureau, *Croquis approximatif de la situation le 23ᵉᵐᵉ jour (2ᵉᵐᵉCas). Joint à la note de Juin 1911* (undated), SHAT 7N 1537/5; Fairholme to Bertie, 24 August 1911, PRO FO 800/100 nos. 258–259. Cf. Fuller, *Strategy and Power*, 444.

27. Wilson to Committee of Imperial Defence, *Note by the Director of Military Operations*, 12 August 1911, PRO CAB 4/3 no. 130-B Appendix A; Callwell, *Sir Henry Wilson*, 1:98–99.

28. Caillaux, *Agadir*, 144.

29. Wilson, *Policy of the Entente*, 17–36; Williamson, *Politics of Grand Strategy*, 142–145.

30. Asquith to Grey, 5 September 1911, PRO FO 800/100 nos. 260–261; see also Wilson, *Policy of the Entente*, 28.

31. Grey to Asquith, 16 April 1911, PRO FO 800/100 nos. 236–238.

32. William Nicholson (Chief of the Imperial General Staff), *Action taken by the General Staff since 1906 in preparing a plan for rendering assistance to France in the event of an unprovoked attack on that Power by Germany*, 6 November 1911, PRO WO 106/49A no. 1; Callwell, *Sir Henry Wilson*, 1:89–90.

33. E.g., Pellé to Min. Guerre, 7 March 1911, SHAT 7 1110/1 no. 25.

34. Callwell, *Sir Henry Wilson*, 1:78–79.

35. Conseil Supérieur de la Guerre, *Procès-verbal*, 19 July 1911, SHAT 1N 10/12 pp. 184–215; Min. Guerre, *Grande Guerre*, 1.i:Carte No. 5; Joffre, *Mémoires*, 1:19.

36. Callwell, *Sir Henry Wilson*, 1:97.

37. Ibid., 1:98–99.

38. Fairholme to Bertie, 24 August 1911, PRO FO 800/100 nos. 258–259.

39. Callwell, *Sir Henry Wilson*, 1:104–105.

40. Committee of Imperial Defence, *Minutes of the 114ᵗʰ Meeting*, 23 August 1911, PRO CAB 2/2 nos. 125–134; see also Winston S. Churchill, *The World Crisis*, 2 vols. (1923; reprint, New York, 1949), 1:38–43; Callwell, *Sir Henry Wilson*, 1:99–100; Williamson, *Politics of Grand Strategy*, 87–194.

41. Churchill, *World Crisis*, 1:40–41.

42. Callwell, *Sir Henry Wilson*, 1:109–111.

43. Sir Reginald McKenna (First Lord of the Admiralty) to CID, *The Military Aspect of the Continental Problem*, 21 August 1911, PRO CAB 4/3 no. 131-B.

44. Nicholson to CID, *The Military Aspect of the Continental Problem: Memorandum by the General Staff*, 13 August 1911, PRO CAB 4/3 no. 130-B; Wilson to CID, *Note by the Director of Military Operations*, 12 August 1911, PRO CAB 4/3 no. 130-B Appendix A; Churchill to CID, *Military Aspects of the Con-*

tinental Problem. Memorandum by Mr. Churchill, 13 August 1911, PRO CAB 4/3 no. 132-B.

45. CID, *Military Aspects of the Continental Problem: Memorandum by Mr. Churchill*, 13 August 1911, PRO CAB 4/3 no. 132-B.

46. Reichsarchiv, *Der Weltkrieg 1914 bis 1918*, vol. 1, *Kriegsrüstung und Kriegswirtschaft*, 252–255.

47. Moltke, *Bemerkungen des Generals v. Moltke zu der Denkschrift*, 1911, PRO CAB 20/1 no. 1 pp. 104–107; Großer Generalstab, 4. Abteilung, *Denkschrift Lüttich* and *Denkschrift Namur*, 1912, BHStA-KA Generalstab 225, 227.

48. Großer Generalstab, *Allgemeiner Stand der Frage Ende Dezember 1911*, 1912, HStAS-KA M1/3 Bd. 65 nos. 15–16; Generalinspektor des Militär-Verkehrwesens, *Zum Kaiservortrag, gehalten 3.II.12*, September 1911, BA-MA PH 9V/162 no. 131.

49. Winterfeldt to Kriegsministerium, 7 and 19 August 1911, GP XXIX no. 10705, 10715 pp. 323–325, 332–335; Winterfeldt to Kriegsministerium, 30 August 1911, PAAA R6753 no. 42.

50. Alfred von Tirpitz, *Der Aufbau der deutschen Weltmacht* (Stuttgart, 1924), 220; Förster, *Der doppelte Militarismus*, 217–218, 218n.

51. Berghahn, *Germany and the Approach of War*, 98.

52. Wandel, *Tagebuch II*, 31 August 1911, BA-MA N564(Wandel)/4.

53. Pourtalès to Bethmann, 1 September 1911, GP XXIX no. 10732 pp. 354–357.

54. Großer Generalstab, 1. Abteilung, *Die wichtigsten Veränderungen im Heerwesen Russlands im Jahre 1910*, 21 February 1911; idem, *Heerwesen Russlands 1911*, 18 March 1912, BA-MA RM5/1486 nos. 190–216, 220–241; Generalstab, Evidenzbüro, *Jahresbericht über die russische Wehrmacht 1910*, 1 May 1911, KA MKSM 1911 18–2/4–2; idem, *Russische Wehrmacht 1911*, 15 April 1912, KA MKSM 1912 18–2/3.

55. Wandel, *Tagebuch II*, 23 November 1911, BA-MA N564(Wandel)/4.

56. Moltke, *Bemerkungen des Generals v. Moltke zu der Denkschrift*, 1911, PRO CAB 20/1 no. 1 pp. 104–107.

57. Wandel, *Tagebuch II*, 16 August 1911, BA-MA N564(Wandel)/4.

58. Winterfeldt to Kriegsministerium, 24 August 1911, GP XXIX no. 10723 pp. 344–345; Wandel, *Tagebuch II*, 24 and 30 August 1911, BA-MA N564(Wandel)/4; note by Heeringen, 31 August 1911, GP XXIX no. 10726 pp. 346–348; Gebsattel to Bavarian war minister, 3 and 4 September 1911, BHStA-KA M.Kr. 41 nos. 1731, 1737.

59. Reichsarchiv, *Kriegsrüstung*, 1 Anl. abelle 13.

60. Fuller, *Strategy and Power*, 430.

61. Förster, *Der doppelte Militarismus*, 216–220; Reichsarchiv, *Kriegsrüstung*, 1:117–123; Fischer, *War of Illusions*, 112–121; Tirpitz, *Der Aufbau der deutschen Weltmacht*, 200–279; Berghahn, *Germany and the Approach of War*, 98–124.

62. Reichsarchiv, *Kriegsrüstung*, 1:119–120, 119n.; Förster, *Der doppelte Militarismus*, 220.

63. Reichsarchiv, *Kriegsrüstung*, 1:119n.

64. Wandel, *Tagebuch II*, 5 January 1912, BA-MA N564(Wandel)/4.

65. Wilhelm II to Bethmann, 30 November 1911, PAAA R852 no. 2108; Bethmann to Wilhelm II, 30 November 1911, PAAA R852 no. 10890.

66. Fischer, *War of Illusions*, 74–81; Förster, *Der Doppelte Militarismus*, 210–211.

67. Charles à Court Repington, "The German Army Manoeuvres," *The Times*, 12, 14, 17, 19, 24, and 28 October 1911; Bernd Felix Schulte, *Die deutsche Armee 1900–1914: Zwischen Beharren und Verändern* (Düsseldorf, 1977), 11–33.

68. Repington, "The German Army Manoeuvres," 28 October 1911, p. 5.

69. Reichstag, *Stenographische Berichte über die Verhandlungen des Deutschen Reichstages* vol. 268 pp. 7708ff., 9–11 November 1911; Fischer, *War of Illusions*, 87–94; Förster, *Der doppelte Militarismus*, 210–216.

70. Förster, *Der doppelte Militarismus*, 226–233; Roger Chickering, "Der 'Deutsche Wehrverein' und die Reform der deutschen Armee 1912–1914," *Militärgeschichtliche Mitteilungen* 25, no. 1 (1979): 7–33; Marilyn Shevin Coetzee, "The Mobilization of the Right? The Deutscher Wehrverein and Political Activism in Württemberg, 1912–1914," *European History Quarterly* 15 (1985): 431–452; August Keim, *Erlebtes und Erstrebtes* (Hannover, 1925).

71. Friedrich von Bernhardi, *Deutschland und der Nächste Krieg*, 2 vols. (Stuttgart, 1912).

72. Förster, *Der Doppelte Militarismus*, 230.

73. Reichsarchiv, *Kriegsrüstung*, 1:118–119.

74. Ibid., 1:123.

75. Cf. Berghahn, *Germany and the Approach of War*, 101–115; Förster, *Der doppelte Militarismus*, 256–265.

76. Reichsarchiv, *Kriegsrüstung* 1:123–126, Heeringen to Bethmann, 19 November 1911.

77. Ibid., 1:120–121.

78. See also Gebsattel to Bavarian war minister, 19 December 1911, BHStA-KA M. Kr. 42 no. 2615; Wilhelm II to Bethmann, 1 December 1911, PAAA R852 no. 2120.

79. Wandel, *Tagebuch II*, 10–13 September 1911, BA-MA N564(Wandel)/4.

80. Pellé to Min. Guerre, 15 December 1911, SHAT 7N 1110/2 no. 391; idem, 25 February 1912, SHAT 7N1111/1 no. 438.

81. Chef des Generalstabes der Armee, *Die französischen Armeemanöver 1911*, 16 January 1912, BA-MA RM 5/1234 nos. 310–330.

82. Reichsarchiv, *Kriegsrüstung*, 1 Anl. no. 41 pp. 132–135, Wandel, *Denkschrift*, 29 November 1911; see also Wandel, *Tagebuch II*, 23 November 1911, BA-MA N564(Wandel)/4; Gerhard Granier, "Deutsche Rüstungspolitik vor dem Ersten Weltkrieg: General Franz Wandels Tagebuchaufzeichnungen aus dem preussischen Kriegsministerium," *Militärgeschichtliche Mitteilungen* 38, no. 2 (1985): 123–162.

83. Moltke to Bethmann, *Die militär-politische Lage Deutschlands*, 2 December 1911, PAAA R789 no. 957.

84. Cf. Förster, *Der Doppelte Militarismus*, 220–247.

85. Ibid., 233–247; Collenberg, *Die deutsche Armee*, 91–94.

86. Witt, *Die Finanzpolitik des deutschen Reiches*, 342–356; Förster, *Der doppelte Militarismus*, 217–218, 225–226; Treasury-war ministry correspondence 1911–12, Reichsarchiv, *Kriegrüstung*, 1 Anl.:135–138; Wenninger (Bavarian military representative in Berlin) to Bavarian war minister, 24 February 1912, BHStA-KA M.Kr. 42 no. 533.

87. Förster, *Der doppelte Militarismus*, 236, 239–242.

88. Williamson, *Politics of Grand Strategy*, 173–182.

89. William C. Askew, *Europe and Italy's Acquisition of Libya*, (Durham, N.C., 1942); Antonio Malgeri, *La guerra libica (1911–1912)* (Rome, 1970); Sergio Romano, *La Quarta Sponda: la guerra di Libia 1911–1912* (Milan, 1977); Angelo Del Boca, *Gli Italiani in Libia*, 2 vols. (Rome, 1986), vol. 1; David G. Herrmann, "The Paralysis of Italian Strategy in the Italian-Turkish War, 1911–1912," *English Historical Review* 104, no. 411 (April 1989): 332–356.

90. Conrad to Aehrenthal, 24 September 1911, HHStA PA I/488 nos. 560–563; Conrad, *Denkschrift des Chefs des Generalstabes für 1911*, 15 November 1911, KA B/1450:67.

91. Aehrenthal to Franz Joseph, 22 October 1911, HHStA PA I/488 nos. 580–592; Conrad, *Ah. Audienz bei S.M. Schönbrunn 15./11. 1911* (notes), KA B/1450: 68 nos. 362–363; Conrad, *Audienz bei Seiner Majestät, Schönbrunn*, 30 November 1911, KA B/1450:68 no. 364.

CHAPTER 6

1. Albertini, *Origins of the War of 1914*, 1:364–487.

2. L. C. F. Turner, *Origins of the First World War* (London, 1970), pp. 60–61.

3. Pellé to Min. Guerre, 1 April 1912, SHAT 7N 1111/2 no. 454; "La nouvelle loi militaire en Allemagne," *Revue militaire des armées étrangères* 80, no. 1016 (July 1912): 41.

4. Eugene Weber, *The Nationalist Revival in France, 1905–1914* (Berkeley, 1959), 94–128; Gerd Krumeich, *Armaments and Politics in France on the Eve of the First World War: The Introduction of Three-Year Conscription 1913–1914*, trans. Stephen Conn (Dover, N.H., 1984), 30–43.

5. See also Jean-Jacques Becker, *1914: Comment les Français sont entrés dans la guerre* (Paris, 1977), 20–52.

6. Porch, *March to the Marne*, 169–190.

7. Min. Guerre, *Grande Guerre*, 1.i:145n.; Chef des Generalstabes der Armee, *Zusammenstellung der wichtigsten Veränderungen im Heerwesen Frankreichs 1912*, February 1913, BA-MA RM5/1235 nos. 38–78.

8. Maj. Gondrecourt (French military attaché in Rome) to Min. Guerre, 10 March 1912, SHAT 7N 1370/2 no. 91.

9. Maj. Wehrlin (French assistant military attaché in St. Petersburg) to Min. Guerre, 31 January 1913, SHAT 7N 1478/1 no. 37.

10. Conseil Supérieur de la Guerre, *procès-verbal*, 25 January 1912, SHAT

1N 10/13 pp. 16–24; Committee of Imperial Defence, Sub-Committee on Aerial Navigation, *Report of the Technical Sub-Committee*, 27 February 1912, PRO CAB 4/4/33 no. 139-B.

11. "La nouvelle loi russe sur le recrutement de l'armée," *Revue militaire des armées étrangères* 81, no. 1026 (May 1913): 435–461; Großer Generalstab, 1. Abteilung, *Die wichtigsten Veränderungen im Heerwesen Russlands im Jahre 1912*, 7 March 1913, BA-MA RM5/1438 nos. 167–197.

12. D. C. B. Lieven, *Russia and the Origins of the First World War* (New York, 1983), 160; Danilov, *La Russie dans la Guerre Mondiale*, 123–142; Fuller, *Strategy and Power*, 442–444.

13. Williamson, *Politics of Grand Strategy*, 227–248.

14. Joffre and Zhilinski, *Procès-verbal de l'entretien du 13 Juillet 1912 entre les chefs d'Etat-major des armées française et russe*, 13 July 1912, MAE CP Russie NS 41 nos. 131–138; Poincaré, *Entretiens de M. Poincaré, Président du Conseil, Ministre des Affaires Étrangères, avec S. M. l'Empereur de Russie, M. M. Kokoftsoff et Sasonoff: Août 1912*, MAE CP Russie NS 41 nos. 280–297; David N. Collins, "The Franco-Russian Alliance and Russian Railways, 1891–1914," *Historical Journal* 16, no. 4 (December 1973): 786–787.

15. Lamezan (Austro-Hungarian military attaché in Paris) to Kriegsministerium, 1 October 1912, HHStA PA XL/182 no. 4127; Callwell, *Sir Henry Wilson*, 1:116–117; Williamson, "Joffre Reshapes French Strategy," 146.

16. Grey to Cambon, 22 November 1912, BD 10/2 no. 416 pp. 614–615; see also Cambon to Grey, 23 November 1912, BD 10/2 no. 417 p. 615.

17. Tyler, *British Army and the Continent*, 140–148; Williamson, *Politics of Grand Strategy*, 367–372.

18. Schemua to Franz Joseph, *Militaerpolitische Denkschrift anfangs 1912*, 12 February 1912, KA MKSM 1912 25–1/1.

19. *Ministerrat für gemeinsame Angelegenheiten, Protokoll*, 8–9 July 1912, HHStA PA XL/310 no. 46.

20. Rothenberg, *Army of Francis Joseph*, 164–165; Lieut.-Col. Hallier (French military attaché in Vienna) to Min. Guerre, 15 January 1913, SHAT 1131/5 no. 184.

21. General Staff to Ministère des Affaires Etrangères, 2 September 1912, DDF III.3 no. 359 pp. 439–440; see also Joseph-Jacques-Césaire Joffre, *Mémoires du Maréchal Joffre 1910–1917*, 2 vols. (Paris, 1932), 1:139.

22. Wehrlin to Min. Guerre, 21 December 1912, SHAT 7N 1478/1 no. 25; see also Kokovtsov, *Out of My Past*, 344–350.

23. *Ministerrat für gemeinsame Angelegenheiten, Protokoll*, 3 and 8–9 October 1912, HHStA PA XL/310 nos. 58–59.

24. Schemua to Franz Joseph, *Denkschrift über die Lage am Balkan*, 28 September 1912, KA MKSM 1912 25–1/11; Conrad, *Denkschrift*, 20 January 1913, KA MKSM 1913 25–1/5; Conrad to Berchtold, 10 February 1913, KA B/1450:81 no. 51; idem, 11 February, 18 April 1913, KA Generalstab, Operationsbüro 738 nos. 738, 624–626; Conrad, *Unterredung Exc. Conrad mit Gf. Berchtold*, 24 April 1913, KA Generalstab, Operationsbüro 738; Conrad to Berchtold, 28 July 1913, KA MKSM 1913 69–5/9–2.

25. Schemua to Franz Joseph, *Denkschrift zur Balkankrise*, 9 November 1912, KA MKSM 1912 25-1/11 no. 4611.

26. *Ministerrat für gemeinsame Angelegenheiten, Protokoll*, 2 May 1913, HHStA PA XL/311 no. 506.

27. Hallier to Min. Guerre, November-December 1912, SHAT 7N 1131/3; Rothenberg, *Army of Francis Joseph*, 167.

28. Moltke to Kiderlen, 19 November 1912, PAAA R10430 no. 17546; Gen. de Laguiche (French military attaché in St. Petersburg) to Min. Guerre, 16 December 1912, 17 January 1913, SHAT 7N 1478/1 nos. 23, 32.

29. Kriegsministerium, *Referat betreffend Beschleunigung des Ausbaues der Landwehrartillerien*, 24 October 1912, KA MKSM 1912 4-4/3 no. 2528; *Ministerrat für gemeinsame Angelegenheiten, Protokoll*, 4 January, 3 October 1913, HHStA PA XL/311 nos. 8, 62.

30. *Ministerrat für gemeinsame Angelegenheiten, Protokoll*, 4 January 1913, HHStA PA XL/311 no. 8.

31. Kriegsministerium, 5. Abteilung, *Extraktbogen für die Militärkanzlei betreffend a.u. Vortrag über Rekrutenkontingentserhöhung*, 22 August 1913, KA MKSM 1913 82-1/2-3.

32. Wolfgang J. Mommsen, "Der Topos vom unvermeidlichen Krieg," in *Bereit zum Krieg: Kriegsmentalität im wilhelminischen Deutschland 1890–1914*, ed. Jost Dülffer and Karl Holl (Göttingen, 1986), 194–224.

33. Schemua, *Bericht über meinen Aufenthalt in Berlin am 22. d. M.*, 27 November 1912, KA Generalstab, Operationsbüro 737 nos. 429–430.

34. John C. G. Röhl, "An der Schwelle zum Weltkrieg: Eine Dokumentation über dem 'Kriegsrat' vom 8. Dezember 1912," *Militärgeschichtliche Mitteilungen* 21, no. 1 (1977): 77–134; idem, "Die Generalprobe: Zur Geschichte und Bedeutung des 'Kriegsrates' vom 8. Dezember 1912," in *Industrielle Gesellschaft und wirtschafliches System: Festschrift für Fritz Fischer zum 70. Geburtstag*, ed. Dirk Stegmann, Bernd-Jürgen Wendt, and Peter-Christian Witt (Bonn, 1978), 357–373; Egmont Zechlin, "Die Adriakrise und der 'Kriegsrat' vom 8. Dez. 1912," in *Krieg und Kriegsrisiko. Zur deutschen Politik im Ersten Weltkrieg: Aufsätze*, 115–159 (Düsseldorf, 1979); Bernd Felix Schulte, "Zu der Krisenkonferenz vom 8. Dezember 1912," *Historisches Jahrbuch* 102 (1982): 183–197; Fischer, *War of Illusions*, 161–164; Wolfgang J. Mommsen, "Domestic Factors in German Foreign Policy Before 1914," in *Imperial Germany*, ed. James J. Sheehan (New York, 1976), 250–251; Förster, *Der doppelte Militarismus*, 252–254.

35. Müller, *Tagebuch*, 169–171, 8 December 1912, BA-MA N159(Müller)/4.

36. Bienerth to Conrad, *Bericht über eine Unterredung mit dem Chef des Generalstabes*, 26 February 1913, KA B/1450:81 no. 75; Albertini, *Origins of the War of 1914*, 1:433–440.

37. Förster, *Der doppelte Militarismus*, 257–263.

38. Heeringen to Bethmann, 13 March 1913, BA R43F/1252/1 nos. 79–80; Reichsarchiv, *Kriegsrüstung*, 1:154–146.

39. Bethmann file note, 14 December 1912, PAAA R853 no. 2003.

40. Heeringen to Bethmann, 13 March 1913, BA R43F/1252/1 nos. 79–80; Reichsarchiv, *Kriegsrüstung*, 1:155–156.

41. Reichsarchiv, *Kriegsrüstung*, 1:156–166; Wandel, Wandel, *Tagebuch II*, 26 November, 21 December 1912, BA N564(Wandel)/4.

42. Moltke to Kriegsministerium, 25 November 1912, Reichsarchiv, *Kriegsrüstung*, 1 Anl. no. 48 pp. 146–148; Heeringen to Bethmann, 2 December 1912, BA R43F/1252/1 nos. 24–28.

43. Reichsarchiv, *Kriegsrüstung*, 1 Anl. no. 50, p. 150, Moltke to Heeringen, 2 December 1912.

44. Bethmann file note, 14 December 1912, PAAA R853 no. 2003.

45. Reichsarchiv, *Kriegsrüstung*, 1:170–171; Förster, *Der doppelte Militarismus*, 264.

46. Bethmann file note, 14 December 1912, PAAA R853 no. 2003.

47. Bethmann to Prussian ambassadors in Munich, Stuttgart, Dresden and Karlsruhe, 8 February 1913, PAAA R853 no. 139.

48. Bundesrat, *Entwurf eines Gesetzes zur Ergänzung des Gesetzes über die Friedenspräsenzstärke des deutschen Heeres*, 1913, BHStA-KA M.Kr. 1136 no. 462.

49. Von Graevenitz (Württemberg military representative in Berlin) to Württemberg foreign minister and minister-president, 24 April 1913, HStAS-KA M 10/41 nos. 1–8; see also Dieter Groh, "Die geheimen Sitzungen der Reichshaushaltskommission am 24. und 25. April 1913," *Internationale Wißenschaftliche Korrespondenz zur Geschichte der deutschen Arbeiterbewegung* 11, no. 12 (1971): 29–38.

50. Von Graevenitz to Württemberg foreign minister and minister-president, 24 April 1913, HStAS-KA M 10/41 nos. 1–8.

51. Reichsarchiv, *Kriegsrüstung*, 1:172–189; Förster, *Der doppelte Militarismus*, 265–274.

52. Heeringen to Moltke, 9 December 1912, Reichsarchiv, *Kriegsrüstung*, 1 Anl. no. 53 pp. 155–156.

53. Moltke to Heeringen, 25 November 1912, ibid., 1 Anl. no. 48 p. 147.

54. Moltke to Bethmann, 21 December 1912, ibid., 1 Anl. no. 54 p. 169; see also Moltke to Kriegsministerium, 14 January 1913, ibid., 1 Anl. no. 55 p. 176; Moltke to Bethmann, 30 January 1913, ibid., 1 Anl. no. 61 p. 187.

55. Moltke to Bethmann, 21 December 1912, ibid., 1 Anl. no. 54 p. 170.

56. Eckart Kehr, "Zur Genesis des Königlich Preußischen Reserveoffiziers" (1928) and "Klassenkämpfe und Rüstungspolitik im kaiserlichen Deutschland" (1932), both in *Der Primat der Innenpolitik: Gesammelte Aufsätze zur preußisch-deutschen Sozialgeschichte im 19. und 20. Jahrhundert*, ed. Hans-Ulrich Wehler, 2nd rev. ed. (Berlin, 1970), 87–110; Karl Demeter, *Das deutsche Offizierkorps in Gesellschaft und Staat 1650–1945*, 4th rev. ed. (Frankfurt am Main, 1965), 19–33; Craig, *Politics of the Prussian Army*, 232–254; Martin Kitchen, *The German Officer Corps, 1890–1914* (Oxford, 1968), xiii-xxix, 1–48; Wehler, *German Empire*, 157–163; Schulte, *Die deutsche Armee*, xxxiv-xxxviii; Förster, *Der doppelte Militarismus*; Berghahn, *Germany and the Approach of War*, 7–17; David Schoenbaum, *Zabern 1913: Consensus Politics in Imperial Germany* (London, 1982).

57. Wildman, *End of the Russian Imperial Army* vol. 1, *The Old Army and the Soldiers' Revolt*, 22; Demeter, *Das deutsche Offizierkorps*, 29.

58. Reichsarchiv, *Kriegsrüstung*, 1 Anl. no. 56 p. 180, Heeringen to Moltke, 20 January 1913. Virtually every scholarly work that refers to the social-political hypothesis concerning the war ministry's resistance to expansion cites this single passage. See Kehr, "Klassenkämpfe und Rüstungspolitik," 101; Craig, *Politics of the Prussian Army*, 251–252; Kitchen, *German Officer Corps*, 35; Wehler, *German Empire*, 160; Förster, *Der doppelte Militarismus*, 271; Granier, "Deutsche Rüstungspolitik vor dem Ersten Weltkrieg," 151n.

59. Von Einem to Schlieffen, 19 April 1904, Reichsarchiv, *Kriegsrüstung*, 1 Anl. no. 26 p. 91.

60. Roger Chickering, "Der 'Deutsche Wehrverein' und die Reform der deutschen Armee 1912–1914," *Militärgeschichtliche Mitteilungen* 25, no. 1 (1979): 9–10, 16.

61. Heeringen to Moltke, 9 December 1912, Reichsarchiv, *Kriegsrüstung*, 1 Anl. no. 53 p. 156; see also Wandel, *Tagebuch II*, 9 January 1913, BA-MA N564(Wandel)/4.

62. Heeringen protocol, March 1913, Reichsarchiv, *Kriegsrüstung*, 1 Anl. no. 64 pp. 190–191.

63. Heeringen to Moltke, 23 January 1913, ibid., 1 Anl. no. 58 p. 184; see also Heeringen to Moltke, 23 January 1913, ibid., no. 59 p. 185; Wilhelm II to Heeringen, 25 January 1913, ibid., no. 60 pp. 185–186; Wandel, *Tagebuch II*, 23 January 1913, BA-MA N564(Wandel)/4.

64. Wandel, *Tagebuch II*, 9 January 1913, BA-MA N564(Wandel)/4.

65. Reichsarchiv, *Kriegsrüstung*, 1:177–180.

66. Heeringen to Moltke, 20 January 1913, Reichsarchiv, *Kriegsrüstung*, 1 Anl. no. 56 p. 180.

67. Heeringen to Bethmann, 2 December 1912, ibid., 1 Anl. no. 51 p. 152.

68. Wandel, Tagebuch II, 26 November 1912, BA-MA N564(Wandel)/4.

69. Heeringen to Moltke, 20 January 1913, Reichsarchiv, *Kriegsrüstung*, 1 Anl. no. 56 p. 179.

70. Ibid., 1:181–182, 188.

71. Heeringen to Moltke, 23 January 1913, Reichsarchiv, *Kriegsrüstung* 1 Anl. no. 58 p. 184.

72. Arden Bucholz, *Moltke, Schlieffen and Prussian War Planning* (New York, 1991).

73. Moltke to Bethmann, 21 December 1912, Reichsarchiv, *Kriegsrüstung*, 1 Anl. no. 54 p. 176; Förster, *Der doppelte Militarismus*, 275–296.

74. Moltke to Bethmann, 1 and 5 March 1913, Reichsarchiv, *Kriegsrüstung*, 1 Anl. nos. 62, 63 pp. 188–189.

75. Witt, *Die Finanzpolitik des deutschen Reiches*, 356–376; Förster, *Der doppelte Militarismus*, 280–294; Berghahn, *Germany and the Approach of War*, 153–159.

76. Mommsen, "Der Topos vom unvermeidlichen Krieg."

77. Laguiche to Min. Guerre, 14 February 1913, SHAT 7N 1478/1 no. 43.

78. Cambon to foreign minister, 12 February 1913, MAE CP Allemagne NS

105 nos. 16–17; see also Maj. Serret (French military attaché in Berlin) to Min. Guerre, 6 March 1913, MAE Papiers Jules Cambon 13/2 nos. 77–79.

79. Krumeich, *Armaments and Politics in France*; Georges Michon, *La Préparation à la Guerre: la Loi des Trois Ans (1911–1914)* (Paris, 1935).

80. Cambon to Pichon, 12 February 1913, MAE CP Allemagne NS 105 nos. 16–17; Serret to Min. Guerre, 27 February 1913, MAE Papiers Jules Cambon 13/2 nos. 65–66; Serret to Min. Guerre, 14 March 1913, SHAT 7N 1112/1 no. 56.

81. Serret to Min. Guerre, 31 January, 1 March 1913, SHAT 7N 1112/1 nos. 46, 53.

82. Conseil Supérieur de la Guerre, *Procès-verbal*, 4 March 1913, SHAT 1N 10/13 pp. 54–62.

83. Commission de l'Armée, minutes of session, 11 March 1913, AN C7421 vol. 2 Annexe.

84. Ibid., 11–14 March 1913.

85. Ibid., 18 March 1913. Cf. Porch, *March to the Marne*, 191–192, 210–212.

86. Krumeich, *Armaments and Politics in France*, 51–52.

87. Ibid., 100–101; Weber, *Nationalist Revival in France*, 120–128.

88. Min. Guerre, *Grande Guerre*, 1.i:Carte No. 7.

89. Troisième Bureau, *Plan XVII, Bases du Plan: Avant-Propos*, 1913, SHAT 7N 1771/2; Joffre, *Mémoires*, 1:141–206.

90. Troisième Bureau, *Plan XVII, Bases du Plan. Avant-Propos*, 1913, SHAT 7N 1771/2; see also Troisième Bureau, *Plan XVII, Bases du Plan*, 18 April 1913, SHAT 1N 11/143 no. 845.

91. Delcassé to Ministère des Affaires Etrangères, March 1913, MAE Papiers Delcassé vol. 19 no. 108; Wehrlin to Min. Guerre, 1 March 1913, SHAT 7N 1478/1 no. 51; Paléologue (foreign ministry) to Min. Guerre, 20 March 1913, SHAT 7N 1535 no. 347.

92. Delcassé to Ministère des Affaires Etrangères, March 1913, MAE Papiers Delcassé vol. 19 no. 108.

93. Delcassé to Ministère des Affaires Etrangères, 24 March 1913, MAE Papiers Delcassé vol. 19 no. 114; see also idem, 26 March 1913, MAE Papiers Delcassé vol. 19 no. 122.

94. Krumeich, *Armaments and Politics in France*, 26–30.

95. Zhilinski and Joffre, *Procès-verbal des entretiens du mois d'Août 1913 entre les Chefs d'Etat-major des armées française et russe*, 9 September 1913, MAE CP Russie NS 42 nos. 146–155.

96. Kokovtsov, *Out of My Past*, 339–340.

97. Danilov, *La Russie dans la Guerre Mondiale*, 84.

98. E.g., Fuller, *Strategy and Power*, 457.

99. Kokovtsov, *Out of My Past*, 362–364.

100. Ibid., 229, 314.

101. "La nouvelle loi russe sur le recrutement de l'armée," *Revue militaire des armées étrangères* 81 no. 1026 (May 1913): 435–461; SHAT 7N 1478/1 no. 111, Laguiche to Min. Guerre, 26 June 1913.

102. Stone, *Eastern Front*, 35.

103. Moltke to Auswärtiges Amt, 24 October 1913, PAAA R10432 no. 17468[iv]; Großer Generalstab, 1. Abteilung, *Die wichtigsten Veränderungen im Heerwesen Rußlands im Jahre 1913*, March 1914, BA-MA RM5/1486 nos. 257–282; Generalstab, Evidenzbüro, *Jahresbericht über die russische Wehrmacht 1913*, 31 December 1913, KA MKSM 1914 18-2/3–1.

104. Delcassé to Ministère des Affaires Etrangères, 24 and 26 March 1913, MAE Papiers Delcassé vol. 19 nos. 114, 122; Zhilinski and Joffre, *Procès-verbal des entretiens du mois d'Août 1913 entre les Chefs d'Etat-major des armées française et russe*, 9 September 1913.

105. Minutes of conference at the foreign ministry, 10 November 1913, MAE CP Russie NS 65 nos. 425bis-425[5]; see also Russian embassy typescript, *Paris, le 2 Juillet 1913*, MAE CP Russie NS 42 no. 45; Sazonov-Delcassé agreement, 30 December 1913, MAE CP Russie NS 42 nos. 208–209.

106. Minutes of conference at the foreign ministry, 10 November 1913, MAE CP Russie NS 65 nos. 425bis-425[5]; Collins, "The Franco-Russian Alliance and Russian Railways," 787–788.

107. Laguiche to Min. Guerre, 26 June 1913, SHAT 7N 1478/1 no. 111.

108. Wehrlin to Min. Guerre, 6 November 1913, SHAT 7N 1478/1 no. 137.

109. Joffre to Renouard, 26 June 1913, SHAT 1N 17/3; Delcassé to Ministère des Affaires Etrangères, 12 August 1913, MAE CP Russie NS 42 nos. 91–92; Maj. von Eggeling (German military attaché in Petersburg) to Kriegsministerium, 28 August 1913, PAAA R10432 no. 35; Joffre, *Mémoires*, 1:131–133.

CHAPTER 7

1. "Le budget de l'Empire Allemand pour 1913 (Part 2)," *Revue militaire des armées étrangères* 83, no. 1034 (January 1914): 1–23.

2. Militärgeschichtliches Forschungsamt, ed., *Die Militärluftfahrt bis zum Beginn des Weltkrieges 1914*, 3 vols. (Freiburg im Breisgau, 1965–66), 1:193, 3:103; Serret to Min. Guerre, 17 April, 24 May 1914, SHAT 7N 1112/2 nos. 179, 193.

3. Meier-Welcker and von Groote, *Handbuch der deutschen Militärgeschichte*, 5:178; Reichsarchiv, *Der Weltkrieg 1914 bis 1918*, vol. 1, *Kriegsrüstung und Kriegswirtschaft* (Berlin, 1930), 1:253–255.

4. Pellé to Min. Guerre, 1 April 1912, SHAT 7N 1111/2 no. 454; Serret to Min. Guerre, 14 March, 10 October 1913, SHAT 7N 1112/1 nos. 56, 111.

5. War Office General Staff, *Special Military Resources of the German Empire*, February 1912, PRO WO 33/579; Conrad to Franz Joseph, *Wahrnehmungen Manöver in Deutschland 1913*, 20 September 1913, KA MKSM 1913 29–10/3–4 no. 3720; Serret to Min. Guerre, 10 October 1913, SHAT 7N 1112/1 no. 111; Deuxième Bureau, *Note au sujet des manoeuvres impériales allemandes en 1913*, December 1913, SHAT 7N 673/1; Comando del Corpo di Stato Maggiore, Riparto Operazioni, Scacchiere Orientale, *Bollettino N. 53: Germania, manovre imperiali del 1913*, September 1913, AUSSME G-22/7 no. 53.

6. Hallier to Min. Guerre, 15 January 1913, SHAT 7N 1131/5 no. 184; idem, 21 January 1914, SHAT 7N 1132/3 no. 380.

7. Rothenberg, *Army of Francis Joseph*, 149, 164.

8. Hallier to Min. Guerre, 10 July 1912, SHAT 7N 1131/3 no. 93; Conrad, *Denkschrift vom Jänner 1914: II Die Allgemeinen Kriegsvorbereitungen*, January 1914, KA Generalstab, Operationsbüro 742 nos. 779–797; Rothenberg, *Army of Francis Joseph*, 174.

9. Schoen (German ambassador in Paris) to Bethmann, 8 August 1913, PAAA R6750 no. 283; Winterfeldt to Kriegsministerium, 20 August 1913, PAAA R6756 no. 39; Chef des Generalstabes der Armee, *Die französische Armee nach Durchführung der dreijährigen Dienstzeit*, February 1914, HStAS-KA M1/4 Bd. 794 nos. 33–49.

10. Reichskriegsministerium, *Vergleichende übersicht des Zahlenverhältnisses zwischen Offizieren, Unteroffizieren und Mannschaften in Deutschland, Frankreich, Österreich und Rußland*, April 1913, BHStA-KA M.Kr. 1136 no. 9578/1; Chef des Generalstabes der Armee, *Die französische Armee nach Durchführung der dreijährigen Dienstzeit*, February 1914, HStAS-KA M1/4 Bd. 794 nos. 33–49.

11. Großer Generalstab, *Die französischen Truppenübungsplätze und ihre Ausnützung*, 15 January 1912, BHStA-KA Generalstab 165 no. 380[ii]; Joffre, *Mémoires*, 1:79–84.

12. Wandel to Heeringen, 21 February 1912, BA-MA PH 2/87; Chef des Generalstabes der Armee, *Zusammenstellung der wichtigsten Veränderungen im Heerwesen Frankreichs 1913*, 15 February 1914, BA-MA RM5/1235 nos. 107–140.

13. Chef des Generalstabes der Armee, *Französische schwere Artillerie und Belagerungs-Artillerie*, 29 November 1912, BA-MA RM5/1235 nos. 2–12; Joffre to Gens. Abinal and Boucher de Morlaincourt, 2 May 1913, SHAT 7N 51/2; Joffre, *Armement et organisation de l'Artillerie*, September 1913, SHAT 50/1; Troisième Bureau to Senator Charles Humbert, September, November 1913, SHAT 7N 53; Conseil Supérieur de la Guerre, *Procès-verbal*, 15 October 1913, SHAT 1N 10/13 pp. 84–89; Min. Guerre, *Projet d'organisation de l'artillerie lourde dans le Plan XVII*, 1914, SHAT 7N 50/1; Chef des Generalstabes der Armee, untitled report, 31 July 1914, HStAS-KA M 1/4 Bd. 794 nos. 138–139; François-Léon-Emile Rimailho, *L'artillerie de campagne* (Paris, 1924), 107; Joffre, *Mémoires*, 1:61–73; Porch, *March to the Marne*, 232–235.

14. Messimy, *Mes souvenirs*, 117–120.

15. Serret to Min. Guerre, 10 October 1913, SHAT 7N 1112/1 no. 111.

16. Chef des Generalstabes der Armee, *Die französischen Armeemanöver 1912*, 3 December 1912, BA-MA RM5/1235 nos. 15–36; idem, *Die französischen Armeemanöver 1913*, December 1913, BA-MA RM5/1235 nos. 83–100; Comando del Corpo di Stato Maggiore, Riparto Operazioni, Ufficio Scacchiere Orientale, *Relazione sulle grandi manovre del 1913 in Francia*, 3 December 1913, AUSSME G-23/131.

17. Großer Generalstab, 4. Abteilung, *Ergänzungen zu den Zusammenstellungen der 4. und 7. Abteilungen vom November 1912 über die wichtigsten*

Veränderungen im Festungswesen der fremden Staaten, 14 June 1913, BHStA-KA Generalstab 489 no. 966; Großer Generalstab, 1. Abteilung, *Die wichtigsten Veränderungen im Heerwesen Rußlands im Jahre 1913*, March 1914, BA-MA RM5/1486 b, 257–282; Generalstab, Evidenzbüro, *Jahresbericht über die russische Wehrmacht 1913*, 31 December 1913, KA MKSM 1914 18–2/3–1.

18. Deuxième Bureau, *Note sur les projets de renforcement de l'Armée russe*, 6 July 1914, SHAT 7N 1535; Danilov, *La russie dans la Guerre Mondiale*, 85; Suchomlinow, *Erinnerungen*, 342; Fuller, *Strategy and Power*, 437.

19. Capt. Langlois, Ecole Supérieur de la Guerre, *Conférence sur l'Armée russe*, 1912/13, SHAT 7N 1535; Großer Generalstab, *Mitteilungen über russische Taktik*, 22 May 1913, HStAS-KA M1/4 Bd. 739 nos. 258–277; Generalstab, Evidenzbüro, *Jahresbericht über die russische Wehrmacht 1913*, 31 December 1913, KA MKSM 1914 18–2/3–1; Großer Generalstab, 1. Abteilung, *Die wichtigsten Veränderungen im Heerwesen Russlands im Jahre 1913*, March 1914, BA-MA RM5/1486 nos. 257–282.

20. Committee of Imperial Defence, Sub-Committee on Aerial Navigation, *Report of the Technical Sub-Committee*, 27 February 1912, PRO CAB 4/4/33 no. 139-B; la Panouse to Min. Guerre, 19 January 1914, SHAT 7N 1228/5 no. 252; Committee of Imperial Defence, *The Royal Flying Corps: Second Annual Report by the Air Committee*, 1 May 1914, PRO CAB 4/5 no. 190-B.

21. Chef des Generalstabes der Armee, *Die Taktik der englischen Armee*, February 1912, HStAS-KA M1/4 Bd. 739 nos. 162–172; Gen. C. W. Douglas, *Annual Report of the Inspector-General of the Home Forces for 1912*, 15 October 1912, PRO WO 163/18 Appendix 1; la Panouse to Min. Guerre, 13 October 1913, 19 January 1914, SHAT 1228/1 no. 225 and 1228/5 no. 252.

22. Stato Maggiore, *La Mobilitazione e la radunata generale dell'Esercito nelle condizioni attuali*, 1912, AUSSME F-4/11; Generalstab, Evidenzbüro, *Jahresbericht über die Wehrmacht Italiens 1913*, December 1913, KA MKSM 1914 18–2/2–3; Brusati to Giolitti, March 1914, ACS Salandra 4/30; Lieut.-Col. Gondrecourt (French military attaché in Rome) to Min. Guerrre, 7 January, 16 April 1914, SHAT 7N 1370/4 nos. 310, 340; Pollio to Gen. Brusati, 15 May 1914, ACS Brusati 11/vii-1–45 no. 51.

23. Spingardi to Giolitti, 29 April 1913, AUSSME F-4/77 no. 38; Pollio to Gens. Porro and Grandi, *Programmi vari per migliorare le attuali condizioni dell'Esercito e l'organizzazione difensiva dello Stato*, 20 March 1914, AUSSME F-4/12; Pollio to Salandra, *Cenni sui provvedimenti indispensabili per migliorare le condizioni dell'Esercito*, 30 March 1914, AUSSME F-4/12.

24. Pollio to Spingardi, 29 January 1912, AUSSME F-4/27/3 no. 2; Zupelli (war minister) to Salandra, 28 November 1914, ACS Salandra 8/56 nos. 128–134.

25. Gondrecourt to Min. Guerre, 20 April, 28 December 1912, SHAT 7N 1370/2 nos. 107, 187; Generalstab, Evidenzbüro, *Jahresbericht über die Wehrmacht Italiens 1912*, January 1913, KA MKSM 1913 18–2/2–4; Gondrecourt to Min. Guerre, 7 and 8 January 1913, SHAT 7N 1370/3 nos. 191, 192.

26. Generalstab, Evidenzbüro, *Jahresbericht über die Wehrmacht der Balkanstaaten 1913: Allgemeiner Teil*, February 1914, KA MKSM 1914 18–2/9–1.

27. Ibid.; Maj. Jellinek (Austro-Hungarian military attaché in Belgrade) to Kriegsministerium, *Resumé über die serbische Armee nach ihrem Feldzug gegen Bulgarien im Sommer 1913*, October 1913, KA MKSM 1913 18-2/6-2; Generalstab, Evidenzbüro, *Jahresbericht über die Wehrmacht Serbiens 1913*, and *Jahresbericht über die Wehrmacht Montenegros 1913*, both January 1914, KA MKSM 1914 18-2/9-1.

28. Conrad to Franz Joseph, 20 September 1913, KA MKSM 1913 29-10/ 3-4 no. 3720; *Verbale riservatissimo della seduta tenuta in Roma dai comandanti designati di armate in guerra e dal Capo di Stato maggiore dell'esercito il 18 dicembre 1913*, 18 December 1913, AUSSME H-5/12/11; Rome-Vienna correspondence, December 1913-June 1914, KA Generalstab Operationsbüro 737.

29. Callwell, *Sir Henry Wilson*, 1:149-151; Williamson, *Politics of Grand Strategy*, 312-316.

30. Schlieffen, *Denkschrift (letzte Niederschrift vom 28. Dezember 1912)*, footnote added by Moltke, who received the document on 8 February 1913, PRO CAB 20/2 no. 1.

31. Reichsarchiv, *Der Weltkrieg 1914 bis 1918*, vol. 1 *Die Grenzschlachten im Westen* (Berlin, 1925), 17.

32. Copy of Russian intelligence report from Berlin, 23 March 1913, enclosed in Laguiche to Min. Guerre, 25 April 1913, SHAT 7N 1478/1 no. 78.

33. Winterfeldt to Kriegsministerium, 20 August 1913, PAAA R6756 no. 39; Chef des Generalstabes der Armee, *Die französische Armee nach Durchführung der dreijährigen Dienstzeit*, February 1914, HStAS-KA M1/4 Bd. 794 nos. 33-49.

34. Großer Generalstab, 9. Abteilung, *Die Neugestaltung der belgischen Armee*, November 1913, BHStA-KA Generalstab 223.

35. Albertini, *Origins of the War of 1914*, 2:120-686; Imanuel Geiss, *Julikrise und Kriegsausbruch*, (Hannover, 1963).

36. Conrad, *Besprechung bei Berchtold am 13. Oktober 1913 von* $\frac{1}{2}$ 3-$\frac{1}{2}$ 5 *nm.* (notes), KA Generalstab, Operationsbüro 738 nos. 730-731.

37. Conrad, *Denkschrift vom Jänner 1914*, January 1914, KA Generalstab, Operationsbüro 742 nos. 769-806; Kageneck to Kriegsministerium, 17 March 1914, PAAA R10433 no. 18; Conrad, *Unterredung mit Moltke am 12./5 in Karlsbad*, 1914 (notes), KA B/1450:103 no. 317; Conrad to Berchtold, 22 June 1914, KA MKSM 1914 25-1/3.

38. Conrad, *Besprechung bei Berchtold am 13. Oktober von* $\frac{1}{2}$ 3-$\frac{1}{2}$ 5 *nm.* (notes), KA Generalstab, Operationsbüro 738 nos. 730-731.

39. Tisza, *Zur auswärtigen Lage*, 15 March 1914, HHStA Geheimakten der Kabinettskanzlei 20.

40. Conrad, *Rapport bei Sr. Majestät in Schönbrunn. 5. Juli 10^h vm.*, 5 July 1914, KA B/1450:109.

41. Conrad, *Aus meiner Dienstzeit*, 4:36.

42. *Ministerrath für gemeinsame Angelegenheiten, Protokoll*, 7 July 1914, HHStA PA XL/312 no. 58.

43. Tisza to Franz Joseph, 25 July 1914, HHStA Geheimakten der Kabinettskanzlei 20.

44. Conrad, *Aus meiner Dienstzeit*, 3:669–663; Maj. Bienerth (Austro-Hungarian military attaché in Berlin) to Conrad, *Bericht über eine Unterredung mit dem Chef des Generalstabes*, 26 February 1913, KA B/1450:81 no. 75; Conrad, *Unterredung mit Moltke am 12./5 in Karlsbad*, 1914 (notes), KA B/1450: 103 no. 317.

45. Berchtold, *Tagesbericht*, 28 October 1913, HHStA PA I/494 nos. 842–849.

46. Albertini, *Origins of the War of 1914*, 2:133–164.

47. Ibid., 2:298–301.

48. Ibid., 2:485–490.

49. Ibid., 2:488–489; Kitchen, *German Officer Corps*, 111–114.

50. Kurt Riezler, *Tagebücher, Aufsätze, Dokumente*, ed. Karl Dietrich Erdmann (Göttingen, 1972), 182–183.

51. Ibid., 184.

52. Ibid., 187.

53. D. W. Spring, "Russia and the Coming of the First World War," in *The Coming of the First World War*, ed. R. J. W. Evans and H. Pogge von Strandmann (Oxford, 1988), 57–86, 66–72, 77–86; Fuller, *Strategy and Power*, 448–449.

54. Lieven, *Russia and the Origins of the First World War*, 141–144; Suchomlinow, *Erinnerungen*, 357–360.

55. Cited in Lieven, *Russia and the Origins of the First World War*, 143.

56. Suchomlinow, *Erinnerungen*, 359–360.

57. Spring, "Russia and the Coming of the First World War," 72–74.

58. Geyer, *Russian Imperialism*, 293–317.

59. Albertini, *Origins of the War of 1914*, 2:295, 618.

60. Joffre, *Mémoires*, 2:207–208.

61. Arthur Nicolson (permanent undersecretary at the Foreign Office) to Grey and Crowe to Grey, both 31 July 1914, PRO FO 800/94 nos. 518–519, 520–527.

62. Grey, *Twenty-Five Years*, 1:302, 2:34–39.

63. Ibid., 2:1–3.

64. Wilson, *Policy of the Entente*, 135–147; Zara S. Steiner, *Britain and the Origins of the First World War* (New York, 1977), 229–239.

65. Cf. Antonio Salandra, *La neutralità italiana* (Milan, 1928), 218, 258–259.

66. Brusati to Giolitti, March 1914 (copy to Salandra, 27 March 1914), ACS Salandra 4/30; Pollio to Salandra, *Cenni sui provvedimenti indispensabili per migliorare le attuali condizioni dell'Esercito*, 30 March 1914, AUSSME F-4/12; Pollio to Brusati, 15 May 1914, ACS Brusati 11/viii-1–45 no. 51; note by Salandra, 27 July 1914, ACS Salandra 4/30 no. 74.

67. Cadorna to Victor Emanuel, *Memoria sintetica sulla nostra radunata nord ovest e sul trasporto in Germania della maggiore forza possibile*, 31 July 1914, AUSSME H-5/12/10.

68. Cadorna to Grandi (war minister), 2 August 1914 (forwarded to Salandra, 4 August 1914), ACS Salandra 4/30.

69. Luigi Cadorna, *La guerra alla fronte italiana fino all'arresto sulla linea*

del Piave e del Grappa (24 Maggio 1914–9 Novembre 1917), 2 vols. (Milan, 1921), 1:15–19; SHAT 7N 1370/4 no. 377, Gondrecourt to Min. Guerre, 20 August 1914; De Chaurand, *Come l'esercito italiano entrò in guerra*, 269–278.

70. Cf. Marc Trachtenberg, "The Coming of the First World War: A Reassessment," in Trachtenberg, *History and Strategy* (Princeton, 1991), 70.

71. Conrad, *Aus meiner Dienstzeit*, 4:72.

72. Fischer, *War of Illusions*, 468–470.

73. Cf. Marc Trachtenberg, "The Meaning of Mobilization in 1914," *International Security* 15, no. 3 (Winter 1990–91): 120–150.

74. Riezler, *Tagebücher*, 185.

75. Stone, *Eastern Front*, 35.

76. Moltke to Bethmann, May 1914, Reichsarchiv, *Kriegsrüstung*, 1:205–211, 1 Anl. no. 65 pp. 192–193; Falkenhayn to Bethmann, 8 July 1914, Reichsarchiv, *Kriegsrüstung*, 1 Anl. no. 66 pp. 193–195.

77. Conrad, *Denkschrift vom Jänner 1914: II. Die Allgemeine Kriegsvorbereitungen*, January 1914, KA Generalstab, Operationsbüro 742 nos. 779–797; Conrad to Berchtold, 22 June 1914, KA MKSM 1914 25–1/3; Rothenberg, *Army of Francis Joseph*, 173–174.

78. Krumeich, *Armaments and Politics*, 181–230; Becker, *1914*, 62–82.

79. Stone, *Eastern Front*, 50.

80. Rimailho, *Artillerie de Campagne*, 108–142.

BIBLIOGRAPHY

OFFICIAL DOCUMENTS

Austria-Hungary

Ministerium des K. und K. Hauses und des Äussern. *Österreich Ungarns Außenpolitik von der Bosnischen Krise 1908 bis zum Kriegsausbruch 1914.* 9 vols. Edited by Ludwig Bittner, Alfred Pribram, Heinrich Srbik, and Hans Uebersberger. Vienna, 1930.

France

Assemblée Nationale. *Journal officiel de la République Française.* Paris, 1903–14.

Institut National de la Statistique et des Etudes Economiques. *Annuaire statistique de la France.* Paris, 1904–15.

Ministère des Affaires Etrangères, Commission de Publication des Documents Relatifs aux Origines de la Guerre de 1914. *Documents diplomatiques français (1871–1914).* 2nd and 3rd series. Paris, 1901–14.

Ministère de la Guerre. *Les armées françaises dans la Grande Guerre.* Vol. 1, *La guerre de mouvement.* Paris, 1922.

Ministère de la Guerre. *Décret du 3 Décembre 1904 portant règlement sur les manoeuvres de l'infanterie.* Paris, 1904.

Germany

Auswärtiges Amt. *Die Grosse Politik der europäischen Kabinette 1871–1914. Sammlung der Akten des Auswärtigen Amtes.* Edited by Johannes Lepsius, Albrecht Mendelssohn Bartholdy, and Friedrich Thimme. Berlin, 1925.

Kaiserliches Statistisches Amt. *Statistisches Jahrbuch für das Deutsche Reich.* Berlin, 1904–15.

Reichsarchiv. *Der Weltkrieg 1914 bis 1918: die militärischen Operationen zu Lande.* Vol. 1, *Die Grenzschlachten im Westen.* Berlin, 1925.

———. *Der Weltkrieg 1914 bis 1918.* Vol. 1, *Kriegsrüstung und Kriegswirtschaft.* Berlin, 1930.

Reichstag. *Stenographische Berichte über die Verhandlungen des Deutschen Reichstages.* Berlin, 1871–1938.

Great Britain

Foreign Office. *British Documents on the Origins of the War, 1898–1914.* Edited by G. P. Gooch and Harold Temperley. London, 1926–.

Italy

Ministero della Guerra, Comando del Corpo di Stato Maggiore, Ufficio Storico. *L'esercito italiano nella Grande Guerra (1915–1918).* Vol. 1, *Le forze belligeranti.* Rome, 1927.

ARTICLES AND BOOKS

Albertini, Luigi. *The Origins of the War of 1914*. 2 vols. Translated by Isabella M. Massey. London, 1957.

Andrew, Christopher M. "France and the German Menace." In May, *Knowing One's Enemies*, 127–149.

———. *Théophile Delcassé and the Making of the Entente Cordiale: A Reappraisal of French Foreign Policy, 1898–1905*. London and New York, 1968.

Angell, Norman. *The Great Illusion*. London, 1910.

Ardant du Picq, Charles Jean Jacques Joseph. *Etudes sur le combat; combat antique et combat moderne*. 6th ed. Paris, 1904.

Askew, William Clarence. *Europe and Italy's Acquisition of Libya*. Durham, N.C., 1942.

Bald, Dettlef. *Der deutsche Offizier: Sozial- und Bildungsgeschichte des deutschen Offizierkorps im 20. Jahrhundert*. Munich, 1982.

Becker, Jean-Jacques. *1914: Comment les français sont entrés dans la guerre*. Paris, 1977.

Behnen, Michael. *Rüstung, Bündnis, Sicherheit: Dreibund und informeller Imperialismus*. Tübingen, 1985.

Berghahn, Volker R. *Germany and the Approach of War in 1914*. New York, 1973.

———. *Rüstung und Machtpolitik: Zur Anatomie des "Kalten Krieges" vor 1914*. Düsseldorf, 1973.

———. *Der Tirpitz-Plan: Genesis und Verfall einer innenpolitischen Krisenstrategie unter Wilhelm II*. Düsseldorf, 1971.

Bernhardi, Friedrich von. *Deutschland und der nächste Krieg*. 2 vols. Stuttgart, 1912.

Bloch, Jean de. *La guerre*. 6 vols. Paris, 1898–1900. Reprint, New York, 1973.

Boetticher, Friedrich von. "Der Lehrmeister des neuzeitlichen Krieges." In *Von Scharnhorst zu Schlieffen 1806–1906: Hundert Jahre preußisch-deutscher Generalstab*, edited by Friedrich Ernst Eduard Arnold von Cochenhausen, 249–318. Berlin, 1903.

Bonnal, Henri. *La récente guerre Sud-Africaine et ses enseignements*. Paris, 1903.

Bosworth, Richard J. B. *Italy and the Approach of the First World War*. London, 1983.

———. *Italy, The Least of the Great Powers: Italian Foreign Policy before the First World War*. Cambridge, 1979.

Brodie, Bernard. *Sea Power in the Machine Age*. 1941. Reprint, New York, 1969.

Bucholz, Arden. *Moltke, Schlieffen and Prussian War Planning*. New York, 1991.

Bülow, Bernhard von. *Denkwürdigkeiten*. 4 vols. Edited by Franz von Stockhammern. Berlin, 1930–31.

Cadorna, Luigi. *La guerra alla fronte italiana fino all'arresto sulla linea del Piave e del Grappa (24 Maggio 1914–9 Novembre 1917)*. 2 vols. Milan, 1921.

Caillaux, Joseph. *Agadir: Ma politique extérieure*. Paris, 1919.

Callwell, Charles E. *Field Marshal Sir Henry Wilson: His Life and Diaries*. 2 vols. London, 1927.

Carrias, Eugène. *La pensée militaire française*. Paris, 1960.

Chickering, Roger. "Der 'Deutsche Wehrverein' und die Reform der deutschen Armee 1912–1914." *Militärgeschichtliche Mitteilungen* 25, no. 1 (1979): 7–33.

Choucri, Nazli, and Robert C. North. *Nations in Conflict: National Growth and International Violence*. San Francisco, 1975.

Churchill, Winston Leonard Spencer. *The World Crisis*. 2 vols. New York, 1949.

Clausewitz, Karl von. *On War*. Translated and edited by Michael Howard and Peter Paret. Princeton, 1984.

Coetzee, Marilyn Shevin. "The Mobilization of the Right? The Deutscher Wehrverein and Political Activism in Württemberg, 1912–14." *European History Quarterly* 15 (1985): 431–452.

Collenberg, Ludwig Rüdt von. *Die Deutsche Armee von 1871 bis 1914*. Berlin, 1922.

Collins, David N. "The Franco-Russian Alliance and Russian Railways, 1891–1914." *Historical Journal* 61, no. 4 (December 1973): 777–788.

Connaughton, Richard Michael. *The War of the Rising Sun and the Tumbling Bear: A Military History of the Russo-Japanese War*. New York, 1988.

Conrad von Hötzendorf, Franz. *Aus meiner Dienstzeit*. 4 vols. Vienna, 1921–23.

Contamine, Henri. *La Revanche 1871–1914*. Paris, 1957.

Craig, Gordon A. *The Politics of the Prussian Army 1640–1945*. New York, 1955.

Craig, Gordon A., and Alexander L. George. *Force and Statecraft: Diplomatic Problems of Our Time*. Oxford, 1983.

Cruccu, Rinaldo. "L'Esercito nel periodo Giolittiano (1909–1914)." In *L'Esercito italiano dall'Unità alla Grande Guerra*, 257–269.

Danilov, Youri. *La Russie dans la Guerre Mondiale (1914–1917)*. Paris, 1927.

Deák, István. *Beyond Nationalism: A Social and Political History of the Habsburg Officer Corps, 1848–1918*. Oxford, 1990.

De Chaurand de Saint-Eustache, Felice. *Come l'esercito italiano entrò in guerra*. Milan, 1929.

Dehio, Ludwig. *The Precarious Balance: Four Centuries of the European Power Struggle*. Translated by Charles Fullman. New York, 1962.

Deist, Wilhelm. "The Kaiser and His Military Entourage." Translated by Angela Rutter and John C. G. Röhl. In *Kaiser Wilhelm II: New Interpretations*, edited by John C. G. Röhl and Nicholas Sombart, 169–192. Cambridge, 1982.

Del Boca, Angelo. *Gli Italiani in Libia*. Vol. 1, *Tripoli bel suol d'amore, 1860–1922*. Rome, 1986.

Demeter, Karl. *Das deutsche Heer und seine Offiziere*. Berlin, 1935.

———. *Das deutsche Offizierkorps in Gesellschaft und Staat 1650–1945*. Frankfurt am Main, 1965.

De Napoli, Domenico. "Il caso Ranzi ed il modernismo militare." In *L'Esercito italiano dall'Unità alla Grande Guerra*, 221–244.

Dobrorolski, Sergei. *Die Mobilmachung der russischen Armee 1914*. Berlin, 1922.

Dülffer, Jost. *Regeln gegen den Krieg? Die Haager Friedenskonferenzen von 1899 und 1907 in der internationalen Politik*. Berlin, 1981.

Dülffer, Jost, and Karl Holl, eds. *Bereit zum Krieg: Kriegsmentalität im wilhelminischen Deutschland 1890–1914*. Göttingen, 1986.

Dunlop, John Kininmont. *The Development of the British Army, 1899–1914*. London, 1938.

Einem, Karl von. *Erinnerungen eines Soldaten*. Leipzig, 1933.

Eley, Geoff. "Sammlungspolitik, Social Imperialism and the Navy Law of 1898." *Militärgeschichtliche Mitteilungen* 15, no. 1 (1974): 29–63.

Ellis, John. *The Social History of the Machine Gun*. New York, 1975.

Epkenhans, Michael. "Großindustrie und Schlachtflottenbau 1897–1914." *Militärgeschichtliche Mitteilungen* 43, no. 1 (1988): 65–140.

L'Esercito italiano dall'Unità alla Grande Guerra (1861–1918). Esercito, Corpo di Stato Maggiore, Ufficio Storico, Italy. Rome, 1980.

Evans, Richard J. W., and Hartmut Pogge von Strandmann. *The Coming of the First World War*. Oxford, 1988.

Falls, Cyril. *The Great War*. New York, 1959.

Farrar, Lancelot L. *Arrogance and Anxiety: The Ambivalence of German Power, 1848–1914*. Iowa City, 1981.

——. *The Short-War Illusion: German Strategy and Domestic Affairs, August–December 1914*. Santa Barbara, Calif., 1973.

Ferrero, Guglielmo. *Il militarismo: dieci conferenze*. Milan, 1898.

Fischer, Fritz. *Germany's Aims in the First World War*. New York, 1967.

——. *War of Illusions: German Policies from 1911 to 1914*. Translated by Marian Jackson. London, 1975.

Foch, Ferdinand. *Des principes de la guerre: Conférences faites à l'Ecole Supérieure de la Guerre par F. Foch*. Paris, 1903.

Foerster, Wolfgang. *Aus dem Gedankenwerkstatt des Deutschen Generalstabes*. Berlin, 1931.

——. "Ist der deutsche Aufmarsch 1904 an die Franzosen verraten worden?" *Berliner Monatshefte* 10, no. 11 (November 1932): 1053–1067.

Förster, Stig. *Der doppelte Militarismus: Die deutsche Heeresrüstungspolitik zwischen Status-quo-Sicherung und Aggression 1890–1913*. Stuttgart, 1985.

French, David. *British Economic and Strategic Planning, 1905–1915*. London, 1982.

Fritzsche, Peter. *A Nation of Fliers: German Aviation and the Popular Imagination*. Cambridge, Mass., 1992.

Fuller, William Charles. *Civil-Military Conflict in Imperial Russia, 1885–1914*. Princeton, 1985.

——. *Strategy and Power in Russia, 1600–1914*. New York, 1992.

Gat, Azar. *The Development of Military Thought: The Nineteenth Century*. Oxford, 1992.

——. *The Origins of Military Thought: From the Enlightenment to Clausewitz*. Oxford, 1989.

Geiss, Imanuel. *Julikrise und Kriegsausbruch 1914*. Hannover, 1963.

Geyer, Dietrich. *Russian Imperialism: The Interaction of Domestic and Foreign Policy 1860–1914*. Translated by Bruce Little. New York, 1987.

Geyer, Michael. *Deutsche Rüstungspolitik, 1860–1980*. Frankfurt, 1984.

Gilbert, Georges. *La Guerre Sud-Africaine*. Paris, 1902.

Giolitti, Giovanni. *Memorie della mia vita*. 2 vols. Milan, 1922.

Girault, René. *Emprunts russes et investissements français en Russie 1887–1914*. Paris, 1973.

Gleason, William. "Alexander Guchkov and the End of the Russian Empire." *Proceedings of the American Philosophical Society* 73, part 3, pp. 1–35. Philadelphia, 1983.

Gollin, Alfred. *No Longer an Island: Britain and the Wright Brothers, 1902–1909*. London, 1984.

Goltz, Colmar von der. *Das Volk in Waffen*. Berlin, 1883.

Gooch, John. *Armies in Europe*. London, 1980.

———. *Army, State and Society in Italy, 1870–1915*. Basingstoke, Eng., 1989.

———. *The Plans of War: The General Staff and British Military Strategy c. 1900–1916*. London, 1974.

Granier, Gerhard. "Deutsche Rüstungspolitik vor dem Ersten Weltkrieg: General Franz Wandels Tagebuchaufzeichnungen aus dem preussischen Kriegsministerium." *Militärgeschichtliche Mitteilungen* 38, no. 2 (1985): 123–162.

Grey of Fallodon, Edward Viscount. *Twenty-Five Years, 1892–1916*. 2 vols. London, 1925.

Groh, Dieter. "Die geheimen Sitzungen der Reichshaushaltskommission am 24. und 25. April 1913." *Internationale Wißenschaftliche Korrespondenz zur Geschichte der deutschen Arbeiterbewegung* 11, no. 12 (1971): 29–38.

Guchkov, Alexander. "Types of Russian Parliamentary Oratory: Speeches on the Naval and Military Estimates of 1908." *Russian Review* 2, no. 1 (1913): 111–121.

Gudmundsson, Bruce I. *On Artillery*. Westport, Conn., 1993.

———. *Stormtroop Tactics: Innovation in the German Army, 1914–1918*. New York, 1989.

Hallgarten, G. W. F. *Das Wettrüsten, seine Geschichte bis zur Gegenwart*. Frankfurt am Main, 1967.

Halpern, Paul G. *The Mediterranean Naval Situation, 1908–1914*. Cambridge, Mass., 1971.

Henderson, George Francis Robert. *The Science of War. A Collection of Essays and Lectures 1892–1903*. London, 1905.

Herrmann, David Gaius. "The Paralysis of Italian Strategy in the Italian-Turkish War, 1911–1912." *English Historical Review* 104, no. 411 (April 1989): 332–356.

Herwig, Holger H. "The Dynamics of Necessity: German Military Policy during the First World War." In Millett and Murray, *Military Effectiveness*, vol. 1, *The First World War*, 80–115.

Herwig, Holger H. *"Luxury" Fleet: The Imperial German Navy 1888–1918*. London, 1980.

Herzfeld, Hans. *Die deutsche Rüstungspolitik vor dem Weltkriege*. Bonn and Leipzig, 1923.

Hölzle, Erwin. *Die Selbstentmachtung Europas: Das Experiment des Friedens vor dem ersten Weltkrieg*. Göttingen, 1975.

Howard, Michael Eliot. *The Franco-Prussian War: The German Invasion of France, 1870–1871*. New York, 1979.

Howard, Michael Eliot. "Men against Fire: The Doctrine of the Offensive in 1914." In Paret, *Makers of Modern Strategy*, 510–526.

———. *War in European History*. Oxford, 1976.

Huntington, Samuel P. "Arms Races: Prerequisites and Results." In *Power, Action and Interaction: Readings on International Politics*, edited by George H. Quester, 499–541. Boston, 1971.

Jäckh, Ernst. *Kiderlen-Wächter: der Staatsmann und Mensch. Briefwechsel und Nachlaß*. 2 vols. Berlin and Leipzig, 1924.

Jervis, Robert. "Intelligence and Foreign Policy: A Review Essay." *International Security* 2, no. 3 (Winter 1986–87): 141–161.

———. *Perception and Misperception in International Politics*. Princeton, 1976.

Joffre, Joseph-Jacques-Césaire. *Mémoires du Maréchal Joffre 1910–1917*. 2 vols. Paris, 1932.

———. *1914–1915: La préparation de la guerre et la conduite des opérations*. Paris, 1920.

Joll, James. *1914: The Unspoken Assumptions*. London, 1968.

———. *The Origins of the First World War*. New York, 1984.

Kehr, Eckart. *Battleship Building and Party Politics in Germany, 1894–1901*. Translated by Pauline R. Anderson and Eugene N. Anderson. Chicago, 1973.

———. *Der Primat der Innenpolitik: Gesammelte Aufsätze zur preußisch-deutschen Sozialgeschcihte im 19. und 20. Jahrhundert*. Edited and with an introduction by Hans-Ulrich Wehler. 2nd rev. ed. Berlin, 1970.

Keim, August. *Erlebtes und Erstrebtes*. Hannover, 1925.

Kennedy, Paul M. "Arms-Races and the Causes of War, 1850–1945." In Kennedy, *Strategy and Diplomacy 1870–1945: Eight Studies*, 163–177. London, 1983.

———. "The First World War and the International Power System." In Miller, *Military Strategy and the Origins of the First World War*, 7–40.

———. *The Rise and Fall of British Naval Mastery*. London, 1983.

———. *The Rise of the Anglo-German Antagonism, 1860–1914*. London, 1980.

———, ed. *The War Plans of the Great Powers, 1880–1914*. London, 1985.

Kennedy, Paul M., and Anthony Nicholls, eds. *Nationalist and Racialist Movements in Britain and Germany before 1914*. Oxford, 1981.

Kitchen, Martin. *The German Officer Corps, 1890–1914*. Oxford, 1968.

Kokovtsov, Vladimir Nikolayevich. *Out of My Past*. Translated by Laura Matveev. Stanford, 1935.

Krumeich, Gerd. *Armaments and Politics in France on the Eve of the First World War: The Introduction of Three-Year Conscription 1913–1914*. Translated by Stephen Conn. Dover, N.H., 1984.

Kuhl, Hermann von. *Der deutsche Generalstab in Vorbereitung und Durchführung des Weltkrieges*. Berlin, 1920.

Lambi, Ivo Nikolai. *The Navy and German Power Politics, 1862–1914*. Boston, 1984.

Langhorne, Richard. *The Collapse of the Concert of Europe: International Politics, 1890–1914*. New York, 1981.

Langlois, Hippolyte. *Enseignements de deux guerres récentes: Guerres Turco-Russe et Anglo-Boer.* Paris, 1904.

La Panouse, Colonel de. "L'Organisation militaire." *Revue des deux mondes* 21, no. 2 (May 1904): 318–352.

Lebow, Richard Ned. "Windows of Opportunity: Do States Jump Through Them?" In Miller, *Military Strategy and the Origins of the First World War,* 147–186.

Liddell Hart, Basil H. *History of the First World War.* 1930. Reprint, London, 1972.

Lieven, Dominic C. B. *Russia and the Origins of the First World War.* New York, 1983.

Luntinen, Pertti. *French Information on the Russian War Plans, 1880–1914.* Helsinki, 1984.

Luvaas, Jay. *The Military Legacy of the Civil War: The European Inheritance.* Chicago, 1959.

Macdiarmid, Duncan Stewart. *The Life of Lieut. General Sir James Moncrieff Grierson.* London, 1923.

McNeill, William H. *The Pursuit of Power. Technology, Armed Force, and Society since A.D. 1000.* Chicago, 1982.

Malgeri, Francesco. *La guerra libica (1911–1912).* Rome, 1970.

Marder, Arthur J. *The Anatomy of British Sea Power: A History of British Naval Policy in the Pre-Dreadnought Era, 1880–1905.* Hamden, Conn., 1964.

———. *From the Dreadnought to Scapa Flow: The Royal Navy in the Fisher Era, 1904–1919.* 5 vols. Oxford, 1961–70.

May, Ernest R., ed. *Knowing One's Enemies: Intelligence Assessments before the Two World Wars.* Princeton, 1984.

Mazzetti, Massimo. "L'Esercito nel periodo Giolittiano (1900–1908)." In *L'Esercito italiano dall'Unità alla Grande Guerra,* 247–256.

———. "I piani di guerra contro l'Austria dal 1866 alla Prima Guerra Mondiale." In *L'Esercito italiano dall'Unità alla Grande Guerra,* 161–182.

Meier-Welcker, Hans, and Wolfgang von Groote, eds. *Handbuch der deutschen Militärgeschichte 1648–1939.* 5 vols. Munich, 1979.

Menning, Bruce W. *Bayonets before Bullets: The Imperial Russian Army, 1861–1914.* Bloomington, Ind., 1992.

Messimy, Adolphe-Marie. *Mes souvenirs.* Paris, 1937.

Michon, Georges. *La préparation à la Guerre: la Loi des Trois Ans (1911–1914).* Paris, 1935.

Militärgeschichtliches Forschungsamt, ed. *Die Militärluftfahrt bis zum Beginn des Weltkrieges 1914.* 3 vols. Freiburg im Breisgau, 1965–66.

Miller, Steven E., ed. *Military Strategy and the Origins of the First World War.* Princeton, 1985.

Millett, Allan R., and Williamson Murray, eds. *Military Effectiveness.* Vol. 1, *The First World War.* Boston, 1988.

Mommsen, Wolfgang J. "Domestic Factors in German Foreign Policy before 1914." In *Imperial Germany,* edited by James J. Sheehan, 223–268. New York, 1976.

Mommsen, Wolfgang J. "Der Topos vom unvermeidlichen Krieg." In Dülffer and Holl, *Bereit zum Krieg*, 194–224.

Moritz, Albrecht. *Das Problem des Präventivkrieges in der deutschen Politik während der ersten Marokkokrise.* Frankfurt, 1974.

Naroll, Raoul. *Military Deterrence in History.* Albany, N.Y., 1974.

Négrier, François Oscar de. "Le moral des troupes." *Revue des deux mondes* 25, no. 1 (1 February 1905): 481–505.

Ninčić, Momčilo. *La crise bosniaque (1908–1909) et les puissances européennes.* 2 vols. Paris, 1937.

Oncken, Emily. *Panthersprung nach Agadir. Die deutsche Politik während der Zweiten Marokkokrise 1911.* Düsseldorf, 1981.

Pakenham, Thomas. *The Boer War.* London, 1979.

Paléologue, Maurice. "La démission de M. Delcassé en 1905." *Revue des deux mondes* 101, no. 3 (15 June 1931): 761–802.

———. "Un prélude à l'invasion de la Belgique (1904)." *Revue des deux mondes* 102, no. 11 (1 October 1932): 480–524.

Paret, Peter, ed. *Makers of Modern Strategy from Machiavelli to the Nuclear Age.* Princeton, 1986.

Pelet-Narbonne, Gerhard von, ed. *Von Löbells Jahresberichte über die Veränderungen und Fortschritte im Militärwesen.* Berlin, 1904–14.

Perrins, Michael. "The Council for State Defence, 1905–1909: A Study in Russian Bureaucratic Politics." *Slavonic and East European Review* 58, no. 3 (1980): 370–398.

Porch, Douglas. "The French Army in the First World War." In Millett and Murray, *Military Effectiveness*, vol. 1, *The First World War*, 190–228.

———. *The March to the Marne: The French Army, 1871–1914.* Cambridge, 1981.

Rapaport, Anatol. "Lewis F. Richardson's Mathematical Theory of War." *Journal of Conflict Resolution* 1, no. 2 (1957): 249–299.

Répaci, Francesco A. *La finanza pubblica italiana nel secolo 1860–1960.* Bologna, 1962.

Rich, Norman. *Friedrich von Holstein: Politics and Diplomacy in the Era of Wilhelm II.* 2 vols. Cambridge, 1965.

Riezler, Kurt. *Tagebücher, Aufsätze, Dokumente.* Edited by Karl Dietrich Erdmann. Göttingen, 1972.

Rimailho, François-Léon-Emile. *Artillerie de campagne.* Paris, 1924.

Ritter, Gerhard. *The Schlieffen Plan: Critique of a Myth.* Translated by Andrew and Eva Wilson. New York, 1958.

———. *The Sword and the Scepter.* 4 vols. Translated by Heinz Norden. Munich, 1959.

Rochat, Giorgio, and Giulio Massobrio. *Breve storia dell'esercito italiano dal 1861 al 1943.* Turin, 1978.

———. "L'Esercito italiano nell'estate 1914." *Nuova Rivista Storica* 45, no. 2 (May-August 1961): 295–348.

Röhl, John C. G. "An der Schwelle zum Weltkrieg. Eine Dokumentation über den 'Kriegsrat' vom 8. Dezember 1912." *Militärgeschichtliche Mitteilungen* 21, no. 1 (1977): 77–134.

———. "Die Generalprobe. Zur Geschichte und Bedeutung des 'Kriegsrates' vom 8. Dezember 1912." In *Industrielle Gesellschaft und wirtschaftliches System: Festschrift für Fritz Fischer zum 70. Geburtstag*, edited by Dirk Stegmann, Bernd-Jürgen Wendt, and Peter-Christian Witt, 357–373. Bonn, 1978.

Romano, Sergio. *La Quarta Sponda: la guerra di Libia 1911–1912*. Milan, 1977.

Ropponen, Risto. *Die Kraft Russlands. Wie beurteilte die politische Führung der europäischen Grossmächte in der Zeit von 1904 bis 1914 die Kraft Russlands?* Helsinki, 1968.

Rothenberg, Günther E. *The Army of Francis Joseph*. West Lafayette, Ind., 1976.

———. "The Austro-Hungarian Campaign against Serbia in 1914." *Journal of Military History* 53, no. 2 (April 1989): 127–146.

———. "Moltke, Schlieffen and the Doctrine of Strategic Envelopment." In Paret, *Makers of Modern Strategy*, 296–325.

Russett, Bruce M. *The Prisoners of Insecurity: Nuclear Deterrence, the Arms Race, and Arms Control*. San Francisco, 1983.

Sagan, Scott D. "1914 Revisited: Allies, Offense, and Instability." *International Security* 11, no. 2 (Fall 1986): 151–173.

Salandra, Antonio. *La neutralità italiana*. Milan, 1928.

Schlieffen, Alfred von. "Der Krieg in der Gegenwart." *Deutsche Revue* 34, no. 1 (January 1909): 13–24.

Schmitt, Bernadotte Everly. *The Annexation of Bosnia*. Cambridge, 1937. Reprint, New York, 1970.

Schoenbaum, David. *Zabern 1913: Consensus Politics in Imperial Germany*. London, 1982.

Schorske, Carl E. *German Social Democracy, 1905–1917: The Development of the Great Schism*. Cambridge, Mass., 1983.

Schulte, Bernd Felix. *Die deutsche Armee 1900–1914: Zwischen Beharren und Verändern*. Düsseldorf, 1977.

———. "Zu der Krisenkonferenz vom 8. Dezember 1912." *Historisches Jahrbuch* 102 (1982): 183–197.

Senghaas, Dieter. *Rüstung und Militarismus*. Frankfurt am Main, 1972.

Showalter, Dennis E. "Army and Society in Imperial Germany: The Pains of Modernization." *Journal of Contemporary History* 18, no. 4 (1983): 583–618.

———. "The Eastern Front in German Military Planning, 1871–1914: Some Observations." *East European Quarterly* 15, no. 2 (June 1981): 163–180.

———. *Railroads and Rifles: Soldiers, Technology, and the Unification of Germany*. Hamden, Conn., 1975.

Showalter, Dennis E. *Tannenberg: Clash of Empires*. Hamden, Connecticut, 1991.

Snyder, Jack. *The Ideology of the Offensive: Military Decision Making and the Disasters of 1914*. Ithaca, N.Y., 1984.

Spring, David W. "Russia and the Coming of the War." In *The Coming of the First World War*, edited by R. J. W. Evans and Hartmut Pogge von Strandmann, 57–86. Oxford, 1988.

Steinberg, Jonathan. *Yesterday's Deterrent: Tirpitz and the Birth of the German Battle Fleet*. New York, 1965.

Steiner, Zara S. *Britain and the Origins of the First World War*. New York, 1977.

Stern, Fritz. *The Politics of Cultural Despair: A Study in the Rise of the Germanic Ideology*. Berkeley, 1961.

Stone, Norman. *The Eastern Front, 1914–1917*. London and New York, 1975.

———. "Moltke-Conrad: Relations between the Austro-Hungarian and German General Staffs, 1909–1914." *Historical Journal* 9, no. 2 (1966): 201–228.

Strachan, Hew. *European Armies and the Conduct of War*. London, 1983.

Stromberg, Roland N. *Redemption by War: The Intellectuals in 1914*. Lawrence, Kans., 1982.

Suchomlinow, Wladimir Aleksandrowitsch [Sukhomlinov, Vladimir Aleksandrovich]. *Erinnerungen*. Berlin, 1924.

Sumida, Jon Tetsuro. *In Defence of Naval Supremacy: Finance, Technology and British Naval Policy, 1889–1914*. Boston, 1989.

Tannenbaum, Jan Karl. "French Estimates of Germany's Operational Plans." In May, *Knowing One's Enemies*, 150–171.

Taylor, Alan John Percivale. *The Struggle for Mastery in Europe, 1848–1918*. Oxford, 1954.

Tirpitz, Alfred von. *Der Aufbau der deutschen Weltmacht*. Stuttgart, 1924.

———. *Erinnerungen*. Leipzig, 1919.

Trachtenberg, Marc. "The Coming of the First World War: A Reassessment." In Trachtenberg, *History and Strategy*, 47–99. Princeton, 1991.

———. "The Meaning of Mobilization in 1914." *International Security* 15, no. 3 (Winter 1990–91): 120–150.

Trebilcock, Clive. "Legends of the British Armaments Industry, 1890–1914: A Revision." *Journal of Contemporary History* 5, no. 4 (1970): 3–19.

Turner, Leonard Charles Frederick. *Origins of the First World War*. London, 1970.

———. "The Significance of the Schlieffen Plan.' In Kennedy, *The War Plans of the Great Powers*, 199–221.

Tyler, John Ecclesfield. *The British Army and the Continent, 1904–1914*. London, 1938.

Van Creveld, Martin L. *Supplying War: Logistics from Wallenstein to Patton*. Cambridge, 1980.

Van Evera, Stephen. "The Cult of the Offensive and the Origins of the First World War." In Miller, *Military Strategy and the Origins of the First World War*, 58–107.

Wallace, Michael. "Arms Races and Escalation: Some New Evidence." *Journal of Conflict Resolution* 23, no. 1 (March 1979): 3–16.

Wandruszka, Adam, and Peter Urbanitsch. *Die Habsburgermonarchie 1848–1918*. Vol. 5, *Die bewaffnete Macht*. Vienna, 1987.

Warner, Denis Ashton, and Peggy Warner. *The Tide at Sunrise: A History of the Russo-Japanese War, 1904–1905*. New York, 1974.

Weber, Eugene. *The Nationalist Revival in France, 1905–1914*. Berkeley, 1959.

Wehler, Hans-Ulrich. *The German Empire 1871–1918.* Dover, N.H., 1985.

Whittam, John. *The Politics of the Italian Army, 1861–1918.* London, 1977.

Wildman, Allan K. *The End of the Russian Imperial Army.* Vol. 1, *The Old Army and the Soldiers' Revolt (March-April 1917).* Princeton, 1980.

Williamson, Samuel R. "Joffre Reshapes French Strategy, 1911–1913." In Kennedy, *The War Plans of the Great Powers* , 133–154.

———. *The Politics of Grand Strategy: Britain and France Prepare for War, 1904–1914.* Cambridge, Mass., 1969.

Wilson, Keith Malcolm. *The Policy of the Entente: Essays in the Determinants of British Foreign Policy 1904–1914.* Cambridge, 1985.

Witt, Peter-Christian. *Die Finanzpolitik des deutschen Reiches von 1903 bis 1913.* Lübeck, 1970.

Wohlforth, William C. "The Perception of Power: Russia in the Pre-1914 Balance." *World Politics* 39, no. 3 (April 1987): 353–381.

Zechlin, Egmont. *Krieg und Kriegsrisiko. Zur deutschen Politik im Ersten Weltkrieg. Aufsätze.* Düsseldorf, 1979.

Aachen, 49–50

Adua, battle of, 35

Aehrenthal, Alois Lexa von, 110–11, 135, 137, 172, 177; and annexation of Bosnia-Herzegovina, 115–17, 120–21, 123, 125–26, 128, 130, 212

aeroplanes, 150; equipment with, 158–59, 183, 201–3, 205–7; testing and development of, 21, 79, 138–45

Agadir, 148–50, 155

Algeciras conference, 39, 54, 57–59, 118, 148

Alldeutscher Verband. *See* Pan-German League

American Civil War, 22

Anastasia, Grand Duchess, 176

André, Louis, 30

Angell, Norman, 29

Anglo-Boer War, 4, 15, 32, 42, 64, 113, 235–36; lessons derived from, 22, 24, 26–27, 67–68, 70–71, 81, 87, 94–96, 112

Anglo-French entente. See *entente cordiale*

anti-Semitism, 30, 186–87

antimilitarism, 29, 36, 60, 67, 83–84, 86, 184, 186–87

Antoinette aircraft manufacturers, 140

army law of 1912, German, 171, 180, 184–85, 190, 200–201, 228–29; origins of, 147–48, 161–70, 172; repercussions of, 172, 174–75, 189, 197

army law of 1913, German, 187–91, 200–201, 228–29; origins of, 174, 180–82; repercussions of, 191–95

Army League, German. *See* Wehrverein

artillery tactics, 18, 24–25; at maneuvers, 80, 86, 93–94, 96, 100–102, 124, 202, 206. *See also* heavy field artillery; quick-firing artillery; siege artillery

Asquith, Herbert Henry, 154, 156–57, 216

Auffenberg, Moritz von, 177–78

Austro-Prussian War, 22, 190

automobiles. *See* motor vehicles

aviation, 5–6, 21, 51, 138, 152, 160, 163, 168, 222. *See also* aeroplanes; dirigible airships

Balfour, Arthur James, 31, 43

Balkan Wars, 3–4, 125, 173, 195–96; strategic situation resulting from, 173–74, 177–82, 185, 189, 197–98, 201, 205, 207, 209

Barrère, Camille, 53

Barthou, Louis, 193

Bassermann, Ernst, 164, 182

battleships. *See* naval armaments

Bebel, August, 183

Beck-Rzikowsky, Friedrich von, 97–98

Belfort, 47, 50, 140, 160, 194

Belgium, 52, 155, 160, 183, 216, 221; in German war plans, 49–51, 151–52, 158, 201; military preparations of, 51, 167, 169, 209

Berchtold, Leopold von, 120, 177–78, 211–13, 228

Berlin, treaty of, 114

Bernhardi, Friedrich von, 164, 170, 181

Berteaux, Maurice, 76, 150

Bethmann Hollweg, Theobald von, 135–36, 137, 180, 220, 228; and 1912 army law, 161–63, 165, 169–71; and 1913 army law, 181–83, 185, 189–91, 194; and July crisis, 213–14, 219, 226; and second Moroccan crisis, 149, 160, 164

Bihourd, Georges, 52

Bilínski, Leon von, 212

Bismarck, Otto von, 57, 184

Blériot, Louis, 139–40, 145

Bloch, Ivan Stanislavovich, 24–26, 29

Boer War. *See* Anglo-Boer War

Bompard, Maurice, 41

Bonnal, Henri, 27–28, 71

Bosnia-Herzegovina annexation crisis, 3, 113–28, 134, 145–46, 225, 226; in relation to subsequent crises, 160, 180, 210, 213–14; repercussions of, 131, 135–37, 145, 147

British expeditionary force to France, 51,
  160, 206, 234–36; genesis of, 43–44,
  55–56, 58, 64, 137, 154–58, 171, 208
Brugère, Henri de, 45–46, 49–50
Brun, Jean, 60, 68
Buchlau, 117
Bulgaria, 173, 183, 207
Bülow, Bernhard von, 32–33, 62, 65,
  135, 163, 229; and annexation of Bosnia-Herzegovina, 115, 117–21, 123,
  125–26, 128, 180, 213; and first Moroccan crisis, 38–41, 44, 52–54, 56–57,
  149

Cadorna, Luigi, 216–17
Caillaux, Joseph, 148, 150–54, 193
Cambon, Jules, 76, 149, 192
Cambon, Paul, 53, 176, 208
Campbell-Bannerman, Henry, 55, 64
Caucasus, 13, 61, 234
cavalry, 9, 12, 20, 34, 42, 52, 70, 72, 75,
  202, 205, 223; German, 85–86, 88–89,
  185, 202, 206; tactics of, 24, 26, 27,
  89, 96, 100, 102
Center Party, German, 32, 164, 183, 191
Chatalja, 173
Churchill, Winston S., 157
Claß, Heinrich, 163, 180
Clausewitz, Carl von, 23, 28
Clemenceau, Georges, 60, 76
Cockburn, George, 139
colonial warfare, 4, 10–11, 15, 21–22, 35
Combes, Emile, 30
Committee of Imperial Defence, 32, 43,
  55–56, 137, 155–57
Congo, 149, 158
Conrad von Hötzendorf, Franz, 98–99,
  137, 170, 176, 178, 220–21, 227–28;
  and annexation of Bosnia-Herzegovina,
  115–16, 121–26, 128–30, 146, 209;
  and confrontation with Italy, 106, 108–
  11, 172, 202; and July crisis, 211–12,
  218
Conseil Supérieur de la Guerre, 30, 45–
  46, 49, 60, 69, 91, 151–52, 192–93,
  194
Conservative Party, British, 31, 216
Constantinople. See Istanbul; Turkish
  straits
Council of State Defense, Russian, 63,
  113
Crowe, Eyre, 216

Cuorgné mutiny, 104
Curtiss, Frank, 139–40
Custozza, battle of, 105

Delcassé, Théophile, 38–40, 42, 45, 49,
  52–56, 194–96
Deport, Joseph-Albert, 17, 107, 137–38,
  207, 217
Desio, 111
dirigible airships, 21, 75–79, 138–39,
  141–45, 158, 230
Döberitz, 85, 89
Dreadnought-type battleships, 59, 64–65,
  137, 232
Dreyfus affair, 30, 35, 60, 73, 99, 187
Dual Alliance, 44, 118, 130, 161; military
  agreements ensuing from, 120–22, 126,
  213
Dubail, Auguste, 154–55
Durkheim, Emile, 23

East Prussia, 132–33, 160, 208
Edirne (Adrianople), 173
Ehrhardt steelworks, 19
Einem, Karl von, 52, 65–67, 71–72, 77,
  91, 188
engineers, 10, 12, 31, 73, 221; German,
  90, 201
entente cordiale, 3, 31–32, 37, 39, 40–44,
  55, 58. *See also* Triple Entente
entrenchment, 26–27, 90, 92, 95, 223
Erzberger, Matthias, 183
Etienne, Eugène, 193
European war, predictions of, 122–23,
  125–26, 128–31, 146–47, 159, 161,
  164, 166–70, 172, 174, 177–80, 183–
  84, 191, 198–200, 208–13, 226

Fairholme, W. E., 155
Falkenhayn, Erich von, 220–21
Fallières, Armand, 152
Farman, Henri and Maurice, 140, 145
Ferrero, Guglielmo, 29
Fez, 148, 150, 158
first Moroccan crisis, 3, 37–40, 52–59,
  101; in relation to other crises, 160,
  225, 227; repercussions of, 55–56, 64–
  65, 67, 111–12, 208
Fisher, John, 64
Foch, Ferdinand, 28, 81, 155
fortresses, 8, 10, 12, 15, 20, 22, 228; Aus-
  tro-Hungarian, 34, 107, 178; Belgian,

50–51, 65, 158, 160, 201; French, 46, 49–51, 53, 65, 182–83, 204; German, 184–85; Italian, 34–35, 106–8, 202, 206–7; Russian, 61, 119, 132–34, 136, 169
Franco-Austrian War, 22
Franco-Prussian War, 41, 80, 84, 157; lessons derived from, 11, 22, 25, 27, 29, 45, 87, 91, 190
Franco-Russian Alliance, 29, 31, 37, 40–41, 44, 47, 120, 135, 160, 215; military agreements ensuing from, 60–61, 136, 153, 194–97, 208
Franz Ferdinand, Archduke, 110, 123, 125–26, 199–200, 211
Franz Joseph, 33–34, 97, 116, 176; and prospect of war, 108–10, 126, 128–29, 172, 211
Frederick the Great, 22, 186
Freud, Sigmund, 23

Galicia, 132, 178–79
Gilbert, Georges, 27
Giolitti, Giovanni, 35, 107, 111, 207
Girodou, Capt., 98–100
Gnôme-le Rhône manufacturers, 141
Goltz, Colmar von der, 23, 25, 29
"Great Program" of Russian rearmament, 205, 220–21; origins of, 191, 195–96, 220–21; repercussions of, 197, 209
Greece, 173, 207
Grey, Edward, 55, 154, 156–57, 176, 208, 215–16
Grierson, James M., 43, 55–56
Groß, Hans, 76–77, 138, 140, 142
Guchkov, Aleksandr Ivanovich, 113, 127–28, 131

Hafid, Mulai, Sultan of Morocco, 38, 148
Hagron, Alexis-Auguste-Raphaël, 91
Haldane, Richard Burdon, 55–56, 64–65, 137, 155–56, 171
Hammerstein-Equord, Baron von, 101, 104–5
Harmsworth, Alfred, 145
heavy field artillery, 10, 13, 138, 221, 223; Austro-Hungarian, 202; British, 42, 97, 206; French, 91–92, 150–51, 203–4; German, 47, 90–92, 137, 150–51, 201; Italian, 107, 207; Russian, 118, 134–35, 159, 169, 205
heavy mortars. See siege artillery

Heeringen, Josias von, 137, 160; and army laws of 1912/13, 162, 165–67, 169, 180–82, 185–90
Herero rising, 4, 33
Hervé, Gustave, 60
Heydebrand und der Lasa, Ernst von, 164
Hintze, Paul von, 127–28, 130–31
Holland, 167, 169
Holstein, Friedrich von, 38–39, 44, 56–57
Honvédség, 34, 98, 177, 201, 220–21
Hotchkiss manufacturers, 20
Hubertusstock, 180–81
Huguet, Victor, 44, 55, 96–97
Hungary, separatism of, 33, 34, 36, 97–99, 107–11, 178, 201

Indian army, 19, 32, 42–43, 56, 234, 236
irredentism of Italy, 34, 106
Istanbul, 115, 118, 173. See also Turkish straits
Italian-Turkish War, 4, 15, 161, 167, 169, 171–73, 182, 206–7, 216–17, 221, 231, 234
Izvolsky, Aleksandr Petrovich, 117–20, 126–28, 130–31, 153, 178

Japan, 13, 132, 136. See also Russo-Japanese War
Jaurès, Jean, 53, 151, 192–93
Jena conference of German Social Democratic Party, 57
Joffre, Joseph-Jacques-Césaire, 152–53, 160, 168, 203, 215; and joint war plans with Entente partners, 155–56, 176, 196–97; and Plan XVII, 181, 194–95, 204; and three-year service law, 192–94
Johannistal, 140–41
Jullian, Lt.-Col., 105
July crisis, 59, 199–202, 204, 210–20, 225–30

Kageneck, Karl von, 122
Karadgeorgević, King Peter, 34, 124
Karlsbad, 212
Keim, August, 164, 170, 181
Kiderlen-Wächter, Alfred von, 119, 126, 128, 135, 180; and second Moroccan crisis, 148–50, 159–60, 163–64, 167, 171–72

Kirk-Kilise, battle of, 173, 178
Kokovtsev, Vladimir Nikolaevich, 63, 175, 195–97, 205
Krobatin, Alexander von, 212
Krupp steelworks, 19, 65, 107, 134, 138, 158, 201, 205, 207, 217
Kumanovo, battle of, 173, 178
Kuropatkin, Aleksei Nikolaevich, 41, 93

Lacroix, Henri de, 56, 81, 89
Laguiche, Col. (later Gen.) de, 77, 85–86, 88, 90, 191–92, 197
Lamsdorff, Vladimir Nikolaevich, 41
Landwehr, Austrian, 34, 98–99, 177, 220–21
Langlois, Hippolyte, 25, 27–28, 91
Lansdowne, Henry Petty-Fitzmaurice, fifth Marquess of, 42
Latham, Hubert, 140, 142
Lauenstein, Lt.-Col., 92–93
Lebaudy, Pierre and Paul, 75–76, 78, 139
Lefèbvre, Eugène, 140
Legrand-Girarde, Gen., 193
Liberal Party, British, 55, 64, 149, 154, 216
Libya. See Italian-Turkish War
Liège, 50–51, 158, 160, 201
Lloyd George, David, 149, 154
lois des cadres, 30, 60, 137, 175, 182, 202, 243n.58
Lorraine, 50–51, 55, 152, 160, 176, 208
Loubet, Emile, 46, 53
Louis, Georges, 153
Louis Napoleon Bonaparte, 29
Ludendorff, Erich, 181, 184–85, 189–90
Luxembourg, 49
Lyncker, Moritz von, 140

Macedonia, 173
machine guns, 5–6, 25, 51, 138, 222, 230; development and testing of, 19–21, 68–70, 100, 252n.54; equipment with, 66, 117, 124, 158, 168, 171, 183, 189, 201–3, 206–7, 217, 221
Madrid, treaty of, 38
Manchuria. See Russo-Japanese War
maneuvers, 15–16, 70, 72; Austro-Hungarian, 99–100, 123–24, 145, 202; British, 95–97, 206; French, 81–83, 91, 138–39, 142–43, 176, 204; German, 21, 85–91, 138, 142–43, 151, 164, 166, 201; Italian, 101–5, 145, 207; Rus-

sian, 93–95, 134, 145, 159, 197, 206; Serbian, 124
Mansion House speech, 149, 150, 159
Marconi, Guglielmo, 21, 73
Maxim, Hiram, 19–20
Mazzini, Giuseppe, 23
Messier de St. James, Lt.-Col., 101–4
Messimy, Adolphe-Marie, 150–52, 154–55, 203–4, 215
Metz, 47, 78, 152
Meuse river, 49–50, 55, 65, 158, 160, 201
Michel, Paul-Henry, 96, 151–52, 155
military budgets, 3–4, 8, 14, 59, 111, 138, 230, 234–37, 241n.9; Austro-Hungarian, 33, 68, 98, 107–8, 123, 137, 177–79, 221; British, 32, 64–65, 137, 206; French, 30, 193–94; German, 32–33, 65–67, 137, 162–68, 170–71, 182, 184, 189–90, 221; Italian, 35, 68, 103, 107, 137; Russian, 62–63, 114, 131, 135, 183, 195–97, 228
military laws. See army law of 1912; army law of 1913; three-year military service law
Millerand, Aléxandre, 176
Miquel, Johannes von, 229
mobilization. See war plans
Mogador, 148, 150
Moltke, Helmuth von, 61, 75–76, 89–90, 120–22, 129–30, 135, 159, 227–28; and 1912 army law, 165, 169–70; and 1913 army law, 181, 184–90; and outbreak of war, 179–80, 191, 209, 212–13; and Schlieffen Plan, 65, 122, 208
Monis, Ernest, 150
Montenegro, 115–16, 122–25, 128–29, 136, 146, 173–74, 177, 207–8
Moroccan crises. See first Moroccan crisis; second Moroccan crisis
motor vehicles, 5–6, 10, 21, 52, 74–75, 138, 158, 202, 205, 217
Moulin, Brig.-Gen., 41, 60–61, 69, 93–95
mutinies, 31, 62, 99, 104, 187, 202
Mutius, Capt. von, 81–84

Namur, 50–51, 158, 160, 201
Napoleonic Wars, 22–23, 25, 27–28, 80, 152, 186
Narev river, 132
"national character," 80–88, 93–97, 99, 103–5, 112

nationalist revival in France. See *réveil national*

naval armaments, xi, 3–5, 8–9, 35, 58–59, 111–12, 149, 174–75, 225, 232; British, 31–32, 64, 137; German, 32–33, 38, 56, 65, 67, 136–37, 150, 161–66, 170–72, 179, 190, 221, 229; Italian, 109; Russian, 195

Navy League, German, 163

Négrier, François Oscar de, 46, 53

Nicholas II, 56, 63, 106, 131, 175, 194–97; and prospect of war, 119–20, 153, 214

Nicholas Nikolaevich, Grand Duke, 63, 87, 176, 197, 214

Nicholson, William, 155–57

Nicolson, Arthur, 119, 136

Nietzsche, Friedrich, 23

noncommissioned officers, 8, 11–13, 60, 93–94, 98, 104, 119, 202–3, 206, 223; German, 46, 86, 188–89, 203

Obrenović, King Alexander, 34, 124

Octobrist Party, Russian, 113, 127, 131

offensive, doctrine of, 4–5, 22–29, 67, 70, 93–96, 168, 229–30

Ottoman Empire, 113–14, 126, 131, 167, 169, 171, 173, 198, 206, 208

Paléologue, Maurice, 215

Palitsyn, Fyodor Fyodorovich, 60–62, 84, 94

Pan-German League, 163, 182

Pan-Slavism. See Slavic nationalism

Panther, German cruiser, 148–50, 155, 159

Paris Commune, 29

Parseval, August von, 76–78, 140, 142

Paulhan, Louis, 140

Pelet-Narbonne, Gerhard von, 233

Pellé, Lt.-Col., 140–41, 192

Pendezec, Jean, 45–46, 49–50

Perino manufacturers, 70

Persia, 32, 119

Piave river, 35, 106, 138

Picq, Charles Jean-Jacques Joseph Ardant du, 23

Picquart, Georges, 76

Plan XVII. See war plans: French

Poincaré, Raymond, 171, 174–78, 196, 208; and three-year service law, 193–94, 197, 215

Poland, 41, 132–34, 136, 161, 209

Pollio, Alberto, 137, 206

Port Arthur, 41, 92, 195

Posadowsky-Wehner, Maj. von, 62, 117–19, 122–23, 135

Pourtalès, Friedrich von, 119, 130, 213

"preventive war," 5, 105–6, 108–12, 114, 116, 122–23, 125–26, 128–29, 146, 170, 177, 191, 198–200, 209–14, 225–28, 230

Pripet marshes, 133

Putilov steelworks, 19

quick-firing artillery, 8, 17–19, 25, 68, 124, 222, 230; Austro-Hungarian, 19, 98, 100, 108–9, 123–24, 202; British, 19, 42, 56, 206; French, 17–19, 30, 46–47, 51, 80, 204; German, 19, 47, 56, 60, 66, 88, 151, 204; Italian, 19, 107–9, 137–38, 207, 217; Russian, 19, 31, 118–19, 134, 169, 205; in Russo-Japanese War, 27, 88

Quinquennat. See military budgets: German

Racconigi, 106

Radical Party, French, 30, 35, 60, 73, 83, 174–75, 193–94, 197, 220

radios. See wireless telegraphy

Radolin, Hugo von, 40, 42, 54

railroads, 8, 10, 12–14, 16, 73, 189, 194, 230; Italian, 35, 106–7, 138; Russian, 31, 62, 132, 136, 169, 176, 196–97, 205

Ranzi, Fabio, 103

Rediger, Aleksandr Fyodorovich, 63, 118, 122, 127, 131, 214

Reims, 49, 139–40

Repington, Charles à Court, 164, 166

reservists, 8–9, 11–13, 16, 43, 62, 64, 74, 93, 119, 124, 207, 221–23; Austro-Hungarian, 220; French, 44–45, 49–50, 151–52, 192–94, 203; German, 44–46, 90, 158, 160, 165, 168, 185, 188, 193, 201; Italian, 104, 206, 217; Russian, 127, 131–32, 134, 136, 169, 205

réveil national, 171, 174, 204, 208, 215

rifles, 8–9, 19, 22, 24–26, 51, 68, 70, 87, 124, 138, 217, 223

Rocques, Pierre Auguste, 142

Rohne, Heinrich von, 25

Rouvier, Maurice, 40–42, 46, 53–54

Rumania, 13, 61, 207
Russian revolution of 1905, 7, 31, 41, 51,
    56, 63, 103, 225
Russo-Japanese War, 4, 7, 63, 91–92,
    101, 103, 113; lessons derived from,
    22, 24, 26, 27–28, 67–74, 87–95, 99,
    112, 206; recovery of Russian army
    from, 114, 129–31, 134–35, 147, 158,
    167, 169, 181–83, 194, 200, 225, 231;
    weakness of Russian army after, 5, 7,
    31, 35, 37, 41, 50–51, 55, 57–59, 61–
    62, 106, 112–13, 115–23, 127–28,
    135, 153–54, 160
Russo-Turkish War, 11, 22

Sainte-Claire Deville, Charles Etienne,
    17
Sakharov, Viktor Viktorovich, 41
Salandra, Antonio, 216
Saletta, Tancredi, 101–2, 104–6
Salonika, 173
San Giuliano, Antonino di, 216
San Marzano, Alessandro Sigrai Asinari di,
    98–100
Santos-Dumont, Alberto, 75
Sarajevo, 199, 211, 213, 225
Sazonov, Sergei, 176, 194–95, 214–15
Schemua, Blasius, 176–79
Schlieffen, Alfred von, 29, 41, 45–46, 50–
    52, 65; after retirement, 61, 130, 191,
    208
Schlieffen Plan. See war plans: German
Schneider-Creusot industries, 107, 124,
    134–35, 138, 205
Schönaich, Franz von, 128
Schwarzlose manufacturers, 69
second Moroccan crisis, 3, 147–50, 152,
    155–61, 201, 205; repercussions of,
    161–65, 172, 174–75, 197, 202, 208,
    226–27
Selves, Justin de, 153
Serbia, 34, 136, 183, 207–8, 221; and an-
    nexation of Bosnia-Herzegovina, 113–
    18, 120–30, 146, 227; and Balkan
    Wars, 173–74, 178; in July crisis, 199,
    210–14, 218–19, 226
Sergei Mikhailovich, Grand Duke, 134
siege artillery, 10, 31, 92, 108, 118, 135,
    169, 204; German, 50–51, 65, 151,
    158, 160, 201–2, 205
Škoda steelworks, 202

Slavic nationalism, 34, 113–15, 119, 127,
    131, 208, 214–15
social Darwinism, 4, 23, 79, 164, 170,
    229
Socialists, 33, 53, 56, 84, 104, 148, 164,
    171, 183, 186–87, 191, 220
Sorel, Georges, 23
Spingardi, Paolo, 137, 206–7
Stengel, Hermann von, 33
Stolypin, Piotr Alexandrovich, 63, 113
Stürgkh, Joseph von, 211–12
Sukhomlinov, Vladimir Aleksandrovich,
    131–36, 178, 191–92, 195–96, 205,
    214
Szögyény, Laszlo von, 118, 120, 126,
    211, 213

Tangier, 38–39
taxation. See military budgets
telephones, field, 5, 10, 21, 52, 66, 73–
    74, 90, 96, 124, 204, 222
three-year military service law, French, 30,
    191–95, 220–21, 228–29; repercussions
    of, 197, 202–3, 208–9
Tirpitz, Alfred von, 32, 38, 67, 136, 182,
    190, 229; and 1912 naval law, 162–63,
    165, 170–72; and prospect of war, 150,
    159, 179
Tisza, István, 34, 177, 211–12
Tittoni, Tommaso, 111
Togo, Heihachiro, 7
traditionalism of armies, 9–11, 35, 71, 73,
    134, 186–87; in Germany, 66, 68, 71–
    72, 86–89, 163–64, 184, 186–88, 231,
    281n.58
Treitschke, Heinrich von, 23
trenches. See entrenchment
Trieste, 111
Triple Alliance, 34, 44, 105, 111, 167,
    169, 181, 208, 211
Triple Entente, 58, 116, 120, 148, 150,
    153, 157–58, 160, 174, 177, 218–19,
    221; German and Austrian perceptions
    of encirclement by, 129–30, 147, 149–
    50, 159, 166–72, 180, 183, 191–92,
    199–200, 208–11, 214, 226; joint
    strategy of, 175–76, 194, 198, 208–9,
    225
Tripoli. See Italian-Turkish War
Tsarskoe Selo, 128, 195
Tsushima, battle of, 41, 195

Turkish straits, 41, 115–17, 173
Tyrol, 106, 179

uniforms, 10, 12, 134; design and testing of, 70–73, 95, 204; supply and issue of, 119, 137–38, 189, 201–2, 217
United States of America, 19, 21–22

Verdun, 47, 49–52, 55, 79, 156
Vickers steelworks, 70
Victor Emanuel III, 106, 216
Vistula river, 132–33
Viviani, René, 208

Wandel, Franz von, 141, 159, 167–68, 171, 189–90
"War Council" of 8 December 1912, 179–81, 191, 209
war plans, xi, 4–5, 11, 13, 16–17, 111, 208, 229–30; Austro-Hungarian, 13, 106, 122–23, 125, 161; British, 43, 156–57, 176; French, 44–45, 47–50, 55, 61, 151–52, 155–56, 160, 166, 194; German, 13, 29, 44–51, 65, 121–22, 158, 160, 184–85, 208–9, 246n.39, 247n.58; Italian, 34–35, 106; Russian, 13, 61, 119, 131–34, 154, 160–61. *See also* British expeditionary force to France; Dual Alliance; Franco-Russian Alliance; Triple Entente

Weber, Max, 23
Wehrlin, Maj., 197
Wehrverein, 164–65, 170, 180, 182, 188
Wermuth, Adolf, 137, 162–63, 171
Wilhelm II, 67, 71–72, 87–89, 106, 130, 136, 191, 213; and annexation of Bosnia-Herzegovina, 119–20, 123, 126, 128, 131; and aviation, 78, 140–41, 143; and expansion of army, 147, 163, 171, 179–82, 186, 189–90, 220; and first Moroccan crisis, 37–40, 52, 54, 56–57; and naval construction, 32, 162, 165; and second Moroccan crisis, 149, 159–60
Wilhelm, Crown Prince of Prussia, 56
Wilson, Arthur K., 156
Wilson, Henry Hughes, 137, 155–56, 176, 228
Winterfeldt, Maj. von, 139–40, 142
wireless telegraphy, 5, 21, 52, 73, 143–44, 222
Wright, Orville and Wilbur, 21, 139–41, 145

Young Turks, 115

Zeppelin, Ferdinand von, 75, 77–78, 139
Zhilinski, Iakov Grigorievich, 153–54, 160, 195–97
Zipfel, Armand, 139

About the Author

DAVID G. HERRMANN is Assistant Professor of History
at Tulane University.